Psychosocial and Legal Perspectives of Marital Breakdown

Margit Gaffal

Psychosocial and Legal Perspectives of Marital Breakdown

With Special Emphasis on Spain

UCLM
UNIVERSIDAD DE CASTILLA-LA MANCHA

Springer

Prof. Dr. Margit Gaffal
Universidad de Castilla-La Mancha
Facultad de Ciencias Jurídicas y Sociales
Cobertizo de San Pedro Mártir s/n
45071 Toledo, Spain
margit.gaffal@uclm.es

ISBN 978-3-642-13895-9 e-ISBN 978-3-642-13896-6
DOI 10.1007/978-3-642-13896-6
Springer Heidelberg Dordrecht London New York

Library of Congress Control Number: 2010938730

Cover design: WMXDesign GmbH, Heidelberg, Germany

Printed on acid-free paper

Springer is part of Springer Science+Business Media (www.springer.com)

Acknowledgements

A few words about the intention to write this book may help explain the form that it has. When I gave a talk at the International Colloquium of Family Law at the University of Castilla-La Mancha in Toledo some years ago, Professor Dr. Carrasco Perera asked me whether I would be interested in writing a systematic treatise on the complex and paradox phenomenon of marital breakdown in Spain. This proposal met with my interest because I had already carried out a study on the impact of divorce on children and adolescents at the University of Salzburg. When I started to work on the present book I came across some rather contradictory facts. On the one hand, there were cases of gender violence and even domestic homicide, high divorce rates, traditional gender roles, uncompromising attitude to conflicts and lack of communication. On the other hand, a forward-looking government has implemented the most progressive laws on gender equality, rapid divorce procedure, same-sex marriage and on family mediation within the past few years. But how do these laws fit to a society with its present conditions? In other words, what is the efficacy of the laws for the problems mentioned? How can the knot be untied? In this book I have intended to follow some of the strings of this knot.

I would like to thank several people who helped me with the information presented in this book. First of all, I thank Professor Dr. Ángel Francisco Carrasco Perera, Chair of Civil Law at the University of Castilla-La Mancha in Toledo, for encouraging me to pursue my studies for the Master Thesis and for inspiring me to specialize in family law. I would also like to thank Professor Dr. Manuel Jesús Marín López for his suggestions referring the manuscript.

Particular thanks go to Professor Dr. Dagmar Coester-Waltjen for giving me worthy proposals and for allowing me to research at the University of Munich. Special thanks go to Professor Dr. Nigel Lowe (University of Cardiff) for his essential annotations and encouraging comments. I am also indebted to Professor Dr. Miquel Martin Casals (University of Girona), Professor Dr. Josep Ferrer i Riba (University Pompeu Fabra) and Professor Dr. María Paz García Rubio (University of Santiago de Compostela) for giving me suggestions for improvement. Moreover, I am also obliged to thank Professor Dr. Wolfgang Servatius (University of Regensburg) and wiss. Ass. Dr. Katharina Hilbig (University of Munich).

I wish to express my gratitude to Amethyst Royal for helping me with the editing of the text. Special thanks go also to the Associate Editor at Springer Publishers, Mrs. Anke Seyfried who has been very supportive.

Finally, I could not have managed this work without the encouragement of my family. Therefore I thank especially my husband, Prof. Dr. Jesús Padilla Gálvez for his unconditional support and our daughter Dafne for her patience at times when I was working on the manuscript. I am also indebted to the University of Castilla-La Mancha for providing support of this work.

Toledo
June 2010

Dr. Margit Gaffal

"To untie a knot one needs
to know how it was made".
(Aristoteles)

Contents

Introduction

Divorce has long been viewed as a single phenomenon affecting two individuals without considering the framework conditions in which it occurs. Due to the increase of divorce rates in the past decades researchers have changed their perspective and have concentrated on the view of divorce as a personal experience that is greatly affected by the socials and economic environment. The aim of this thesis is to investigate divorce that has become a mass phenomenon in our present society. The assumption is that in order to understand the grounds for divorce and its consequences, we have to view divorce as a phenomenon that occurs at the intersection of personal, socio-economic and legal factors.

Family disputes involve persons who have interdependent and continued relationships and arise in a context of distressing emotions. Separation and divorce affect all the members of the family, especially children. The study presents a comprehensive analysis of divorce as a psychological process that is situated within a social and a legal context. It presents a comprehensive view of divorce as a psychosocial, economic and legal phenomenon and contains a review of the research literature about divorce and its consequences for parents and children. Moreover, it describes divorce by proposing conceptual frames and explanatory models.

For this multifaceted view of divorce the investigation uses an interdisciplinary approach including the fields of psychology, socio-economics and law. The reason for the interdisciplinary approach is that divorce is a complex phenomenon in which legal, socio-economic and psychological factors play a role. In contrast to the research tools of a single academic discipline the interdisciplinary approach allows us to view divorce in its entirety. In the present study we apply the *ceteris paribus* principle in order to single out particular variables from a set of interdependent variables. Thus, an individual's psychological reaction is conditional on the socio-economic and legal circumstances. By focusing on the each of these variables the interdependence among the factors shall be analysed.

We are interested in the grounds for divorce by referring to both, the individualistic and the social dimension. Furthermore, we want to know how legal systems have responded to divorce as a social phenomenon. Does the legal frame enable ex-spouses to adequately rebuild their post-divorce lives? This is especially relevant as the fundament of society is the family rather than the single individual. Cohesion is as essential value that arises from family relations and develops within the family context. Divorce produces changes in many respects and affects the legal, socio-economical and psychological relationships among family members. If parents separate the well-being of all family members is harmed. Therefore we are interested in the legal, socio-economic and psychological consequences that divorce has for mothers, fathers and children.

In Spain divorce rates have been particularly high within the last decades. Therefore the thesis analyses a significant number of divorce sentences brought to Spanish Courts of Appeal in the year 2007. Reference is made to the reform of Spanish Family Law in 2005. We seek to answer whether the introduction of the joint custody regime as a post-divorce parenting option has led to a preference of this regime among divorced parents.

Chapter 1 addresses the question of why so many marriages end in divorce. To know why so many marriages end in divorce we have to ask for the criteria for marital stability. Thus, the chapter provides a descriptive analysis of the grounds for divorce, by relating to socio-environmental, personal, pair-related and systemic factors. We give a detailed description of how these factors contribute to the destabilisation of the institution of marriage. After the presentation of these risk factors we propose a model of family functioning.

Chapter 2 presents the factors that influence the former spouses in their process of adjustment to divorce. In particular we analyze the factors that either facilitate or impede the adaptation to divorce. The chapter presents several conceptual models from which these factors can be understood. These include personal, relational and cultural factors.

Chapter 3 deals with children and adolescents and their process of adjustment to divorce. Whereas the former spouses freely decide about their lives, children and adolescents of divorced parents do not form part of the decision-making process but are still confronted with a whole range of consequences resulting from the divorce. The chapter presents a theoretical model of mediating and moderating factors that have some bearing on adjustment. It provides a comprehensive view of the socio-economic and psychological changes that children and adolescents experience as a reaction to parental divorce. Special reference is made to different custody regulations and their effect on child well-being.

The main purpose of Chap. 4 is to offer the reader a theoretic model of factors that play a role in decisions on custody arrangements in divorce sentences. On the basis of this model legal several aspects such as legal authority, custody and the liquidation of the matrimonial union are analyzed. We are particularly interested whether the introduction of the joint custody regime has led to a preference of parents to opt for this regime in the regulating agreement.

Chapter 5 investigates the role of family mediation in the divorce process. According to the recommendation of the Council of Europe the Member States should take measures to allow access to family mediation in order to achieve a resolution of family disputes in a consensual manner. The chapter presents an overview of mediation techniques and gives a detailed description of the mechanisms that come into effect during the mediation process.

It is the overall aim of the thesis to provide a comprehensive framework within which divorce can be understood.

Chapter 1
Grounds for Divorce

1.1 Introduction

In the last few decades divorce figures have risen considerably in many European states.[1] Due to the advances in society, the family dyad is exposed to many changes and influences from outside. New forms of life have emerged while traditional forms of relationships have remained. These days a couple may opt for one of several accepted forms of life ranging from the traditional marriage, or forms of temporal cohabitation[2] or negotiated partnerships. Marriage can be defined as a legal, social and religious union among adult individuals that creates an intimate relationship. A marriage can be recognized by the state and/or by religious authorities. Civil marriage is a legal institution that creates obligations among the spouses according to the legal dispositions of marriage in jurisdiction. Thus marriage changes the personal and social status of the individuals who enter a marriage. Whereas a man and a woman traditionally enter into a marriage and form a monogamous relationship, some jurisdictions have also recognized same-sex marriages.[3] National jurisdictions have provided the necessary legal

[1]See: European Statistic Yearbook (2009): 151.

[2]Within the European Union 12 Member States allow unmarried couples of the same or different sex to have their partnership registered in the form of a civil union, a registered partnership or unregistered cohabitation. In Spain cohabitating couples are considered as "*parejas de hecho*", which is a stable marriage-like union among two individuals of the same or different sex. They may have their union registered at the city authorities and there are certain legal regulations that apply to this union. For more details see García Rubio (2006): 113–138. In Germany the legislator has allowed registered partnerships ("*Eingetragene Lebenspartnerschaft*") for same-sex couples since 2001. In the United Kingdom the *Civil Partnership Act 2004* grants civil partnerships similar rights and responsibilities as a civil marriage.

[3]Same-sex marriage is a marriage between two individuals of the same gender that is legally and socially recognized. In Europe, there are six countries that have legalized same-sex marriages. The Netherlands was the first country to allow same-sex marriages in 2001, followed by Belgium in 2003, Spain in 2005, Sweden and Norway in 2009 and Portugal in 2010.

M. Gaffal, *Psychosocial and Legal Perspectives of Marital Breakdown*,

DOI 10.1007/978-3-642-13896-6_1, © Springer-Verlag Berlin Heidelberg 2010

instruments to recognize these new forms of life and to facilitate legal procedures dealing with these partnerships.[4]

This chapter seeks to answer the question of why so many marriages end in divorce. More specifically, what are the reasons for the mass phenomenon of divorce? On revising the research literature it can be noticed that researchers often focus on the analysis of one aspect of divorce and tend to lose sight of the whole family context. The difficulty and impracticality of studying the entirety of family dynamics has led to a partial analysis of the mass phenomenon of divorce.

1.2 Theoretical Considerations

To know why so many marriages end in divorce we have to ask which factors actually cause marital (in)stability. There are many aspects that play a role in this field; therefore we need a theoretical concept that takes the complexity of the phenomenon into account. The relationship among family members has a legal, an economic, a social and a psychological dimension. From the methodological point of view, we will therefore use an interdisciplinary approach that includes the fields of law, family sociology, home economics and personality psychology. This methodological approach is justified because it permits the examination of the problem from several angles. We will present a multidimensional model that is based on these fields and that will provide an insight into the dynamics of marital decisions. We will concentrate on the following questions: Which factors are relevant for marital (in)stability? How do spouses evaluate these factors in the process of marital decisions?

Before we deal with these questions we will provide definitions for marriage and family. Definitions of family usually include the following elements: first, family members are related by blood, marriage, or some other legal bond such as adoption, second, the spouses are intimate partners and there exists trust among all family members, third, they share a common household and fourth, the individuals have daily interactions with one another.[5]

---

[4]The following amendment to Article 44 of the Spanish Civil Code on the legalisation of same-sex marriages was introduced by the Ley 13/2005 of 1 July (published in BOE, Nr. 157, de 02-07-2005, pp. 23632–23634): "Artículo 44.

El hombre y la mujer tienen derecho a contraer matrimonio conforme a las disposiciones de este Código. El matrimonio tendrá los mismos requisitos y efectos cuando ambos contrayentes sean del mismo o de diferente sexo." (Código Civil, Art. 44). Similarly, the expressions of "man" and "woman" were replaced by "spouse" in Articles 66 and 67 of the Spanish Civil Code to refer to both, marriages among people of the same or different sex.

[5]These two elements go back to the view of family in the Roman tradition, whose family concept was based on the biological unit of parents, children and relatives (related by blood) living in the same socio-economic community or household (Sandkühler 1990: 17).

Within the family political and economic structures are conserved and cultural practices are transmitted with the aim of regulating relationships in the reproduction and education of children.[6] It has the following characteristics:

- The family is a cooperative union freely chosen by two adult individuals who create and raise human beings. In the family division of labour typical for the industrial society is reflected.
- The family has a key role in the accumulation and distribution of property through marriage and heritage.
- Within the family interpersonal skills, patterns of socially accepted conduct as well as ways of thinking and evaluating are transmitted in explicit and implicit ways. These abilities determine an individual's attitude not only towards himself or herself but also towards society and the social order.
- The family forms a system of interpersonal relations among its members within which individuals develop and are shaped, according to the conditions of the surrounding social system.[7]

Many of the definitions of family reflect this traditional idea of the family and the family members' social roles on the condition of the parents' legal bond of marriage. Burgess et al. give the following definition of the family:

> "The family is [...] a group of persons united by ties of marriage, blood, or adoption; constituting a household; interacting and communicating with each other in their respective social roles of husband and wife, mother and father, son and daughter, bother and sister, and creating and maintaining a common culture." (Burgess et al. 1971: 2)

This definition represents a view of family in which ties are characterized by "marriage", "blood" or "adoption". It describes a model example of the bourgeois or civil nuclear family embedded in a modern democratic state with a capitalistic economic order. The definition by Bidwell and Vander Mey introduces the new element of "affinity" as an additional family feature.[8] The interaction of family members rests on social roles, a common identity as well as responsibilities. The authors underline also the parents' responsibilities for children and include the economical dimension that is involved in the family structure:

> "Family refers to a collection of people, related to each other by marriage, ancestry, adoption, or affinity, who have a commitment to each other and a unique identity with each other. This collection forms an economic unit. The adults in the collection have varying degrees of responsibility for young members that might be a part of the collection." (Bidwell and Vander Mey 2000: 3)

---

[6]See the definition of family of the United Nations: "The family is the natural and fundamental group unit of society and is entitled to protection by society and the State" United Nations, 1948.

[7]See: Mies (1990): 16.

[8]Affinity in sociological terms refers to "kinship of spirit", interest and other interpersonal commonalities. It is characterized by high levels of intimacy and sharing, usually in close groups, also known as affinity groups. It differs from affinity in law and canon law which generally refer to the marriage relationship. Social affinity is generally thought of as "marriage" to *ideas*, *ideals* and *causes* shared by a tight community of people. See: Bidwell and Vander Mey (2000): 45f.

The definition of the family varies according to the theoretical perspective that one takes. Hanson and Lynch use a situational definition of family by introducing the notion of "commitment" among family members. They state that family is:

> "... any unit that defines itself as a family including individuals who are related by blood or marriage as well as those who have made a commitment to share their lives." (Hanson and Lynch 1992: 285)

If we take a diachronic perspective it becomes obvious that the family model has undergone significant transformations in its structure especially since the 1970s. Societal changes have contributed to a reduction in traditional family forms such as the extended family, which was gradually replaced by the nuclear family. In fact, statistic research in European countries shows that within a period of 25 years (1980–2005) the average size of European households has decreased from almost three persons (2.82) to 2.4 members per household. The bar diagram shows the number of family members in different countries (Fig. 1.1).

The results show that Germany, Denmark, Finland and Sweden are the countries with the lowest number of members per household. In contrast, Malta, Cyprus, Romania and Spain are the countries with the highest number of members per household.[9]

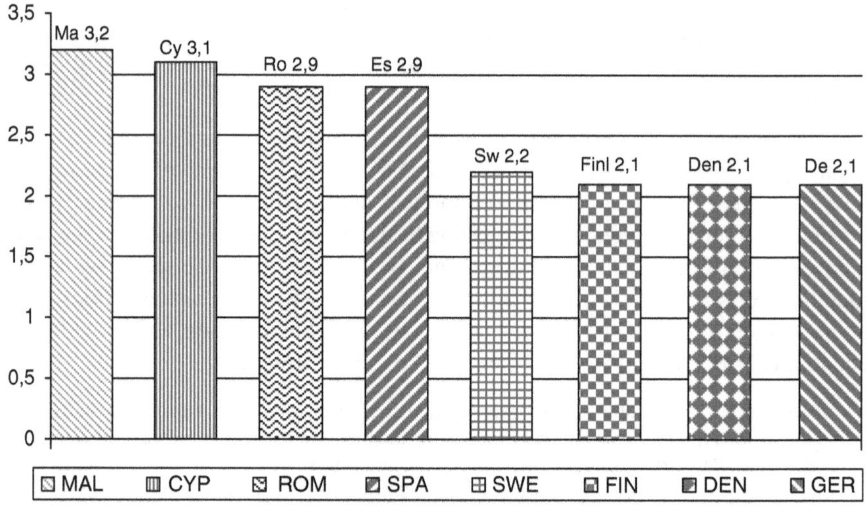

Fig. 1.1 Number of family members per household[10]

---

[9]According to EU-statistics of the year 2008 the average rate of family members per household ranges between two and three people (2.5) living in one household. Denmark, Sweden, Germany and Finland have lower rates (between 2 and 2.2) whereas in Cyprus, Slovakia, Malta, Poland and Spain the amount is slowly higher (2.8–3). See: European Statistic Yearbook (2008): 234.

[10]See: Report on the Evolution of the Family in Europe, Institute for Family Policies, (2008): 32, http://www.ipfe.org.

Since the 1970s European households have undergone significant changes not only as refers the number of family members but also as refers the family form. In fact, the definitions mentioned earlier mostly disregard the post-modern family forms, such as non-married cohabitating couples,[11] one-parent (or lone-patent) families, stepfamilies[12] or blended families (patchwork family).[13] These new family forms have brought about modifications in the organization of relationships referring relational patterns and forms of communication. The tendency towards individualization has led to a considerable amount of one-person households. European statistics show that nearly one third (27.7%) of European households have only one person which corresponds to a number of 54 million European citizens living alone. The pie chart shows the occurrence of five different forms of life in European societies (Fig. 1.2).

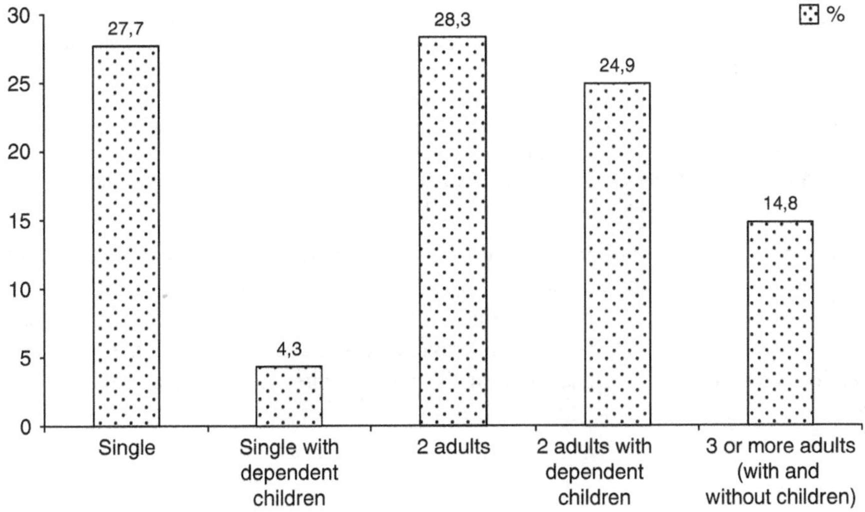

Fig. 1.2 Distribution of family forms in Europe[14]

[11]Within the group of non-married cohabitating couples two forms are possible, such as the registered partnership and non-marital cohabitating couple. In a registered partnership two people live as a couple and have their union registered with a public authority established by the law of their Member State.

[12]A stepfamily is formed when a person gets married to somebody who enters this marriage with a child or children stemming from a former partner.

[13]A blended family is a family that includes children of a previous marriage of one spouse or both. The parent's significant other takes over the role of full- or part-time caregiver without adopting the child. Children of blended families live together without being stepbrothers or stepsisters. Children experience dual socialization because they have a relationship to the biological parent and to the parent's new mate. They have to make continuous flexible adjustments between these spheres.

[14]See: European Statistic Yearbook (2008).

The chart illustrates that nearly one third of European citizens live in a pair relationship, followed by a slightly smaller number of people living in single households. One quarter of people live as families with dependent children. Nearly 15% of people live in households of three or more people with or without children. A minority of people (4.3%) lives as single parents with dependent children. According to the European Statistic Yearbook 2009 there are generally more households and households of a smaller average size, as a higher proportion of people live alone. In fact, the highest proportion of people living alone is found among the elderly.[15]

The following views of family are of the U.S. Supreme Court and reflect the traditional view of family as well as different attributes of the family by including the "individualist" model:

> "1. (...) a traditional "nuclear family" of two parents and their children, and where the parents are presumed to be acting in the best interests of their children. In such a family, there is no need to give the children their own voice – even when parents do such things as institutionalize their children"
> 2. An extended-kind model of family made up of a community of parents, siblings, grandparents and other relatives which should be recognized as a primary family, even if the blood-ties are not as strong as a nuclear family; and
> 3. An individualist model where family members are fairly autonomous and that individuality should be respected." (Dolgin 2002: 379f)

For a realistic assessment of the phenomenon of divorce researchers should consider both the old and new family forms by acknowledging the variety of possible family forms. This variety is important as it is positively correlated with the acceleration of divorce rates that began in the second half of the last century. In the following section we shall have a closer look at the divorce rates in Europe and the United States.

1.3 Divorce Statistics

From the beginning of the 1960s divorce rates have gradually increased in many European countries as well as in the United States. Nowadays, on the average, nearly every third marriage ends in divorce and in urban areas this tendency is even higher. According to the European Statistic Yearbook 2009 the average number of divorces in all 27 Member States EU-27 grew steadily and exceeded one million a year in 2005, which corresponds to 42 divorces per 100 marriages.[16] However, a more detailed analysis of the evolution of the figures within a decade (from 1997 to 2007) shows interesting results. Three groups of significant developments can be made out: the first group of countries including Belgium, Denmark and Germany

[15]See: European Statistic Yearbook (2009): 149.

[16]See: European Statistic Yearbook (2009): 151.

has high divorce rates with a rising tendency.[17] The second group of countries, such as Luxembourg and Hungary (2.4), Austria and Sweden (2.3–2.4), and Finland (2.6) have considerably high divorce rates that have remained relatively constant over the period mentioned. And there is a third group of countries including Spain and Portugal in which the divorce rate was below the European mean rate but rose drastically within a decade, with an increase of 0.9–1.7 in Spain and 1.4–2.4 in Portugal. In the Netherlands (2.2–2.0) and the Czech Republic (3.2–3.0)[18] a slight decrease of divorce rates can be noticed.[19]

The diagram shows the amount of marriages, separations, divorces and nullities in Spain within a period of more than two decades over 26 years from 1982 to 2008 (Fig. 1.3).

The graphs show that over a decade (from 1995 to 2005) the divorce rate in Spain has risen by 81%. At the same time a decrease in the number of marriages may be noted. Although the Spanish population has augmented by over 7 million

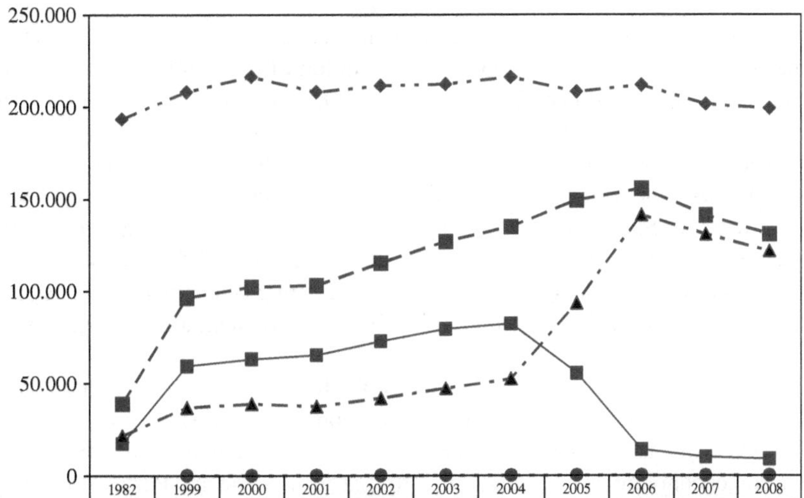

	1982	1999	2000	2001	2002	2003	2004	2005	2006	2007	2008
Marriage	193.319	208.129	216.451	208.208	211.492	212.300	216.149	208.146	211.818	201.579	199.145
Separation	17.445	59.503	63.377	65.527	73.032	79.423	82.340	55.632	14.158	10.211	9.071
Divorce	21.463	36.900	38.973	37.571	42.017	47.319	52.591	93.536	141.317	130.897	121.814
Nulity		133	145	152	229	191	190	199	153	196	175
Total	38.908	96.536	102.495	103.250	115.278	126.933	135.121	149.367	155.628	141.304	131.060

Fig. 1.3 Marriages, separations, divorces and nullities in Spain[20]

[17]See: Table 3.14 Divorces (per 1,000 persons), in Belgium the rate went up from 2.6 to 2.9 and in Denmark and Germany the rates went up from 2.4 to 2.6 (See: European Statistic Yearbook 2009: 157).

[18]The Czech Republic (3.0) together with Lithuania (3.4) and Lativa (3.3) have noticeably high divorce rates.

[19]See: European Statistic Yearbook (2009): 157.

[20]See: Spanish National Institute of Statistics INE (*Instituto Nacional de Estadı́sticas*), 2009.

people in the last 25 years the marriage rate has not increased respectively. In fact, the number of marriages in 1,000 people has fallen from 5.88 to 4.70 over the last 25 years. It has however remained relatively constant within the last decade (from 4.96 in 1997 to 4.61 in 2007).[21] Within the last decade, Hertfelder de Aldecoa summarizes the results from a study on family life in Spain. He states that within a period of 12 years the divorce rate has increased by nearly 80%. This has put Spain together with Belgium on the list of those 27 European countries with the highest numbers of divorces:

> "La ruptura familiar se ha disparado (146.919 rupturas en el 2006), de manera que se rompe un matrimonio cada 3.6 minutos en España, es decir, 17 matrimonios cada hora y 408 matrimonios al día, con un crecimiento vertiginoso: En 12 años (1995–2006): la ruptura familiar ha crecido en casi el 77% (76.9%). En tan solo los últimos 6 años (2000–2006) la ruptura se ha incrementado en un 42.5%. Ya se ha superado el millón de divorcios en España (1,018,877), que ha afectado a más de 1,750,000 niños, convirtiendo a España, junto con Bélgica, en el país de la UE27 con mayor tasa de rupturas/matrimonios." (Hertfelder de Alcedoa 2009: 3)

This development goes along with the tendency that people in Europe get married at a later age. A report on the evolution of the family carried out in 2006 stated that over a period of 23 years the age at first marriage has increased by nearly 5 years (4.9 years for women and 4.5 years for men). European statistics on the female mean age at first marriage show that within a period of 29 years (1975–2004) the women's age at first marriage had gone up from 24.4 years to 29.2 years. In Spain women's mean age at first marriage is slightly higher than in the rest of Europe and had risen from 22.9 years in 1975 to 28 years in 2004. Accordingly, the mean age of women at childbearing is among the highest in Spain together with Ireland, the Netherlands, Sweden and Denmark with approximately 31 years.[22]

In many European countries marriage is often preceded by cohabitation which implies that a couple actually starts a relationship some years prior to marriage. However, this is relatively rare in Spain. In their investigation on women's changing socioeconomic position and union formation in Spain and Portugal Domínguez-Folgueras and Castro-Martín showed that 70.1% of Spanish women and 53.3% of Portuguese women in their 20s had never entered a conjugal union.[23] The authors name several reasons for this trend that have to do with longer formation times, later access to the labour market and a significant change of gender roles. Longer education times create better job opportunities and produce an independence effect, whereby better educated Spanish women are less likely to enter into a marriage. Women having lived independently for some time prior to union formation tend to prefer cohabitation to marriage. The authors prove this trend by the following statistic data:

---

[21]See: Table 3.13 on Marriages (per 1,000 people) in European Statistic Yearbook (2009): 156.

[22]See: Fig. 3.15: Mean age of women at childbearing, European Statistic Yearbook (2009): 155.

[23]Domínguez-Folgueras and Castro-Martín (2008): 1525.

> "The odds of entering marriage among college educated women are 31% lower than among women with primary schooling in Spain and 59% lower in Portugal. (...) In Spain, the odds of entering marriage relative to remaining single are 11% higher among employed than unemployed women, but at the same time, the odds of entering cohabitation relative to entering marriage are 61% higher among employed than unemployed women." (Domínguez-Folgueras and Castro-Martín 2008: 1532)

One reason for this trend may be that the institution of marriage has lost its importance at least as financial protection and social safeguard. It may further suggest that women with higher education are less prepared to make fundamental concessions which increases the risk of divorce in the case of conflict.

Another significant aspect in the discussion of grounds for divorce is the duration of marriage. A longer life expectancy leads to a longer duration of marriage in number of years. However, contrary to this assumption statistics of the year 2002 prove that there is a tendency that marriages last fewer years. According to the European Statistic Yearbook 2009, the mean duration of each marriage exceeds 10 years in every Member State, rising to nearly 17 years in Italy. Spain is the country where marriages last 13.8 years in contrast to, for instance, the Netherlands (12.9 years), the United Kingdom and Hungary (10.9 years) and Germany (10.4 years). In Austria marriages last on the average under 10 years (9.4) and in Cyprus they last only 7 years.[24]

All these facts clearly indicate that marriage and family have undergone significant changes. Despite extensive research on separation and divorce, the acceleration of divorce rates has not yet been explained systematically and profoundly. However, scholars have agreed on a number of influences that are responsible for the amount of stability in partnerships. The following section gives an overview of the possible reasons for divorce.

1.4 Grounds for Separation and Divorce

There are many reasons why people get divorced which can be influenced by a person's character, age, status, education or religion. For instance, one or both spouses may have few skills in the commitment to marriage or they have deficiencies in the communication of problems. They may have different expectations about rearing children or rely on traditional role models that impede personal growth. Other reasons include divergent ideas of personal and career goals or else a couple may have financial problems which in turn provoke crisis and lead to divorce.

For the analysis of the grounds for divorce it is pertinent to briefly address the factors that play a role in a person's decision to enter a relationship. As such decision is a highly private matter research in this field seems difficult. There are,

[24]See: European Statistic Yearbook (2009).

however, certain factors that appear to play a decisive role in the mating process. Similar and homogeneous standards in the following areas are considered to have a stabilizing effect in a pair relationship: education, way of life, political convictions, religious beliefs, attitude towards marriage and family (e.g. children, private property), educational level, employment and the environment, such as living in urban or rural areas.[25]

The notion that homogenous standards within a relationship contribute to stability was taken up by Esser who proposed the frame-selection theory.[26] This theoretical foundation takes all relevant motives into consideration, such as economic, psychological and sociological conditions. According to his model marital stability is related to the quality of a couple's common frame. A frame represents the abilities and skills learned during socialisation, life experiences, and through acquired knowledge. More specifically, it contains mental convictions, norms, values, beliefs and emotional patterns for social interaction. If a person is confronted with a certain situation, he or she would automatically activate the frame that matches the situation. Situations usually involve typical objects or significant symbols that determine the choice of the appropriate frame. Within this frame the person can then choose from several scripts or proven programmes of conduct that best match a situation.[27] As such, a person's actual conduct is founded on the chosen frame and script. Accordingly, the more homogamic people are in their values, backgrounds and life goals, the more likely they seem to enter into a successful marriage. People who share common backgrounds and similar social networks are probably better suited as marriage partners than people with heterogamic backgrounds and networks.

A perfect framing is not only seen as the foundation for a stable marriage but is also fundamental for the spouses' expectations of future events. Marital stability is supposed to depend on framing as a steadfast institution especially at the beginning of the relationship. In the case of a strong frame the efforts invested in the relationship are considered worth while. This assumption is verified by a study carried our by Lauer and Lauer in which 351 couples in long-term marriages (of 15 or more years) were asked to report on relevant stabilizing factors in their relationships.[28] The researchers divided the couples into three groups, such as the happy, unhappy, and mixed (one partner happy and one unhappy) marriages, who gave different reasons for their marital stability. For happy couples, the most frequently mentioned reason for staying together was the perceived nature of the relationship and the belief in marriage as a long-term commitment. One fifth (19%) of parents living in mixed marriages and nearly a half of the spouses (47%) in unhappy marriages said the children kept their marriage together.

---

[25]See the studies of White (1990): 904–912, Karney and Bradbury (1995): 3–34; Beck and Hartmann (1999): 655–680.

[26]See: Esser (2002a, b): 472–496.

[27]See: Esser (2002a, b): 62.

[28]See: Lauer and Lauer (1986): 382–390.

The assumption that people do not mate randomly but rather assortatively has been shown in the sociological research literature.[29] The authors Esteve and Cortina focused on the Spanish situation and analysed the criteria that underlie the process of partner search and mating. The authors showed that there has long been a general trend that people with higher education are more likely to form homogamic unions compared to people with lower educational attainment. However, within the last decades a changing trend of mating practice has been noticed in Spanish women: whereas in earlier generations women preferred a hypergamic pattern whereby they married up, women with higher education nowadays prefer either a homogamic or a heterogamic relationship. The authors summarize their results in the following way:

> "Patterns and trends of educational homogamy in Spain are consistent with those found in the literature and with our initial research expectations." As in those societies where the educational structure has expanded, in Spain we observe that (a) educational diversification has led to a reduction of global homogamy levels, (b) an increase of the number of highly educated people increases the propensity for them to marry homogamously with each other and (c) the reduction in differences between the educational distribution of men and women has reduced the pattern of female hypergamy." (Esteve and Cortina 2006: 425)

On the whole women seem to be more susceptible to changes in gender roles than men. As women have reached a higher level of education in the last decades they do not longer follow the traditional hypergamic pattern. In contrast, men might not have changed their heterogamic mating practices accordingly. Therefore higher educated women are confronted with a reduced pool of possible partners with a comparable educational background. Statistic analysis of the data for marriages of the year 2008 (194,022 marriages) show that within the group of spouses who have a doctoral degree both, men and women had married down. Interestingly, in general more women (1,224) have a doctoral degree than men (1,185).[30]

Investigation on the grounds for divorce seems complex because it involves the fields of socio-economy, psychology and law. Each of these fields has its special research methods. Research on this issue entails two types of knowledge: subjective and objective knowledge.[31] A person's assessment of a problem is always subjective and incomplete despite the intention of striving for objectivity. As such, subjective knowledge always has an explicit and an implicit dimension which complicates investigations.[32] A difference can often be noticed between a person's

[29]See: Oppenheimer (1994): 293–342; Kalmijn (1998): 395–421.

[30]See: Data of the Spanish National Institute of Statistics (INE), Table: Matrimonios de diferente sexo por Nivel de estudios de la esposa y Nivel de estudios del esposo. (http://www.ine.es/jaxi/tabla.do).

[31]Whereas an objective fact denotes a truth that remains true everywhere, independently of human thought or feelings, a subjective fact is only true for an individual person in relation to place and time.

[32]Explicit knowledge is codified knowledge that can be articulated and may be transmitted to others. Implicit or tacit knowledge is knowledge that a person carries in mind and that provides the context for people, places, ideas, and experiences. It is difficult to access implicit information as

subjectively perceived reasons and the objective causes for crisis and divorce. The reasons explicitly named represent only a part of the whole picture.

For methodological reasons de Graaf and Kalmijn distinguish between the motives for and causes of divorce. Whereas cause points to statistically significant factors that are associated with divorce, motive refers to a spouse's subjective view. People who have experienced a divorce give motives in order to understand and justify what has happened. The authors say this of divorce:

> "Motives to divorce should not be equated to the causes of divorce (Kitson 1992). Causes of divorce are factors that increase the likelihood of divorce. We speak of a cause of divorce only if certain features or variables are present among divorced couples and are not present or are present to a lesser extent among married couples. The study of causes is always comparative and objective. Motives, in contrast, are reasons given by former spouses themselves for why they got divorced. There is no comparison with married couples, and by definition, the information is subjective. Not every motive is a cause, and not every cause is a motive." (de Graaf and Kalmijn 2006: 484)

This distinction has implications for the investigation of the grounds for divorce. There are certain socio-economic conditions, individual predispositions and recurring psychological patterns that are likely to cause conflicts.[33] We shall call these conditions risk factors. There is never just one assignable cause for a relationship crisis, instead, there are several factors that either cause problems or make an already existing crisis worse, especially when they act in combination. The risk factors may cause problems on the following overlapping and interacting levels, such as the biological level (intimacy, age, fertility), the psychological level (individual dispositions, patterns and mechanisms of interaction), the economic level (education, working life, household organisation), and the societal level (religion, cultural background, family identity interacting with society). Based on this distinction we will present a classification of risk factors that may occur in different spheres of life. In the diagram these spheres are depicted as concentric circles (Fig. 1.4).

The inner circle represents personal factors such as individual dispositions that commonly count as risk factors. The next circle represents risk factors that concern the management of the relationship and includes such aspects as the commitment to the marriage and the organisation of the common household. Other risk factors may be related to the family system as a whole and are due to normative and non-normative life events. The systems surrounding the family such as relatives and friends who may also be a source of crisis and may have a destabilizing influence on the partnership or the family. Finally, the outmost circle stands for the socio-environmental factors, such as demographic facts or social and economic conditions. In the following section the risk factors will be described in detail.

---

people are often unaware of the knowledge they actually possess. Transfer of implicit knowledge among individuals generally requires a certain amount of personal contact and trust.

[33]Conflict may be defined as a process of long or short term interaction in which one or both marital partners feel discomfort about one aspect of their relationship and which they attempt to resolve.

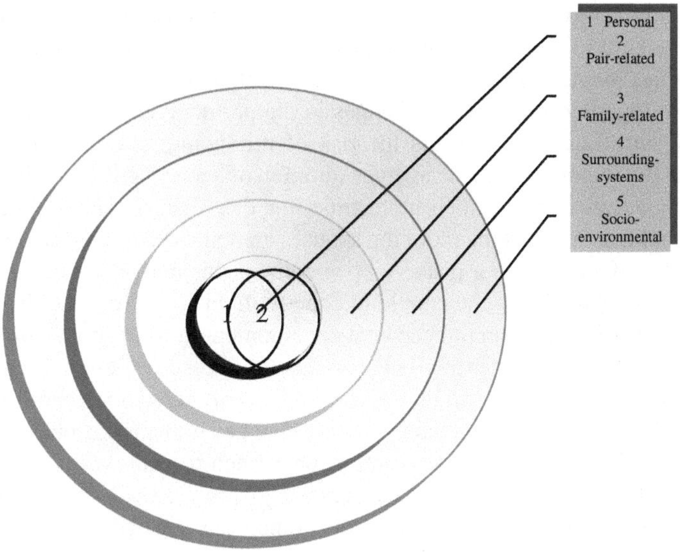

Fig. 1.4 Diagram showing classification of risk factors for divorce

1.4.1 Socio-environmental Factors

In modern societies the family has become ever more susceptible to influences from outside. The ongoing differentiation of society has brought about a process of individualisation.[34] Along with the development of individualisation, human relationships have become more complex in two ways: there are more possibilities for impersonal relationships in the public sphere and there is a tendency to have more personal relationships in privacy. As a result of the increasing complexity of society in its stratification and functional diversification, the individual has a need of a familiar surrounding and reliable relationships represented by the family.

Within the social environment, some factors are considered as static risk factors because they are outside an individual's domain of control. On the contrary, the relationship and personal factors are considered as dynamic risk factors because they are basically changeable. Each generation is confronted with specific socio-economic conditions that determine the frame within which individuals develop and organize their lives. These conditions include the economic and political situation of a country, as well as environmental and cultural conditions. Part of

[34]Beck-Gernsheim and Beck define individualisation as a process during which the influence of customs and traditions becomes weaker on an individual's biography. They describe the process in the following way: "(...) die Biographie der Menschen aus traditionalen Vorgaben und Sicherheiten, aus fremden Kontrollen und überregionalen Sittengesetzen herausgelöst, offen wird und gleichsam als Aufgabe in das Handeln jedes einzelnen gelegt wird." Beck-Gernsheim and Beck (1998): 12–13.

these conditions lie outside one's personal domain and constitute chances as well as limitations. Due to the demographic fact of a longer life-expectancy, marriages nowadays last longer than in earlier times. In fact, this longer duration in number of years spent together brings about changes in the partners' expectations and hopes associated with marriage. It bears the risk of producing new kinds of conflicts. Within the last hundred years the average duration of a marriage has doubled, which means that couples spend much more time together than in earlier times.[35] The longer a couple is married the more the spouses are exposed to the changing values and attitudes of society. In a positive development this may cause closer ties and more stability which helps the couple to cope with changes. On the other hand, it also bears the risk of differential personal development in which both partners react differently to new circumstances. Therefore more divorces of long-term marriages can be noticed in countries with highly dynamic socio-economic conditions.

Within the last decades gradual economic changes in many European countries and the United States have made it easier for women to gain access to the labour market due to political measures, education and professional specification. The increasing labour market participation of women has changed family life. This change together with a demographic pressure from an ageing population has made the reconciliation of work and family one of the major topics on the European social agenda. In 2005 the European Commission adopted the Framework of Actions on Gender Equality as proposed by the European social partners:[36]

> "With regard to supporting work-private life balance, the Framework of Actions identifies three key elements as follows: considering flexible working arrangements that can be taken up on a voluntary basis by both women and men, including leave arrangements, designed in a way that does not undermine their long term participation and position on the labour market (...); promoting a more balanced take-up of possibilities to ease work-private life balance; and jointly approaching public authorities to develop instruments that help increase the availability of accessible and affordable child care facilities of good quality and seeking innovative ways of providing essential private household or caring services." (Communication from the Commission 2006)[37]

The economic changes have several implications on the relationship between husband and wife. The way in which the spouses distribute paid and unpaid work among them has repercussions on the power dynamics that exist between them. Women have gained access to the labour market which has brought about a

[35]From a comparative historic point of view a couple who got married in 1870 would spend an average time of 23.4 years together, around 1900 it would be 28.2 years. Around the year 1930 a couple spent approximately 30 years together whereas a couple getting married in 1970 would spend a total amount of 43 years together. Lutz quoted in Sieder (1987): 262.

[36]The European social partners are: UNICE (Union of Industrial and Employers' Confederation), UEAPME (European Association of Craft, Small and Medium-Sized Enterprises), CEEP (European Centre of Enterprises with Public Participation and of Enterprises of General Economic Interest), ETUC (European Trade Union Confederation).

[37]See First-Stage Consultation of European Social Partners on Reconciliation of Professional, Private and Family Life (http://ec.europa.eu/employment_social/news/2006/oct/consultation_reconciliation_en.pdf).

modification of gender roles. In this context we have to distinguish between gender role and gender stereotype.[38] Research has shown that biological sexuality is not linked to different types of character.[39] Rather, there exists a broad range of psychological characteristics whereby femininity and masculinity partially merge and overlap. Gender differences are not biologically or genetically determined but are culturally transmitted. In fact, the male nature contains female features the same as the female nature contains male characteristics. Nevertheless, every society holds some sort of gender ideology for men and women which results in gender stereotypes that are commonly held and are adopted by many people. But this does not necessarily mean that the majority of men and women exactly show these characteristics.

Gender stereotypes tend to be formed at an early age with men and women being identified with particular qualities. Stereotypes are used to quickly process information about a person and to keep the effort for thought as low as possible. Therefore gender stereotypes are problematic in two respects, first because they often hold outdated and obsolete views and values that have been uncritically adopted and second, stereotypes are resistant to change, even if personal experience shows otherwise.[40]

Although men and women are equal before the law women's discrimination is still present in our society. This becomes manifest in the form of job discrimination, fewer women occupying higher posts in politics, social, cultural or the economic area. A severe form of discrimination is domestic violence.[41] Therefore the motives for the introduction of the Law on Gender Equality, introduced in Spain in 2007, was to guarantee gender equality in public life and to promote it in people's private lives.[42] In the introduction to the law some of the motives for its implementation are mentioned:

> "El pleno reconocimiento de la igualdad formal ante la ley, aun habiendo comportado, sin duda, un paso decisivo, ha resultado ser insuficiente. La violencia de género, la discriminación salarial, la discriminación en las pensiones de viudedad, el mayor desempleo femenino, la todavía escasa presencia de las mujeres en puestos de responsabilidad política, social, cultural y económica, o los problemas de conciliación entre la vida personal, laboral y familiar muestran cómo la igualdad plena, efectiva, entre mujeres y hombres, (...), es

---

[38]Gender role is a sociological construct that describes a set of recognized norms of conduct that are associated with men and women in a society. Within gender roles biological sexuality is transformed into specific forms of male and female behaviour. Gender roles vary according to culture and social class, although there are also similarities among what is expected from men and women in different social and cultural contexts.

[39]See studies of Kürthy (1987): 23, Oerter and Montada (1982): 20.

[40]See: Dema-Moreno and Díaz-Martínez (2010).

[41]'Gender-based violence' and 'domestic violence' are used synonymously to denote abusive behaviour by one or both partners in an intimate relationship. Both terms refer mainly to violence against women because women suffer higher rates of injury or assault than men.

[42]Ley Orgánica 3/2007, de 22 de marzo, para la igualdad efectiva de mujeres y hombres, BOE, 71, 23.3.2007: 12611–12645.

todavía hoy una tarea pendiente que precisa de nuevos instrumentos jurídicos. Resulta necesaria, en efecto, una acción normativa dirigida a combatir todas las manifestaciones aún subsistentes de discriminación, directa o indirecta, por razón de sexo y a promover la igualdad real entre mujeres y hombres, con remoción de los obstáculos y estereotipos sociales que impiden alcanzarla." (Ley Orgánica para la igualdad efectiva de mujeres y hombres)

As was mentioned before, the economic changes go along with new demands and require a modification of gender roles. Nevertheless, the role distribution in a couple's private sphere often tends to be a traditional one which results in a double burden for women trying to manage job and household duties. Therefore the law makes also reference to the organisation of family duties and pleads for the principle of co-responsibility among husband and wife.[43]

From a sociological perspective stereotypes are used by the more influential group of society against the group who is less significant in terms of influence and power. The aim is a consolidation of power relations and to prevent change. Gender stereotypes can degenerate into a prejudiced belief of the pre-eminence of one's own gender and result in male or female chauvinism. A special form of gender denigration is sexism which denotes the belief that one gender is superior to the other. There is a risk that gender stereotypes turn into a barrier for men and women to develop their individual talents and qualities without constraints. Therefore the Law on Integral Protective Measures against Gender Violence,[44] introduced in Spain in 2004, makes special reference to the fields of media and mainstream and states that women's dignity and their right to a non-discriminatory and non-stereotypical image must be respected in both, the public and the private sphere. The law contains guidelines for the prevention of violence at all levels of society.[45]

The future developments of gender roles will increasingly become an indicator for family wellbeing. Beck analyses the socio-economic changes from a socio-historic perspective and points to two opposing tendencies that have influenced society since the 1950s, industrialisation on the one hand and individualisation on the other hand. Post-War industrial societies are based on the division of labour and

---

[43]See the following claim for co-responsibility in the distribution of household duties: "Especial atención presta la Ley a la corrección de la desigualdad en el ámbito específico de las relaciones laborales. Mediante una serie de previsiones, se reconoce el derecho a la conciliación de la vida personal, familiar y laboral y se fomenta una mayor corresponsabilidad entre mujeres y hombres en la asunción de obligaciones familiares, criterios inspiradores de toda la norma que encuentran aquí su concreción más significativa." (Ley Orgánica 3/2007, de 22 de marzo, para la igualdad efectiva de mujeres y hombres, BOE, 71, 23.3.2007:12612.

[44]Ley Orgánica 1/2004, de 28 de diciembre, de Medidas de Protección Integral contra la Violencia de Género, BOE, 313, 29.12.2004: 42166–42197.

[45]The law states the following: "En el campo de la publicidad, ésta habrá de respetar la dignidad de las mujeres y su derecho a una imagen no estereotipada, ni discriminatoria, tanto si se exhibe en los medios de comunicación públicos como en los privados. De otro lado, se modifica la acción de cesación o rectificación de la publicidad legitimando a las instituciones y asociaciones que trabajan a favor de la igualdad entre hombres y mujeres para su ejercicio." For a more detailed discussion of the phenomenon of gender violence see Chapter 2.

the citizens' dependence on paid work. The division of labour is mirrored in the family organization and is translated into traditional gender roles of male work outside the house and female housework. On the contrary, since the 1960s our society has undergone a continuous tendency of individualization, according to which individuals tend to construct and modify their lives according to personal preferences, wishes and needs. These two tendencies do not only produce tensions in society but also affect the private sphere. In other words, what appears as a private conflict about gender roles between two people has a societal as well as a political dimension.

Traditional gender roles have been changing, mainly as a reaction to women's labour market participation. A dual-earner couple being confronted with job, child-care and housework can only effectively manage their duties if both spouses work together. This requirement is explicitly mentioned in Article 68 of the Spanish Civil Code, which was modified by the Ley 15/2005 of 8 July.[46] The article states that the spouses are obliged to live together, be faithful and mutually support one another. Additionally, they should share housework and participate in the care of people who are dependent on them.

Likewise, Delgado Martín speaks of new democratic values in the family which were the inspiring motives for the reform of Spanish Family Law. He states that freedom and equality among women and men have replaced traditional attitudes such as authoritarian style and obedience. The new democratic family model has taken the place of the patriarch family. He points out that women's access to the labour market has changed the distribution of family duties. Conversely, he notices an increasing participation of fathers in domestic responsibilities:

> "En la sociedad española actual, así como en los países de nuestro entorno, existe una tendencia de mayor implicación del padre en las responsabilidades del hogar familiar, aunque todavía quede un largo camino por andar para conseguir una auténtica efectividad del principio de corresponsabilidad doméstica que consagra el último inciso del artículo 68 del Código Civil (. . .). Esta constatación se confirma si se tiene en cuenta el escaso número de permiso de paternidad solicitados por los padres en caso de nacimiento de hijo (. . .), así como el hecho de que en la gran mayoría de los procesos de separación o divorcio se atribuye a la madre la guarda y custodia.(. . .)." (Delgado Martín 2008: 158)

In a study on the evaluation and distribution of family work, Thompson found three factors that contribute to women's sense of fairness: Outcome values, comparison referents, and justifications.[47] Women sense an injustice if they lack some outcome they desire, have a high standard for comparison, and believe there is no acceptable justification for being deprived of desired outcomes. To understand women's sense of fairness, researchers need to consider (a) valued outcomes

---

[46]"See Article 68 CC: Artículo 68

Los cónyuges están obligados a vivir juntos, guardarse fidelidad y socorrerse mutuamente. Deberán, además, compartir las responsabilidades domésticas y el cuidado y atención de ascendientes y descendientes y otras personas dependientes a su cargo." (Article 68, Spanish Civil Code).

[47]See: Thompson (1991): 181–196.

other than time and tasks, (b) gender comparison referents, and (c) gender-specific justifications for men's contribution to family work.

A working woman's financial contribution to the family budget usually has a stabilizing effect on the economic household situation. However, the mere fact that separation has become economically possible for women seems to have considerable influence on the equilibrium between spouses. The organisation of a relationship and the family requires indispensable contributions from both sides. Nevertheless it is the economically more powerful spouse who is able to increase the value of a couple's tangible assets.[48] In their study about the influence of the division of household labor on marital stability, Nock and Brinig demonstrate the economic aspect:

> "For example, building an addition on a house or installing thermally efficient windows will increase the home's resale value. (It will also increase the share of the property allocated to whoever did or financed the improvement, should the couple divorce). Doing work on an automobile may save costly repairs and may increase the car's resale or trade-in value. On thc other hand, ironing shorts or keeping a spotless home assets in a much less direct and tangible way." (Nock and Brinig 2002: 186)

Traditional role models rely on the separation of tasks into household duties and work outside of the house. From the economic point of view, marriage is a long-term contract which entails monogamy and couple-specific investments that are supposed to increase the value of marriage across time. The economist Becker argues that this value can be best achieved if men specialize in 'market production'[49] whereas women concentrate on 'household production'[50] once the marriage begins. He states that women's ability of childbearing gives them a comparative advantage by which they can invest in human capital. Husbands, however invest their labour force in market production. He considers the traditional marriage as more efficient than dual-worker marriages, where housework is shared:

> "Since married women have been specialized to childbearing and other domestic activities, they have demanded long-term "contracts" from their husbands to protect them against abandonment and other adversities. Virtually all societies have developed long-term protection for married women; one can even say that "marriage" is defined by a long-term commitment between a man and a woman." (Becker 1991: 31f)

The home-economist's approach to the study of marriage has provided relevant insight into the dynamism of cost and benefit calculation of family roles. Economic family theories hold that the division of labour and specialization within the family increases its productivity. According to this view, a family functions similar to economies of scale, referring to organisation and consumption of goods. This perspective is described by Carrasco who points to the advantage of marriage in providing the most favourable conditions for the production of goods and services:

---

[48]Tangible asset refers to material property such as money or real estate. Intangible assets include immaterial values such as patents, copyrights etc.

[49]Becker (1991): 312ff.

[50]Becker (1991): 3f.

"El matrimonio produce economías de escala. El matrimonio (la relación de pareja) no es solo una unidad de gestión del afecto y de la pulsión sexual, ni un mecanismo (el más barato y eficaz de los descubiertos hasta ahora) de producir descendientes de la especia humana. Es también una unidad productiva de bienes y servicios. El matrimonio (la relación de pareja) produce bienes y servicios y consume inputs externos para programar esta producción, entre ellos, y muy importante, el trabajo en casa de uno o de ambos cónyuges. El matrimonio tiene una gran ventaja frente al resto de las formas productivas de naturaleza societaria: la extremada eficiencia en conseguir economías merced a una especialización adecuada de cada uno de los miembros de la pareja." (Carrasco 2006: 20)

However, the question remains if there are other criteria, apart from those of efficiency and output, which have an effect on marital stability. Nock and Brinig take up the notion of individualism and see it related to an egalitarian distribution of resources and duties. This concept is contrary to the traditional gender roles. They summarize their view in the following statement:

"This alternative assumes individualism within the marriage, equality among spouses, roughly equivalent earning capacity between spouses, and a need for flexibility over the life cycle. Those who advocate a more egalitarian marriage presume that, as married women enter the labour force, their husbands will pick up a fair share of household tasks." (Nock and Brinig 2002: 172)

In their study on the effect of egalitarian division of household labour on marriage, the authors focused on the spouses' individual evaluations of fairness of this division. They received rather astonishing results stating that, "marriages benefit when husbands and wives agree that wives are treated unfairly, but suffer when they agree that husbands are treated unfairly."[51] They concluded from their outcomes that if American marriages followed an asymmetric relational pattern which is inherently unfair, the result is stability. Economic dependence seems to contribute to marital stability. Conversely, stable marriages may not always be experienced as fair marriages by both spouses.

In a study on the role of egalitarianism for marital stability, Wilcox and Nock[52] came across two crucial issues: First, the dyadic commitment to institutional ideals about marriage and second, women's contentment with the division of household tasks. They also showed that men's marital emotion work is a very important determinant of women's estimated marital quality. They concluded that women experience marriage as happiest when it combines both, traditional and new elements, such as gender equality as well as normative commitment to the institution of marriage. These results are also confirmed by a study on divorce motives carried out by de Graaf and Kalmijn[53] who state that problems in the realm of work and household labour have become more important motives for divorce. This is consistent with the increase in emancipatory attitudes in the past decades. The authors state that:

[51]See: Nock and Brinig (2002): 188.

[52]See the study of Wilcox and Nock (2006): 1321 ff.

[53]See: de Graaf and Kalmijn (2006): 483.

> "Women's attitudes and ideas on gender roles became more egalitarian in the course of time, suggesting that women have also become more sensitive toward the way household labor is divided in marriage. In addition, changes in the actual practice of marriage have been less marked than changes in attitudes, particularly when focusing on how much men contribute to domestic chores and child rearing. This discrepancy, together with growing sensitivity toward gender issues, may lead to growing discontent about the division of labor in the home.
>
> Our hypothesis is that motives related to how the household is organized have become increasingly important across time, especially for women. This can be expected to lead to growing dissatisfaction with the role of men in child rearing and domestic chores and with men who spend too much time at work. This is the emancipation hypothesis." (de Graaf and Kalmijn 2006: 488)

A relevant aspect in this context seems to be the amount of equality and bargaining power that each partner has in the case of conflict.[54] The relevant components of the bargaining model are a spouse's earning power (income), the amount of working hours (full-time, half-time employment) and education or level of formation. Any change in earning power, working hours and education results in a change of an individual's threat point.[55] If we start from a traditional distribution of gender roles an increase of women's earning power tends to reduce the gains from home specialization.[56] A relative balance in the amount of bargaining power is supposed to be more advantageous for both in terms of equality. On the contrary, such relationships tend to be more susceptible to conflicts of interest than relationships involving traditional role models. Lehrer analyzed the difference in effects that a high earning potential has for husbands and wives. Whereas a husband's high income in a marriage with traditional role distribution enables a high living standard that alleviates economic tensions and leads to stable unions, it seems to have the reverse effect for married women:

> "While an increase in the wife's earning capacity generates an income effect similar to that associated with the husband's earnings, an "independence effect" exerts a countervailing influence: a higher wage rate increases a woman's ability to support herself and her children outside of marriage. Thus among unhappily married women, those with a higher earning potential can more easily terminate their unions." (Lehrer 2006: 5)

An additional risk factor lies in the little time that dual-earner couples have for their relationship.[57] Full-time working couples spend probably the same amount of time with their colleagues at work as with each other. The better economic conditions have an adverse effect by enabling easier separation for couples. As the relationship often acts to absorb social stress from outside of the marriage, the

[54]Bargaining or negotiation power in relationships denotes the power that one has in order to pursue his or her interests. It includes a person's power in economic terms as well as communication skills such as persuasiveness or art of reasoning.

[55]The threat point denotes the position in negotiations until a person is willing to make concessions in order to reach an agreement.

[56]See: Anxo and Carlin (2004): 32.

[57]This risk will be discussed in detail in Sect. 2.4 in connection with the structure–functional theory of family.

organization of work, running costs and child rearing make great demands. The less the spouses are socio-economically dependent on each other, the more frequently they may consider separation to end an unhappy marriage.[58] Several studies have shown the significantly high ratio between women's employment and divorce rates. In a study carried out in the United States, Greenstein points to a parallel increase of both divorce rates and female employment over time:

> "... we find that both indicators have been generally increasing since the late nineteenth century; that both indicators have increased sharply since the 1950s; and that the relative increases in the indicators have been approximately equal." (Greenstein 1990: 659)

Other factors that contribute to this trend are the secularization process, an increasing mobility due to urbanization and the individualization of life concepts. People have to be increasingly flexible and react to changes on the labour market. During the process of secularization, institutions throughout society were removed from the control of religion. This applies also to the institution of marriage.

However, a brief insight into Spanish history shows that divorce has only been legally permitted for three decades. It had been allowed during the Second Spanish Republic (1931–1939) when the Courts had approved a divorce law under an article of the Constitution of 1931, which provided for the dissolution of marriage. During the long period of Francisco Franco y Bahamonde's dictatorship (1939–1975) state and church were not separate. Therefore the only way for a couple to end their marriage was to prove that it had totally failed and had to be declared null and void under canonical proceedings. It was not until 1981 that divorce was re-legalised and introduced by Law 30/1981.[59]

For instance, de Ussel summarizes that two or three generations ago marriage was strongly related to customs and tradition. This attitude has changed fundamentally. Church has lost its influence on privacy and the state no longer interferes in the assessment of divorce grounds. Therefore legal systems have introduced the non-fault regime in divorce procedures. Nowadays, on the contrary, the greater diversity puts couples willing to get married in the role of pioneers. He states:

> "La familia y el matrimonio (también las relaciones de pareja) son hoy, y cada vez mas, construcciones individuales en un escenario donde se cuenta con elementos de hostilidad cultural. Es una realidad mas diversa – si se quiere mas adaptable a las opciones personales – pero incrementa las dificultades de armonización entre las partes involucradas." (de Ussel 2005: 42)

---

[58]Ninety percent of the divorces are submitted by women. This seems to indicate that for women, marriage as an institution has lost its importance and function as a life-long relationship. Middle class wives with work formation and in non-tenured employment living in urban areas most frequently file for divorce. Lowest divorce rates are to be noticed with non-working wives. See: Sieder (1987): 261.

[59]See: Ley 30/1981, de 7 de julio, por la que se modifica la regulación del matrimonio en el Código Civil y se determina el procedimiento a seguir en las causas de nulidad, separación y divorcio. In the year 1981, a total number of 202,037 couples got married and 16,334 couples divorced or separated.

Nowadays partners tend to negotiate the organisation of their relationship in terms of personal expectations and distribution of duties. Relationships of this kind are characterized by a more flexible organisation of family roles and by negotiation of family tasks and duties. People seem to have become more suspicious of institutional constraints obviously verified by the number of people who opt for non-marital partnerships or for staying single.[60] Accordingly, a greater variety of forms of life have developed, especially among couples without children. There are several new forms of relationship that do not fit into the traditional frames such as weekend relationships, negotiated partnerships, and temporal partnerships based on mutual consent.[61] The variety of family forms that exists nowadays is due to the fading influence of religion and tradition, a change in the biological conditions, and exchange with other cultures. However, the tendency towards individualization carries the risk of isolation.

The separation of public and private sphere leads to an alienation between family and society. As the welfare state has become the provider of security and care, the family has lost its political importance. As a consequence, this has led to an internalization of family relations and a tendency to closer and more reliable relationships:

> "Verinnerlichung der familiaren Beziehungen ist ein Kennzeichen dieses Funktionswandels. Die Partnerwahl gewinnt den Rang einer einzigartigen persönlichen Entscheidung der Ehegatten füreinander; die Kernfamilie konstituiert sich als Intimgruppe, die ihre Bewahrung in stärkerem Masse, als es die funktionsgesättigte Grossfamilie einst tat, in der Harmonie ihrer Gefühle findet. [...] Die mit diesem Funktionsverlust verbundene "Ausgliederung der Familie ins Private" (Schelsky) erscheint in dieser Intimisierung der personalen Beziehungen folgerichtig zu Ende gefuhrt." (Gernhuber and Coester-Waltjen 2006: 5)

A further aspect refers to a greater social acceptance of divorce these days as compared to earlier times.[62] Until the 1970s, divorce was socially unaccepted and legislation made it difficult for couples to divorce. It was seen as a pathologic development caused by the spouses' personal failure and divorced people were often discriminated. However, within the last two decades the cultural and normative significance of marriage has decreased and has diminished its importance as a life-long institution.

---

[60]In this context it is interesting to consider the motives for marriage over time. Historically we may distinguish between four types of marriages. The first type is characterized by economic calculation where marriage was considered as security for women and was a possibility of transmitting land property. Due to political and economic changes in the nineteenth century the economically inspired marriage was replaced by an institutional legal model. The family was considered as the core of society and people married to have a family. In both forms marriage and family were legally and socially controlled by state and church. After the Second World War two aims dominated the partners' decision to get married, emotional reasons and the desire to found a family. During the post-war years, state and church had considerable influence on the construction of parent role models. See: Sieder (1987).

[61]See: Gernhuber and Coester-Waltjen (2006): 4.

[62]According to the Christian view marriage is an inseparable band and divorce is considered a moral failure that has to be sanctioned.

Today divorce tends to be more and more accepted as a solution to an irrevocable breakdown of marriage. Divorce is less considered as personal failure, but is now associated with the principle of freedom of choice and self-responsibility. In fact, sociologists see a trend in our society where the lifelong institution of marriage will be more and more replaced by a 'serial monogamy' with more than one temporary relationship. Sociologists and psychologists have reflected on the high divorce rate and conclude that divorce is no longer an isolated issue but rather a phenomenon that affects a growing number of couples. Napp-Peters even speaks of divorce as a mass phenomenon and pleads for the parents' rights to receive competent advice during the family transition.[63]

As a result of the increasing number of divorced people the normative status of marriage has changed. In Spain divorce was first introduced in 1981 by the Law 30/1981 which contained the guilt-principle according to which the one who contravened Article 82 was legally sanctioned.[64] In contrast to the previous legislation the new legal provisions of Law 15/2005 enable the spouses to divorce unilaterally without having to account for their decision. Article 82 was annulled and the non-fault regime was introduced, according to which marital breakdown is considered sufficient proof.[65]

We have listed some relevant sociological and economic aspects that affect the pair relationship. However, there are certain individual dispositions and peculiarities in a person's conduct that are likely to cause conflict. The economic status of society has reached a level at which people's primary needs are generally satisfied. Individual well-being and attainment are sometimes more important for individuals than family life and compromise. Therefore a spouse's personality traits play a decisive role in the choice of a partner. In the following section we will present some personal dispositions that count as risk factors for crisis.

---

[63]See: Napp-Peters (1988), Amato (1993): 50 f. and Fthenakis (1985a, b).

[64]Among the reasons for separation Article 82 of the Law mentioned a spouse abandoning home without justification, marital infidelity or any other gross violation of marital duties. See: Article 82 of Ley 30/1981, de 7 de julio, whereby the regulation of marriage was modified in the Civil Code. BOE, 20. 1. 1981.

[65]This legal modification has provoked a debate among scholars whether the new legislation would be responsible for the increase in divorce rates. Studies carried out on this issue over the last two decades can be divided into two groups, with the first group of studies where researchers suggest that no-fault divorce did not have any impact on divorce rates. See: Peters (1986): 437–454; Ellman and Lohr (1998): 341–359; Gray (1998): 628–642. Another group supports the view that these laws have had a significant impact on divorce rates. See: Allen (1992): 679–685; Brinig and Buckley (1998): 325–340; Friedberg (1998): 608–627). For instance, González and Viitanen (2006) investigated to which extent reformed divorce laws facilitating non-fault and unilateral divorce have contributed to increasing divorce figures. By analyzing the changes in legislation of 18 European countries within the last 50 years they found out that the introduction of no-fault, unilateral divorce is positively correlated with divorce rates.

1.4.2 *Personal Factors*

This section is devoted to the description of pathological processes within the relationship and the family-structure that may provoke mental disturbances in the partners and their children. Marital crises do not only affect the spouses but usually have a negative impact on the functioning of the whole family. A conflict situation may lead to problems such as psychosomatic and psychological illnesses, behaviour and personality disturbances, sexual dysfunctions or addictions. The reason why a problem emerges among spouses is usually from the complex process of individual dispositions interweaving with partnership related factors. A problem caused by one of the partners nearly always affects also the other and requires conflict solving strategies on both sides.

The following factors exert an influence on the quality and stability of relationships: personality traits (e.g. unsolved psychological conflicts, depression, lack of self-esteem), style of emotional ties (closeness versus distance), biographical experience (e.g. age and maturity, divorce of parents), educational and professional resources, and demographic facts (e.g. age at which marriage is contracted). We will describe some of these aspects in more detail. Several studies have shown the positive correlation between divorce rates and young age at the time of marriage. People who get married at their early twenties tend to have inadequate self-knowledge and are often uncertain about their potential and future plans. They are probably less able to judge their partner's personality characteristics and are therefore prone to making a wrong decision. A spouse's high expectations of the respective other and unrealistic ideas about marriage and sharing life together are often the reason for conflict.[66] In her study exploring the relation between age at marriage and marital stability, Lehrer explains the lower divorce rate in the United States since the 1980s by assuming that marriages contracted by spouses who are in their thirties tend to be more stable than those contracted at a very younger age.[67] She says:

> "While the age at marriage-marital instability curve flattens in the early thirties, the strongly favorable effect of postponing marriage is the most salient pattern in both cycles: the unions of women who delay entry into marriage are more stable than those of their counterparts who wed in their teens by a wide margin. This age at marriage – divorce connection, coupled with the trend towards delayed marriage, is undoubtedly a major force

---

[66]The following misconceptions about love and relationship are typical ingredients of conflicts: "Who loves, automatically knows what the partner wishes, wants, feels and thinks. – In a loving relationship the spouse considers the other's needs more important than the own, wants to make him happy and always wants to be close. – One partner is incomplete without the other. – In a good marriage there are no problems and conflicts. – Partners always have the same views, aims and ideals. – A good marriage comes about by itself without the spouses' effort to make the relationship work – the relationship is static and does not change over time. – Having divergent opinions about something is not favourable and should be avoided. In such a case only one can be right (lack of tolerance)".

[67]See also the studies of Oppenheimer (1988): 563–591 and Becker et al. (1977): 1141–1187.

> in the overall decline in the rate of marriage dissolution in the United States since the early 1980s (. . .)." (Lehrer 2006: 22)

Certain personality characteristics create risk factors for the functioning of the relationship, such as egocentrism, unsolved internal psychological conflicts in one partner, dependence on family of origin (e.g. sub-conscious delegations or instructions) and forms of mental disorder (such as perception disorder or thought disorder). Egocentrism or narcissism is the inability to understand or perceive someone else's point of view.[68] It has a negative effect on relationships because of an egocentric person's primary interest in his or her own needs and the extreme concentration of attention upon the self. In her study on therapeutic strategies when working with high conflict personalities Nichols views egocentrism as a counter-reaction to deep-rooted feelings of inferiority. She gives the following description of a narcissistic personality:

> "The driving force in the Narcissistic personality is a fear of inferiority. This sense of inferiority causes the person to constantly demand attention and exaggerated respect. They feel they are victims when others do not hold them in the esteem they feel they deserve. (. . .) Any criticism will be met with extremely negative reactions and they will not hesitate to be disrespectful and arrogant to you or others." (Nichols 2007: 231)

The behaviour of a narcissistic family member is opposed to the view of the family as a system of relations based on mutual exchange of resources[69] and support. An egoistic person's constant demand for attention is therefore likely to produce conflicts. Another personality disorder that affects the family is antisocial personality disorder (ASPD). The person with ASPD is characterised by self-interest and will hurt others in ordered to reach his or her goals. It is assumed that this disorder has its origin in childhood and becomes worse across time. Unlike the narcissistic personality the antisocial person has a fear of being dominated which in turn provokes him or her to dominate and control others in order to avoid this feeling. Nichols says about the antisocial personality:

> "This drive manifests itself in (. . .) taking advantage of other people (. . .). They win people over with charm and good deeds while underneath lurk their true intentions and bad acts. Chronic lying and manipulation are key characteristics of the antisocial personality. They will often accuse another person of being guilty of behavior that is actually their own." (Nichols 2007: 232)

---

[68] Other expressions with similar meanings are egocentricity, egoism, self-centeredness or selfishness. An egocentric person has an exaggerated belief in his or her own importance and tends to strive for the satisfaction of own needs with little or no concern for others.

[69] Mental resources include a person's conceptual and professional knowledge as well as practical skills such as operational and cognitive skills, relationship skills and attitudes. Resources enable a person to establish competencies in specific fields of action. For instance, relationship resources concern a person's readiness to support and encourage the other and provide help. They refer to the amount of time, attention and affection dedicated to the other, the sense of a common bond, or the steadiness of trust and reliance someone is willing to invest in a relationship.

Unsolved psychological conflicts are often the origin of partner problems. Leaving aside what the contents may be, in such cases, the internal conflicting urges and motivates clash with family rules, values and social norms. The affected person usually attempts to solve the conflict by trying to impose a logical structure on it. However, it is rather difficult to solve such conflict without a therapist's help, especially if it dates back to earlier events in a person's life.

Another psychological problem is a person's thought disorder which denotes the difficulty to distinguish between a certain event and its personal experience, to comprehend its cause and draw conclusions for one's conduct. Thought processes may also either be too abstract or too concrete or may be characterised by irrational attitudes. Thought disorders often go along with perception disorders[70] in which people tend to cut out certain impressions and emotions or perceive a distorted picture of reality. Such disorders often have a long history and impede on the resolution of conflicts.

In his pioneering book on the analysis of dual relationship, Willi presented a profound analysis of frequent behavioural patterns.[71] The reason why we present this concept in the section on personal factors is because the concept starts from an individual's predispositions as a main motive for partner selection. By making use of a combined systemic-psychodynamic approach to marital therapy, Willi introduces the concept of the 'collusion'. In this context collusion is defined as the interplay of two people's desires and needs that proceeds on a subconscious level. According to this concept, the emotional attraction in the selection of a mate is based on a fascinating, mutual theme shared by both partners in order to be mastered together. According to the author collusion means:

> "(...) ein uneingestandenes, oft unbewusstes Zusammenspiel von Partnern, das sie zur Abwehr und Bewältigung von miteinander geteilten Ängsten und Schuldgefühlen inszenieren und aufrechterhalten und durch das sie sich unentrinnbar aufeinander bezogen fühlen." (Willi 1998: 286)

The partners subconsciously start colluding in order to compensate for former frustrations and to repress fears of intimacy. The partners experience this perfect interplay as harmony and interpret it as love. However, across time the collusion can turn into a trap from which it seems difficult to escape. This is because the interplay has gathered momentum and each of the two has undergone emotional change. Thus, the spouses may enter into an escalation of the dysfunctional interaction pattern which is difficult to solve without the help of a therapist.[72] Willi identifies four different types of collusions, each type of which contains two

[70]Perception disorder is a disturbance in the processing of sensory impressions and denotes a disordered process in the perception, evaluation and interpretation of impressions.

[71]See: Willi (1998): 35 f.

[72]A partner therapy based on the concept of collusion aims at improving the intradyadic and extradyadic boundaries and the depolarization of extreme progressive-regressive behaviour. These goals can be reached by both systemic and psychodynamic techniques. See: Willi (1998): 16.

Type of collusion	narcissistic collusion	oral collusion	phallus-oedipal collusion	anal-sadistic collusion
Motto: love as...	being as one	caring for each other	male self-affirmation	belonging to each other

Fig. 1.5 Model of four partner-collusions according to Willi

roles such as a "progressive" and a "regressive" role.[73] The four collusions are the (1) narcissistic collusion, (2) the oral collusion, (3) the phallus-oedipal collusion and (4) the anal-sadistic collusion. The roles within these collusions fit perfectly together, with those played by individuals who share the same type of collusion in a complementary way. The table shows the four collusions (Fig. 1.5).

In the narcissistic collusion the motto is 'love as being one', which indicates a symbiotic attitude towards the relationship. The progressive partner tends to see the other as part of himself rather than as a separate individual. The regressive partner, on the contrary admires the other and his or her life revolves around the partner's life. The second, oral collusion, centers on the theme of caring for each other and denotes an asymmetric relationship in which the regressive partner expects the progressive to unconditionally care for him without asking for anything in return. In a phallus-oedipal collusion both partners have a problematical attitude towards their respective gender roles. The woman suppresses characteristics that are viewed as masculine and her male partner suppresses his feminine qualities. This attitude has its origin in a conflicting relationship to the opposite-sex-parent.[74] A solution to this conflict is difficult because both reject the possibility to identify with the same-sex-parent.

In the anal-sadistic collusion the progressive partner has the powerful, autonomous and active role, whereas the regressive partner shows passive and submissive behaviour. The dynamism behind this collusion is that the dominant partner tends to ward off his or her own fear of being dominated. The submissive partner, on the other hand, avoids any confrontation and signals the other that he may be sure of his or her obedience. Yet, the submissive partner indirectly dominates the other through his or her obedience.[75]

A further relevant aspect is the partners' aim of finding an appropriate form of emotional bonding, such as the acceptable degree of closeness and distance

[73]In Willi's concept of the collusion the actors have the characteristics of the Freudian psychosexual stages. See: Mitscherlich et al. (1975): 119 ff.

[74]Freud called this phenomenon Oedipus conflict (derived from the Greek myth of Oedipus, who unknowingly killed his father and marries his mother) which refers to a stage of psychosexual development in which boys regard the father as an adversary and competitor for the exclusive love of their mother. It is assumed that the successful resolution of the Oedipus complex is a key element in the development of gender roles and identity. See: Freud (1972): 254 ff.

[75]This type of collusion can take several forms such as the ruler-obedient or the sado-masochistic relationship as well as the jealousness-infidelity collusion. In the case where the fear of being dominated is present in both partners, the collusion degenerates into a power struggle. This is associated with antagonist feelings in the sense that the constant struggle unites and at the same time separates the two.

between the spouses. This is not only important for the couple but their conduct also serves as a model for the children. Some family members distance themselves too much from others by hiding their thoughts and emotions and shutting themselves off. This leads to an unproductive constellation in which the family members tend to impede each other. In this context Fromm speaks of two kinds of unproductive families, such as the withdrawing and the symbiotic family.[76] Although withdrawal as a family style is accepted if it occurs in certain intervals, it may also become a dominant style, involving indifference or even hatefulness among partners or family members. Parents are usually demanding of their children who are expected to live up to high standards. Deviant behaviour is punished with the use of guilt and withdrawal of affection. This behaviour is considered destructive because it views rules more important than the individual.

Another problematic constellation is the symbiotic family. Fromm defines symbiosis as a relationship of two or more people who cannot live without each other. In a symbiotic family, some members of the family are prevented from fully developing personalities of their own. In such cases the child would be forced into the role of becoming merely a reflection of the parent's wishes. A further characteristic of the symbiotic family is a tendency of one partner inundating the other with personal thoughts and feelings and constantly striving for affection and recognition. Paradoxically, in this case intimacy presents a superficial contradiction. That is to say, a high grade of intimacy and self-disclosure usually leads to more intensive feelings of investment and concern. It may lead to a beneficial symbiotic relationship where both mutually benefit. On the contrary, however, it may as well generate a relationship of mutual dependence where feelings of love can easily turn to feelings of hate. In other cases partners tend to fluctuate between isolation and intensive involvement, which can be especially irritating for younger children.

Another complex problem is a partner's emotional dependence on the family of origin. This dependence has its origin in a person's biography and individual experience of a spouse's own parent–child relationship. It goes back to early parental delegations or instructions which tacitly have influenced a child's behaviour. These delegations may contain expectations referring to a profession or discouraging statements. Adult sons or daughters may still be bound to their parents by feelings of guilt or hatred because of earlier traumata. Due to the subconscious nature of this problem it is difficult to treat because the affected person tends to avoid or even negate the whole problem. However, if such conflicting relationship is not reflected upon, the person affected may later project similar feelings on his or her partner.[77]

---

[76] See: Fromm (2004).

[77] According to Freud projection is one of the ego defence mechanism in which one attributes to others one's own unwanted thoughts or emotions. Projection reduces anxiety by allowing unwanted subconscious impulses to be expressed in the context of the other without the own self recognizing them (Freud, 1975).

1.4.3 Pair-Related Factors

We will now deal with the factors that concern the functioning and management of the pair relationship. A meaningful criterion for the quality and stability of relationships is the extent to which the partners are well matched in the following aspects: personality traits and physical appearance, preferences concerning way of life, social networks and attitude towards sociological roles. Communication is the fundament for interactions. However, communication does not always follow a strict logical order and is therefore susceptible to misunderstandings. Nichols puts it like this:

> "All behaviour is considered communication. One "cannot not communicate" (. . .) according to one of the axioms of communication theory that has become a staple of family systems approaches. Patterns of communication and the accompanying metacommunications (communications about how to perceive and respond to the message) define rules, roles, and relationships (including boundaries) within the family and between the family and external systems." (Nichols 1989: 71)[78]

Certain constellations and mechanisms that may cause conflicting situations shall be described. The interaction among the factors mentioned above is guided by the mechanisms of symmetry and complementary. A relationship may have a relatively clear symmetric or complementary structure, but it may also take the form of a paradox meta-complementary structure. All messages delivered in relationships have two sides: the content and the communication style that reveal the quality of the relationship.[79] For a better understanding of interactions, Schulz von Thun has pointed out the two aspects of every message, the content and the communication style, both of which reveal the speaker's attitude towards the receiver of the information. Communication is always in the form of meta-communication because the speaker's style determines the contents.

The diagram shows four patterns of communicative interaction, such as the symmetric, the complementary (or asymmetric), the meta-complementary pattern and meta-communication (Fig. 1.6).

A relationship is called symmetric if both partners allow each other to choose from the same range of possible conduct (e.g. make suggestions, criticize, give advice). Both spouses have the similar resources and perceive their power base as more or less equal. Conflict here might escalate rapidly because each believes that he or she can win. In a complementary relationship, A's conduct would differ from B's conduct under the condition that these different ways of conduct complement

[78]Nichols (1989): 67–97.

[79]For a better understanding of interactions, Schulz von Thun (1981) added more notions to the relational aspect of a message, such as self-disclosure and appeal. These meta-communicative indicators give the reveal the receiving person information about how the content of the message shall be understood and treated.

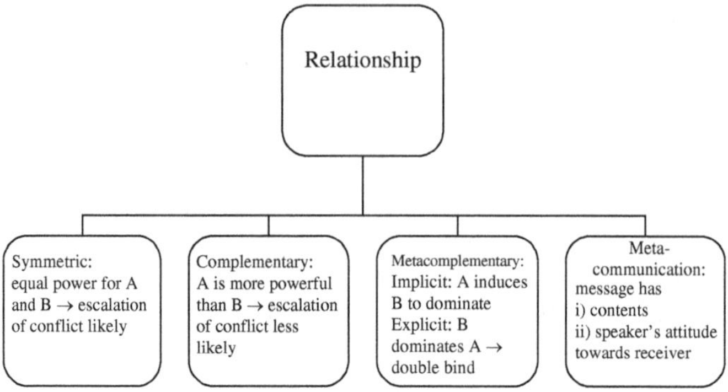

Fig. 1.6 The four components of a relationship

each other or are tailored for each other (e.g. A asks and B answers, A gives orders and B obeys, etc.). Both spouses have a different amount of resources because one is superior to the other which generates both dominant and submissive behaviours. Escalation of conflict is not as likely because one member is perceived as more powerful.

A traditional division of labour among spouses may be considered as asymmetrical relationship. If such a relationship is analyzed in terms of private autonomy or personal freedom, it can be described as a game where one spouse sacrifices autonomy to the benefit of the other. This agreement is commonly known as the 'housewife family model'[80] where wives follow a role that is tacitly and explicitly established in our society. On the contrary, a husband would use his freedom of movement to follow a profession and to establish societal contact. The rules of the game are based on the agreement that one is willing to deliberately constrain his freedom for the sake of the other. This rule remains normally implicit first, because it is based on tradition and second, because it belongs to the private sphere. This is also the reason why a change of this rule is likely to result in conflict.[81] The risk with an asymmetrical relationship lies in the fact that the spouse who is in control of the family resources (e.g. money) usually has more bargaining power in the case of

[80]One of the aims of the reform of German family law was to replace the traditional concept of the 'housewife family model' (*Hausfrauen-Ehe* or *Versorgungsehe*) by a model based on women's economic independence and self-responsibility. Accordingly, Gerngruber and Coester-Waltjen say about this principle: "Nachehelicher Unterhalt wird nur auf Grund bestimmter, in den §§ 1570–1576 abschliessend geregelter Tatbestände geschuldet; (...). Wenn überhaupt, so mag der Norm Bedeutung zugestanden werden als gesetzlicher Ausdruck des Vorrangs der Eigenverantwortung (mit besonderer Betonung der Erwerbstätigkeit in den „folgenden Vorschriften") vor der Fremdversorgung und als Träger eines Enumerationsprinzips, das jedes Bemühen um weitere Anspruchsgrundlagen (etwa aus § 242) ausschliesst." Gerngruber and Coester-Waltjen (2006): 292. See also the principle of 'self-sufficiency' referring maintenance between former spouses in the Principles of European Family Law (Part II, Chap. I, Principle 2:2).

[81]See: Padilla-Gálvez (2008): 57ff.

conflict. Parkman points to the risk of underestimating the contribution of the economically weaker part:

> "Over the duration of marriage, the potential contributions of both spouses create the incentives that are the basis for the marriage, but the asymmetry of their contributions can create incentives for the income-earning spouses, for example, to dissolve their marriage later [...]. To increase the gains from marriage, it is important to encourage spouses to search diligently for a spouse, to appreciate the benefits of their actions to others, and to anticipate that their sacrifices will be reciprocated by the actions of others." (Parkman 2002: 60)

At first sight, it seems that only one of either possibilities, either the symmetric or the asymmetric model can exist in a marriage. However, an interaction becomes complex when A induces B to guide, dominate, or help. This implies that B has the upper hand. On a meta-level, however, A has the upper hand by having induced B to this kind of complementary relationship. This is called a meta-complementary relationship.[82] Once this knot is tied it is difficult to untie it because the interaction is implicitly created without the actors being fully aware if its implications. This kind of interaction takes a paradox turn if A (who has indirectly induced B to a dominant behaviour) later criticizes B's behaviour and demands a more egalitarian treatment. Consequently, B is in a dilemma because his or her conduct is considered wrong in any case. Such paradox interaction is called "double bind" because a person is bound to opposing or contradicting possibilities.[83]

In their study on satisfaction and stability in marriage, Karney and Bradbury proposed a theory that incorporates personality, family variables and life events into a framework.[84] In their "Vulnerability-Adaptation-Stress Model" they take a process-oriented view of relationships and underline the importance of adaptive processes when dealing with conflicts and critical life events. They identified the following three skills that optimise the processes by which marital satisfaction and stability change over time: (1) Enduring vulnerability denotes the individual strengths and weaknesses each spouse brings to the relationship, such as their personality, beliefs and attitudes about marriage, their family of origin and social background; (2) Coping with stressful life events is the ability of dealing with incidents, transitions, or circumstances encountered by the couple that can impinge on their relationship and create tensions or stress; (3) Adaptive processes are characterized by ways in which a couple addresses conflict, how they communicate, how they support each other and the ways in which they think about marriage.

[82]See: Olson (1972): 69–94.

[83]Double bind denotes a contradiction in the communication process in which a person receives two or more inconsistent messages, with one message negating the other. The receiver of such information finds himself or herself in a dilemma because if he or she responds to one message then automatically says the opposite to the other. See: Watzlawick et al. (2009).

[84]See: Karney and Bradbury (1995): 3ff.

They point out that dysfunctional patterns of communication may increase the likelihood of relationship problems and produces declines in satisfaction over time.[85]

Conflicts usually follow certain patterns of interaction. If they cannot be solved the pathogenic effects may lead to the splitting of the family, to alliances with outsiders (grandparents, friends) or to the expulsion of a family member. Expulsion may occur in the form of separation and divorce, unsocial behaviour or even mobbing in relationships.[86]

1.4.4 Family Related and Systemic Factors

There are family conflicts due to normative life events (transitions in the life- and family cycle) or non-normative life events (unforeseen events, e.g. unemployment, illness, change of job). Many family conflicts are provoked by either refusing a certain family role or by neglecting family duties. For example, a woman may withdraw herself from her husband in her role as a wife because she has made her role as mother absolute. Family members may lack a clear concept of the skills and duties that are associated with a particular role.

The quality of the relationship decreases if a spouse fills his or her role only insufficiently or excludes parts of it. This applies for instance, to cases of marital infidelity when one spouse starts an extramarital affair with another partner. A closer look on the phenomenon of infidelity shows, however, that it is rather the consequence to earlier changes in the relationship than its actual cause. In most cases there is a past record of disappointment with the relationship in one or both spouses and a lack of hope for change that induce infidelity. As such infidelity stands for loss of love, betrayal of trust, indifference or the spouses' impression of drifting apart. As a consequence infidelity often leads to deterioration in the affective and emotional realm of the marriage.[87]

---

[85]Here are some examples of communication traps that often lead to misunderstandings: A person may send vague or indefinite messages that contain ambiguous terms or incomplete sentences. Or else a sender gives only insufficient information to express a complex matter assuming that the perceiving person will guess the contents. Verbal messages may contradict nonverbal ones, which produces confusion on the side of the person receiving the message. In many cases the receiver does not ask for an explanation but tries to decode the message based on his or her experience. In such cases, the irritated receiver who is unable to decode the message tends to react by interrupting and disqualifying the sender's statements. Another conflict may be produced when family members use different channels of communication, such as one speaks in the name of the other or two family members communicate via a third member. It is obvious that such conduct produces misleading information which results in misunderstandings, wrong reactions, and discussions.

[86]The phenomenon of "mobbing" is known in the context of working life but may also occur in personal relationships where the economically more dominant partner uses unsocial behaviour to put the respective other under pressure. See: Schmidbauer (2007): 33ff.

[87]See: Glass and Wright (1997): 483 f.

Within Spanish Family Law the spouses' faithfulness towards one another is defined as obligation. Article 68 CC states that the spouses are obliged to live together, be faithful and should support one another.[88] As a precondition for trust among the spouses it is a constitutive requirement for marriage. Marín Lopez gives the following interpretation of the rule and marks the frame within which it is situated:

> "Los cónyuges deben guardar fidelidad. En sentido negativo, la fidelidad supone la exclusividad de las relaciones sexuales, de modo que los cónyuges deben abstenerse de mantener contactos – homosexuales o heterosexuales – sexuales con terceros. En sentido positivo, la fidelidad implica la disponibilidad sexual recíproca de los esposos. Discutible es si el deber de fidelidad, en su vertiente positiva, incluye esa especie de obligación de mantener relaciones sexuales con el otro cónyuge." (Marín Lopez quoted in Bercovitz Rodríguez-Cano 2006: 188)

Although from the legal point of view faithfuless is considered an obligation, its non-compliance is no longer sanctioned. One aspect of the reform of Spanish Family Law according to Ley 15/2005 of 8 July was the abolition of the fault-regime and the annulment of Article 82 of the Civil Code, which listed the reasons for marital separation.[89] Due to the reform a spouse may unilaterally file for divorce without the other's consent and without giving any reasons.[90] Nevertheless, if the affected spouse can proof that the other spouse's infidelity has caused the

---

[88]See: "Artículo 68

Los cónyuges están obligados a vivir juntos, guardarse fidelidad y socorrerse mutuamente. Deberán, además, compartir las responsabilidades domésticas y el cuidado y atención de ascendientes y descendientes y otras personas dependientes a su cargo." (Article 68, Spanish Civil Code).

[89]This Article has been annulled by the Ley 15/2005, de 8 de Julio on the modification of the Civil Code and the Legal Procedure in the field of separation and divorce (BOE núm. 163, de 09-07-2005, pp. 24,458–24,461): 82: "Artículo 82 Son causas de separación:

1. El abandono injustificado del hogar, la infidelidad conyugal, la conducta injuriosa o vejatoria y cualquier otra violación grave o reiterada de los deberes conyugales. No podrá invocarse como causa la infidelidad conyugal si existe previa separación de hecho libremente consentida por ambos o impuesta por el que la alegue.

2. Cualquier violación grave o reiterada de los deberes respecto de los hijos comunes o respecto de los de cualquiera de los cónyuges que convivan en el hogar familiar.

3. La condena a pena de privación de libertad por tiempo superior a seis años.

4. El alcoholismo, la toxicomanía o las perturbaciones mentales, siempre que el interés del otro cónyuge o el de la familia exijan la suspensión de la convivencia.

5. El cese efectivo de la convivencia conyugal durante seis meses, libremente consentido. Se entenderá, libremente prestado este consentimiento cuando un cónyuge requiriese fehacientemente al otro para prestarlo, apercibiéndole expresamente de las consecuencias de ello, y éste no mostrase su voluntad en contra por cualquier medio admitido en derecho o pidiese la separación o las medidas provisionales a que se refiere el artículo 103 en el plazo de seis meses a partir del citado requerimiento.

6. El cese efectivo de la convivencia conyugal durante el plazo de tres años.

7. Cualquiera de las causas de divorcio en los términos previstos en los números 3., 4. y 5. del artículo 86".

[90]See Civil Code, Article 81.

disruption, disregard of Article 68 may entail legal consequences. As such the one spouse who has contravened the rule may face disinherison (Article 855.1.), loss of spousal support (Article 154.4.), and restitution of the donations made at marriage (Article 1343.II, III).[91]

Due to a significant increase in the number of divorces in Spain in the year 2003 the Spanish Ministry for Social Affairs engaged the Institute for Family Policy to carry out an investigation on the satisfaction of couples with family life.[92] The aim of the study was to analyse the reasons for pair conflicts, to find out which factors contribute to a deterioration of conflicts and lead to a break-up, and to investigate supportive mechanisms and resources that help to tackle pair conflicts. A representative sample of 400 spouses of different age groups, half of them with children and half of them without children participated in this study. They were asked to give evaluations on a rating scale on a number of issues. One issue concerned the reasons that the spouses considered responsible for marital discussions and family conflicts. When the spouses were asked which factors they considered as contributing to marital stability the majority viewed mutual support, fidelity, personal realisation, joint life experiences, love and children as most relevant elements. On the other hand, when they were asked to evaluate the grounds for conflict the spouses considered factors such as unsocial behaviour (abuse), lack of communication and infidelity as most detrimental. The bar diagram shows the results (Fig. 1.7):

The results show three most frequently mentioned pair-related grounds for conflicts such as infidelity, not to be able to solve a problem and not investing enough time in the relationship. Among the external reasons the interviewed spouses named three reasons that were supposed to produce conflict such as

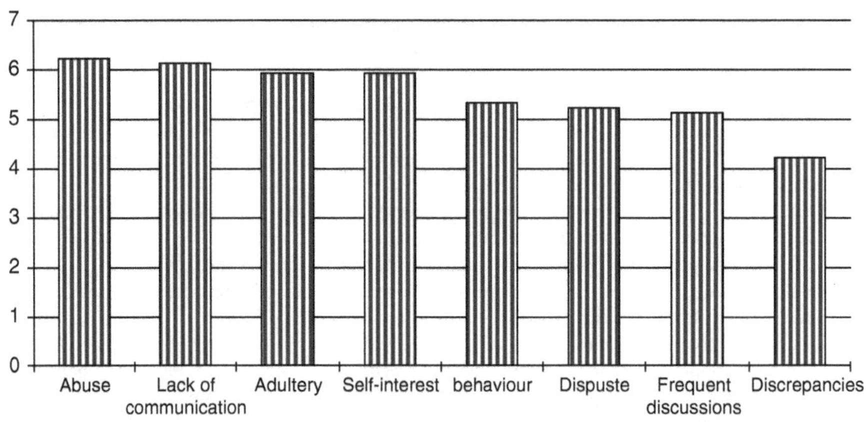

Fig. 1.7 Causes for conflict

[91]See comments to Article 68 CC of M. J. Marín Lopez in Bercovitz Rodríguez-Cano (2006): 188.
[92]See: Hertfelder de Ardecoa (2004).

addictions or substance abuse, economic difficulties and job loss. In fact, many family problems arise from insufficient fulfilment of family functions. Some couples may simply be overstrained with the management and organisation of a household (e.g. running of household budget, distribution of household labour, etc.). Other families neglect leisure time activities, which leads to boredom, dissatisfaction, or excessive media consumption.

Conflicts may also have their roots in the systems that surround the family. In the following section some of these causes will be addressed. A spouse's relation to the family of origin, when dysfunctional, may lead to marital conflict. A spouse may be involved in symbiotic relations with his or her parents. As a result the parents intervene in their offspring's family life and treat him or her (or even the son- or daughter-in law) like children and not like adults. In other cases the biggest part of the family life takes place in the residence of the family of origin. It seems particularly problematic if parents make demands or provide financial support in return for maintaining a close relationship to their son or daughter. If the spouses are not aware of these dysfunctions, they tend to enter alliances with their parents when marital conflicts arise.

Likewise, a spouse's relationship to the family system as a whole may be problematic. Some family members have extremely close relations to third persons outside the family who alienate them from their family. On the contrary, a family member may virtually have no social contact outside the family, so much so that they are completely dependent on his or her family. In other cases a friend or somebody from the circle of acquaintances interfere in marriage problems and thereby cause detrimental consequences.

Pathogenic influences can have their roots in professional life. A competitive economic climate that is associated with increased pressures and extra hours of work have an effect on family life.[93] Thus, the spouses may suffer from conflicts with superiors, colleagues, or subordinates and transfer these conflicts to the private sphere. Pressure may come through stress, continuous and excessive demands, or from the change of workplace. Tensions can spill over into family life and lead to lack of time spent with the family and, less available emotional and physical energy to invest in the partnership and family life. All these constellations are likely to produce dissatisfaction or marital conflict.[94]

In the previous section, we presented several categories of possible reasons for divorce. However, these reasons offer little information about the factors that actually contribute to the stability of a marriage. Therefore, the next section is devoted to the explanation of family functioning in general. Knowledge of the dynamism and mechanisms that stabilize a marriage is a pre-requisite for further investigations in the field of family mediation. We will present a Model of Relationship and Family Dynamism by making reference to the theoretical approaches that exist in the field of family sociology.

---

[93]See: Glezer and Wolcott (1999): 69–74.

[94]See: Thompson (1997): 273–290 and Glezer and Wolcott (1999): 69–74.

1.5 Explanatory Models for Family Functioning

If we want to gain insight into the dynamism of family relationships we have to take sociological conditions and psychological predispositions into account and relate them to economic considerations. For an integrated view of the structure and processes involved we present the Model of Relationship and Family Dynamism based on five main elements described by Kelly, Redenbach and Rinaman.[95] Due to the complex nature of the subject an interdisciplinary approach is used that involves the fields of economy, psychology and sociology, in particular that of family sociology. Before the five elements of the model will be explained in detail, they are illustrated by the diagram (Fig. 1.8).

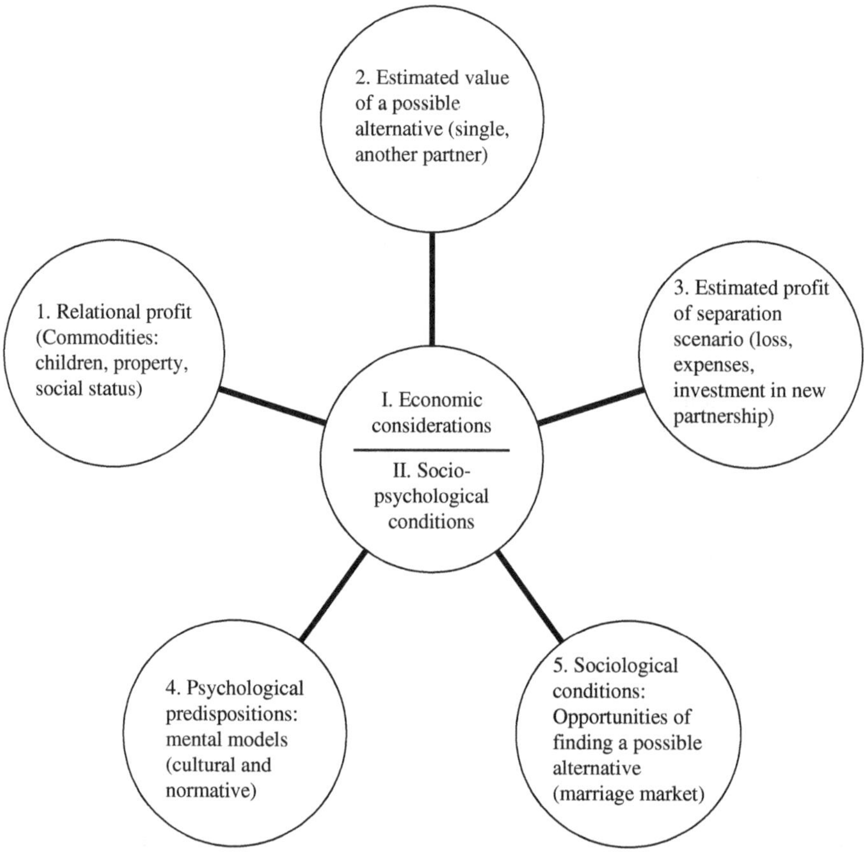

Fig. 1.8 Model of relationship and family dynamism

[95]See: Kelly et al. (2005): 26f.

The model defines the objective situation of a couple. According to this model a spouse would assess the quality of his or her marriage by using both economic and socio-psychological criteria (see I and II). The marriage is evaluated by considering the actual relational profit (1) and putting it in relation to the availability of a possible alternative (2) or a hypothetical scenario divorce (3). Apart from mere economic utility of the quality of marriage, the spouse should not forget to take into account psychological predispositions (4) and the sociological conditions (5), such as the actual state of the marriage market.

The first element of the relational profit is based on the view that the marital relationship is organised and mutually controlled by the spouses. Following the economic approach of Becker marriage is seen as a unit in which relational profit is produced.[96] For our model the relational profit includes children, property and status. It is assumed that marital decisions are guided by the rule of utility maximization,[97] which means that spouses tend to assess their relationship according to a cost-benefit analysis. As part of the rational-choice theories this rule has become very popular in the last few years as an explanation for behaviour within empirical sociological research. It denotes the overall value of a project by comparing all the costs invested to the benefits gained.

The second aspect, the estimated value of a possible alternative is a partner's assessment of the relationship versus the estimated value of a possible alternative form of life (another partner or being single). According to Becker's hypothesis of the 'assortative mating' on the marriage market, partners decide to get married in order to produce goods (commodities) that cannot be easily acquired elsewhere. They do this only if the relational profit in a marriage is expected to be higher than that of remaining single.

Together, with the three additional inter-related factors of organisation and investment, this forms a system of checks and balances by which relationships are organised. The material organisation includes the running of a joint household, agreeing on daily routines (e.g. the use of money) and the division of labour. Investment refers to the accumulation of marriage specific capital (e.g. acquisitions, property) and spare-time activities. Interaction comprises all communicative processes in the organisation of the relationship and sexuality. Relational profit depends on the investment made by the spouses, which in turn depends on the amount of attention they show for each other. In the case of reduced relational profit a spouse would express dissatisfaction (voice). The figure shows the cycle of organising and controlling relational profit (Fig. 1.9).

In economic terms, the estimated profit of a separation scenario equates the total rewards (e.g. commodities) minus all total costs (e.g. investment, attention). A relationship is considered to function well if the rewards make up for the attention invested. On the contrary, a relationship is likely to terminate in divorce if the profit constantly falls below a critical threshold level whereby this level has to be seen in

---

[96]See: Becker et al. (1977): 1141–1187; Becker (1991): 20.

[97]See: Becker (1991): 21f.

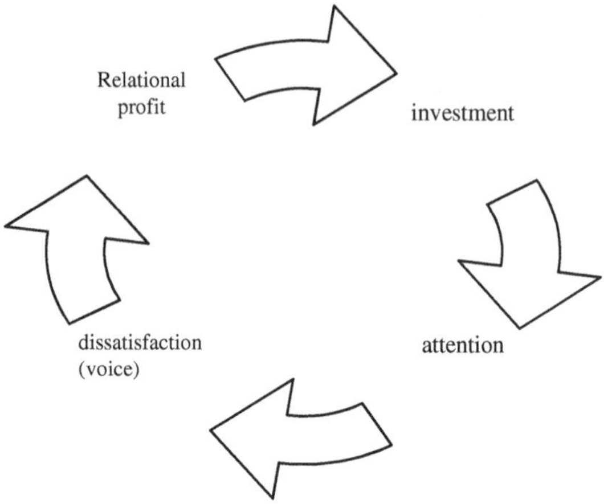

Fig. 1.9 Organisation and control of relational profit

relation to the availability and costs of other alternatives. The four factors tend to undergo changes over time. A high amount of attention might be replaced by the familiarity among the spouses whereas more time is invested in profession and child care.

In order to keep the relational profit on a satisfying level, both partners would have to adapt their organisation (e.g. division of labour) in such a way so that less attention is dedicated to the relationship and more investment is made in family specific capital.[98] If a couple decides to have children they tend to divide labour into work outside and work inside of the house, including various household duties. However, this concept of the traditional family seems to be only possible in the upper middle class and upper class, where the corresponding gender roles are learned during socialisation.

Children are also considered as relational profit and their worth is theoretically recognized in the 'value-of-children' – theory (VOC).[99] According to the VOC-theory children are perceived to enhance not only the family's social recognition (socio-normative utility and increase in status), but also the material utility (income and insurance specific utility) as well as emotional well-being (psychological and emotional utility) of all family members.

Referring the role of children, G. Becker's economic approach has been criticized because he sees the decision for children mainly from a cost-benefit perspective based on the most effective investment and organization of time and money. However, this view presents only an incomplete picture of the spouses' decision process and neglects all psychosocial incentives that play a role in the decision for children. For instance, Friedman, Hechter and Kanazawa point out that economic approaches fail to explain why a couple would choose to have children:

[98]This bears the risk of a possible devaluation of the family specific capital. Such risk is minimized if the spouses are unconditionally committed to marriage as an institution or as a collective unit.

[99]See: Nauck (2001): 407 ff. and Trommsdorff (2001): 36 ff.

> "Models based on instrumental values are effective in explaining the decline of fertility in developed societies, but they cannot explain why anyone under current circumstances would choose to have a child (. . .). Thus the interesting question for instrumental models for fertility is why do people in developed countries have any children at all when the prevailing constraints are inconsistent with this choice?" (Friedman et al. 1994: 380)

Several studies have dealt with the question whether children would raise their parents' subjective well-being. Some researchers assumed that parents with dependent children have lower levels of subjective well-being than those without dependents. This assumption was verified by the outcomes of their empirical study. They interpreted their findings as symptomatic for the decline of fertility levels in most Western nations.[100] However, a more complete assessment of the perceived benefits of children requires adopting a lifetime perspective. Marks and Fleming argued that the relationship between children and parental subjective well-being is likely to depend on the factors age and gender.[101] Nevertheless, while there are a number of studies of the impact of childlessness on the subjective well-being of older adults,[102] we are unaware of any study that has attempted to examine how the impact of children of different ages, including adult children, impacts the subjective well-being within a more general population sample.

Our model on family functioning and in particular the aspect of relational profit includes monetary as well as non-monetary aspects. This is due to the fact that many motives seem to play a role in the explanation of human behaviour. People have diverse reasons for investing in relationships and evaluate relational profit in different ways. In order to understand these motives Weber described four basic motivations for human behaviour: value oriented rationality (*Wertrationalität*), affective action or action motivated by emotions (*Affektualität*), traditional action (*Tradition*), and goal oriented rational action (*Zweckrationlität*). According to Weber, the legitimacy of order may be guaranteed by any of the following motives:

> "Die Legitimität einer Ordnung kann *garantiert* sein:
> I. rein innerlich und zwar
> 1. rein affektuell: durch gefühlsmässige Hingabe;
> 2. wertrational; durch Glauben an ihre absolute Geltung als Ausdruck letzter verpflichtender Werte (sittlicher, ästhetischer oder irgendwelcher anderer);
> 3. religiös: durch durch den Glauben an die Abhängigkeit eines Heilsgüterbesitzes von ihrer Innehaltung;
> II. auch (oder: nur) durch Erwartung spezifischer äusserer Folgen, also: durch Interessenlage; aber: durch Erwartungen von besonderer *Art*.
> Eine Ordnung soll heissen:
> a) Konvention, (...),
> b) Recht (...)." (Weber 1976: 17)

---

[100]See: McLanahan and Adams (1987): 237–257.

[101]The authors assumed that young children are more demanding in terms of time whereas the presence of adolescents implies higher costs. See: Marks and Fleming (1999): 301–323.

[102]See: Koropeckyj-Cox (2002): 957–971 and Zhang and Hayward (2001): 311–320.

A marriage crisis holds the chance of re-defining or re-framing the marriage. In his study on the functions of (re)framing marriage, Esser has analyzed the role of the marriage crises as a ground for divorce.[103] It shows a clear interaction between the quality of the framing of marriage and the couples' susceptibility to crises and divorce. Whereas there are no effects in the case of strong framing, weak framing has an impact especially on younger couples. This can be interpreted as a confirmation of the model of frame-selection and as an argument for the assumption that in the process of increasing diversification of society the demands partners make on their marriage has risen to such an extent that they can hardly be met in the same relationship.

After the exploration of the grounds for divorce the following section presents two sociological theories of family functioning, such as Structural-Functional Theory and Symbolic Interaction Theory.

1.5.1 Structural–Functional Theory

Structural–functional theory is a sociological theory focusing on the organizational structure of societies that consist of interrelated social units.[104] The main idea is that both, individual and group behaviour serve a function for the larger society. Parsons founded the theory on the works of anthropologists who investigated the organisation of primitive cultures.[105] Structural–functional theory defines and explains society as a system with checks and balances.[106] According to this view, individual people interact in a social system within a specific frame of time and place. The interaction is characterized by the use of symbols that are known by the actors. Parsons gives the following definition of the social system:

> "A social system consists in a plurality of individual actors interacting with each other in a situation which has at least a physical or environmental aspect, actors who are motivated in terms of a tendency to the "optimization of gratification" and whose relation to their

---

[103]See: Esser (2002a, b): 27 ff.

[104]Such unit may be a large community (e.g. corporation, factory, university) or a major institution (e.g. economy, religion, politics) as well as a smaller unit such as the family.

[105]Talcott E. F. Parsons (1902–1979), sociologist, studied biology and philosophy in the U.S. and Europe. He obtained his PhD at the University of Heidelberg, where he studied the works of Weber and translated them into English. He founded the Department of Social Relations at Harvard University and developed an interdisciplinary approach based on sociology, anthropology and psychology. See: Parsons (1951, 1986).

[106]'Structure' stands for the static elements of the system whereas 'function' describes its dynamic processes. According to Parsons societal changes proceed in the following four ways: 1. Differentiation, which refers to the increase in complexity of social organizations; 2. Adaptive Upgrading, whereby social institutions become more specialized; 3. Inclusion occurs where groups previously excluded from society because of race, gender or social class etc. are now accepted; and 4. Value Generalization is the development of new values that tolerate and legitimate a greater range of activities.

situations, including each other, is defined and mediated in terms of a system of culturally structured and shared symbols." (Parsons 1951: 5)

Family can be looked at from a structural point of view focusing on its composition, such as the number of family members, their age and gender and their connectedness to the outside world. The family members use patterns of interaction that create bonds. Families use rules and principles to organize their joint activities. The function of the family is to raise children and equip them with the skills necessary for social interaction. The functions performed by the family members are considered to contribute to the stability of the system whereby changes in one part require adjustments in another part in order to keep the balance.

In his analysis of the changes of the family system, Parsons points out that there has been a differentiation of its primary functions for society compared to earlier times. Nowadays, the socialisation of the children and what he calls the "tension-management" among the family members have become more important. This has had an impact on the balance of gender roles and on the way in which the family is connected to its surrounding systems. Whereas all functions associated with children's socialization have become part of the wife-mother-role, the role of the husband-father has turned into that of a "chairman of the advisory board" within the family. This means that the wife and mother is specialized in the field of human relation and tackling of subtile psychological problems. On the other hand the husband-father role has undergone a shift of function which is typical for adaptive processes.[107]

Each social structure is founded on two essential interconnected parts, such as the social position (status) and the conduct expected in this position (role). Social structure arises from the interaction of positions and roles. The family interacts with its surrounding systems, such as the economic, political, religious and education systems. These surrounding systems are also interconnected. Accordingly, Goode described Parsons' view of structural functionalism by comparing society to a human body where all parts work together as a whole:

"The leading thinker of functionalism in America was Talcott Parsons (. . .), who believed that behaviour was driven by our efforts to conform to the moral code of society. The purpose of such codes is to constrain human behaviour in ways that promote the common good. The purpose of an organism is to survive. In order for a society to survive, the subsystems (the family and other institutions) must function in ways that promote the maintenance of society as a whole. This is similar to how a person's organs must function in interrelated ways in order to maintain a healthy body." (Goode 1969: 9)

Society provides a model on the organization of life. The state offers education and formation to its citizens and thus contributes to the socialisation of children. On the political level decisions are taken on issues such as education, economy, law, etc. If the individual complies with the norms of society he or she contributes to the

[107]See: Parsons (1968): 270.

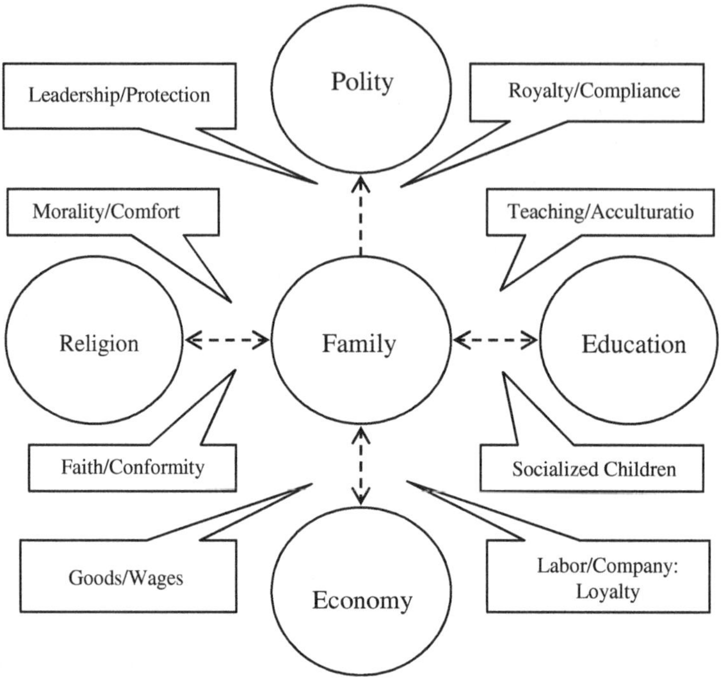

Fig. 1.10 Parson's concept of social integration

functioning of society as a whole.[108] The figure shows Parson's concept of social integration (Fig. 1.10).

As an institution the family represents a model of partner selection and procreation. As such, divorce is not only a single phenomenon that affects particular individuals but it has to be seen in its social context. Divorce has long been viewed as a personal failure of two individuals. However, it may equally be true that certain social ills are to blame for family breakdown. The spouses have to organize their lives according to internal family responsibilities, the requirement of job organization, social limitations and gender roles. Additionally, the influence of mass media and mainstream[109] on the family has increased considerably whereby unrealistic images of family functioning are often transmitted.

[108]In exchange for the loyalty and allegiance of family members, the political institution protects the citizens. In exchange for labour, the economy provides money and goods. The political institution guarantees law and order, protection as well as health care and welfare. The religious institution provides moral standards for behaviour, approval of worthiness, help and empathy.

[109]Mainstream as a sociological term denotes a trend or taste that is followed by a majority of people in society. It is viewed as opposed to individuality and can induce individuals to conform to the standards or ideas set by certain groups in society.

According to Parsons, the individual personality system depends on the surrounding social structure in the sense that our actions and motives can be explained in social terms. This applies event to intimate feelings such as love. The surrounding cultural system offers a set of beliefs (e.g. love is essential in a person's life, everyone should love somebody, etc.) that is related to a series of symbols and standards for the expression of our emotions (accepted behaviour).[110]

This has implications on the individual's process of partner selection. On the cognitive level we understand the concept of love. Still, the individual has to decide who in the population surrounding him or her is actually loveable. Once a person has selected a pool of possible partners he or she intends to establish contact with a possible partner. As love is based on reciprocity and transitivity the other person's feedback is an essential indicator of whether or not the attempt is responded.

The view of family as a system enables us to explain family functioning in socio-economic, psychological and legal terms. However, divorce is not the end of family functioning but rather a phase of transition in which the family system is reorganized and reshaped.

In this section we have presented models of family functioning based on complex interrelated factors. We tried to analyse the rationale behind family decisions and focused on the behavioural dimension of family members.

1.5.2 Symbolic Interaction Theory

Whereas Structural–functional Theory is focused on social units and their functions for society, the Symbolic Interactionalism (SI) arose as a counterpoint to structural functionalism because it concentrates on the individual and the development of self-concepts through interaction with others. The theory is based on three conceptual units that form part of social relationships, such as the role as the cultural component, position as sociological component and the self as a psychological unit. Representatives of Symbolic Interactionalism portray a 'socialized self' and an 'internal self', both of which act simultaneously in the same individual. The creation and understanding of meaning is a central issue. It is supposed that meaning is created in the interactions with other people with whom we share the interpretation of symbols. First we create meaning internally and through processes of interpretation we examine externally whether our meaning is correct. The same is true for our self-concepts, we modify and shape our self-concepts through interaction with others. In this process culture and social processes act as social norms.

One of the representatives of Symbolic Interaction Theory, Mead wrote his recognized book '*Mind*, *Self*, and *Society*' (1934) from the viewpoint of a social

[110]Our emotions do not develop in a sphere that is free of socialisation. On the contrary, we assume beliefs, attitudes and preferences that play an important role for our emotions. In fact, according to Social Interaction Theory our emotions seem to be socially mandated by so-called "socialization agents", such as parents, priests, teachers, who transmit concepts and beliefs.

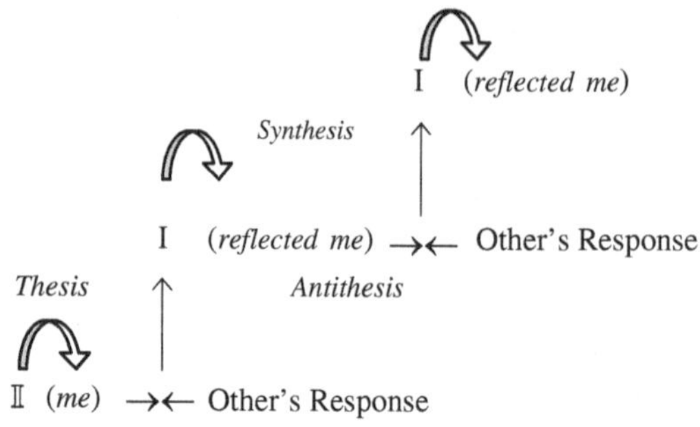

Fig. 1.11 Mead's I-me interaction as procedure

behaviourist.[111] In this book the author conceptualized a definition of two components of the self, such as the socialized self and the internal self, which he named as *Me* and *I*. Whereas the "I" is the individual's self or the knower, the "me" represents the socialised part of the knower that acts upon a thing. In our experience we tend to switch between the "I" and the "me" when we reflect upon ourselves (self-consciousness). The diagram shows the dynamism between the "I" and the "me" (Fig. 1.11).

As the "I" has developed on the basis of interaction with others, the "me" may be considered as a reflection on the interactions or as a kind of reflected behaviour. From this perspective personal autonomy is basically possible but it depends on two aspects, the nature and history of one's self and the type of society in which it develops. Joas describes how Mead views personal autonomy in the context of his theory:

> "For Mead the individual and his property is no longer a presupposition of the formation of society, but rather individualization as a consequence of the structure of socially-organized life processes. It thereby becomes possible, (...), to retain the ideal of the individual's autonomy. However, this autonomy is now no longer an original given that is to be opposed to society. Instead, it requires for its emergence a re-shaping of social life, which must be so organized that free self-determination of all is both possible and necessary." (Joas 1991: 59)

There appears to be a consensus among the persons in a society referring the meanings we give to objects, events, and situations that we experience. The definitions we tend to attribute for instance to intimacy on the individual level depend on the values of the society in which we live, and on specific values of the groups with which we identify. If we experience love it is because we have learned the meanings associated with this particular feeling. As such, two peoples' movement from being strangers to becoming intimates proceeds within well recognized frames. During this process of courtship people tend to offer idealized images of them and accept the idealized images offered by the others.

A central issue is the meaning and interpretation that family members give to their experiences. Such symbolic interactions occur during communication.

[111]George H. Mead (1863–1931), American philosopher, sociologist and psychologist and founder of the Symbolic Interactionist School of Sociology and Social Psychology. He presented a theory of how the mind and self arise from social processes. Mead (1934): Part III, 22–29.

Researchers can only find out about these meanings by observing people while they communicate and observe how they use dialogue to construct meanings. There is an explicit and an implicit dimension to social interactions. In order to understand communication we need to find out about the implicit meanings that the family members use.

1.6 Conclusion

In Chap. 1 the question of why so many marriages end in divorce was addressed. Since the 1950s industrialisation, urbanization and a tendency to individualization have produced many economic and social changes. Due to the political and socio-economic development in Spain, industrialization, women's labour market participation and all its consequences reached the country two decades later than other countries of Western Europe. As a consequence the family has also changed and new ways of pair relationship and family life have emerged.

Since the 1960s divorce rates have increased steadily in many European States. Nowadays, every third marriage ends in divorce, a tendency that is even higher in urban areas. Additionally, marriages tend to last fewer years. There are certain risk factors that undermine marital stability. These include certain personality characteristics and pair-related factors that concern the management of the family. There are also family-related risks that have to do with the internal organisation of the family. Additionally, the socio-economic conditions may also act as risk factors.

As more and more women have entered the labour market gender roles have changed from a complementary relationship to a more symmetric model. Accordingly, Article 68 of the Spanish Civil Code was modified by the reform of Family Law in 2005 which states that the spouses are obliged to share domestic duties and the care for family members. Gender roles are a consequence of the ongoing diversification of the labour market. Whereas they were pre-designed in earlier generations, couples nowadays tend to negotiate their roles and modify them according to their personal preferences. In Spain the legislator introduced the Law of Gender Equality in 2007. At the same time the traditional form of the extended family has been replaced by the nuclear family. In fact, the average number of family members in European households has decreased within the last three decades. New ways of life and forms of living together have emerged and coexist with traditional forms of relationships. In 2005 Spain was among the first countries who legally allowed same-sex marriages.

A central issue for marital stability is the way in which marital decisions are taken and how the spouses deal with problems. It is a spouse's bargaining power that determines the influence that he or she has in order to pursue personal and family-related aims. In order to explain the rationale behind family decisions we offered the Model of Relationship and Family Dynamism which describes how the spouses organize and control relational profit. Basically the spouses tend to cooperate and try to maintain a balance of mutual welfare. A marriage functions well if the relational profit makes up for the time and attention invested in the relationship and family activities. On the contrary, one may consider divorce if the profit falls below a critical level.

Statistics and studies have shown that more women than men initiate divorce. Women take an active role in preparing and planning for divorce and they are more consistent in carrying out their plans. The reason why the majority of divorces is initiated by women may be that wives have enhanced their bargaining power by contributing to the household budget. Therefore they expect their husbands to cooperate more in child care and household activities. It seems, however, that men tend to be more reluctant to adjust their gender role to the new situation. In fact, a woman's earning capacity creates and independence effect that allows her to end an unhappy marriage. Several studies have revealed a significant correlation between women's employment and divorce rate.

As such, it was shown that divorce has to be viewed in its social context rather than as a single individual phenomenon. Finally two sociological theories of family functioning were presented, the Structural–functional Theory and Symbolic Interaction Theory. The theories explicate the function of human behaviour and social interaction in the context of society.

Chapter 2
Factors Influencing Ex-spouses' Adjustment to Divorce

2.1 Introduction

Divorce is a turning point in the life of each individual involved. From the legal point of view divorce is the dissolution of the marital union, whereas psychologically it is more than a legal document and a courtroom event. It is considered a timely process rather than a one time event. In many cases months and sometimes years of tension, unhappiness, and family discord precede the actual decision for divorce. Regardless who initiated divorce, there are emotional ramifications for both partners. The purpose of this chapter is to give an overview of the consequences that divorce has for the ex-spouses. More specifically, we will deal with the factors that have an influence on the process of the ex-spouses' adjustment to the new situation.

Separation and divorce go along with fundamental legal and socioeconomic changes. The ex-spouses have to adapt to these changes by activating skills that help them to cope with the problems arising from these changes. Divorce not only has psychological consequences but also has economical and physical consequences for all the family members involved. As we will deal with the situation of the children in the following chapter, this chapter is especially dedicated to give an overview of the psychological consequences of divorce on the ex-spouses. In particular we will analyse the factors that play a role in the process of divorce adjustment, and how they relate to the skills that facilitate or impede the adaptation to divorce.

Generally, psychological reactions to divorce range from uncertainty, anger, grief and depression to anxiety and the feeling that one's life is getting out of control. Therefore, divorce has long been viewed as producing mainly negative outcomes that leave the divorcees in a state of deprivation. However, a marital dissolution can also be associated with feelings of relief or liberation and may benefit some individuals. If ex-spouses consider divorce not only as the end of a contract, but take a positive attitude and see it as the beginning of family transformation and individual change they tend to recover more easily from the strains of divorce.

Many factors have an impact on divorce adjustment, such as personal, relational and cultural factors. Among the personal factors there are certain facts such as age,

M. Gaffal, *Psychosocial and Legal Perspectives of Marital Breakdown*,
DOI 10.1007/978-3-642-13896-6_2, © Springer-Verlag Berlin Heidelberg 2010

post-divorce options and socio-economic status that mark the frame within divorce takes place. Moreover a number of relational aspects influence the process of divorce adjustment such as mental and emotional functioning prior to divorce or the degree of attachment to former spouse. Psychological conditions such as the level of self-esteem, personal coping skills, initiation of divorce, individual beliefs and attitudes also play a role in the process of adjustment. Several relational factors concerning the individual's connectedness to others in the private and public sphere contribute to divorce adjustment. This includes the support received from children, the family of origin, from close friends, and a possible new relationship. Additionally, cultural factors have influence on divorce adjustment, specifically in relation to the degree of acceptance or stigmatization of divorce within a culture and the measures taken in a national legal system to deal with marriage dissolution (e.g. child custody, division of assets, etc.).

2.2 Theoretical Perspective

The focus of interest is on the question of how the ex-spouses actually manage to adjust to divorce. Adjustment in this context is understood as a process during which a person responds to a difficult life situation and tries to modify, correct and adapt to the circumstances in order to regain control.[1] Two questions are particularly relevant in this context, such as the first: which changes does divorce bring about?, and the second: which resources does the divorced have available in order to cope with these changes effectively?

Form the methodological point of view we will use psychological theories for the explanation of the ex-spouses' functioning after divorce.[2] Psychological investigations focus on three aspects, such as human experience, body processes and overt behaviour.[3] It is supposed that psycho-dynamism[4] comes into effect in the

[1]Adjustment disorder is the incapacitating reaction to a stressful event that lasts usually around six months. Typical reactions include psychological disturbance and personal crisis which produce symptoms such as changes in mood, depression, anxiety, eating disorder or sleeplessness.

[2]Psychology is situated on the intersection between human, natural and social sciences as it employs quantitative as well as qualitative research methods. As an empirical science it describes and explains human experience and behaviour, their development in the course of life and all its relevant internal and external causes and conditions. In our explanations we will draw on the results of studies employing qualitative and quantitative research methods.

[3]As human experience is an inner and invisible process, access to it can only be gained via the theory of mind. In order to describe the relational processes between individuals, we will also employ the theory of mind, which provides hypotheses about the needs, emotions, intentions, expectations and opinions of the other. Body processes can be measured by clinical investigations and behaviourism provides explanations for overt behaviour. For the analysis of the consequences of divorce additional explanations from the fields of individual and developmental psychology will be used.

[4]The idea of a psycho-dynamism is based on the theory of personality and psychoanalysis that investigates the interplay between conscious and subconscious psychological processes.

human psyche when people interact in relationships. This dynamism is based on individual life experience. Everybody has developed a repertoire of interaction patterns that are utilized when they are in contact with others. As a result, when in conflict situations, people recall and utilize problem solving strategies.

We are particularly interested in the human psychological abilities that facilitate the process by which the ex-spouses adapt to the consequences of divorce and regain their personal well-being.[5] In the investigation of these factors, two aspects have to be taken into account: the temporal component and the research perspective being employed. The first aspect relates to a tendency within the last decades to analyse divorce according to a deficit perspective, by which divorce is seen as an event producing mainly negative results leaving the divorced in a state of deprivation. However, recent studies have added a different perspective implying that divorce may also benefit individuals by enhancing self-confidence, self-efficacy, and by producing feelings of relief and liberation when leaving an unhappy marriage. This second perspective entails that divorce adjustment is a process that improves life over time. Many studies have long neglected this time factor thus disregarding the variability of the adjustment process and the temporal recovery.

In our investigation we will apply the Theory of Family Stress and Buffer Factors which was presented by Hill[6] in 1949 and was later further developed by McCubbin and Patterson (1983).[7] Hill developed his model on the basis of experience gained as a psychologist when working with traumatised families during the worldwide economic downturn of the Great Depression in the 1930s. In his work he analysed the factors that had an influence on family stability and he compared broken families to those who remained intact during this time of economic hardship. Concerning research methods he and his colleagues pleaded for a multidisciplinary approach to the study of families that would take a variety of factors into account. At least five aspects were considered relevant in the study of family processes, such as interaction, structural–functional elements, situational components, institutional aspects and developmental features. These different perspectives led to the creation of three major conceptual frameworks for the study of the family environment, such as symbolic interaction, systems theory and exchange theory. Nowadays investigations of the family concentrate on family strength and resources rather than on deficits and pathologic developments.

Psychoanalysis speaks of 'psychological energy' including human urges, desires, motives and emotions, which are considered as the driving force for human behaviour (Freud 1975: 112–114).

[5]Well-being or happiness is the degree to which an individual evaluates the overall quality of life in a positive way. Self-reported well-being measures are thought to be a reflection of at least four factors: objective circumstances, aspirations or expectations, comparisons with others and a person's base-line happiness or disposition.

[6]See: Hill (1949).

[7]See: McCubbin and Patterson (1983): 5–25.

According to this theory the ex-spouses' adjustment to divorce depends on three decisive elements: (1) the accumulation of stressors,[8] (2) the individual's resources for coping with stress and (3) the definition of the incident producing stress. It is assumed that acute stressors, such as divorce and the events surrounding it, can lead to family crisis, especially when the stressors are accumulated. Mederer and Hill describe this process of accumulation in the following way:

> "Hill (...) introduced the notion of "pile up" of stressors to account for the fact that most families can accommodate to one or two stressor events, but are forced into reorganisation if the stress engendered by the stressors exceeds a certain threshold. (...) Hill (1949) defines "crisis" as any sharp or decisive change for which old patterns are inadequate." (Mederer and Hill 1983: 46)

This crisis usually leads to physical, emotional and relational problems. According to the view that several factors interact in the development of stress the activation of an appropriate response the authors called their model "ABCX-theory of family stress", the letters denoting the various factors that influence family stability.[9]

We will briefly explain what is understood by the factors. Factor A stands for the stress producing event (such as job loss, divorce, etc.). On the contrary, the two factors B and C act to buffer the family from these acute stressors reducing the direct correlation between multiple stressors and family crisis. In other words the detrimental effect of divorce may be lessened or buffered by these *protective factors* which help families to persist despite continual and serious stressors. The scheme depicts the ABCX theory of family stress (Fig. 2.1).

Mederer and Hill thought that the two protective factors, internal family resources (i.e. attachment style) and social relationships (B factor) and the family perception and parental self-efficacy (C factor), correlate with the acute stressor of divorce (A factor) and forecast family crisis (X factor). The researchers assumed

---

[8]Stress in general is considered an automatic response to an internal or external stimulus. M. and H. McCubbin distinguish between four levels of stress-intensity, such as *stress*, *eustress*, *distress* and *hyperstress*. Stress and eustress may have a positive effect in that a person activates internal resources to adapt to a change of circumstances or to meet challenges. However, if the tensions produced by these conditions cannot be overcome and the demand exceeds the internal and external resources the authors speak of distress or hyperstress. Common responses to stress include physical tension, irritability, difficulty to concentrate or even anxiety and depression. Family distress denotes the family's feeling of unpleasantness due to hyperstress. See: McCubbin and McCubbin (1989): 11.

[9]S. White and K. Mika recapitulate what is understood by adjustment, reaction to stress and management of resources in the theory of family stress: "In the ABCX model, what is referred to as crisis is, "the amount of incapacitatedness or disorganization in the family where resources are inadequate" (...). Adjustment in this literature refers not only to what characteristics and resources family members bring to situations, but also to what families do in response to a stressful event. An important distinction is made between a family's vulnerability to stress, which is defined as its ability to withstand the initial impact of the stressor, and a family's regenerative power, that is, its ability to recover once there has been some internal stress and disruption (...). In addition, there is a distinction made between reactions to stress, management of existing resources, and more active coping behaviors, such as seeking out new social supports." (White and Mika 1983: 186f.).

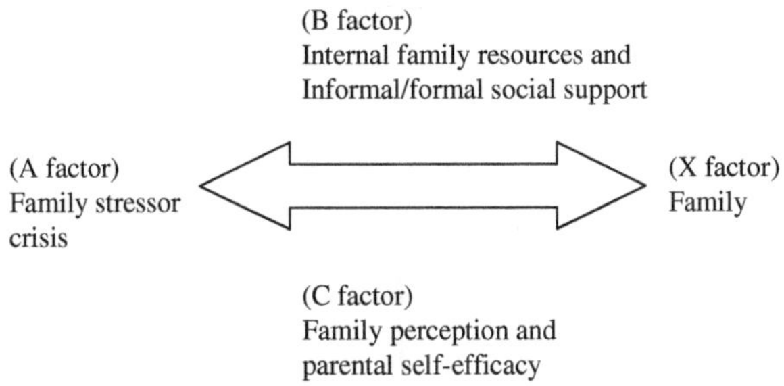

Fig. 2.1 Theory of family stress and buffer factors

that social isolation intensified the impact of divorce on the family functioning. The C factor, which refers to the perception of the stressful event, concerns the spouses' system of values and attitudes toward divorce and whether they perceive the divorce as either a failure or an opportunity. Accordingly the emotions that accompany divorce may range from hope to despair. M. and H. McCubbin give the following description of the C-factor:

> "The family's subjective definition of the stressor, accompanying hardships and their effect on the family comprises the C factor in the Typology Model. Although there are objective cultural definitions of the seriousness of life events and transitions representing the collective judgment of the community, this factor represents how the family defines the seriousness of the experienced stressor. (. . .) The family's appraisal of the situation can range from interpreting a stressor as uncontrollable and contributing to the family's disintegration to viewing the situation as a challenge to be met with growth producing outcomes. (McCubbin and McCubbin 1989: 10)

The theory addresses all relevant factors that play a role in the process of divorce adjustment. A revision of the research literature shows that the theory of family stress and buffer factors is referred to in many studies. Accordingly, most studies in this field mention three groups of factors that influence adjustment to divorce issues, such as personal characteristics, relational patterns and cultural factors. These three groups of factors are depicted in the diagram (Fig. 2.2).

Individual characteristics that are assumed to affect adjustment to divorce include the person's age and psychological qualities (beliefs and attitudes), socio-economic status (education, employment, income). The question of who initiated divorce is also relevant in this context because it allows conclusions to be drawn about the pre-divorce functioning of the marriage.

Several relational factors concerning the individual's connectedness to others, both in the private and public sphere, contribute to divorce adjustment. This includes the support received from children, the family of origin, a possible new relationship and close friends.

Additionally, cultural factors have effects on the process of divorce adjustment, such as the degree of acceptance or stigmatization that divorce is associated with in a culture. Other cultural factors include the measures taken in a national legal

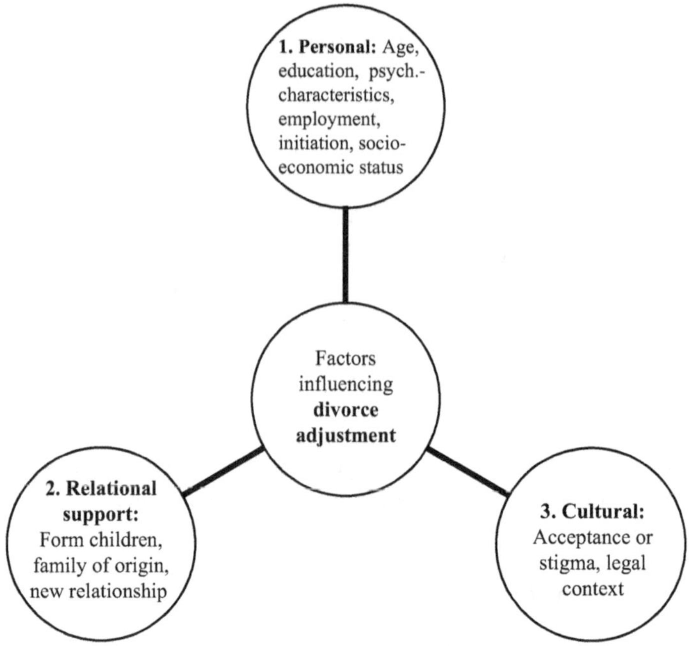

Fig. 2.2 Factors influencing divorce adjustment

system to deal with marriage dissolution (e.g. child custody, division of assets, etc.) and the repartnering options available. The three groups of factors shall now be described in more detail.

2.3 Personal Factors

Among the personal factors that influence an ex-spouse's adjustment to divorce are a person's age and psychological characteristics (e.g. intelligence, individual beliefs and attitudes), his or her socio-economic status (e.g. education, employment) and the post-divorce options. Moreover a number of psychological conditions influence the process of divorce adjustment, such as mental and emotional functioning prior to divorce, the degree of attachment to former spouse, the level of self-esteem as well as coping skills.[10]

[10]Coping skills are cognitive and behavioural processes that are used to respond to stressors. These processes include thinking of alternative strategies, collecting information, cooperating with others or viewing a problem from various perspectives. Coping techniques are selected and constantly tested on reality.

H. and M. McCubbin give the following definition of coping skills: "Coping refers to the family's strategies, patterns and behaviours designed to maintain and/or strengthen the

Referring to the divorced person's age and adjustment studies show different and sometimes even contradictory results. This is probably due to the fact that the framework conditions of the various age groups investigated are quite different. Some studies revealed that it is more difficult for older people to adjust because they have restricted post-divorce options in terms of employment and remarriage.[11] Other studies found better adjustment among older divorced persons because they have fewer parenting problems in concerns of raising children. One study found that young people were more pessimistic than older people when their marriages ended probably because they tend to have high expectations combined with relatively little life experience.[12]

Psychological dispositions such as intelligence, individual attitudes and beliefs[13] play a relevant role in the adjustment to divorce. It is known that our perception is influenced by attitudes, beliefs and individual definitions. Thus, an ex-spouse's subjective interpretation of his or her situation seems to have more influence to adjustment than the factual situation. The actual economic situation is therefore viewed in relative terms. Wang and Amato (2000) found out that a decline in living standard may nevertheless be viewed optimistically because the ex-spouse has more control of the whole situation. They conclude the following:

> "For example, a decline in standard of living might be experienced positively if it also means that people feel that they have more control over their remaining income. (...) This conclusion is consistent with Shapiro (...), for example, who found that people's adjustment to divorce was related more strongly to their subjective perceptions of economic hardship than it was to their objective economic situations." (Wang and Amato 2000: 665)

Personal resources that are needed to cope with stressful life events seem to be related to an individual's level of education. It is assumed that people with longer education and formation times tend to have higher cognitive abilities,[14] a stronger sense of control and self-discipline and a better social network of supporting people than poorly educated individuals.[15] In accordance with Hill's crisis model, these

---

organization and stability of the family unit, maintain the emotional stability and well-being of family members and, obtain and/or utilize family and community resources to manage the situation and initiate efforts to resolve the family hardship created by the stressors/transition." (McCubbin and McCubbin 1989: 10).

[11]See: Kitson and Morgan (1990): 913–924.

[12]See: Kitson et al. (1989): 5–32.

[13]Attitudes are formed by experience and denote personal preferences towards something (a person's behaviour or an event) and likes or dislikes towards somebody (person). Attitudes are based on emotions, cognition and are expressed by a certain conduct. Belief has a wider scope than attitude and means a person's acceptance of something as being true, and being convicted of the actuality and validity of something. If we speak of belief there is always a subject involved, the believer, and an object of belief, such as a proposition.

[14]By cognitive skills we understand the ability of the human mind to process information by learning, understanding and reasoning. Cognitive skills include activities such as differencing, planning, problem-solving, making decisions, abstractions, generalizations and specifications and meta-reasoning.

[15]See: Kitson and Morgan (1990): 913–924, McCubbin and McCubbin (1989): 3–43.

personal resources are relevant because they help to deal with the stressors that usually pile up in the process of divorce. The better the divorced is able to cope with arising problems and take appropriate measures in reaction to these problems, the less the problems will accumulate and thereby worsen the situation. M. and H. McCubbin give a summary of the most relevant personal resources that range from intelligence, skills acquired by experience, character, to health and self-confidence:

> "Some of the important personal resources that may be used by the family in adaptation include (a) innate intelligence, which can enhance awareness and comprehension of demands and facilitate the family's mastery of these; (b) knowledge and skills acquired from education, training, and experience so one can gain employment and perform the tasks necessary for daily living; (c) personality traits (e.g. sense of humor, extroversion), which may facilitate efficacious coping behaviours; (d) physical and emotional health, so that intact faculties and personal energy may be available for meeting family demands; (e) a sense of mastery, which is the belief that one has some control over the circumstances of one's life; and (f) self-esteem, that is a positive judgment about one's self-worth." (McCubbin and McCubbin 1989: 19)

As personal attitudes and beliefs have a key role in the interpretation and attribution of life events they shall be analysed in more detail. A person's beliefs and attitudes are mainly shaped during the socialization process and undergo critical reflection during young adulthood. They have an organizing function for our behaviour and govern an individual's interaction with the world. Beliefs and attitudes affect the mind in three different ways: first, they manipulate our perception of events by controlling the process of receiving information from outside; second, they have some bearing on the evaluation of information concerning conduct; and third, they help to adjust the mental processes to the actual situation. As such they are both, stable and flexible as we need to adapt our behaviour constantly to reality. The stabilizing quality lies in the fact that once they are established they remain relatively steady over a lifetime as a fundamental change would destabilize the whole personality. On the other hand, changes and modifications are inevitable. The diagram shows a circular process that represents the functioning of beliefs and attitudes (Fig. 2.3).

In particular, beliefs and attitudes may be so strict, rigorous or of authoritarian quality, that they impede personal development and inhibit individual growth. In such cases an individual needs to revise them and make essential changes and necessary adaptations. Positive attitudes can act as a buffer which helps one to cope with the difficult consequences of divorce. This view is supported by the study of Wang and Amato who investigated predictors of divorce adjustment by focusing on people's attitudes and emotions concerning divorce. They found out that an ex-spouse can handle a significant amount of trouble if he or she accepts this change and sees it as an opportunity for a second chance. They describe this phenomenon as follows:

> "Indeed, people may be willing to put up with a considerable degree of economic, social, and psychological strain to extricate themselves from an unsatisfying marriage. (...) Furthermore, it may be necessary to understand what these potential stressors mean to the individual. For example, a decline in standard of living might be experienced positively

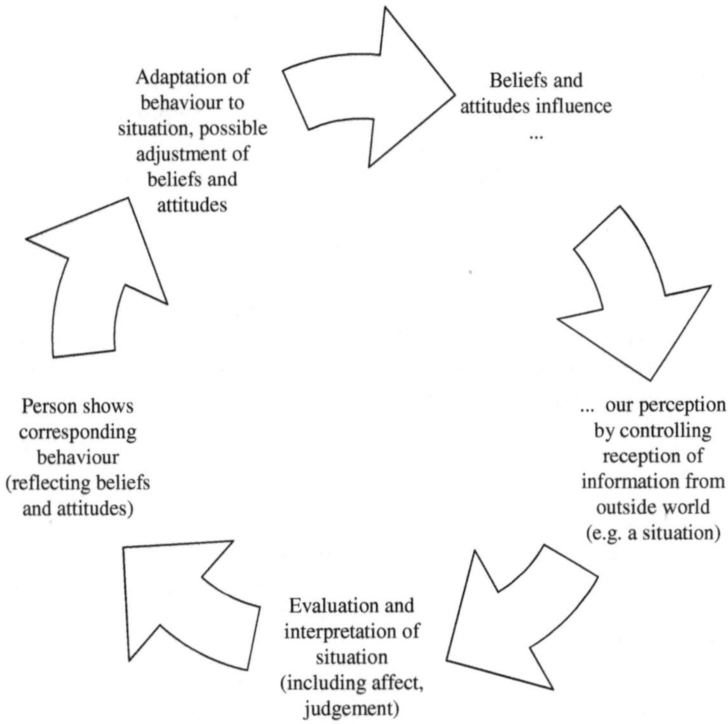

Fig. 2.3 Organisation of human behaviour by attitudes and beliefs

> if it also means that people feel that they have more control over their remaining income. Similarly, losing friends might not be distressing if these friends are viewed as allies of the ex-spouse. Moving might be desirable if it involves relocation away from a home that one found aversive. These considerations suggest that rather than looking at objective events and assuming they are stressful, it may be necessary to obtain peoples' subjective judgments about the extent to which these events are experienced as problematic." (Wang and Amato 2000: 665)

Another relevant aspect referring attitudes and beliefs is the role of attribution[16] that ex-spouses give for the failure of their marriage. In particular, we are interested in what ex-spouses think about their divorce and how they explain the reason for the divorce. This is supposed to have a general impact on the ex-spouse's well-being and is likely to have an effect on the process of adjustment. In their qualitative study on the attribution of responsibility, Newman and Langer explored the attributions that divorced women, aged 24–57 years, gave for the failure of their marriages. They investigated the type of attribution that well-adjusted women gave and related it to other personality characteristics (e.g. self-esteem) and overall happiness.

[16] Attribution means explaining a phenomenon by ascribing one or more reasons to it.

Two different kinds of attributions were distinguished, such as interactive or person related attributions, the first pointing to the dyadic unit that has been established by both spouses and the second concerning mainly characteristics of one spouse. The authors state that ex-spouses may actively promote or exaggerate their own feelings either by recrimination or by self-reproach, which impedes adjustment. They reasoned that ex-spouses would be more prone to make attributions to themselves or the other rather than to their relationship on the whole. This is because it seems easier to blame one person rather than to explain a complex interaction process such as the relationship where many aspects play a role and it is impossible to take an objective perspective. However, using an interactive attribution by putting the blame on the malfunction of the relationship prevents the ex-spouse from self-reproaches and change of conduct. The authors describe the advantages and disadvantages of person attribution:

> "The use of interactive attributions may restore to the divorced individual a greater feeling of control over future interpersonal endeavors through the recognition that undesirable behaviours are changeable. On the other hand, person attributions may foster the irrational belief that oneself or one's ex-spouse caused the marriage to fail because he or she was, in some sense, a "personal failure". Thus person attributions may lead to feelings of self-recrimination, resentment, the unreasonable assumption that people and circumstances cannot be changed, and a hopeless search for "the more perfect person". (Newman and Langer 1981: 225)

Their results confirmed the presupposed correlation between attribution type and self-esteem. Thus, women who made interactive attributions for their divorce instead of using personal attribution had a higher opinion of themselves, were more active and socially skilled, and described themselves as happier with positive feelings for the future.

If we focus on the economic consequences of divorce, one or both ex-spouses may experience a decline in living standard, at least some time after divorce from which they might ultimately recover. Generally, financial matters are crucial in this case, therefore the ex-spouse's factual income must be distinguished form his or her available income.[17] A high factual income may be associated with high obligations and might therefore mean a lower available income. As a consequence an ex-spouse with a reduced available income may refrain from making promises in a possible new relationship in order to avoid further obligations.[18]

Many studies have found a correlation between higher education, employment, better socioeconomic status and successful post divorce adjustment.[19] Dividing one household into two while not increasing resources has, undoubtedly, a weakening

[17] The available income denotes the income that remains after the deduction of all costs and obligations from the factual income.

[18] This can mean that he or she prefers superficial contacts compared to stable relationships or that the commitment in the relationship is restricted to cohabitation rather than marriage.

[19] See studies of Amato and Booth (1991): 895–914, Demo and Acock (1996): 457–488, Gove and Shin (1989): 122–144, Menaghan and Lieberman (1986): 319–328; Plummer and Koch-Hattem (1986): 523–529.

effect on the living standard of both ex-spouses.[20] However, ex-spouses who are employed and have a high income experience less economic hardship in the post divorce phase than those who have a moderate or low level of income.

Several studies found a gender-specific component revealing different economic consequences for men and women.[21] The results showed that in many countries women usually face a decline in their economic situation following divorce, whereas men experience fewer economic changes, less deterioration of their living standard and sometimes even improvement of their economic status. The couples' post divorce adjustment is influenced by the economic hardship that follows over the years, produced depending on the severity and duration of such decline.

In Spain the post-divorce situation is determined by the following socioeconomic characteristics: the application of Articles 90, 92 and 96.1 of the Spanish Civil Code cause that the children have the right to remain in the family accommodation and the parent who primarily exercises child custody remains with them.[22] The non-custodial parent has to find new accommodation and is often confronted with considerable financial commitments. Given the high prices of real estate in Spain it is often difficult or even impossible to cover the costs for two residences. In his comment on the application of Article 96 of the Spanish Civil Code, González del Pozo describes the difficult situation of non-custodial parents from his experience as a judge of the family court:[23]

> "(. . .) el progenitor obligado a abandonar el domicilio conyugal viene obligado a procurarse un nuevo inmueble en que alojarse, y a asumir una carga económica adicional antes inexistente, al tiempo que debe continuar abonando la mitad de la hipoteca del inmueble que constituyó del domicilio conyugal, todo lo cual le coloca en una situación de extraordinaria percariedad economica." (González de Pozo 2009: 16)

The statistical portrait of the income of men and women of the European Commission[24] provides details about earnings and the risk of poverty with reference to single parents. Generally, the hourly wage is higher for men throughout all 25 European countries, with the gap increasing with age. The following details are published by the European Commission:

> "Across the EU as a whole, average gross hourly earnings of women (those between 16 and 64 years old and working 15 h or more a week) were, on average, 15% below those of men in 2005. Women earn less than men in all Member States and in 2005 there were only eight countries out of the 27 and only three – Belgium, Malta and Slovenia – where it was smaller than 9% (. . .). In six countries – Germany, Estonia, Cyprus, Slovakia, Finland and the UK – the gap was 20% or more." (European Commission 2008: 93)

---

[20] See: Duncan and Hoffman (1985): 427 ff.

[21] See: Rogers (2004), Wilcox and Nock (2006), Alwin et al. (1992).

[22] See: González de Pozo (2009): 16.

[23] Several associations of divorced fathers and mothers complain on their homepages about the precarious economic situation that usually affects the non-custodial parents. Some Autonomous Communities have reacted to this situation and provide affordable accommodation for rent to divorced people.

[24] European Commission, (2008).

A detailed analysis of the wage gap with reference to women's age shows that the older women are the greater the difference is between the income of men and women. Thus, women younger than 30 years of age earn 8% less than their male age group while men in their thirties earn 20% more than women. According to the structure of earnings survey the European Commission gives the following data:

> "... women below 30 earned less than men in the same age group through-out the EU, their hourly wages on average being 92% of those of men (...) were only three EU Member States – Greece, France and Hungary — in which women's earnings were more than 95% of those of men and five in which they were below 85%. (...) For those aged 30–39, women on average earned only some 80% of what men earned in the EU. In this case, there were only eight Member States in which their earnings were more than 85% of those of men and none in which they were more than 90%. In Estonia, women's earnings averaged under 75% of those of men and in the Czech Republic and Slovakia, less than 70%" (European Commission 2008: 94)

In 2005 the risk of living in poverty for the working people within European Member States was slightly higher for women than for men.[25] Referring to the relation between risk of poverty and being a single parent, the European Commission found that women living with a dependent child are especially at risk for descending into poverty. Except for five Member States[26], in the remaining 20 European states, more women lived in low income households, although the difference was relatively small (only 1% point). This is shown in the EC statistics (Fig. 2.4).

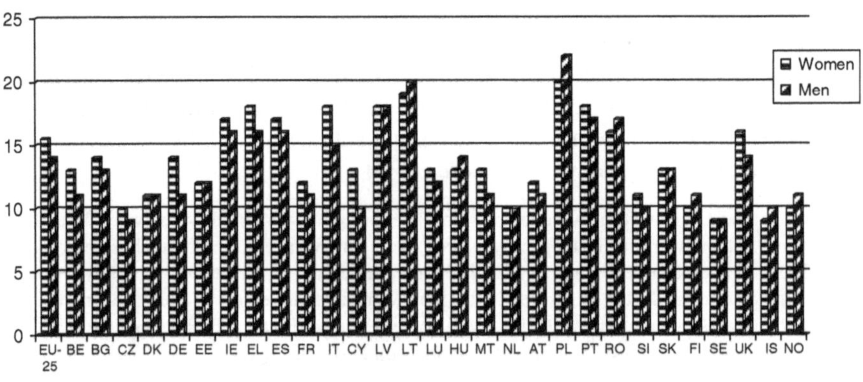

Fig. 2.4 Proportion of lone parents at risk of poverty, 2005

[25]According to the European Union people are considered at risk of poverty, "when they live on an income below 60% of the median household income of their own country." In a press release on the eradication of poverty and the promotion of social inclusion the European Union stated that currently 78 million people in the European Union or 16% of the population and 19% of the children are at risk of poverty. See: European Statistic Yearbook (2008): 91.

[26]See: Andreß et al. (2006): 533–560.

Whereas the average percentage of single parents' at risk for poverty in the Member States is 15% for women and 14% for men, the rate for Spain is slightly higher at 17% for women and 16% for men. Among the Member Sates with a high living standard (i.e. Denmark, France, the Netherlands and Sweden), the risk of poverty for single parents lies below the European average. It may be concluded that these countries have established a system of family support in which the family members in the post divorce phase help the divorced person to cope, at least with economic difficulties.

Undoubtedly, the economic effects of divorce depend to some extent on the socio-economic circumstances and the family policy that a particular state provides. The study of Andreß et al. looks at the relationship between the economic consequences of divorce and the different forms of family policies in European Member States. The authors used Belgium, Germany, Great Britain, Italy and Sweden as representatives of four prototypical models of family support: these are (1) the market model, (2) the extended family model, (3) the male breadwinner model and (4) the dual earner model. The typology goes back to two concepts of welfare states employing either an extensive or a rudimentary family policy. The authors consider models (3) and (4) as part of the continental European and North European states with an extensive family policy where governments provide two different types of family support:

> "…either through financial compensation for children and other dependent household members in the form of cash transfers or tax relief or by support for sufficient care facilities and gainful employment for all adult family members." (Andreß et al. 2006: 536)

On the contrary, of countries with a rudimentary family policy, dominant mainly in the Anglophone and Southern European countries, the few existing benefits have only the aim of preventing poverty by using safeguard measures via the market or by the family. Whereas the market model encourages citizens to find private solutions based on the market rather than utilizing state interventions, in the extended family model, support is supposed to come from the family network rather than from the market. They assume that these four types of family support create specific dependencies within the family, which in the case of separation or divorce, there may be negative consequences for the economically weaker partner. The researchers focus on the question of how much economic autonomy is granted to the weaker family members within each of the four models. The table shows the characteristic features of the four models of family policy and their corresponding states in terms of economic autonomy for women (Fig. 2.5).

A comparison of the four models shows that a high female employment rate is positively correlated with a high amount of family cash benefit and public child care available for young children until the age of three years. Both measures facilitate women's re-entrance into the labour market after maternity leave. Women's economic autonomy appears to be lowest in the extended family model in which low part-time employment is the most frequent job option. A higher income level, privately organised child care and less state intervention is typical for the market

Economic autonomy	Sweden (4)	Belgium (3/4)	Germany (3)	Great Britain (1)	Italy (2)
Cash transfer					
Family cash benefits	++	0	–	0	– –
Child benefits	0	+ +	–	–	– –
Social assistance	0	+	–	0	– –
Public childcare					
0- to 3-year olds	+ +	+	– –	– –	– –
3- to 6-year olds	0	+	0	– –	+
Women's employment					
Employment rate	+ +	–	0	+	– –
Low part-time employment	+	0	0	– –	+ +
Economic autonomy: 3, high; 2, middle; 1, low Rank compared to five-country mean:––, very low; –, low; 0, average; +, high; + +, very high					

Fig. 2.5 Women's economic autonomy in five states[27]

model. The authors assumed that that economic autonomy for the weaker members is highest in Sweden and lowest in Italy with Belgium, Germany, and Great Britain ranging in between. The results show that the post-divorce household income is affected for both genders, however more negatively for women than for men. This can be seen in the diagram that shows the adjusted household incomes of 2004 separately for men and women in each country from 5 years before to 5 years after separation (Fig. 2.6a, b).

On the whole, the study reveals high gender inequalities in economic status after divorce in all five countries. In accordance with European statistics, women turn out to be the losers while the men seem to be better off. In three of five countries (Belgium, Italy and Great Britain) men experience either no income changes or they have an increase in income. However, in Germany men lose 2% of their former income and half of the divorced men in Sweden lose 7%. Their results also show that the women's income decline is highest in Italy and lowest in Sweden, and that British and German women recover rather quickly from the negative economic effects of separation. The dual earner model turns out to have the highest gender equality and both men and women are confronted with long-lasting financial consequences following divorce.

Despite of the fact that the welfare state protection has increased within the last two decades, the Spanish family policy may still be subsumed under the extended family model because it expects the family to internalize welfare responsibilities. In their detailed description of the Spanish family policy model Baizán, Michielin

[27] 1 = market model, 2 = extended family model, 3 = male breadwinner model, 4 = dual earner model. Andreß et al. (2006): 533–560.

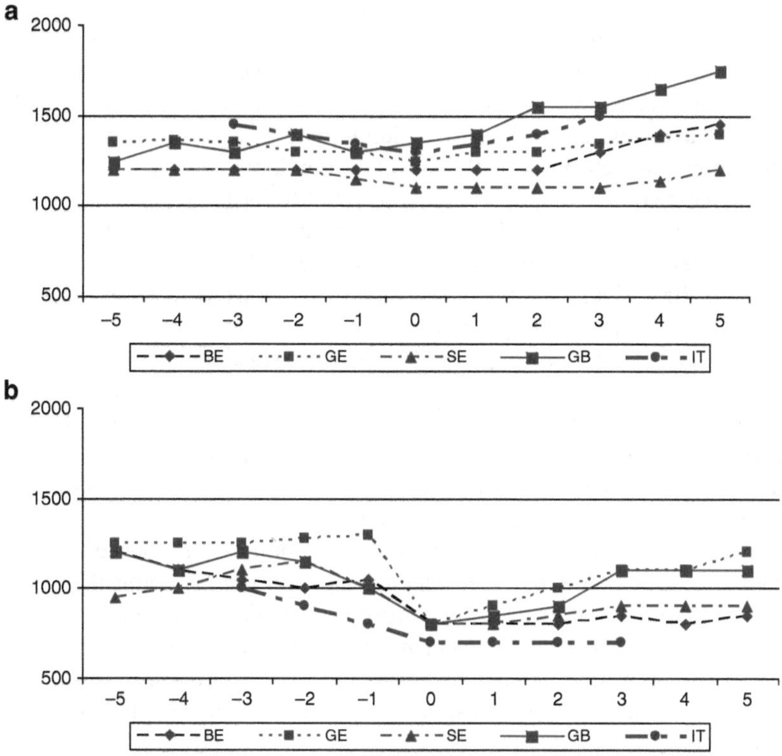

Fig. 2.6 (**a**) Adjusted household incomes for men before and after divorce in 2004. (**b**) Adjusted household incomes for women before and after divorce in 2004[28]

and Billari report that the Spanish family policy had been criticised by the OECD because of its low profile in state intervention. According to the authors, the Spanish family policy may be described by the following features: a low development of active labour market policies and insufficient communication between employers and job seekers. This puts the emphasis on the family as supporting entity for unemployed family members and for finding a job by using private family networks. The housing policy has strengthened the private housing sector and weakened the rental housing market. This puts a heavy economic burden on first household formation as well as on the new start after divorce. The tax system promotes joint taxation among couples, a disincentive for working women, and grants tax reduction for non-working people living in the household. There are few student grants available and private formation is often difficult to afford. A low amount of child benefit and 16 weeks of maternity leave tend to favour the male

[28]Andreß et al. 2006: 533–560.

breadwinner model.[29] In fact, despite of a considerable increase in women's labour market participation within the last decades the female employment rate is still lower than the European average rate. Working women occupy often part-time jobs and the male breadwinner model is still predominant in Spanish society. Public child care is available free of cost for children from the age of three years. Schools are mostly comprehensive schools and often provide catering for pupils, which facilitates the reconciliation of work and private life for families.[30]

The economic side of marital dissolution entails a regulation of the obligations and the property acquired during marriage (Articles 90.E, 91, 95 of the Spanish Civil Code), the attribution of the family accommodation (Article 96), child support (Article 93) and compensatory payments, such as spousal support (Article 90.F, Article 97 CC).[31] The outcome of the spouses' stipulations in the regulating agreement (Article 90) determines to a large extent the economic shape of the post-divorce family. The negotiations concerning property division are often dominated and influenced by emotions. Both spouses are afraid of giving up too much and intend to maximize their gains. Due to these circumstances it often takes a considerable amount of time to settle economic questions.

In a study on gender and the short-run economic consequences of marital disruption, Smock points out that although men do not economically fare well after divorce, women suffer from more serious economic consequences. The author sees a special disadvantage for women who have lived in a marriage with the characteristics of the traditional male breadwinner model. This is because the post-divorce consequences that ex-spouses experience depend mainly on their economic status before the separation:

> "Men and women with similar levels of work attachment before separation or divorce tend to have similar post disruption personal incomes, largely because prior work experience predicts employment and earnings after marital disruption. But the reality is, of course, that few women with young children can achieve this level of labour force attachment. Childless women have significantly more years of work experience compared to women with children, and childless women worked as many weeks as men in the year before marital disruption." (Smock 1994: 258)

In their article on occupation, family and household trajectories among young Spaniards the authors Baizán, Michielin and Billari conclude that the Spanish welfare state is designed for stable families with male breadwinners in which the vulnerable are mainly the elderly. However, in reality it is especially the younger generations who are confronted with all the problems and risks associated with industrialization and globalization, such as requirement for high flexibility, competition and high level of formation. Therefore the increasing risk of unemployment

[29] See: Baizán et al. (2002): 197f.

[30] For a description of the situation of the Spanish family in the European context, see: Ruiz Corbella (2005): 41–62.

[31] The effects of separation and divorce in Spanish Family Law are discussed in more detail in Chapter 4.

affects mainly younger people and women who want to enter the job market. This does not only delay the transition to adulthood and household formation but also complicates the situation for men and women after divorce.[32]

Spanish family law contains several statutory provisions aimed at preventing a precarious post-divorce situation for the economically disadvantaged spouse.[33] As such, Article 97 of the Civil Code takes into account the specific conditions of the marriage. The following criteria are relevant for the attribution of spousal support: agreements made between the spouses, age and state of health of economically weaker spouse, professional qualifications, pre-divorce family organisation and duration of marriage, collaboration in ex-spouse's business and special necessities.[34] Likewise the Spanish Law on Gender Equality contains special provisions in Article 31 on urban policy, territorial organisation and housing which maintain that the government will provide access to accommodation for women who are in precarious situations or at risk of social exclusion. They apply especially to women who are victims of gender violence or custodial mothers of minor children. This is expressed in Article 31, paragraph 2:

> "Artículo 31. Políticas urbanas, de ordenación territorial y vivienda. (...) 2. El Gobierno, en el ámbito de sus competencias, fomentará el acceso a la vivienda de las mujeres en situación de necesidad o en riesgo de exclusión, y de las que hayan sido víctimas de la violencia de género, en especial cuando, en ambos casos, tengan hijos menores exclusivamente a su cargo." (Ley Orgánica para la igualdad efectiva de mujeres y hombres, 2007: 12,618).

Another relevant factor that has some bearing on spouses' adjustment to divorce is the question who initiated divorce. The research literature is based on the observation of the spouses normally confirming that one spouse "left the other".[35]

[32]See: Baizán et al. (2002): 218.

[33]See in particular the Law on Gender Equality, which states that the government will provide access to accommodation for women in precarious situations or at risk of social exclusion. This applies especially to women who are victims of domestic violence or custodial mothers of minor children (Ley Orgánica 3/2007 para la igualdad efectiva de mujeres y hombres, 2007: 12618).

[34]See: "Article 97

El cónyuge al que la separación o divorcio produzca desequilibrio económico en relación con la posición del otro, que implique un empeoramiento en su situación anterior en el matrimonio, tiene derecho a una pensión que se fijará en la resolución judicial, teniendo en cuenta, entre otras, las siguientes circunstancias: 1° Los acuerdos a que hubieren llegado los cónyuges. 2°. La edad y estado de salud. 3°. La cualificación profesional y las probabilidades de acceso a un empleo. 4°. La dedicación pasada y futura a la familia. 5°. La colaboración con su trabajo en las actividades mercantiles, industriales o profesionales del otro cónyuge. 6°. La duración del matrimonio y de la convivencia conyugal. 7°. La pérdida eventual de un derecho de pensión. 8°. El caudal y medios económicos y las necesidades de uno y otro cónyuge. En la resolución judicial se fijarán las bases para actualizar la pensión y las garantías para su efectividad." (Spanish Civil Code, Article 97).

[35]The expression "leave" has four connotations according to the type of relationship. The separating spouses may be subdivided into one of the following four categories depending on their active or passive role: (1) the abandoner and the abandoned denoting the aspect of one partner leaving back the other, (2) the escaped and the escapee, where the conflicts have become unsolvable, (3) the released and the releaser, implying that one exerted control over the other,

In fact, in the majority of cases there is one spouse who initiates the break-up while the other prefers the marriage to continue. Only in a minority of cases the break-up is initiated simultaneously by both spouses. However, not every unilateral divorce necessarily results in non-consensual divorce because most spouses finally reach a consensus on their regulating agreement. In fact, statistic data of the year 2007 show that from the 125,721 couples who got divorced in Spain, a total number of 79,945 divorces were consensual and only 45,776 were non-consensual.[36]

Each spouse's decision to stay or leave is influenced by comparing the utility of the existing marriage to that of a hypothesized alternative. Divorce figures show that a majority of divorces are filed by women in European countries as well as in the United States.[37] There may be several reasons for this. One reason is that husbands tend to avoid separation because the social status of "husband" entails some social recognition.[38] Another explanation is that women are more sensitive to problems and suffer more from an unsatisfactory relationship.

In their investigation on spouses' attitude toward divorce, Crane, Soderquist and Gardner found that women and men use a different mental approach when entering the divorce process and use dissimilar communication patterns. According to their study women tend to be more sensitive to marital quarrels and are more likely to make specific plans for divorcing without communicating said plans with their spouses. Women also are more consistent in carrying out their plans for divorcing. The authors point to the difference between men and women when thinking and communicating about divorce and underline the importance of these results for pre-divorce counselling:

> "Women also think more about divorce and talk to others about divorce and are willing to make these thoughts and desires known to their spouse. Therefore this study indicates that women appear to take a more active role in preparing and planning for divorce or separation. (...) One conclusion related to the results of this study is that wives' statements of distress or divorce intention will occur more frequently than statements from their husbands. Also, given that wives' distress levels are more predictive of divorce than are their husbands' distress levels, clinicians and husbands should pay careful attention to any such statements. Because many women know the costs of divorce in such terms as loss of social and economic status, increased responsibility for children, and custody disputes, their willingness to consider divorce should not be taken lightly." (Crane et al. 1995: 103f)

Another reason why more women file for divorce is that they often have fewer material resources to utilize. As fewer resources translate into restricted bargaining power women have less means that would allow them to effectively change their

---

and (4) the set-up and the setter-upper, indicating that one partner played a trick on the other or used some sort of trap to provoke the end of the relationship.

[36]See: Appendix Divorce Sentences in Autonomous Communities (2007).

[37]See: Brinig and Allen (2000): 126–169.

[38]See: Nock (2001): 756–777.

marriage to a more enjoyable state.[39] Their power to convince and induce their husbands to change is therefore greatly restricted, which then leads to an accumulation of problems and a radical solution for change.[40] This seems logical, as the one who suffers more during the marriage is more likely to initiate the divorce. In their study on motives for divorce, Hetherington and Tyron draw our attention to the amazing difference in perceiving, experiencing and evaluating the quality of marriage between the spouses. They point to two aspects that preoccupy women when they consider divorce, such as the fear to loose child custody and a decline in economic status once they are divorced:

> "Divorced women reported having been dissatisfied longer in their marriages and having considered separation for a longer period than did men. In contrast, about one quarter of the husbands said they were surprised when their wives wanted to divorce and were not sure about the reasons for the sudden degeneration in their marriages. Women usually reported that the main thing that locked them into an unsatisfying marriage was too little independent income to support themselves when they left, and some, in anticipation of the breakup, had prepared by going back to school or to work. Unhappily married men were more likely to fear the loss of their children." (Hetherington and Tryon 1989: 58).

Many people have a high level of distress long before the divorce or during the decision making phase.[41] Thus the initiator has usually finished the mourning process when he or she discloses the wish to divorce and has fewer adjustment problems. Furthermore, the initiator tends to have a feeling of control over the situation whereas the divorcee experiences more distress after the divorce. Basically, both spouses experience distress but the timing and recovery is different. Wang and Amato found that a new relationship had a positive effect on the process of divorce adjustment:

> "Spouses who initiate divorce have completed all or most of their mourning for the marriage by the time the physical separation and legal divorce occurs. In contrast, spouses who resist the divorce must do most of their mourning after the marriage ends. Furthermore, forming a new intimate relationship – especially if it is satisfying one – may be the fastest way for people to soothe the psychic pain associated with a failed marriage." (Wang and Amato 2000: 667)

Researchers found that the experience of control over the divorce process had a positive effect on divorce adjustment.[42] This is confirmed by longitudinal studies

---

[39]Bargaining power is an economic term that is applied to relationships and denotes all the advantages that a person can offer in a negotiation. It is a person's capacity to pursue his or her interests by way of negotiation, persuasion, status or influence, power or a combination of these elements.

[40]This is also due to the tendency that social norms do not encourage women to exert power of their husbands and making compromises is less accepted for husbands. Although there is a tendency towards more gender equality it is still more accepted for women to take over traditional male roles than men taking over typical female roles (e.g. household duties, child care, etc.). See also: Sweeney (2002): 410–440.

[41]See: Kitson (1992).

[42]See the studies of Gray and Silver (1990): 1180–1191; Wallerstein (1986): 65–77.

specifying that unhappily married people tend to adjust comparatively well once the marriage has ended.[43] Furthermore, the authors found two predominant factors facilitating divorce adjustment, such as social resources and the spouses' evaluation and definition of the divorce. They state the following:

> "More important, social resources (such as forming a new relationship) and people's definitions reflected in being the initiator of divorce) consistently predict better divorce adjustment. (. . .) Our measures assume that adjustment involves believing that the divorce was a good idea, perceiving positive outcomes of divorce, no longer being preoccupied with the former spouse and marriage, and psychologically "moving on" with one's life. Given this way of measuring adjustment, it is not surprising that the best adjusted individuals are those who initiated the divorce and are in a new relationship." (Wang and Amato 2000: 666f)

This statement shows that the partners who take an active role and are in a new relationship seem to adapt well to the new situation. However, it was also mentioned that entering into a new relationship always bears the risk of committing the same errors as in the former relationship. Therefore a critical reflection of the own conduct is recommended.

2.4 Relational Support

We will now turn to the relational factors that affect post divorce adjustment, such as the psychological functioning before divorce, including the attachment style and intensity of attachment to the former spouse. Another factor refers to the amount of social support received from both the family and from friends. The quality of the parent–child relationship is a relevant indicator for the well-being of the divorced person. This is influenced by the ex-partner's readiness and ability to separate the role of the parent and from that of the ex-spouse. However, family support may also come from kin such as the family of origin and relatives. The more relationships are negatively affected by the marital breakdown, the more discord and social isolation the divorced person has to face. A simultaneous decline of several sources of social networking has a destabilizing effect on the whole personality. Nevertheless, social support may also come from external sources such as close friends or, sometimes, from colleagues.

A special indicator for divorce adjustment is an ex-spouse's level of psychological functioning before the separation.[44] Not surprisingly, individuals who were emotionally stable before divorce and who have developed helpful coping strategies have valuable pre-requisites for adjusting well to the post divorce situation. Personal resources such as high self-esteem, self-discipline and social skills have a positive effect.

---

[43]See the studies of Aseltine and Kessler (1993): 237–251; Wheaton (1990): 209–223.

[44]See: Tschann et al. (1989): 1033–1046.

A distinctive criterion for post divorce adjustment is the style and degree of attachment to the former spouse.[45] Theoretical approaches in attachment theory distinguish between secure and insecure, disorganized or avoidant attachment styles. A secure attachment is associated with productive communications skills, practical coping strategies, the ability to incorporate conflicting feelings and control negative emotions, and the willingness to solve conflicts beneficially for the individuals involved.[46] Thus research has shown that a secure attachment style helps to deal with divorce and is the basis for shared parenting, whereas an insecure attachment style has a detrimental effect on the family members involved.[47] A cooperative relationship between the ex-spouses has a positive effect on their own adjustment and that of their child(ren). On the contrary, ex-spouses find it difficult to keep in contact on the basis of mutual respect, feeling unable to avoid emotions of anger, hate, resentment, love, etc.[48]

If we assume that the end of a dyadic relationship creates a situation of mental and emotional deprivation, we should know something about the psychological implications that are associated with a long-term relationship.[49] The divorced person may react with feelings of anger against his/her former partner. These reactions are normal or even healthy to a certain extent. However, if the anger turns into hatred and an impulse to insult and mentally destroy the other, it has taken a pathological turn. Such extreme emotional reactions are caused by the ex-spouse feeling offended in the following five respects: (1) self-esteem,[50] (2) sense of justice, (3) breach of trust and confidence, (4) the termination of the sexual relationship and (5) a change in the relationship to the children. A person's self-esteem is affected when he or she is left by a partner. Being rejected by the other creates a feeling of inferiority, which marks the beginning of a fatal spiral of inferiority and consequently compensating it by creating an emotional state of superiority from which it is difficult to escape. The diagram shows the psychodynamics of this spiral (Fig. 2.7).

The diagram depicts the consecutive course of feelings that may be provoked by the separation. The fact that the divorcee (A) has lost interest in the divorced (B) and abandons him/her has an effect on the B's self-esteem and causes feelings of humiliation and shame (stage 1). This induces B to perceive himself or herself in an inferior position. As a consequence, B intends to minimize this feeling of inferiority by contemplating revenge and emotionally attacking A in his/her vulnerable points

[45]Attachment style denotes the type of emotional bonds that persons form in close relationships. In parenting it is the degree to which parents respond to their children. Attachment style is based on deep rooted convictions and experience and is assumed to reflect the view of the self and others.

[46]See: Shaver and Mikulincer (2002): 133–161.

[47]See: Cohn et al. (1992): 417–431.

[48]See: Main and Solomon (1990): 121–160; Bartholomew (1990): 147–178.

[49]By dyadic or intimate relationship we mean a close interpersonal relationship in which the participants know and trust one another and share physical and emotional intimacy.

[50]Self-esteem denotes how much an individual values his or her overall worth as a person.

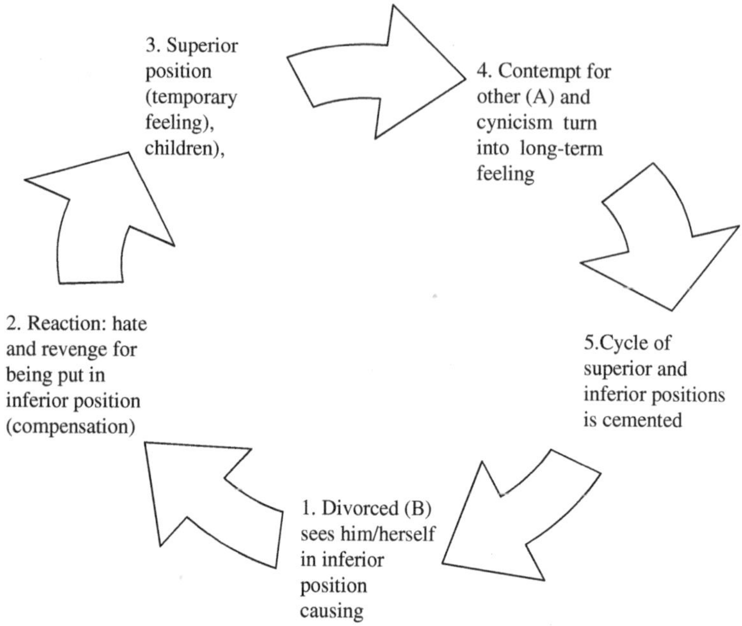

Fig. 2.7 Spiral of inferiority and superiority

(stage 2). This, in turn, puts A in a difficult position who therefore attempts to compensate or outweigh his/her weak position. For B the mere experience of being able to cause problems to A puts him or her in a superior position of control (stage 3). This dynamism occurs sometimes in divorce negotiations especially if feelings of revenge are involved.[51] However, as the feeling of superiority seems only a short-term experience, it is turned into a long-term attitude through continuous contempt and cynicism (stage 4). Unfortunately, the existence of these long-term attitudes cements the original experience of inferiority (5). As described above, the feeling of inferiority provokes a striving for revenge and vengeance. The lower a person's self-esteem is the higher the feeling of revenge tends to be.[52]

---

[51]As a result one spouse may, for instance, tend to make high demands for the regulating agreements and/or may use the best interests of the child in order to pursue his or her goals.

[52]Adler (1870–1937) was an Austrian psychiatrist and founder of individual psychology. He underlined the importance of social equality and democratic family structures in order to prevent psychopathologic personality development. In his psychological investigations of the human character he considered the feeling of inferiority as the basic motivation of an urge for power. In fact, he regarded the feeling of inferiority as a key incentive for personality development and the attempt to overcome it by way of compensation. He saw a parallel between psyche and body in how they react to the frailty of one element in the whole system. The psyche tends to react in the same way as bodily organs, namely that the weakness of one organ would be compensated by a special effort of the others. Accordingly, the psyche tends to react with intense struggle to make up for feelings of weakness, helplessness and vulnerability (Rüedi 2007: 76).

Another relevant factor for post divorce adjustment is the style of attachment to the former spouse. In her qualitative study on certain typical patterns of close relationship, Hetherington was interested in the typology of patterns and how these changed after divorce. In marriages she identified five configurations of couple relationships, such as (1) the pursuer–distancer,[53] (2) the disengaged,[54] (3) the operatic,[55] (4) the cohesive individuated,[56] and (5) the traditional marriages,[57] all of which are associated with certain characteristics. The results of the study show that the pursuer–distancer marriage has the highest risk of instability because the spouses do not seem to have developed joint problem solving strategies. The second highest risk of marital instability is associated with disengaged couples because once the emotional attraction has faded and the children become more independent there is little that holds the spouses together. Operatic marriages have the third highest divorce rate because of the inherent problems associated with this type of relationship as the spouses tend to become involved in cycle of recurring breaks and reconciliations. The cohesive individuated attachment style has one of the lowest divorce rates because their relationship has few immanent risks. The traditional marriage works well if both spouses share the same beliefs and attitudes and there is little change.

Although the number of religious wedding ceremonies has been decreasing in Spain the traditional marriage is still the predominant pattern of relationship. Undoubtedly, a marriage goes through good and bad times depending on the problems that occur and the stress encountered. However, Hetherington underlines the salience of an elaborate attachment style and lists a number of qualities that are pre-requisites for fulfilling relationships. She says:

---

[53]According to the author this type of marriage is characterized by a high amount of nagging, hostile criticism, and contempt on the part of wives and is responded by withdrawal and denial of husbands.

[54]In this type of marriage husbands and wives tend to lead separate or parallel lives, having few interest, activities and friends in common. Due to their few interactions and infrequent communication they rarely have arguments, avoid intimacy (even their sexual relations are occasional and unsatisfying) and companionship.

[55]In an operatic relationship the spouses are not interested in a harmonious family climate but rather constantly seek sensation and diversion. They are fascinated by intense feelings but run the risk of ignoring the limit of what is considered accepted by the respective other. As 'operatics' consider balanced marriages as boring the relationship usually ends when one spouse finds that the excitement has faded.

[56]Typical qualities in the cohesive individuated marriage are warmth, respect, equity, mutual support, autonomy, and relatively low instability. This type of marriage seems to include a high level of tolerance and social skills from both sides, because there is no overall tendency to resolve differences by hostile strategies. The relationship has a balance of the partners pursuing their own interests but also enjoying their relationship together.

[57]Traditional marriages follow the male breadwinner model. If the woman is employed she provides just a supplemental income. Couples usually enjoy their relationship and support each other mutually, provided that the spouses share a traditional view of gender roles. The crucial point lies in change, especially when a spouse's values or attitudes change over time (e.g. when women want to gain more independence, etc.).

> "Generally, marriages that have built up positive emotional bank accounts through respect, mutual support, and affirmation of each other's worth are more likely to survive. Our work and that of other researchers studying marriage and divorce (...) finds that couples who have good problem-solving skills; are able to listen; respond to the other persons' feelings and opinions; express themselves and disagree without contempt, hostility, belligerence, or withdrawal; and are able to de-escalate conflicts when they get too intense are better able to deal with the bumps along the path to marital survival. Individuals who are more socially responsible, are more mature, are better educated, have an internal locus of control, and are religious are less likely to be involved in divorce than those who are immature and antisocial." (Hetherington 2003: 322)

There is general agreement among many authors that the most important influential form of support comes in the form of new relationships. Research consistently shows that new relationships, cohabitation and remarriage, are associated with better post divorce adjustment for both men and women.[58] If mechanisms of the broken relationship are not reflected upon, there is always the danger of mistakes being repeated in a new relationship. Therefore, Hetherington investigated the different ways divorced people coped with the new situation by analysing their post divorce adaptive patterns over time. As a result she found six patterns of adjustment and ascribed them specific psychological characteristics: (1) enhancers, (2) good-enoughs, (3) seekers, (4) swingers, (5) competent loners, and (6) defeated.

The first group called enhancers was predominantly well-adjusted women who had grown more competent over time and succeeded at work, as parent, socially and in their remarriages. She explained their success by drawing on an internal and an external reason. This group scored slightly higher in terms of self-esteem, achievement, social responsibility and self-efficacy, and showed less depression and antisocial behaviour. The external reason was provoked by stressors of divorce such as being a single parent that forced this group to seek further education in order to improve their situation. The author describes the positive effect of their effort:

> "As enhancers improved occupationally, they began to travel in new social circles and meet men of higher socioeconomic status. The second time around, enhancers usually moved up, and their second marriages were usually more successful than their first." (Hetherington 2003: 324)

The relevant factor is that enhancers are described as open for change and prepared to acquire new social skills in the public sphere that enable them to improve their economic situation. The acquisition of skills for the private sphere seems more complicated because they are implicit and need to be deduced from overt behaviour.[59]

The second group called "goodenoughs" represented the average person coping with divorce who had some success, as well as some problems and set-backs.

---

[58]See: Hetherington et al. (1997): 163–172.

[59]This is a multifaceted aspect because social skills depend in part on the socio-economic and educational level of a group in society and they form an implicit code. A precondition for the entrance to such groups is the knowledge of this code. If an enhancer wants to get access to a higher social level he or she has to acquire this implicit knowledge.

Although there were more women than men in the first year after divorce, this difference moderated over time. They try to improve their lives economically and socially, but as they are not as ambitious as the enhancers they usually remain in their social status and tend to choose a new partner similar to former spouse. Consequently, their circumstances after ten years from divorce resembled their old marriage. There is a risk of the goodenoughs to repeat committing the same errors. However, the author describes their positive qualities:

> "However, goodenoughs were frequently competent mothers; their children did nearly as well as children with enhancer mothers. Women in the group also dealt fairly effectively with the normal tensions and challenges of postdivorce life." (Hetherington 2003: 324)

The third group called seekers contains all divorced women and men who aim at finding a new partner as soon as possible mainly in the first year after divorce. Statistical results show that finding a new partner was more important for men's well-being than for women. Male seekers are described as having low autonomy and self-esteem, need a partner who cares form them, and they have difficulties staying alone. Due to these predispositions, seekers are not very selective in choosing a new partner and tend to end up with the same problems that they had in their former marriage. The author characterizes male seekers as follows:

> "Men usually were not interested in real emotional sharing or personal change. They wanted a woman who would be supportive and undemanding, someone who would look after them and would not expect much in return." (Hetherington 2003: 325)

The group called "swingers" is primarily male but for a short period represented both men and women. Swingers dress in a youthful fashion, appear in single bars and have more superficial relationships. They score higher in antisocial behaviour and lower in social responsibility. Once they have liberated themselves from their relatively stable marriage they tend to lead a rather untamed life at least for some time. However, swingers are described as unhappy because of two reasons, firstly they miss their family (e.g. feel depressed) and secondly they feel guilty (e.g. sometimes also experienced as anxiety) for the marital breakdown. Nevertheless, the author depicts them as, "... fairly conventional people, and once they are again in an intimate relationship, they tend to revert to their old selves."[60]

The fifth group named "competent loners" is a group of mainly well-adjusted and socially skilled women who do well in their jobs and lead active social lives, committing their free time to various interests and hobbies. However, their relationships do not usually last long because they are not really interested in sharing life with a partner. They are described as being independent and autonomous and do not need a partner to feel complete. However, they may make an exception and commit to a relationship if they meet an exceptional person.

Representatives of the last group of divorced called "defeated" are characterized as having low self-esteem, low social responsibility, and score high in depression and antisocial behaviours. They do not have the resources to solve their problems,

---

[60]See: Hetherington (2003): 325.

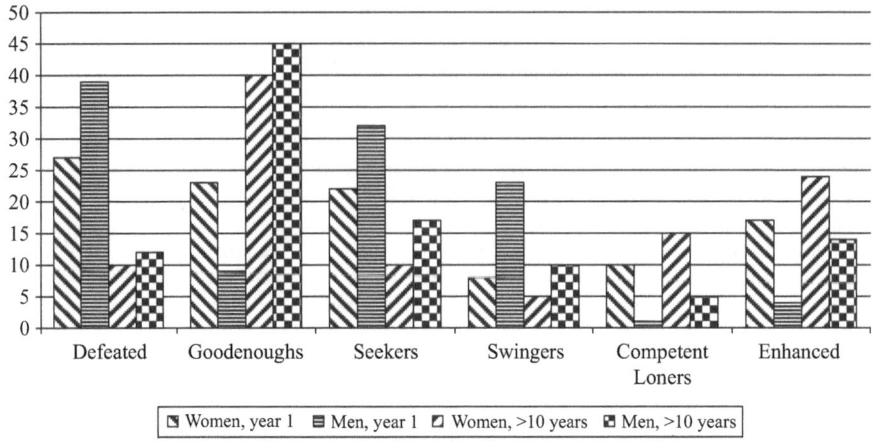

Fig. 2.8 Percentage of women and men in six post-divorce adaptive patterns over time[61]

thus making it difficult for them to build up more satisfying relationships and actively reconstruct their life. The author gives an overview of the percentage of men and women opting for the patterns and compared their adaptive behaviour between 1 year and up to 10 years after divorce. The diagram shows the percentage of men and women in each of the six groups (Fig. 2.8).

If we compare the results for men and women 1 year after divorce we notice that the majority of men and women are found in the group of the defeated which clearly reflects their state of suffering caused by the many changes and stressors they have been confronted with. The biggest difference between male and female adaptive patterns 1 year after divorce was found in the following three groups: whereas 17% of women had enhanced their situation only 4% of the men had done so. This would support the view that more women than men initiate divorce and the initiator tends to feel happier after separation.

The second striking difference can be noticed in the group of competent loners, with 10% women and only 1% men belonging to this group. This implies that divorced women have learned to cope with their lives and do not want to give up their independence whereas a minority of men considers this pattern as preferred option. Perhaps it also means that if women have custody of their children they have restricted options for dating or remarrying in terms of role overload.[62] It makes a difference for a new relationship whether or not the partner has to care for children. On the contrary, the parent who takes care of the children on a weekend basis has more resources (e.g. time, flexibility, etc.) to seek and build up a new relationship. The most outstanding difference is found in the group of the swingers, with nearly a

[61]See: Hetherington (2003): 324.

[62]Role overload means that a person has either not enough time to fulfil the number of role functions or is uncertain about duties associated with a particular role.

quarter being men and just 7% being women. As this behaviour is associated with the variable of social responsibility it entails that women tend to be more socially responsible than men in the year following divorce. The author explains this behaviour as transitionally deviant by making reference to an earlier study and says about male swingers:

> "Swingers tended to become goodenoughs when they married, and their antisocial behavior decreased and social responsibility increased. The incidence of extramarital affairs among remarried former swingers was no higher than among that found in other second marriages. This may simply be a reflection of age. At the time of remarriage, many of our parents were in their late 30s or 40s. It also may be that the early relentless swinging was a temporary aberration produced by the breakdown of the self that also often occurs after divorce." (Hetherington 2003: 325)

After a period of up to 10 years more than half of women (64%) were either in the group of the goodenoughs or the enhanced. As a comparison, more than a half of the men (62%) were either in the group of the goodenoughs or the seekers. A minority of women remained swingers and the same amount of men remained in the group of the competent loners.

In this context it is interesting to know how many divorced people actually take a second chance and decide to remarry. The Spanish National Institute of Statistics reveals remarkable results for the 2008. The table on marriages and the spouses' pre-matrimonial civil status shows that from the 194,022 marriages including all age groups in 2008 it was the second marriage for more men than women.[63] However, a detailed analysis of the different age groups shows a reverse trend for spouses born between 1969 and 1986. In fact, within the age groups of the 22–40 year-olds more women than men had been divorced before they remarried.

The specific conditions of the post-divorce scenario have an effect on the ex-spouse's well-being. The custody regulation stipulates the amount of time that children spend with their parents. Children may be a special source of support. The amount of time that parents and children spend together is an important issue because it determines how long a child is exposed to the influence of the parent. In a study on post-divorce parenting Amato and Gilbreth found that the quality of contact is more important than the amount of contact in terms of positive post-divorce outcomes for children.[64] Thus, it is supposed that parenting that includes warmth and participation, strengthening of psychological autonomy and supervising the setting of limits has a relevant effect on the quality of the relationship. The

---

[63]See: INE, Spanish National Institute of Statistics, Tabla: Matrimonios de diferente sexo por años cumplidos y años de los cónyuges, sexo y estado civil anterior de los matrimonios (http://www.ine.es/jaxi/tabla.do). The statistics reveal the following details: Among the total number of 194,022 marriages in 2008 the spouses' pre-matrimonial civil status was 170,101 single men and 172,839 single women, 1,785 male widowers compared to 1,035 female widowers and 22,076 divorced men compared to 20,148 divorced women.

[64]See: Amato and Gilbreth (1999): 557–573.

supportive effect of children is particularly true for women because in the majority of cases it is them who retain custody.

On the other hand children may also be a source of post-divorce stress. Divorcees often find it difficult to separate their roles as ex-spouses from those of being parents. Therefore psychologists advise parents to reach a non-emotional level or a "business-like relationship" for dealing with educational and organizational matters. This is in fact difficult because parents tend to feel ambivalent toward their children. On the one hand children and the affection they give are a source of emotional support, on the other hand they constantly remind the ex-spouses on the failure of their marriage.[65]

In their qualitative study Cohen and Finzi-Dottan examined the possible contribution of four factors to parental satisfaction with their parent–child relationship one year after divorce. These factors include attachment style, parenting style, perception of own parents' parenting and ex-spouses' assessment of the quality of the parent's parenting.[66] Their results showed that for men and women different factors predict satisfaction with their parent–child relationship. Women tend to gain their satisfaction from how they felt and behaved when they interacted with their children. The more mothers give their children a predominant place in their lives, the less they consider them as a burden, and the more satisfied they tend to be. On the contrary, male satisfaction turned out to be influenced by higher education and by the image they had of their own mothers and their ex-wives. Higher education is correlated with fathers' higher level of satisfaction with parent–child relationship. Furthermore, if fathers experienced their own mothers as less overprotective and felt that their ex-wives appreciated their fathering, they tended to be more satisfied. This result is interesting because it suggests that for fathers a reduced form of contact is helpful for their father–child relationship. The authors give the following explanation for this fact:

> "The finding that greater satisfaction was reported by fathers who believed that their ex-wives thought well of their parenting may be explained in two ways. One is that the ex-wives' appraisal accurately reflects the quality of the fathers' parenting, and the fathers' satisfaction stems largely from their sense of competence and the good relationships they form with their children. The other is anchored in the power and influence mothers have as custodial parents after divorce. Mothers who disapprove of their ex-husband's parenting may put up barriers to access and/or convey their unfavorable opinion to their children, affecting their children's attitudes and creating strains in their relationship with him. Either behavior would lead to frustration and reduced satisfaction on the father's part." (Cohen and Finzi-Dottan 2005: 93)

[65]See the study of Tschann et al. (1990): 1–22.

[66]Despite the end of the marriage it seems to be of importance for the individual parent's satisfaction that the other recognizes and appreciates the own education work. See: Belsky et al. (1996): 921–924; Leite and McKenry (2002): 601–623.

This view is supported by some psychologists who apply a systemic view of relationships and say that a divorce does not end a relationship but rather transforms it. According to this view it is important that ex-spouses recognize that they continue to have an influence on each other after divorce. This systemic approach views family relations as a system of interdependent relationships. Thus, the notion of interdependence is also relevant for post-divorce family relations because there will always be some sort of mutual involvement between ex-spouses via the children.[67] Thus ex-spouses can also serve as a form of help, emotional support or as assistance.

Custodial parents with joint custody often experience the parent role as overload due to the amount of day-to-day task of raising the children. For the non-custodial parent however, usually the father, the reduced contact and influence is associated with higher levels of depression and poorer post-divorce adjustment. In a study conducted by DeGarmo, Patras and Eap, the authors addressed the question of where fathers turn to for social support and how this support can mitigate effects of stress accompanying the changes caused by divorce.[68] The authors wanted to know if social support would buffer the three main stressors associated with divorce such as (1) conflict with the former spouse, (2) daily life and family stressors, and (3) role overload. They used a Stress Buffer Model hypothesizing that social support would buffer the negative impact of common stressors for divorced fathers. The diagram shows the elements of the Stress-Buffer Hypothesis (Fig. 2.9).

Similar to Hill's theory of family stress and buffer factors it is assumed in this model that social support tends to moderate the effects of stressors. People who

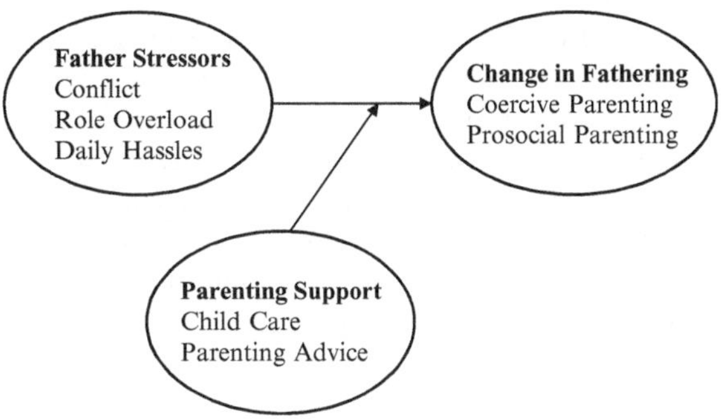

Fig. 2.9 Stress-buffer hypothesis

[67]See: Ahrons (1981): 415–427.

[68]See: DeGarmo et al. (2008): 35–48.

receive a lot of support tend to resist stressors more easily compared to people who receive less or little support. Three stressors are considered to affect the parent's well-being, the first one being the conflict with the former spouse. Research results show that divorcing parents usually experience a high conflict period lasting up to three years. After that, most parents have established a more stable relationship that enables them to cooperate in their parenting.[69] The second stressor concerns the problems of shifts of parenting routines and change of residence. The third and probably most intensive stressor is role overload and changes in the social roles in general. A divorced parent has to give up the role of spouse and at the same time has to set new rules for his role as a parent. Whereas women are usually more prepared for the role of caretaker than men, it means a big change for fathers to be a full or part time caretaker. The authors assume that this stressor would be reflected in the quality of a father's parenting:

> "In general, divorced men are not prepared to assume greater responsibility for parenting even on a part-time basis (...). For divorced fathers, identities, roles, and functions as a parent become significantly altered and potentially ambiguous, resulting in markedly high stress (...). Research shows that divorced fathers report substantially higher levels of parental role strain compared to married fathers (...), and fathers' role strain is associated with poor psychological health (...). We hypothesized that role overload reported by fathers would be associated with poor quality parenting." (DeGarmo et al. 2008: 36)

Their results showed that fathers tend to disengage from parenting over time due to a personal cost-benefit analysis of the investment and the expected outcome and ongoing conflict with the former spouse. Furthermore, it was found that custodial fathers relied more on new partners as a source of social support. A clear correlation between stressors and parenting quality (coercive versus prosocial)[70] was noticed. Thus, role overload and conflict with former spouse induced fathers to a more coercive parenting style. As a consequence the authors of the study concluded that men seem to have a restricted role pattern where non-traditional tasks are considered as a threat to masculinity. They recommend that gender stereotypes can only be prevented by starting parenting education early at school.[71]

We have described the personal and relational factors that have some bearing on ex-spouses' adjustment to the post divorce situation. In the following section an overview of the cultural factors influencing ex-spouses' post divorce lives will be given.

---

[69] See: Braver et al. (2005): 81–96.

[70] Coercive parenting involves the use of power or authority to make a child do something against his or her will. On the contrary prosocial parenting denotes helping, sharing and caring behaviour.

[71] See: Chapter 1 for a reflection on gender roles and the Spanish Law on Gender Equality, Ley Orgánica 3/2007, de 22 de marzo, para la igualdad efectiva de mujeres y hombres, BOE, 71, 23.3.2007: 12611–12645.

2.5 Cultural Factors

Without doubt the cultural context affects adjustment to divorce. In particular this concerns two aspects, such as (1) the amount of stigma[72] associated with divorce, and (2) the amount to which the legislator responds to societal changes in the field of family law. Our society has become more tolerant towards different forms of life other than marriage such as cohabitation, singleness, voluntary childlessness, homosexual marriages or serial monogamy. Divorce is no longer a reason for being morally condemned or excluded from public life as it was centuries ago. The notion of private autonomy has become a leading principle and has replaced fault-based divorce laws in most legal systems.[73] The state has no longer the role of a moralizing punitive institution in the divorce process. It has become possible to divorce unilaterally because it does not make sense to force a spouse to continue marriage against his or her will. It has become easier to follow the individual private autonomy by getting divorced.

However, historically marriage had long been seen as institution in which both spouses were supposed to sacrifice their private interests for the well-being and the future chances of their children.[74] This notion of sacrificing personal interests for the sake of children's well-being is expressed in Weber's considerations on the justification of subjective rights. He argued that the reason for public disapproval and stigmatization of the freedom to divorce is mainly that the future chances of children are put at risk:

> "Für die bürgerliche öffentliche Meinung sind meist die wirkliche und vermeintliche Gefährdung der Erziehungsschancen der Kinder massgebend für die Ablehung der Scheidungsfreiheit, daneben speziell bei den Männern autoritäre Instinkte und, soweit die ökonomische Befreiung der Frau in Frage steht, auch einfache Geschlechtseitelkeit oder Sorge um die in Anspruch genommene Position der Familie." (Weber 1976, 414)

From the methodological point of view, beliefs and attitudes are difficult to measure. By asking direct questions about personal beliefs researchers do not always gain a clear picture of its roots, structure, their state of integration, or embeddedness in the mind. However, researchers examined attitudes in relation to specific aspects. For instance, Martin and Parashar investigated women's changing attitudes toward divorce in a long-term study in the United States. They questioned 4,999 women aged 25–39 years and related their attitudes to their educational attainment over 28 years (1974–2002).[75] The authors hypothesized that highly educated women would have the most permissive attitudes toward divorce because they might be interested in keeping the option of divorce in mind

---

[72]Stigmatization denotes the shame, disgrace or disapproval attached to something regarded as socially unacceptable. In societies where divorce is despised, divorcees will find it more difficult to adjust to the post-divorce phase, because social disapproval creates an additional stressor.

[73]See: Hofer et al. (2005).

[74]See: Carrasco Perera (2006): 116.

[75]Martin and Parashar (2006): 29–40.

if reconciliation is impossible. Furthermore, they mentioned earlier studies showing that highly educated women were very selective in the search for a marriage partner.[76] Recent studies show that women with higher incomes tend to have more stable marriages and improve their gains to stay married.[77] In fact, their results showed a clear correlation between high education and prestige on the one hand and more restrictive attitudes toward divorce on the other. The authors state the following:

> "Consistent with Blankenhorn's (2002) conjecture, we find that highly educated women are adopting restrictive attitudes toward divorce in American society. We also agree that changing attitudes toward divorce might also be reducing divorce rates for those groups of women who are adopting more restrictive attitudes toward divorce. Furthermore, this top educational stratum can have a disproportionate ability to promote family change by shaping laws or influencing the social acceptability of divorce, compared to those in the middle educational levels who are more ambivalent about the availability of divorce, or disadvantaged groups at the lowest education levels who clearly want divorce to remain accessible." (Martin and Parashar 2006: 38)

Traditional or conservative attitudes toward divorce do not only delimit perception but also affect the judgements made and tend to influence our behaviour.[78] A difference in values, beliefs and attitudes toward divorce may be noted between urban and rural areas. People who live in towns or cities are exposed to higher levels of anonymity and social distance and mainstream culture undergoes more rapid changes. The majority of the Spanish population lives in areas with a population density of more than 20,000 inhabitants. As divorce occurs more often in urban areas it is less stigmatized. On the contrary, people who live in rural areas experience a low social distance and tend to disapprove of divorce.[79]

As the issue of gender violence is a complex phenomenon and a profound analysis would go beyond the scope of this study it shall only be addressed briefly in this context. Gender violence can occur in the public sphere (e.g. public spaces, job) or in the private sphere, such as in the family environment and domestic surrounding.[80] A comparative study based on national surveys from several European Member States has shown that the phenomenon of gender violence is just as

---

[76]See: Oppenheimer (1994): 293–342.

[77]See the studies of Rogers and DeBoer (1999): 458–472, Sayer and Bianchi (2000): 906–943, Schoen et al. (2002): 643–662.

[78]If a person's attitude toward divorce includes principles, such as "Marriage is for life, even if the couple is unhappy", or "My wife/husband is the love of my life" or judgements such as "Couples are getting divorced too easily nowadays", he or she will suffer more in the case of divorce than a person with more liberal views.

[79]Especially in rural areas there is a risk that divorce produces hostility not only among the divorced but also among the ex-spouses' families, relatives and friends.

[80]Domestic violence includes forms of denigration and offence, verbal or physical threat, forced limitation of a person's movement, sexual violence (rape), non-sexual physical assault and murder of spouse. See: Data on the number wives (or women) killed by their husbands (or partners) within a period from 1998 to 2001. (Alberdi and Matas 2002: 117)

common in northern as in southern European countries and goes across all class and cultural boundaries.[81] According to this study it is generally assumed that one in five women is exposed to physical violence by a partner. Statistics show that more women than men are affected by gender violence.[82] In 1999 the Association of Women Lawyers (THEMIS) in Spain carried out a study of legal procedures for domestic violence in the Autonomous Community of Madrid. As public awareness concerning gender violence was raised over the last decade more women tend to report incidents of domestic violence to the police. The investigation revealed that in the overall majority of complaints (90%) women reported an incident against a male perpetrator.[83]

Domestic violence occurs in many different forms. It ranges from patriarchal convictions,[84] forms of economic violence and psychological terror to physical violence. As the organisation of a close relationship is a private matter there is a psychological barrier in the affected women to report gender violence to the police. In fact, many women tended to withdraw their reports some time after the incidents.[85] In order to prevent, sanction and eradicate gender violence the Spanish government introduced the Law for the Integral Protective Measures against Gender Violence in 2004, Ley Orgánica 1/2004, de 28 de diciembre, de Medidas de Protección Integral contra la Violencia de Género. The law has the following objectives:

"Artículo 1. Objeto de la Ley.

1. La presente Ley tiene por objeto actuar contra la violencia que, como manifestación de la discriminación, la situación de desigualdad y las relaciones de poder de los hombres sobre las mujeres, se ejerce sobre éstas por parte de quienes sean o hayan sido sus cónyuges o de quienes estén o hayan estado ligados a ellas por relaciones similares de afectividad, aun sin convivencia.
2. Por esta Ley se establecen medidas de protección integral cuya finalidad es prevenir, sancionar y erradicar esta violencia y prestar asistencia a sus víctimas.
3. La violencia de género a que se refiere la presente Ley comprende todo acto de violencia física y psicológica, incluidas las agresiones a la libertad sexual, las amenazas, las coacciones o la privación arbitraria de libertad." (Ley Orgánica de Medidas de Protección Integral contra la Violencia de Género)

---

[81]See: Collins (1999): 8.

[82]According to a study on women's reports of domestic violence against their partners the rate had increased from a total number of 16,657 (in 1991) to altogether 24,158 (in 2001) (Alberdi and Matas (2002): 120). A report of the Spanish General Council of the Judicial Power on domestic homicide stated that in 2009 55 women were murdered by their partners or ex-partners in contrast to 10 male victims. See: Consejo General del Poder Judicial 2009.

[83]According to the study in nearly 70% of cases violence occurred among married couples, in nearly 20% among ex-spouses and in the rest of cases among parents and children. (Themis 1999)

[84]Patriarchy may be defined as a social system in which male individuals have authority over women and children.

[85]In Spain in more than half of reported cases (63.5%) the victims of domestic violence withdrew their charges. (Themis 1999: 89)

The same as in many other countries domestic violence is in Spain considered a serious offence that is sanctioned by penalties. Offences in this context are classified as physical, psychological and sexual crimes and are legally sanctioned according to the Spanish Criminal Law.[86] The main consequences of domestic violence in the victims are symptoms of post-traumatic stress and depression.

The family as a system constitutes a frame within which a range of values, beliefs and attitudes are transferred to the next generation. Whereas a patriarchal conviction is based on male authority over women, traditional values refer to the preservation of established or conventional customs against contemporary, innovative or progressive views. As refers post-divorce recovery, Booth and Amato found out that people with conservative attitudes towards divorce were more depressed and unhappier after marital dissolution than couples with more tolerant attitudes. Likewise, Wang and Amato point out that people with negative attitudes are more likely to blame themselves and view their separation as personal error and moral shortcoming:

> "People who hold negative attitudes toward divorce in general, compared with those who hold positive attitudes, are likely to view their own divorces as moral failures (Amato and Booth 1991). (...) Individuals who want the marriage to end are likely to view divorce differently from individuals who want the marriage to continue. Indeed, following marital dissolution, unhappily married individuals may experience an improvement in well-being, whereas happily married individuals may experience declines in well-being (...)." (Wang and Amato 2000: 656)

In general there does not seem to be any explicit stigmatization of divorce in modern societies nowadays. However, such fundamental processes of cultural development – reflected as changes in the legal system – need to be performed on the individual level by every citizen in order to have an effect. In other words, every individual has to translate these changes into his or her own system of beliefs and attitudes.

2.6 Conclusion

For a long time divorce has been viewed as producing only deficits and negative effects. This has changed and nowadays it is mainly seen as a family transition which develops over time and that may also benefit individuals. In this chapter we

---

[86]The following physical crimes and offences are sanctioned by the Spanish Criminal Law (CP): Homicidio y asesinato (Codigo Penal, Articulos 138, 139, 140), Delito de lesión física (CP, Article 147.1), Delito de violencia habitual (CP, Article 153), Delito de detención ilegal (CP, Article 163), Falta de lesiones (CP, Article 617.1), Falta de maltrato de obra (CP, Article 617.2). The following psychological offences are sanctioned by the Criminal Law: Delito de violencia habitual (CP, Article 153), Delito de amenazas (CP, Article 169), Delito de injurias (CP, Article 208), Delito de trato degradante (CP, Article 173), Delito de coacciones (CP, Article 172), Falta de amenazas (CP, Article 620), Falta de injurias (CP, Article 620), Falta de vejación injusta (CP, Article 620), Falta de coacciones (CP, Article 620). The following sexual crimes are sanctioned by the Criminal Law: Agresión sexual (CP, Articles. 178, 179, 180.4), Abuso sexual (CP, Articles. 181, 182). See: Alberdi and Matas (2002): 171.

analysed the factors that have an effect on the process of adjustment to divorce, which is the way in which the ex-spouses respond to the family transition. Three groups of factors play a role in this process, such as individual dispositions, relational support from family and friends and cultural factors. The theory of family stress and buffer factors was used to explain the complex mechanisms involved in this process.

Among the personal factors we found that the age and the socio-economic status of the divorced have an impact on his or her adjustment. Young people tend to suffer more after their divorce because of shattered dreams and little life experience than people in their late thirties or forties. Ex-spouses with longer education and higher cognitive abilities have an advantage and adjust to divorce more easily. The economically weaker ex-spouse experiences financial disadvantages after divorce in most European countries. The contrary is true for Spanish divorcees because in the majority of divorce cases the family residence is attributed to the children and their custodial mothers.

Women seem to be less satisfied with the quality of their pre-divorce relationship which is reflected in the fact that most divorces are filed by women. Generally, the one who initiates divorce has a temporal advantage because he or she has planned the event earlier and has already thought about the consequences. Additionally, the initiator has already confronted himself or herself with the emotions that go along with the decision. This creates a feeling of being more in control of the situation. As a consequence, it is often women who improve their post-divorce situation in the long run in terms of relationship qualities and personal development in the private and the public spheres. Among the age group of Spanish 22–40 year-old spouses who presently live in a marriage there are more women who had been married before than men.

Concerning the relational support gained from children after the divorce, mothers and fathers have quite different experiences. Divorced fathers tend to loose a considerable amount of influence on their children, even if joint custody is awarded. On the contrary, women receive more social support from their children and from external relations than men. Culturally and traditionally, the role of a divorced mother seems to be more clearly defined than that of the divorced father.

The extent to which divorce is stigmatized in our present society there is a difference between urban and rural areas. A higher social distance together with more diversification and change in urban areas has contributed to a decrease of stigmatization and discrimination of divorcees. In order to prevent, sanction and eradicate gender violence the Spanish government has introduced the Law for the Integral Protective Measures against Gender Violence in 2004.

It may be concluded that divorce as a solution to acute relationship crisis and point of no return seems to be an acceptable solution for most affected couples. The majority of divorced people manage to cope with the crisis and to adapt to the new situation in the long run. If the former spouses consider their divorce as an opportunity for a new start, they reduce any detrimental effects on their children.

Chapter 3
Post-divorce Adjustment of Children and Adolescents

3.1 Introduction

The present chapter is devoted to the factors that influence post-divorce adjustment in the lives of children and adolescents. Whereas ex-spouses are free to make decisions about their lives, children and adolescents from divorced parents find themselves in a less favourable situation. They do usually not form part of the decision-making process but are still confronted with all the resulting consequences of divorce.

This is where the state has a special function of providing protection and safeguard for children whose parents have separated and file for divorce. From a political perspective of family policy many governments are interested in the consequences of divorce and its related effects on children. Each national legal system has an ethical responsibility to protect children's rights and act in their best interests.[1] Therefore research in this field seems highly relevant because scientific results are suited to found and justify legal and political decision-taking. Knowledge of the factors that put children at risk of maladjustment or else protect them from detrimental consequences of divorce enable experts to take appropriate measures and therapeutic steps with children affected. Services provided by governments may range from counselling, that is made available to families in trouble, to legal assistance for children or mediation offered to couples in conflict.[2] As the theme of divorce and its consequences has a high societal relevance, many studies can be found that deal with the effect of divorce on children and adolescents.

In the following sections we will give an overview of the changes that children and adolescents are confronted in the post-divorce phase by reviewing relevant scientific studies. These changes concern the economic situation, parental communication and the parent–child relationship. For the description and explanation of the impact of divorce we will use the theoretical approach of the Divorce-Stress-Adjustment Perspective. Special reference is made to different types of custody regulations and their psychological implications on the offspring.

[1]See: Article 39 of the Spanish Constitution.

[2]See: Marín López (2008).

M. Gaffal, *Psychosocial and Legal Perspectives of Marital Breakdown*,
DOI 10.1007/978-3-642-13896-6_3, © Springer-Verlag Berlin Heidelberg 2010

3.2 Theoretical Perspective

Parents and children usually experience the most stressful time in the period leading to divorce and the time immediately following it. The parents' disclosure of their intention to separate sets a series of irreversible events into motion. Once the decision to separate has been taken one or both spouses may file for divorce and the legal processes are initiated. Then the legal processes follow and with it the search for a new residence and the redefinition of parental roles. Additionally the higher costs associated with the legal procedure and the change of residence often requires the ex-spouses to look for better job opportunities. All these life-altering changes are considered as family transition rather than as family breakdown. Although it has a deep impact on all the family members it also contains the chance for a new start with new perspectives and possibilities.

A review of the research literature shows that because of the political relevance of divorce numerous studies have been carried out on this topic. A comparison of these investigations shows that many of them produce inconsistent results. One group of studies that have measured the difference in well-being between children from intact and divorced families identified a lower level of well-being in children from divorced families.[3] Another group of studies did not provide proof for this assumption but rather suggested that the majority of children and adolescents ultimately recovered from the disadvantages experienced by parental separation and showed no differences in well-being.[4] Some studies pointed to the fact that in the case of intense conflict, parental divorce turns out to be more advantageous for the offspring because it means an escape from a discordant setting. Furthermore, several studies revealed that children and adolescents tended to mature more rapidly and often develop close and mutually helpful relationships with their custodial parents.[5]

The reason for the contradictory results may be explained by the fact that the methodology used in earlier studies on divorce has undergone a change in the last decades. If we take into account that for instance in the 1960s almost 90% of all children and adolescents in the United States lived together with their biological married parents in a common household, it is not surprising that the theoretical approach to the investigation of divorce was dominated by the so-called 'deficit perspective'. This meant that the focus was on the imperfect family structure and the negative consequences resulting from an incomplete socialisation process and the traumatic event of divorce. It was assumed that a child socialized in a one-parent

---

[3]See studies of Amato (2000): 1269–1287, Fürstenberg and Kiernan (2001): 446–457, Simons et al. (1999): 1020–1033, Zill (1986): 295–307.

[4]See: Edwards (1987): 355–372, Emery (1988).

[5]See studies of Arditti (1999a, b): (109–119, 35–56), Amato et al. (1995): 895–916, Hanson (1999): 1283–1316.

household, usually headed by mothers, and the absence of the father would produce severe harm in children. This perspective is considered out-dated nowadays and has been replaced by a multi-faceted perspective of the changes that take place in the course of the family transition. Hetherington and Stanley-Hagen criticize the scientific insufficiency of these earlier studies, conducted between the 1950s and 1970s, because they used a prejudiced research design and insufficient samples. They summarize their objections as follows:

> "Moreover, many of these early studies were methodologically flawed. Almost all were cross-sectional and used nonrepresentative, ill-defined, often clinical samples, and many relied on single informants or limited unvalidated measures. Most failed to investigate significant mediating or moderating factors that accompany divorce, such as economic declines or residential mobility, often involving moves to les desirable housing, neighbourhoods, schools and peer groups." (Hetherington and Stanley-Hagan 1999: 130)

On the contrary, studies conducted since the 1980s employed a different research approach concentrating mainly on three aspects, that is to say the variety of modes how people adjust to divorce,[6] the change of adjustment over time and the relevance of the family structure (e.g. the number of siblings) for the adjustment process. This new approach has also brought about a shift in methodology preferring cluster analysis to analysing mean differences between divorced and intact families as well as the use of observations and longitudinal studies.[7]

As a consequence, the contradictory outcomes produced by the majority of studies seem to have inspired Amato and Keith[8] in their attempt to gain a clearer picture of the impact of divorce on the well-being of children and adolescents. Therefore they conducted a meta-analysis [9] in which they reviewed altogether 92 studies that investigated 13,000 children on their scores of well-being and related aspects. In their meta-analysis they listed the most relevant eight indicators for adjustment, such as (1) academic achievement, (2) conduct (misconduct, aggression), (3) psychological adjustment (personal contentment, unhappiness, anxiety) and (4) social adjustment (group recognition, isolation, cooperativeness),

---

[6]For instance, the study of Demo and Acock showed that there are considerable variations in the adjustment process of children and adolescents that range from having low self-esteem or problems with their peer group to unsocial behaviour. However, there are as well children who adjust easily without any psychological disturbance. See: Demo and Acock (1996): 457–488.

[7]In a cluster analysis a representative set of data is divided into subsets in which the subjects share specific traits. In a mean difference the statistic distribution is measured in relation to the absolute difference between two variables. Cluster analysis in contrast to measuring mean differences allows for a more complex view on a phenomenon and reveals more detailed results.

[8]See: Amato and Keith (1991a): 26–46.

[9]A meta-analysis involves the comparison of the results of a number of studies with similar research hypotheses that show divergent results. Its aim is to highlight the conditions that cause problems and tendencies within the reactions to it. The authors found out that the studies with a well-substantiated methodology gained less significant results. On the contrary, those studies with a less refined methodology and lower validity showed more significant results. This indicated that in human sciences the choice of a suitable methodology is a crucial issue and inappropriate research methods tend to produce incorrect results.

(5) self-concept (self-esteem, competence), (6) mother–child and (7) father–child relations and (8) other relationships. A comparison of the results of all the studies supported the assumption that children from divorced families experienced lower levels of well-being compared to children with an intact family background. Although this difference proved significant as a general outcome, a detailed analysis revealed that some criteria were more remarkable than others. Specifically, the father–child relationship and children's conduct turned out to be most affected. Conversely, minor differences in children's well-being were noticed for psychological adjustment and self-concept. Therefore the authors concluded that divorce tends to affect mainly children's behaviour and the relationship to their fathers whereas it seems to have little or no impact on children's self-concepts and their process of adjustment to parental divorce. Subsequent studies added that these adjustment problems may persist in the long term and might even continue into the next generation.[10]

Various scientific approaches have been used to investigate and explain the impact of parental divorce on children.[11] A relevant shift in paradigm was created by the view of the family as a system or the systemic perspective of family.[12] This approach takes the complexity of the family system into account and allows for an understanding of the mutual influence of individual behaviour within the family. From the methodological point of view it has stimulated the consideration of more interrelated criteria and has brought about the application of more complex methods of data evaluation.

In the majority of studies divorce is viewed as a stressful event of life transition that both, adults and children have to cope with. The most appropriate theoretical model for the description of such family transition contains elements of stress and coping theory.[13] The view of children as mere victims of the family transition has been replaced by a perspective according to which children and adolescents are

---

[10]See studies of Kiernan and Hobcraft (1997): 41–55, O'Connor et al. (1999): 777–790, Amato and Keith (1991a): 26–46.

[11]Amato (2000: 1270) provides an overview of the various research approaches and the corresponding studies carried out by their representatives, such as feminist theory (Carbonne 1994: 183–209), attachment theory (Hazan and Shaver 1992: 90–110), attribution theory (Grych and Fincham 1992: 267–290), systems theory (Emery 1994) and symbolic interactionism (Orbuch 1992: 90–110).

[12]Systems theory is an interdisciplinary concept that enables psychologists and sociologists to gain insight into the functioning of complex systems. The family is considered a system in balance which can only be maintained if the family members take the others' individual needs, expectations, emotions and roles into account. The parts of the system interact and interrelate in many ways and on many levels. Interactions take place on the intrapersonal level (such as the individual psyche), the interpersonal level, the sociological level (roles), the family life cycle and the institutional level. Systems theory was inspired by Bateson and Mead and provides helpful insights into family and group dynamism. See: Mead (1934).

[13]See: Hill (1949), McCubbin and Patterson (1983): 5–25.

ascribed the ability of actively constructing their adaptation to divorce.[14] Parental divorce may also bring positive alterations for them, such as the end of parental dispute and the experience of clearer relationship structures. Thus the view of divorce as a traumatic life event may be changed to a prospect where the family members have an opportunity of enhancing personal well-being.

Taking these methodological alterations into account we will use the theoretical approach of the Divorce-Stress-Adjustment Perspective for the description and explanation of the effect that divorce has for children and adolescents.[15] This theoretical approach is described by Amato in his article on the consequences of divorce for adults and children. The model provides an integrated view of all relevant factors associated with divorce. As the changes take place on several levels it combines relevant economic factors with psychological aspects, such as individual and relational characteristics of the people involved. The figure shows the elements of the model and their interrelations (Fig. 3.1).

The model includes *mediating factors* (*mediators*) that stand for all the stressful changes that go along with divorce. These stressors include, firstly, limited support

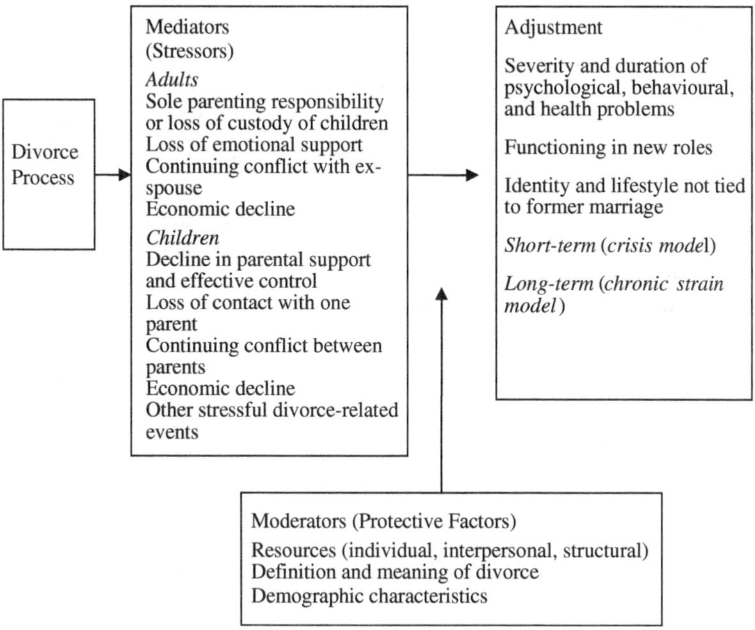

Fig. 3.1 The divorce-stress-adjustment perspective

[14]This new perspective was also taken as fundament in the Spanish law on legal protection applying to children and adolescents until the age of 18 years, Ley Orgánica 1/1996 de Protección Jurídica del Menor. The legislator states that the legal order and the present law in particular are based on a view of underage children as active and creative subjects who dynamically participate in the organisation of their lives.

[15]See: Amato (2000): 1271.

or even loss of contact to the non-resident parent, secondly, ongoing conflict between parents, especially if divorce related disputes cannot be resolved. A third stressor concerns the costs of divorce together with additional expenses that arise because one household is divided into two. This often leads to economic decline. A fourth stressor that has a destabilizing effect is the change of the child's peer group due to removal.

On the other hand appear certain moderating or protective factors (moderators) that are activated by each child or adolescent in order to compensate the negative effect of such changes. According to Rutter these moderators act as, "shock absorbers and weaken the links between divorce-related events and people's experience of stress, and hence the extent to which divorce is followed by negative emotional, behavioural, or health outcomes."[16] Moderators do not only include a person's mental resources (e.g. social and coping skills, self-efficiency) but also include support that comes from related people (e.g. family members, relatives, and friends). The amount and quality of the resources that children and adolescents have available and can thus retrieve during the crisis depends mainly on the experience that they have stored in their minds up to then.[17] For children the event of divorce is not tied to any experience and therefore it may provoke feelings of existential threat. Particularly, as younger children cannot image any concrete consequence of parental divorce their fear may aggravate into anxiety. However, the reactions to the event depend mainly on the children's age and developmental stage. Amato points to children's different reactions according to age and mental development:

> "For example, an older child might experience stress prior to the divorce, during the period when the parents' marriage is unravelling. For this older child, the physical separation of constantly warring parents might come as a relief. For a younger child in the same family, however, the departure of one parent from the household might be a bewildering event that generates considerable anxiety. In other words, members of divorcing families can experience different trajectories of stress and adjustment." (Amato (2000): 1272)

Additionally certain demographic characteristics such as children's age, gender, ethnicity and cultural background can moderate their well-being after divorce. Amato points to the relevance of the new family and school environment. An important aspect is the extent to which a child's identity is tied to the pre-divorce family system.[18] The interplay between mediators and moderators influences the process of adjustment and determines to which extent negative consequences are produced in the short or even in the long run:

> "The severity and duration of these negative outcomes varies from person to person, depending on the presence of a variety of moderating or protective factors. Successful

---

[16]See: Rutter quoted in Amato (2000): 1272.

[17]In a parent–child relationship of high quality (in terms of attachment style, devotion, time spent together, etc.) more positive experiences are stored in a child's mind. Such positive emotional accounts can be retrieved in case of crisis and may reduce its negative impact.

[18]Therapeutic interventions with children of divorced parents aim to help them create positive images of the post-divorce constellation and to develop separate relations to mother and father.

> adjustment occurs to the extent that individuals experience few divorce-related symptoms, are able to function well in new family, work, or school roles, and have developed an identity and lifestyle that is no longer tied to the former marriage (...)." (Amato 2000: 1271)

In our investigation we will focus on the four mediators mentioned in the model, such as (1) the decline in the socio-economic status, (2) parental dispute, (3) changes in the parent–child relationship with special reference to the non-resident parent, and (4) the consequences of custodial arrangements. The fourth aspect requires a more detailed analysis, in which we will refer to the types of custody arrangements, the factors influencing its choice and their effects on parents and children.

3.3 Economic Changes

One of the consequences of divorce is often a deterioration in financial circumstances which is supposed to cause a range of problems in children and adolescents. For children to live in a household with sufficient income is one of the most important factors for well-being. Several studies have supported the hypothesis that post-divorce financial decline creates disadvantages for children and adolescents. These disadvantages range from reduced overall well-being, to lower educational and occupational attainment to weak relationships with parents and other relationships in adult life. Conversely, children seem to benefit from adequate child support in several ways, such as it supports their cognitive development, and helps adolescents in their school attainments and motivates young adults to attend college or university. More specifically, Argys, Peters et al. found out that a father's child support payment reduces the stress that children are exposed to during and after divorce. Moreover in the long run it leads to higher school attainment:

> "Children whose parents divorce or separate or whose parents never marry face many problems not experienced by children in intact families. In addition to the emotional upheaval that surrounds marital dissolution and the absence of one parent from the household, children from single parent households are more often raised in families with low incomes. (...) Some recent empirical studies have found that child-support income is more beneficial to children than other sources of income. (...) They found that child support was positively related to more years in school, even after controlling for income level and receipt of welfare. Graham et al. (1994) found that child-support income had a significantly greater positive effect on educational attainment than did other types of income (...)." (Argys et al. 1998: 159)

In Spain the rights and duties associated with legal authority are regulated in Articles 154–156 of the Civil Code. Parents who do not pay judicially ordered child or spousal support after divorce face heavy penalties and are sanctioned according to Article 227 of the Criminal Law.[19]

---

[19]See: "Artículo 227. 1. El que dejare de pagar durante dos meses consecutivos o cuatro meses no consecutivos cualquier tipo de prestación económica en favor de su cónyuge o sus hijos,

As an additional positive effect the authors found that fathers who pay child support tend to be more emotionally involved with their children. A longitudinal study conducted by Ruschena et al. investigated the impact of family transitions on the lives of Australian children and adolescents.[20] The researchers assumed that children who had experienced parental divorce or separation would have lower outcomes in the fields of family attachment, educational attainment, social competence and psychological adjustment. However, the results showed no significant developmental differences between children of divorced and intact families. Their outcomes suggested rather that children in a family transition do not seem to function in a different way than their peers from intact families. They regard the quality of the parent–child relationship a relevant condition for post-divorce adjustment and underline that it is more important than the economic family status:

> "The child's temperament would clearly have a powerful effect upon the type of relationship he or she has with a parent, which would in turn affect adjustment outcomes for the child. (...), adolescents who have a warm and supportive relationship with at least one parent show better adjustment on a variety of measures than those who do not. For example, possessing the trait of persistence, i.e., the ability to follow through on a task even when circumstances are difficult, may enable a person to trial different coping strategies, if one proved to be unsuccessful, or to just keep persevering. Being able to approach others for help or to allow the approach of others is likely to be another factor involved in optimal coping. Social and personal networks can allow young people to access help during hardship. Moreover, children and adolescents with positive temperamental styles are more likely to have developed warm, supportive parental relationships that would be invaluable during any period of difficulty." (Ruschena et al. 2005: 361)

Concerning the Divorce-Stress-Adjustment Perspective the authors see relevant links between the mediators of economic decline and inter-parental conflict on the one hand and the moderating effect of a constructive parent–child relationship on the other hand. They point out that it is not the financial loss itself that automatically produces negative consequences for children. It seems more significant how the parents react to this strain, which in turn has an impact on children. The same seems to be true for the role of parental conflict during the phase of family transition. It is not the conflict itself that produces harm but rather the parents' lack of coping strategies which results in unpredictable, incoherent behaviour and deficiencies in emotional care. Divorcing parents are often overburdened by the family transition which influences their parenting. As a consequence a decline in the quality of parenting may be noticed during the family transition, which the authors explain in the following statement:

---

establecida en convenio judicialmente aprobado o resolución judicial en los supuestos de separación legal, divorcio, declaración de nulidad del matrimonio, proceso de filiación, o proceso de alimentos a favor de sus hijos, será castigado con la pena de prisión de tres meses a un año o multa de seis a 24 meses." (Codigo Penal)

[20]The study is considered representative as altogether 2,443 families (1,310 parents and 1,260 children and adolescents) participated and interviews and tests were conducted in intervals over a time of 18 years (Ruschena et al. 2005: 353–363).

"Another theoretical stance contends that it is not the divorce per se which leads to poorer outcomes for children, but the influence of inter-parental conflict. Indirectly, conflict may diminish parents' emotional energy and interfere with their ability to respond sensitively to their children's emotional needs. Parents in high conflict marriages engage in more erratic disciplinary practices and are more likely to use anxiety or guilt-inducing techniques to discipline their children than parents in low-to-moderate conflict marriages, according to Kelly (. . .)." (Ruschena et al. 2005: 353)

Ruschena and his colleagues see the effects of economic decline and parental conflict in relative terms and suggest that they can be outweighed by appropriate parental reactions and the acquisition of problem solving skills. Another study on the same issue was conducted by Thomson et al. (2003) who were interested in the effects that the two factors economic resources and parental behaviour had on children's adjustment. According to the results of earlier studies they assumed firstly, that children in single parent families would be disadvantaged in several aspects of well-being compared to children living in original two parent families. Secondly, they hypothesized that remarriage or cohabitation of a single parent does not significantly minimize this disadvantage. They view economic resources and parental behaviour as two relevant determinants of well-being that are transmitted in the form of time and money dedicated to children.

Financial resources allow parents to provide not only for primary needs (e.g. food, accommodation, and clothing) but also for "high quality neighbourhoods and schools" as well as spare-time activities that foster the children's cognitive development. When parents dedicate time to their children they do this usually in order to contribute in joint activities during which they also supervise and control their children. The authors point to the interdependence of time and money in that parents bestow their time to earn money and conversely use the money for spare-time activities. They explain this relation and its effect on child well-being in the following quotation:

"Effects of parents' time and money on child well-being are likely to be interrelated. Bronfenbrenner (. . .), for example, views economic resources as enablers for optimal parent–child relationships. Parents under economic stress are less able than other parents to provide adequate levels of support and control (. . .). Coleman (1988) sees parents' time with children as a form of "social capital" expended on children, which enables the intergenerational transmission of parents' economic resource (including human capital and financial capital). Both money and parental time are associated with family structure in ways that could explain poorer outcomes for children in single-parent families and step-families. Economic resources are the predominant explanation for problems of children of mother-only households, since single mothers have much lower incomes than married couples." (Thomson 2003: 178)

Their outcomes confirm the assumption that economic decline is responsible for lower scores in school performance of children in single parent families compared to children living in original two parent families. Although they supposed children in step- or cohabitating families to be equally disadvantaged, the results showed no significant differences in academic performance between step- or cohabitating families and families with biological parents. However, a difference was noticed in problematic behaviour and temperament where children from stepfamilies scored higher. The authors explain this effect by presupposing some ambiguity in stepfamily relationships compared to original ones.[21]

A key consequence of limited financial resources in the post-divorce household is the need to move residence shortly after divorce. Due to the lower income these moves are in many cases to neighbourhoods characterized by a lower living standard. A recurrent theme in studies carried out in the United States and in Great Britain is the requirement of removal due restricted economic resources. Several authors make a link between the economic decline after divorce and the subsequent detrimental consequences for children and adolescents.[22] It is argued that financial loss, parent's employment instability, the change of familiar surroundings and peer-groups, pose special risks for children or adolescents in a phase when they are most vulnerable. As a consequence such moves are often to a neighbourhood with low professional schools and peers who tend to show more adverse behaviour. Authors such as Hetherington and Stanley-Hagan (1999) reason that even the most caring home environment could not make up for the detrimental influences associated with such a surrounding. An explanation for this argument may be that the parent–child relationship is more susceptible to crisis during the family transition and children and adolescents tend to seek more frequently the company of their peers. Thus the influence from friends seems more dominant than that exerted by parenting in the home environment.

The notion of residential mobility due to parental divorce and its consequences for children was also investigated in a longitudinal study carried out by South et al.[23] The study conducted in the United States lasted for 20 years (from 1968 until 1988) and included 7,000 families representing a total number of 37,000 individuals. The authors started out from the fact that a majority of divorced parents is forced to move into another neighbourhood with lower socio-economic conditions. The authors wanted to know which impact this change of residence and surrounding neighbourhood would have on the offspring. Earlier studies had shown that a change of residence meant a disruption of the favourable "social capital"[24] offered to children in the environment they had lived in before parental divorce. These assumptions are explained as follows:

> "Residential mobility is problematic for the children's development because it disrupts these social relations that bind parents, children, teachers and other community adults. To the extent that parental divorce encourages residential mobility, it thus places the children of divorce at a dual disadvantage, because it disrupts both the social capital of the family (when one parent leaves the household) and the child's access to community-based social

---

[21]This ambiguity results probably from the fact that the relationship in a stepfamily is newer and the stepfamily members do not have an equally long common history together. This often involves a feeling of alienation between step-parent and step-child because both do not have any emotional relation per se but rather live together in a step-family because of one parent's decision.

[22]See: Astone and McLanahan (1994): 575–584, McLanahan and Sandefur (1994).

[23]See: South et al. (1998): 667–693.

[24]Coleman defines social capital as all the relations within the family and the community that have a positive influence on a child's social and cognitive development. (Coleman 1998: 92–120).

> capital, as neighborhood ties are severed upon moving. (...) If children's downward economic mobility caused by parental divorce results in downward neighborhood mobility – that is, in moving to a poorer neighborhood – then divorce also exacts a cost to children by exposing them to disadvantaged neighbourhood conditions." (South et al. 1998: 669)

Their results confirmed the assumption that a reduced family income induces divorced parents to move to neighbourhoods with lower socio-economic status than children living in stable two-parent families. Consequently this new neighbourhood represents a further disadvantage and creates inequality among children of a divorced parent and those living in intact two-parent households. On the contrary, the latter group tends to increase the family income over the years and move upward in living standard.

According to Spanish Family Law, the main determinant for the attribution of the family accommodation is the interest of those family members, the children, who mostly need protection (Articles 90, 96). It is therefore common practice that the children remain in the family accommodation after parental divorce and with them the parent who exercises custody at longer intervals. The application of the principle of the best interest of the child concerning the use of the family accommodation is summarized by González del Pozo:

> "Ante todo, la satisfacción de ese superior interés del menor exige, en primer lugar, garantizar al mismo su derecho de habitación o posibilidad real de alojarse en una vivienda digna que les sirve de sede física en que vivir, crecer y desarrollarse en todos los órdenes: personal, familiar, educativo, relacional, afectivo, etc." (González de Pozo 2009: 16)

Due to this legal rule children do not normally have to mover residence after parental divorce. The family accommodation is a stable point of reference for the offspring in times of emotional turmoil. A relevant specification within the effects of divorce on children's well-being is made by Ram and Hou[25] by their longitudinal study conducted in 1994. They investigated the effects of changes in the family structure, namely from two-parent to lone-parent or step-family, on the children's cognitive and emotional development. Their results supported the assumption that children living with a lone parent or in a stepfamily showed generally poorer results than children from intact families. However, the authors state that a decline in family income is only related to lower scores in tests measuring cognitive abilities. On the other hand a deterioration of family resources (such as ineffective parenting) is more responsible for lower scores in the field of emotional development and behaviour. In other words, economic decline does not affect children's emotions and conversely, poor parenting does not necessarily produce cognitive drawbacks. These results led the authors to raise a methodological problem associated with previous studies on this issue. They criticize that many of the earlier studies did not recognize that many of the problems of the post-divorce phase had already existed prior to divorce. This leads to an overestimation of the detrimental consequences of parental separation for children. They conclude that in most cases it is not the family disruption itself that causes problems, but rather there are certain

[25]See: Ram and Hou (2003): 309–330.

pre-existing family characteristics that are responsible for the divorce and its consequences.

The argument that many problems, such as children showing adverse behaviour or poor school records are often present before divorce seems convincing. In fact, children and adolescents being exposed to marital conflict probably experience their parents' divorce as relief from a frustrating family situation. From this perspective divorce is seen as putting an end to a long phase of unsuccessful, deficient or flawed development in the marital relationship. Thus researchers concentrate more on children's adjustment problems to marital conflict prior to divorce. Consequently it is pertinent to highlight those conditions under which divorce is detrimental or favourable for children.

3.4 Parental Conflict

Several studies have shown that conflict among parents has a strong influence on children's well-being.[26] Certainly in many families parental conflict does not start with the divorce but has usually persisted months and years before separation. Conflict is a relevant aspect because it is always associated with a lack or loss of social capital.[27] Coleman views 'social capital' in the family as deriving from relationships based on cooperation and mutual trust. In the family context it means that father and mother communicate about child-related aspects, such as supervision, education, health and also values that they consider important for their child's development. Children who experience their parents communicating learn interpersonal skills, conflict solving and making compromise. In the case of parental conflict a child's access to social capital is reduced or not available.

Several studies have investigated the impact of parental conflict on child well-being. Investigations deal mainly with three aspects, such as frequency and intensity of the conflict, its style and content, and how it is resolved. We are interested in the interplay between these characteristics and how children and adolescents react to it. Generally, parental conflict affects children in direct and indirect ways. When exposed to conflict, children run the risk of imitating negative behaviour and fail to acquire constructive interaction skills.

---

[26]See the studies of Amato (1993): 50–54, Amato and Keith (1991a): 26–46, Amato and Rezac (1994): 191–207, Buchanan et al. (1991), Camera and Resnick (1989): 560–574, Hanson et al. (1996): 141–154, Johnston et al. (1989): 576–592, Kline et al. (1989): 430–435.

[27]According to R. Putnam social capital includes interpersonal communication skills that increase group cohesion and promote participatory democracy, which in return benefits the individuals. He defines social capital: "Social capital refers to features of social organization such as networks, norms, and social trust that facilitate coordination and for mutual benefit (. . .). Networks of civic engagement foster sturdy norms of generalized reciprocity and encourage the mergence of social trust." (Putnam 1995: 67)

An indirect effect is produced via their parents who are demoralized by constant marital discord that undermines the quality of their parenting. As marital conflict is rather tiring, parenting behaviour deteriorates and parents show less affection, use less consistent disciplinary techniques or even withdraw from their parenting role. The child psychologists Garrity and Baris summarize the effects of high parental conflict:

> "Parental conflict interrupts many of the critical tasks of psychological development. It changes the nature of the parent–child relationship, creates anxiety and distress, over stimulates and frightens children, weakens parents' protective capacity, and compromises identity formation. Most of all, it leaves children powerless to do anything about it." (Garrity and Baris 1995: 26)

Conflicts occur in every relationship therefore it is relevant how a couple uses conflict solving strategies to terminate it. A quarrel may be intense and highly emotional but this does not necessarily lead to irreconcilability or diminish the spouses' feelings for one another. Although the style in which the conflict is dealt with matters, its outcome seems more important. A positive solution by way of negotiation and compromise tends to make up for the excitement provoked by the argument. If, on the other hand, ongoing marital conflict remains repeatedly unresolved, children seem to be more affected than if parental conflicts are brought to a positive end. This was especially shown by Davies et al. who analyzed the responses of children and adolescents to different marital conflict scenarios. The authors point to the importance of a positive conflict resolution:

> "The results indicate that both children and adolescents respond to the emotionality of conflict endings. Harmonious (positive) emotional endings elicited more positive, and less negative, Reponses that did hostile (negative) emotional endings across a range of responses hypothesized to reflect emotional security. Consistent with Cummings et al. (...), explicit verbal resolution of conflict issues was not necessary to reduce children's emotional insecurity when faced with analogous of marital conflict; changes in the emotionality of the interactions were sufficient." (Davies et al. 1996: 14)

Another relevant aspect is the content of marital dispute. The more the content refers to child-related topics, the more detrimental the consequences are for the child because it induces feelings of self-blame and fear of being drawn into the conflict. High conflict marriages may deteriorate and lead to the use of violence and threat, in the majority of cases by the husband against his wife. A child who experiences his father acting violently against his mother is much more seriously affected than a child witnessing just a verbal conflict. Repeated exposure to domestic violence against the other is likely to produce a posttraumatic stress disorder in the child.[28] Furthermore, a parent using violence against the other

[28]Post-traumatic stress disorder occurs after a person's experience of a traumatic event that the human psyche cannot overcome. It is a reaction to an overwhelming event which the mind cannot process because it provokes intense emotions. Reactions among individuals vary according to type of trauma, a person's age, intelligence and cognitive abilities.

often does not shrink back from also acting violently against the child.[29] Not surprisingly, children living with violent and high conflict parents show more adjustment problems than children in non-violent high conflict families.[30]

It would go beyond the scope of this study to analyse the complex phenomenon of violence in families. However, it shall be mentioned that there are certain indicators that may predict gender violence. It was already outlined in chapter one that gender roles have undergone a considerable change within the last decades. This means that a role has lost some of its inherent functions and required that new skills had to be included in the role. A parent's reluctance to react to these changes and inability to acquire new skills may generate role confusion and produce tensions. If an individual cannot resolve this conflict he or she may react by externalizing these tensions and vent the rage on the respective other.[31] In Spain the legislator has reacted to cases of gender violence and introduced the Law of Integral Protective Measures against Gender Violence, Ley Orgánica 1/2004.[32] This law is designed to prevent gender violence at all levels of society. Additionally, in the exposition of its motives it is mentioned that the aim of the Law is also to protect children who are indirect or direct victims of a violent family environment:

> "Las situaciones de violencia sobre la mujer afectan también a los menores que se encuentran dentro de su entorno familiar, víctimas directas o indirectas de esta violencia. La Ley contempla también su protección no sólo para la tutela de los derechos de los menores, sino para garantizar de forma efectiva las medidas de protección adoptadas respecto de la mujer."

From the psychological point of view, marital conflict affects children on the cognitive and the emotional level. They use their cognitive abilities and activate mental processes such as assimilation and appraisal in order to understand and solve the conflict.[33] As a reaction to the impossibility of disentangling the knot, children develop so-called internalizing behaviour.[34] On the other hand, the failure to solve conflicts together with emphatic feelings for the parents produce emotional reactions in the child. More specifically, children often experience this impossibility as personal failure, which produces feelings of self-blame and guilt, shame or

[29]In a high conflict marriage one or both spouses usually show the following behaviours: anger and mistrust, verbal and/or physical aggression, problems in the communication about children and consequently problems in the organization of parenting, one parent interfering in the other's relationship to the child, etc. (McIntosh 2003: 64)

[30]See: McNeal and Amato (1998): 123–139.

[31]See: Parsons (1968): 267.

[32]See: Ley Orgánica 1/2004, de 28 de diciembre, de Medidas de Protección Integral contra la Violencia de Género, BOE, 313, 29.12.2004: 42166–42197.

[33]A logic analysis of a conflict is based on the existence of one or more propositions that lead to a conclusion. However, as the child will never know all the relevant propositions it cannot draw any conclusions.

[34]The child's intention to solve parental conflict becomes a paradox for two reasons. Firstly, a child has not got the cognitive skills that are necessary for the solution of a conflict. Secondly, a third person will never have a complete picture of the reasons that led to a conflict.

anxiety.[35] The problem is that especially younger children tend to mix the cognitive and the emotional dimension which should be kept apart.

From their experience of working with children who were exposed to parental conflict the psychologists Harold and Shelton developed a checklist for the measurement of child-wellbeing that addresses the following components:[36] children's psychological symptoms, such as depression, anxiety, conduct problems or hostility, their perception of parental conflict and the risks related to it, their perception of the parent–child relationship, children's perception of support from family and friends and their perception of their general well-being. In their study on the impact of parental conflict on children and adolescents the authors found that conflicting parents tend to be less available for their children, which in turn creates a feeling of being rejected in the children. They say the following:

> "Couple conflict can lead parents to withdraw from their children's lives, for example, being less available to provide instrumental support to children in their day-to-day routine or not knowing their friends' names. Children, it is suggested, could experience this withdrawal as parent rejection." (Harold and Shelton 2008: 721)

Whereas internalizing behaviour may be considered as aggression against oneself, externalizing behaviour means that the problem is shifted outside and is projected onto other people or in interaction with others. Thus children may show forms of antisocial behaviour against others, which means they subconsciously apply a mechanism where they enhance their well-being at the cost of another person feeling worse. This detrimental psycho-dynamism is related to the principle that if the other feels worse, then the individual feels better.

Accordingly, the research literature shows that there are two theoretical models that aim at explaining the effects of marital conflict on children and adolescents. These models are the Cognitive-contextual Theory and the Emotional Security Hypothesis. The Cognitive-contextual Theory developed by Grych and Fincham starts from the assumption that children's appraisal, that is the way in which they understand and interpret parental conflict, affects their coping efforts. These appraisals take place in two stages – the primary appraisal, referring to an initial estimation of the importance of the conflict and its actual threat for the child. And the secondary appraisal the child uses to try to understand the reason for the conflict and who is responsible for it. This is the stage where children run the risk of being thrown into the conflict. As a reaction, they tend to blame themselves, which has especially detrimental consequences on the emotional level, producing feelings of sadness or depression. The author describes this process in the following quotation:

> "Even before stable patterns of responding to events have emerged, appraisals of conflict as destructive and threatening may mediate the impact of conflict on children's adjustment. Indeed, children's experiences with conflict may contribute to the emergence and stability of negative affective responding. The study also suggests that self-blame appraisals play a

---

[35]Other associated reactions include social withdrawal, loneliness and isolation or even sadness and depression.

[36]See: Harold and Shelton (2008): 712–724.

less prominent meditational role than threat appraisals in younger children, (...)." (Grych and Fincham 1990: 290)

Another approach to the investigation of the consequences of marital discord is the Emotional Security Hypothesis presented by Davies and Cummings. Similar to the previous model, the authors consider the children's evaluation of the meaning and its threat for them predominant. However, children tend to assess mainly how threatening the conflict is for their emotional security[37] and the integrity of the whole family unit. The authors ascribe emotions a central role in the regulation of human action. They define emotional security as the interaction between socio-economic and biological processes viewing it as a system which regulates social interactions and is at the same time regulated by them. The authors give the following definition of emotional security:

"Emotional security is a latent construct that can be inferred from the overall organization and meaning of children's emotions, behaviours, thoughts, and physiological responses, and serves as a set goal by which children regulate their own functioning in social contexts, thereby directing social, emotional, cognitive and physiological reactions." (Davies and Cummings 1994: 388)

The need of safety is certainly one of the basic human needs. In the case of parental conflict the need of safety is affected which may provoke reactions of fear, anxiety and depression. Maslow viewed human needs in a hierarchical order in which a higher need would only become dominant if the subordinate lower one is satisfied.[38] A person's need for safety includes the security of body and health, employment and resources, property, of morality and the family. For children, the feeling of safety seems to be mainly associated with a kind of daily routine, which is affected by parental divorce. Maslow (1943: 378) describes a child's typical reaction if this routine is disturbed:

"Another indication of the child's need for safety is his preference for some kind of undisrupted routine or rhythm. He seems to want a predictable, orderly world. (...) Young children seem to thrive better under a system which has at least a skeletal outline of rigidity, in which there is a schedule of a kind, some sort of routine, something that can be counted upon, not only for the present but also far into the future. Perhaps one could express this more accurately by saying that the child needs an organized world rather than an unorganized or unstructured one." (Maslow 1943: 377)

Davies and Cummings assume that emotional security also builds on the quality of the parent–child relationship, especially if that relationship features a secure or

[37]The authors name three fundamental assumptions on which the concept of social security is based. First, they ascribe emotions a central role in the organization of human action, second characteristic aspects of emotional security point out that a child's emotional security depends on the functioning of three regulatory mechanisms, such as emotion regulation, the internal representation of family relationships, and regulation of exposure to family affect. (Davies and Cummings 1994: 387–411)

[38]See: Maslow (1943): 370–396.

insecure attachment style.[39] Secure attachment is supposed to induce attachment security and leads to emotional well-functioning. The marital relationship seems to be an additional factor that influences children's emotional security, as the authors describe in the following quotation:

> "We propose that children's emotional security also derives from the quality of the marital relationship. Children have sound bases for concern about the quality of marital relations. Marital conflict can cause family life to be emotionally unpleasant, threaten the child's emotional or even physical well-being, result in a breakdown of discipline practices, and reduce the emotional availability or sensitivity of parents. (..) Marital conflict may have negative implications for the future intactness of the family, with children taking the blame for marital problems (. . .)." (Davies and Cummings 1994: 389)

Research results have shown that there is also a gender-specific aspect in children's reactions to parental conflict. Whereas girls tend to feel responsible and develop more internalizing problems, boys seem to be more prone to externalizing behaviour, such as anger and aggressiveness. This is shown by the results of a study on the role of gender and children's appraisal of marital conflict by Cummings.[40] Whereas girls tended to react with internalizing behaviour whereas boys showed more externalizing behaviour. These typical reactions are an indictor for subsequent adjustment problems. The following quotation explains these correlations:

> "Children's appraisals were also significantly related to child outcomes for both boys and girls. In keeping with predictions, threat was a stronger predictor for boys, whereas self-blame was a better predictor for girls. For boys threat predicted internalizing problems, externalizing problems, and the total behaviour problem score. (. . .) For girls, self-blame was associated with internalizing problems and the total behaviour problem score. None of these relations was significant for boys." (Cummings et al. 1994: 145)

The amount of adjustment problems a child or an adolescent may develop depends on many factors, such as age and developmental stage, coping skills, intelligence, temperament, gender, self-confidence gained from other social relations and others. The longer the offspring is exposed to conflict the more severe the consequences seem to be. However, children have a high capacity to recover from these consequences once the conflict is resolved. We will now turn to the question which particular impact parenting behaviour has on children and adolescents in the post-divorce phase.

---

[39]Attachment style is understood as a lasting emotional relationship between individuals that is based on the exchange of attention, security and enjoyment. The roots of attachment theory go back to Freud, who described the early object-relations of the child as motivated by human urges and desires. (Freud 1982, I: 501 f.) This concept was further developed by Klein, who brought the theory of object into a social context. She assumed that the way in which a person perceives and experiences his or her environment depends largely on the quality of his or her first close relationship called 'object' (usually the mother) during early infancy. (Segal 2004: 28 ff.)

[40]See: Cummings et al. (1994): 145.

3.5 Post-divorce Parenting

Until the end of the adolescence, parents are the most important caregivers in the life of sons and daughters. Parents usually provide them with love, support, attention and guidance, all of which form part of what is normally subsumed under the term "parenting". It can be considered a transmission of two types of know-how from parents to children. First, by experiencing the relation to their parents children acquire a particular attachment style, which is later applied to other relationships in adult life. Second, parents transfer interpersonal know-how to their children by applying and demonstrating social skills in the interaction with others.

We will describe these two aspects in more detail. Bowlby[41] developed a theory of attachment ascribing the first relationship a primary importance in a person's life. The same as stable bonding between infant and mother gives a child confidence in other relationships, a traumatic experience of loss and disruption may later cause behaviour disturbances. Thus an adult has a basic experience of a specific attachment style that he or she would diversify and adapt to the following relationships in later life. Bowlby describes this in the following quotation:

> "A young child's experience of an encouraging, supportive, and co-operative mother, and a little later, father, gives him a sense of worth, a belief in the helpfulness of others, and a favourable model on which to build future relationships (. . .) by enabling him to explore his environment with confidence and to deal with it effectively, such experiences also promote his sense of competence." (Bowlby 1982: 378)

The author described four different styles of attachment, such as secure,[42] ambivalent,[43] avoidant,[44] and disorganized attachment.[45] Securely attached adults tend to have long-lasting relationships, have a higher self-esteem and enjoy social contact. Several authors consider a parent's secure attachment style as beneficial for the parent–child relationship.[46] Parents with secure attachment tend to have helpful communication skills and practical coping abilities. They are able to deal with negative and contradictory emotions and are more often willing to be a cooperative ex-spouse. In their qualitative study on the parent–child relationship during the

---

[41]Bowlby (1907–1990) was a British medical doctor, psychoanalyst and pioneer in the investigation of attachment. He assumed that humans are equipped with a genetic system for attachment which is activated and influenced by the quality of the first relationship to the caregiver, the mother. See: Bowlby (1958): 350–373.

[42]Parents who are securely attached to their children spend more time with them and are responsive to their children's needs.

[43]Ambivalent attachment style occurs when the caregiver is less responsive and children are not sure of his or her affection.

[44]A person with an avoidant attachment style does not invest much time and effort in relationships and does not excessively suffer if a relationship terminates.

[45]Children with a disorganized attachment style tend to show different patterns of interaction and have parents who use opposing parenting techniques such as support and fear. See: Bowlby (1982).

[46]See studies of Cohn et al. (1992): 417–431, Crowell and Feldman (1988): 1273–1285, Ward and Carlson (1995): 69–79.

divorce process, Cohen and Finzi-Dottan report that securely attached mothers were less rejecting and their child-relationship had a central position in their life. They explain this in the following quotation:

> "For instance, securely attached mothers, compared with insecure mothers, appeared to show more warmth and supportiveness during a challenging activity and to provide clearer and more helpful assistance which encouraged learning and mastery in their children, while insecure mothers appeared to switch between overprotecting their children and inviting role reversal child parentification." (Van Ijzendoorn quoted in Cohen and Finzi-Dottan 2005: 85).

The authors summarize that parents' satisfaction with the parent–child relationship generally tends to be higher if they respect their child's autonomy, show interest in their development and are less distant and have their relationship built on trust. Adults with an ambivalent attachment style tend to be insecure in closer relationships fearing that the other might not reciprocate their feelings. Children showing an avoidant attachment style do not actively seek a parent's attention and do not especially feel comfortable in the company of others. They have difficulties sharing feelings with others and sometimes prefer staying alone. In view of this description, it is important to note that a person's attachment style is very much likely to undergo changes over their lifetime. Individual factors, such as character, education and experiences, play a role in the process of change. However, the style experienced by primary caregivers seems to shape a person to a certain extent.

The transmission of social skills is another component of parenting. Social skills include a range of accepted conduct used in the interaction with other people.[47] Generally, children tend to model their behavior after their parents. On the other hand, parents actively intervene and encourage children to learn what they consider appropriate behaviour. A child's knowledge of social skills depends on the age and the demands of a particular situation. A child acquires interpersonal skills and internalizes them, which becomes a pool of available mental resources over lifetime.

We will now turn to the question which impact divorce has on parenting? Divorce tends to affect the parent–child relation on the emotional level. Cohen and Finzi-Dottan point to an ambivalent feeling that parents often experience towards their children after divorce. Parents tend to see themselves in their children and at the same time, children symbolize the ex-spouse and thus remind them of the broken marriage. This creates a certain feeling of ambivalence also because every parent–child contact may involve seeing the ex-spouse. The authors say:

---

[47]Examples for situations and speech acts that require social communication skills are: greeting, introducing yourself and others, having a conversation, listening to others, getting along with others, staying calm in a difficult situation, managing impulsivity, following instructions, asking for help or for permission, apologizing, accepting criticism, etc. Social competence is based upon the knowledge of social skills and denotes the ability to choose the appropriate behaviour in an interpersonal situation.

"Hence, divorced parents often fantasize their children not being there. The degree of satisfaction with their children may thus be a measure of how well divorced parents have managed their ambivalence." (Cohen and Finzi-Dottan 2005: 82)

This ambivalence seems to be also true for adolescents, who often experience contradictory feelings towards each parent.[48] As the identity of younger children is still linked to their parents' matrimonial union and its functioning, divorce affects them directly and they tend to react with self-doubt and self-blame. This is because divorce is a situation where the needs of parents and children clash. Whereas parents have the undisputable right to reorganize their lives separately, adolescents want to maintain the family system, which means stability for them. Similarly, adolescents are often insecure about how their role would change once the parental alliance is ruptured. Therefore the legislator has taken special measures to protect the child's right to be heard in family matters as well as in the course of any administrative legal procedure that affects his or her personal, social or family environment. This right is guaranteed in Article 9.1. of the Law of the Juridical Protection of the Minor Child and the Partial Modification of the Civil Code and Civil Procedure:[49]

Artículo 9. Derecho a ser oído.

1. El menor tiene derecho a ser oído, tanto en el ámbito familiar como en cualquier procedimiento administrativo o judicial en que esté directamente implicado y que conduzca a una decisión que afecte a su esfera personal, familiar o social. (...)
2. Se garantizará que el menor pueda ejercitar este derecho por sí mismo o a través de la persona que designe para que le represente, cuando tenga suficiente juicio.

No obstante, cuando ello no sea posible o no convenga al interés del menor, podrá conocerse su opinión por medio de sus representantes legales, siempre que no sean parte interesada ni tengan intereses contrapuestos a los del menor, o a través de otras personas que por su profesión o relación de especial confianza con él puedan transmitirla objetivamente.

3. Cuando el menor solicite ser oído directamente o por medio de persona que le represente, la denegación de la audiencia será motivada y comunicada al Ministerio Fiscal y a aquéllos." (Ley Orgánica de Protección Jurídica del Menor)

Post divorce parenting may take several forms and includes sole or exclusive custody (custodia exclusive/unilateral), joint or shared custody (custodia compartida) or less frequently split custody (custodia repartida).[50] Custody is based on the legal principle of legal authority, the "patria potestad" (Article 156 CC). According

[48]As the identity of younger children is linked to their parents' functioning marriage, divorce affects them directly and they tend to react with self-doubt and self-blame.

[49]See: Ley Orgánica 1/1996, de 15 de enero, de Protección Jurídica del Menor, de modificación parcial del Código Civil y de la Ley de Enjuiciamiento Civil, BOE núm. 15/1996, de 17 de enero de 1996.

[50]A split custody arrangement applies to families with more than one child and corresponds to the Spanish option of "*custodia repartida*", whereby one child resides with one parent and the other child with the other parent. As Article 92.5 of the Spanish Civil Code states that when judges reach a decision on custody they should take care that brothers and sisters are not separated. Therefore the split custody regime or 'custodia repartida' is not a recognized legal concept within Spanish

to this legal rule both parents are entitled and obliged to hold legal authority, except for cases in which this would be harmful to the child. In Spain custody is therefore always joint in the sense that both parents have the right and duty to exercise it. As such joint physical custody is a parent-chosen and court-ordered custody according to which the child stays with both parents at alternating intervals of days, weeks, months or even whole terms. Taking into account this provision legal practitioners speak of sole custody when the child resides with one parent during the week and sees the other parent at alternating weekends with or without overnight stays. On the contrary joint custody refers to a parenting regime in which the child has a residence in with both parental homes at certain, more or less equally divided intervals (e.g. days, weeks, months, trimesters).

In 2008, Arch Marin and Jarne Espacia carried out a pilot study in which they analyzed how psychologists and legal practitioners evaluated different custody settings according to the experience when working with divorced families.[51] They interviewed forensic psychologists, judges and lawyers and asked them about their professional experience with the functioning of sole and joint custody. The authors grounded their analysis on several custody arrangements, such as three exclusive custody options and four types of joint custody settings depending on the amount of parent–child contact. The table shows this distinction (Fig. 3.2).

According to their distinction, exclusive custody included three possibilities: (1) the child living exclusively with the custodial parent without having contact to the non-custodial parent, (2) the child lives with the custodial parent and visits the other parent on weekends without staying overnight, and (3) the child living with the custodial parent sees the non-custodial parent on weekends including overnight stays. Within the joint custody arrangement, four options are distinguished, depending on the amount of time dedicated to the alternating stays at parental homes that range from days (CD) or weeks (CS) to months (CM) or even trimesters (CT).

Exclusive / sole custody (EC)	Joint custody (JC)
1. EC – weekend visits (Excl. sin Inters.)	A) JC days (CC días)
2. EC + weekend visits – overnight stays (Excl. Inters. sin pernoc.)	B) JC weeks (CC semanas)
3. EC + weekend visits + overnight stays (Excl. Inters. con pernoc.)	C) JC months (CC meses)
	D) JC trimesters (CC trimestres)

Fig. 3.2 Exclusive/sole custody and joint custody[52]

family law. Nevertheless it is legally allowed and there are cases in which such regime is preferred and exercised by the former family (e.g. SAP Cordoba 132/2006 de 12 junio, JUR\2007\78867).

[51] See: Arch Marin and Jarne Esparcia (2008): 25–33.

[52] + With, – without

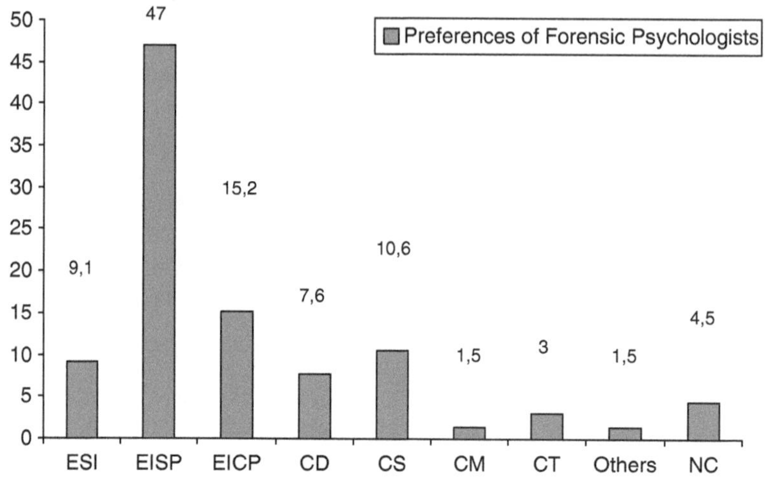

Fig. 3.3 Preferences of forensic psychologists[53]

The results of the study showed that representatives of all three groups of professions showed a clear preference for exclusive custody with extensive contact options between child and non-custodial parent. The diagram shows the distribution of the different custody settings according to the preferences of forensic psychologists (Fig. 3.3):

Nearly half of the group of forensic psychologists (47%) preferred exclusive custody with weekend visits but without overnight stays (EISP) on the assumption that the child needs a stable point of reference during the turmoil of the family transition. They argued that children should not to be viewed at as 'suitcases' and therefore exclusive custody with weekend visits but without overnight stays is the most feasible alternative and most common option. Only a minority (15.2%) of psychologists viewed exclusive custody including overnight stays (EICP) as beneficial for the children. In reference to the joint custody option, slightly more than one fifth (22.7%) of the psychologists considered joint custody (CC) with various types of dual residence for the children (CD, CS, CM, CT) as a positive option for parents and children.

These findings appeared as a contradiction especially when psychologists were asked for their own experience on the actual functioning of joint custody in divorced families. More than half of the psychologists (56.1%) stated that joint custody worked: very well, (10.6%) or moderately well, (45.5%) and a quarter (25.8%) reported it as functioning neutrally (10.6%) or moderately badly (15.2%).[54] The authors of the study pointed to the contradiction that psychologists

[53]See: Arch Marin and Jarne Esparcia (2008): 28.

[54]A group of psychologists corresponding a percentage of 18.2 did not give a definite answer.

did not recommend joint custody although it seemed to work fairly well in practice. They comment on this contradiction in the following statement:

> "Como puede apreciarse, si sumamos el porcentaje de ≪ resultado muy bueno ≫ y ≪ moderadamente bueno ≫ se alcanza un porcentaje del 56.1% de la muestra, dato que resulta contrario a la opinión expresada en cuanto a las preferencias. Es decir, aunque los psicólogos forenses expertos en guarda y custodia no prefieren inicialmente le opción de recomendar una custodia compartida, su valoración en tanto el resultado que esta teniendo en los casos que conocen es positiva." (Arch Marin and Jarne Esparcia 2008: 29)

In fact, only a minority of psychologists and lawyers was in favour of the joint custody option and none of the judges showed a preference for it. However, judges and magistrates approved of the possibility of the child staying overnight in the non-custodial parent's residence. This led the authors to the assumption that family judges tend to consider a lack of parental cooperation more detrimental to the child than the negative consequences that may arise from a restricted parent–child contact. They give the following explanation:

> "En este sentido, el análisis de las manifestaciones aportadas por los participantes nos conduce a hipotizar que, en el caso de los jueces, su preferencia podría estar más influida por la creencia de cierta falta de capacidad de los adultos para manejar un sistema que requiere de alto nivel de acuerdo interparental que no con la creencia de que el contacto igualitario del niño con ambos progenitores pueda resultarles perjudicial." (Arch Marin and Jarne Esparcia 2008: 32)

We will now concentrate on the functioning of the primary resident parent, mostly the mother, and analyze if divorce has an effect on the relationship to her child. Several studies have shown that it is beneficial for children's well-being if the primary residential parent is satisfied with the post-divorce situation.[55] This is not surprising because a parent's problems in the social, economic or emotional sphere might have negative effects on the relationship to his or her child. However, many mothers in this situation take up this challenge and activate their resources by turning to social networks and trying to improve their professional life. Steward[56] underlines that, without downplaying the reality of divorce, custodial mothers are sometimes capable of making profit within a difficult situation:

> "With the stress associated with increased demand on time and family schedules, increasing child care costs, and foregone education and employment opportunities, the single custodial females have learned to look for and use social support networks. Many of these women commented that they were able to rely on friends and family for both, social and financial support. They seemed also to have relied on themselves, especially in their determination to reduce debts and move to a more secure financial setting. Many of these women took additional training to equip them better to compete in the work force. The most common positive response by these women to their divorce was the reference to their new-found degree of personal control and efficacy." (Steward 1991: 313)

---

[55]See: Thomson et al. (1994): 221ff.

[56]See: Steward (1991): 296–317.

The custodial parent's satisfaction will depend largely on how she or he copes with the challenges of the post-divorce changes. Successful management of the problems depends on a person's age, cognitive abilities and education as well as support from the family of origin.

A special kind of role reversal seems to affect the mother–child relationship after divorce.[57] There is general agreement among authors that custodial mothers have an inclination to forge close relationships with their children, especially during the post-divorce phase.[58] And adolescents often undertake the active role by comforting and encouraging their mothers, partly replacing the mother's absent partner.[59] In a retrospective study Hughes explored how adult children of divorce perceived their mothers, especially their mothers' managing of the post-divorce phase. The research literature had provided some evidence that adolescents undertaking the role of confidants experienced themselves as being important for their mothers' well-being.[60] In turn this created a temporary increase of self-esteem in daughters and sons. The relationship was characterized by more intimacy and reduced distance, more communication, problem disclosure and efforts for empathy. Hughes refers to this role reversal by the following quotation:

> "...the decomposition of the authority structure and group size increases communication and disclosure. Indeed there is some evidence that single mother parent–child relationships are characterised by greater equality, more frequent interaction, more discussion, and greater intimacy and companionship – especially with older children who are more in touch with a parent's emotional state." (Hughes 2007: 565)

In particular, the author of the study wanted to know how this role reversal was actually evaluated by adult children looking back at the post-divorce phase. Her in-depth interviews revealed that the majority of adult children of divorced parents experienced conflicting impulses towards their mothers. These resulted from the son's and daughter's desire for personal growth and autonomy on the one hand and the experience that this was hindered by the family breakdown and their mothers' subsequent dependence on them. They considered their mothers as helpless, deprived and dissatisfied and felt their mothers' demand for support. In contrast to the traditional social roles of earlier generations, they had grown up in a time when roles were negotiable. These dissimilar role models led to conflicting views and divergent expectations.

There are divergent views among scholars about the impact of role reversal between mother and adolescent after divorce. Some authors such as Arditti (1999a,

---

[57]If we start from the assumption that certain tasks and functions are expected with a specific role, role reversal means that a family member undertakes a role that is normally assumed by another family member.

[58]See: Aquilino (1994): 295–314, Arditti (1999a, b): 109–119, 35–56.

[59]See: Johnston (1990): 405–414.

[60]A mother enlisting her daughter as a confidant means that she frequently discloses and discusses her personal fears, concerns or grievance with the daughter.

b) see positive effects for adolescents granting support to their divorced mothers because it enhances their feeling of competence and maturity.[61] Other authors see more negative consequences, especially when divorced mothers disclosed personal problems to their children.[62] It is often said that the mother–daughter relationship is characterized by intense bonds and that daughters are in general more susceptible to their mother's demands than sons. This theme inspired Silverberg Körner, Wallace et al. to investigate the specific influence of post-divorce, mother-to-daughter relationship on adolescent daughters and their adjustment to divorce. The authors wanted to know first, if the mother-to-daughter disclosure would benefit daughters, in terms of a positive feeling of closeness. And second, they were interested if the inclination of divorced mothers to enlist the daughter as a confidant would cause worry and lead to daughters' psychological distress. Their results showed that more disclosure produced more psychological distress in daughters but did not result in closer feelings towards the mother. The authors summarize their results as follows:

> "Specifically, in our sample of adolescent girls whose mothers had been divorced between 5 and 20 months, we found evidence that detailed mother-to-daughter disclosure regarding four of the five sensitive topics (i.e., financial concerns, negativity toward ex-husband, job ups-and-downs, personal concerns) was positively and robustly associated with daughter psychological distress. Greater depth of maternal disclosure about those topics was not, however, related to greater feelings of mother–daughter closeness. (...) For example, detailed mother-to-daughter disclosure about parenting challenges was significantly and *negatively* associated with perceived mother–daughter closeness." (Silverberg Koerner et al. 2002: 479)

One explanation that the authors give for daughters' distress is that mothers' negative reports about their ex-husbands may destabilize the image of the whole family and of the father in particular. In fact, there is a completely different psychodynamism between ex-spouses than between father and daughter.[63]

We will now focus on the relevance of the father for the child's development by analyzing, first, the pertinence of the father–child relationship and subsequently name the factors that influence their post-divorce relationship. Relying on the predominance of attachment theory in psychological research until the beginning of the 1970s, scholars concentrated almost exclusively on the investigation of the mother–child relationship. More explicitly, the role of the father was considered insignificant and therefore hardly any studies were carried out on the father–child relationship. This view is reflected in the following statement by the founder of attachment theory Bowlby on the predominant role of the mother in a child's life:

> "If growth is to proceed smoothly, the tissues must he exposed to the influence of the appropriate organizer at certain critical periods. In the same way, if mental development is to proceed smoothly, it would appear to be necessary for the undifferentiated psyche to be

[61]See: Arditti (1999a, b): 109–119, 35–56.

[62]See studies of Teyber (1983): 305–310, Weltner (1982): 203–210.

[63]Whereas a divorce eventually eliminates any responsibility of the ex-spouses for each other, the family bonds between father and daughter persist for life.

exposed during certain critical periods to the influence of the psychic organizer – the mother." (Bowlby 1951: 53)

As Bowlby was influenced by the Freudian psychoanalysis, he assumed that in the early years of a child, the mother represented both, a child's ego and super-ego. According to this view the child takes her as a model and later internalizes these maternal functions. The author describes this process:

"It is not surprising that during infancy and early childhood these functions [that of the ego and the super-ego] are either not operating at all or are doing so most imperfectly. During this phase of life, the child is therefore dependent on his mother performing them for him. She orients him in space and time, provides his environment, permits the satisfaction of some impulses, and restricts others. She is his ego and his super-ego. Gradually he learns these arts himself, and as he does, the skilled parent transfers the roles to him. This is a slow, subtle and continuous process, beginning when he first learns to walk and feed himself, and not ending completely until maturity is reached. (. . .)." (Bowlby 1951: 53)

Since the middle of the 1970s the view of the role of the father for a child's development has changed fundamentally. Five factors play a causal role in this change, such as women's movement, birth control and family planning, de-ideologization of motherhood, the increase of divorce rates and the beginning of men's movement.[64] Psychologists' interest in the father–child relations grew steadily and led to an increase in publications.[65] One focal point was the question of whether fatherhood would be genetically determined, similar to motherhood. Research on this question has shown that a baby is equipped with a behavioural preparedness or susceptibility to gain benefits from its interaction with the caregiver. It was found out that babies tend to react to any caregiver visible to them.[66] This meant that the father has an equally important role as the mother if he undertakes the role of primary caregiver.[67]

[64]Inspired by the women's movement men have become aware of the restrictions that the traditional male role has imposed and imposes on them and that they want to get rid of. This is reflected in men's growing awareness of the pertinence of fatherhood and their active participation in child care and household duties.

[65]Scholars then focused on the following questions: Does the father play an equally important role for the infant as the mother? Does the infant show a preference for the mother or the father at any time during its development? During which developmental stage does the parent-infant bonding exactly occur? Are there differences in the interaction of fathers and mothers with their infants? Further reasons for the general neglect of the father-relationship are described in Gaffal (1990): 11f.

[66]See: Papoušek and Papoušek (1984): 127–163.

[67]These results highlighted not only that fathers can have equal importance for the child but also implied that the relationship between a non-biological parent and his or her adopted child can have equal quality and significance than that between a biological parent and child.

Research on father involvement in child upbringing has been developed around three aspects, such as engagement, accessibility and responsibility.[68] Research results have shown that fathers are generally less involved in their children's lives than mothers.[69] However, Lamb pointed to the tendency that a more egalitarian role distribution among mothers and fathers leads to slightly more father involvement:

> "In two parent families with employed mothers, the average levels of paternal engagement and accessibility are both substantially higher than in families with unemployed mothers. In such families paternal involvement in direct interaction or engagement and accessibility average 33 and 65% of the relevant figures for mothers, respectively. Even when both fathers and mothers are employed 30 or more hours per week, however, many fathers assume little responsibility for child care. (...) Thus, fathers are proportionally more involved when mothers are employed, even though the extent of their involvement, in absolute terms, increases quite modestly, if at all. Over time, levels of paternal involvement in dual-earner families have increased, but the changes are much smaller than popular accounts often suggest." (Lamb 2004: 2)

The author draws the attention to the historical interdependence of socio-economic conditions and father role expectations. Father roles underwent a substantial change over time, especially in the last century. Towards the beginning of the last century, a father had the role of a family patriarch, supervising his children's acquisition of moral values and appropriate behaviour. During the time of industrialization, fathers mainly undertook the role of the earner and breadwinner to support the family. It was not until the 1970s that the role of the nurturing father – who took a more active part in his children's lives, emerged. As a conclusion, the modern father represents several roles and is not restricted to being the breadwinner or educator. Thus it seems pertinent to study father involvement by including all his possible sociological roles. This new research perspective is underlined by Lamb:

> "In contrast to earlier conceptualizations of earlier father roles, that often focused quite narrowly on breadwinning, researchers, theorists and practitioners no longer cling to the simplistic view that fathers fill a unidimensional and universal role in their families and in their children's eyes. Instead, they recognize that fathers play a number of significant roles – companions, care providers, spouse, protectors, models, moral guides, teachers, breadwinners – whose relative importance varies across historical epochs and sub-cultural groups. Only by considering the father's performance of these various roles and by taking into account their relative importance in the socio-ecological contexts concerned can researchers evaluate fathers' impact on child development." (Lamb 2004: 4)

[68]Engagement means the amount of time and quality of interaction a father is prepared to grant to his child. Accessibility refers to a father being generally available and at short notice whenever his child addresses him. Responsibility denotes a father's participation in decision-taking in all kinds of child-related matters.

[69]See: Lamb et al. (1987): 111–142.

In 1990, I carried out an empirical investigation on the quality of the father–child-relationship from the perspective of 15 year-old pupils in Austria.[70] In this study, 125 pupils from different sociological backgrounds[71] were asked to write an essay titled "My father and I," in which they should write everything down that came to their minds when thinking of their fathers. The essays were coded after psycholinguistic and sociolinguistic criteria. One focus of interest was the sociological roles in which the pupils observed their fathers. Accordingly, each essay was evaluated by recording the role in which the father was described. These roles included: the husband, the caregiver (or home husband), the educator, the breadwinner, son (of his own parents), the beloved of his daughter,[72] the spare-time person, and the friend.

The outcomes showed that the majority of pupils saw their fathers in the role of a friend (76%), the role of an educator took the second rank (68%), followed by that of the breadwinner (56.8%). It was noticeable that girls described their fathers in more detail and in a reflexive style, in texts double the size than those of the boys. Girls also mentioned more sociological roles in their descriptions. Interestingly, the girls described their fathers particularly in their role as caregiver. In the comparative study on the mother–child relationship boys behaved similarly and described their mothers more often in the role of the housewife. Consequently, girls seem to appreciate their fathers acting as caregivers. The results also showed that boys tended to describe their fathers more frequently in the role of the educator controlling them and encouraging them to performance and competition.

Adolescents who lived with their divorced parent (mostly the mother) described their fathers in shorter texts with fewer sociological roles. Their father image appeared vague in the sense that they were lacking an apparent idea or model of father behaviour. More adolescents from divorced families described their father-relationship as ambivalent and avoided any remark about their own self-concepts, seeing themselves as sons or daughters of their fathers. Yet, rarely did any adolescents express the desire for more contact with the father. Thus, fewer expectations are associated with father roles. Some revealed conflicting feelings between the biological father and their step-father or their mother's cohabitating partner. The style which adolescents from divorced parents used was remarkable, because they described their family situation in a very realistic and adult way, avoiding

[70]The study, a Master thesis, was embedded in a broader research project by E. Neubauer and R. Wodak, who conducted an overall study on the mother-child-relationship. The aim was to compare the results gained from both studies and draw conclusions about the importance and the functions of the father in the lives of sons and daughters. See: Neubauer (1988), Wodak (1981): 39ff.

[71]The ten year-old pupils attended a primary school (*Volksschule*) and the 11–15 year-old pupils attended either a secondary modern school (*Hauptschule*) or a grammar school (*Gymnasium*), the latter two groups representing two sociological classes.

[72]This category was used to address the special father-daughter-relationship. According to S. Freud's theory of the Oedipus, there is a phase in a daughter's life during which she develops intense affection for her father and subconsciously wants to replace her mother. During this phase a daughter idealizes her father and seeks closeness. See: Freud (1972): 264f.

emotional references. It seemed as if some had assumed part of the responsibility for their parents' problems. This aspect is in accordance with research results stating that adolescents living with their divorced parent tend to take the role of confidants and mature earlier. The father appears to have an important function for the child as he acts as a role model for sons and daughters and transmits interpersonal skills. Father absence leads to role diffusion, lack of encouragement and deficient social competence.

It seems relevant to raise again the notion of the vague father image. Ahrons and Tanner point to the limited characteristics that fatherhood is still associated with in many societies.[73] Many non-residential fathers have to redefine their new role after divorce. This process requires from a father the reflection of the traditional role model and the search for those father functions that he is willing to undertake. Avoidance of such redefinition may lead to withdrawal from parental and co-parental interaction, as is described by the authors:

> "Because the role of the noncustodial father is undefined, ambiguous, and complex, it can result in difficulties with performance of his parenting role and decreased involvement with his children (...). Unfortunately, paternal identity often is viewed in terms of financial contributions, and this becomes more pronounced in divorce. As a result, fathers may believe that their emotional and nurturing contributions are unimportant, and this may cause some to disengage (...)." (Ahrons and Tanner 2003: 349)

The same as father absence seems to have detrimental consequences for sons and daughters, children profit from fathers who stay involved in their children's lives. In a recent investigation, Sarkadi, Kristiansson, et al. reviewed 24 long-term studies on the consequences of father absence that were carried out in Sweden, Israel, the United Kingdom and the United States.[74] Their outcomes revealed that children in intact two parent families showed fewer conduct and psychological problems than children living in father-absent families. In order to measure a father's involvement in a child's life, the authors subdivided the concept into the three aspects; accessibility, engagement and responsibility.[75] They concluded that several studies lacked a clear definition of father engagement but also conceded that it is subject to individual habits and influenced by social and cultural norms. However, the conclusion is that children benefit if their fathers participate in their lives. This is described as follows:

> "(...), what is especially promising with the effects of father engagement is that it seems to differentially influence desirable outcomes. Father engagement reduces the frequency of behavioural problems in boys and psychological problems in young women; it also enhances cognitive development while decreasing criminality and economic disadvantage in low SES families." (Sarkadi et al. 2008: 157)

---

[73]Ahrons and Tanner (2003): 349f.

[74]From altogether 63 studies 24 studies were selected and these included a total amount of 22,300 individual datasets.

[75]The authors used a comprehensive definition of child well-being for the investigation, including: educational attainment, cognitive skills, intelligence, externalizing and internalizing behaviour, psychological state, and social skills.

Fathers seem to have a key role for the development and acquisition of a child's gender role. Although there are gender stereotypes for men and women in every society this does not imply that the majority of men and women show exactly these characteristics. This view is particularly supported by Silverstein and Auerbach who criticized the neo-conservative attitude towards the family in their sensational article, "Deconstructing the Essential Father". The aim of their article was to support fathers in their parenting role without discriminating against single mothers, step-parents or same sex couples. They question traditional gender stereotypes and believe that:

> "(...) parenting involves a series of care giving functions that have developed as adaptive strategies to specific bioecological contexts. These care giving functions can be performed by parenting figures of either sex, whether or not they are biologically related to the child." (Silverstein and Auerbach 1999: 401)

What does it actually mean for a child to adopt a gender role? It is the process during which a child develops gender-specific personality characteristics and forms of conduct and includes them in his or her repertoire of roles. Thereby, a child models his or her behaviour on parents or other caregivers, integrating motives, views and strategies into their personality. Gender roles are acquired in two ways, by imitation and identification. Research outcomes have shown that a father's restrictive parenting is only beneficial for sons if it is embedded in a loving relationship. The more a father's parenting style is characterized by punishing and restrictions, the less the son identifies with him.[76] If sons experience the father in the role of the caregiver, bestowing warm-heartedness and affection, it promotes their cognitive development. Additionally, these parenting characteristics help sons in the development of a marked male identity.[77] The assumption that successful gender role acquisition depends on a positive parent–child relationship is also emphasized by the study of Watson and Greeff. They presumed that children tend to imitate behaviour only if they relate well to their parents:

> "Should learning theory be found to explain variance in adjustment to divorce, a child whose parent(s) adjust well to being divorced is likely to, him/herself, be better adjusted to divorce than is a child whose parent(s) experience problems in adjusting to divorce. In short, it is widely acknowledged that the parent–child relationship is integral to the adjustment of adolescent children of divorce. This study takes this link as its point of departure. It aims, by investigating the parent–child relationship, the child's attitude to divorce, the child's adjustment, as well as the interrelationships between these variables, to see whether either schema or learning theory is able to adequately explain the variance found in adolescent adjustment to divorce." (Watson and Greeff 2004: 439)

They investigated three aspects; the quality of the mother–child relationship, the father–child relationship; and the adjustment attitude toward divorce in 38 adolescents (17–22 years old) from married parents and 39 children and adolescents (2–20 years old). Their results show that there is a significant relation between the

[76]See: Biller (1981): 319–358, Bandura and Walters (1963).

[77]See: Hardesty et al. (1995): 283–297.

adjustment of mothers and that of their adolescent sons and daughters, whereas there is no such relation between father and son. The authors explain that mothers were the primary caregivers in the cases investigated and thus had more influence on their offspring. However, in cases where a mother experienced adjustment problems, their daughters and sons did not automatically show the same difficulties, as the learning theory suggests. This is probably due to the tendency that a good relationship to that parent may limit or even outweigh such difficulties and facilitate adolescents' individual adjustment process.

The influence of the father for a daughter's adoption of her gender role is less well documented. According to Biller, three parenting skills are beneficial for daughters; warm-heartedness, father's positive attitude towards women and encouragement of independence and self-realization.[78] Another study revealed that both parents tended to attach the importance of achievement and competition for sons but not for daughters. They accepted more aggressive utterances from boys, were less tolerant towards their sons' emotions and used stricter punishment. The reason for increased aggressiveness in sons from divorced parents is seen as a consequence of the father's absence and inconsistent contact with the father. Moreover, co-resident mothers were often unable to provide appropriate models for the male gender role in their sons. It may generally be concluded that fathers, compared to mothers, seems to have more traditional ideas about gender roles and transmit these to their daughters.[79]

Several studies have concentrated on the question how parental divorce affects the father–child relationship. Shapiro and Lambert were interested in the long-term effects of divorce on the father–child relationship and on fathers' well-being. The authors assumed that mothers and fathers would experience and judge the quality of their parent–child relationship according to the specific gender roles they had during marriage. These gender roles would act as a kind of filter or restricted perception:

> "This perspective suggests that reactivity to parent–child relationship stressors corresponds to the socially structured roles that men and women play in the family, particularly in a married-couple household. For example, men may be more reactive to financial or occupational stressors because men's family roles typically involve financial provision for the family. Similarly, because women's family roles typically involve responsibility for the emotional and physical well-being of family members (...), women may be more reactive than men to stressors related to parenting (...)." (Shapiro and Lambert 1999: 400)

Basically, their results showed that divorced non-resident fathers experienced a decrease in the level of relationship quality with their child over time. Conversely, the relationship quality to the child of co-resident fathers was similar to that of continuously married fathers. The authors reason that non-resident fathers have often the feeling of losing influence and control over their children's lives due to the physical distance. Moreover, they add another interesting element, namely, that fatherhood and father identity appear to be mainly linked to marriage. Thus divorce

[78]See: Biller (1974).

[79]See: Fthenakis (1985a, b): 319.

may produce some kind of role uncertainty, especially in non-resident fathers. Referring to fathers' psychological well-being, the outcomes show that divorced fathers tended to be more depressed than married fathers. Divorced fathers often find it rather demanding to care for their children when they stay with them. The following two explanations are given by the Shapiro and Lambert:

> "First, children in the home impose demands of time and energy and limit social and personal choices, especially on divorced parents (...). Second, single parenthood may be more emotionally taxing for males than for females. Men have smaller confidant networks than females (...) and the parental role may not be well integrated into the male role as a result of differential gender socialization (...)." (Shapiro and Lambert 1999: 406)

Due to the limited forms of behaviour associated with traditional gender roles, a non-resident parent may find it difficult to undertake tasks that were earlier carried out by the ex-spouse. Thus it may be rather demanding for a non-resident father to exercise the role of a primary caregiver that he is not familiar with. However, a certain amount of role flexibility and improvisation benefits both parents and children. We will deal with this aspect in more detail in the last section on non-resident fathers' involvement.

3.6 Custody Regulations

Many legal practitioners took the theoretical implications of attachment theory until the late 1970s as a basis for court decisions. Additionally, following the disorganization model, divorce was seen as the end of the intact family and the aim was to strengthen the rest of the family or the remaining one-parent family.[80] On the basis of these theoretical approaches, the majority of courts considered sole custody arrangement least disruptive to the child's life. The predominant parenting pattern awarded by courts until the early 1980s was that of sole custody to mothers with fathers being granted visitation rights. Therefore research conducted at that time concentrated mainly on the consequences of father absence and the conditions of divorced custodial mothers.

The systemic family perspective, a higher acceptance of divorce in society, and the change of gender roles seem to have induced courts to apply more egalitarian custody arrangements such as joint custody. In the following section, we will explain the different types of custody, their advantages and disadvantages.

Although traditional role models have changed, custody is in the majority of cases exercised mainly by mothers who are more available in terms of time. Therefore in the case of separation, the father–child relationship is mainly affected

---

[80]The disorganisation model was proposed by Goldstein et al. (1974) in their book called "*Jenseits des Kindeswohls*" in which the authors recommended that the custodial parent should be given a primary decision making right in settling questions of children's contact with the non-resident parent. Their view was inspired by the assumption that this would have a calming effect on children after the turbulences of divorce.

by a restriction of contact time. Several studies have investigated the amount of time that divorced fathers spent with their non-resident children. A widely cited study by Fürstenberg and Nord, states that within the period of five years (1980–1985) more than half of all fathers investigated had no contact with their children at all and another fifth had not met their children within a few years after divorce.[81]

In a joint legal custody regime, both parents have the authority to make decisions on behalf of the child in reference to education, religion, health and his or her general well-being. A possible danger associated with this arrangement is that it may provoke conflicts among parents in educational matters. Joint physical custody implies that each parent is given the right to have the child reside with him or her and the obligation to provide daily care and supervision of the child. As the child has two residences with both parents, the notion of "visiting a parent" is actually replaced by the notion of "dual residence." A predisposition for this arrangement is that the two households are close enough and both parents have enough time available to make the arrangement work.

The advantage of this custody arrangement is that it guarantees children ongoing contact with both parents. The disadvantages of joint legal custody are that there are higher costs to provide two fully equipped households to accommodate children and also the continuous negotiation between ex-spouses. If parents do not cooperate, this arrangement can be detrimental to children.

We want to analyze if joint legal and physical custody have any significant effect on the well-being of children and adolescents. Generally, there is agreement among authors that in joint custody arrangements, fathers spend more time with their children and are more involved in their offspring's lives.[82] Compared to sole maternal custody, where a decrease of father–child contact can be noticed 1 year after separation,[83] there is less variation of parent–child contact in joint custody settings.[84]

The well-being of children has been measured in various details including behaviour problems (externalizing behaviour), psychological state (internalizing problems, self-esteem), social relations (family relations and peers) and educational attainment. Taking the considerations about the importance of the father for a child's development into account, one would clearly expect a joint custody arrangement to be more advantageous to children. However, the research literature provides rather contradictory results. Although several studies have revealed positive effects, there are others that report no effects of joint custody on children. We will present some relevant investigations.

---

[81]For Germany a study conducted by Napp-Peters (1988) revealed that more than half of the divorced fathers (54%) broke off the contact to their children within two years after divorce.

[82]See: Arditti (1992): 23–42, Kline et al. (1989): 430ff.

[83]See: Seltzer et al. (1989): 1013–1032; Maccoby et al. (1993): 24–38.

[84]See: Coysh et al. (1989): 52–71; Kline et al. (1989): 430ff.

Three studies have shown that joint custody arrangement is beneficial for children's well-being and helps them to adapt to the post-divorce situation. The first investigation is a meta-analytic review carried out by Bauserman, in which 33 studies investigating children's adjustment to divorce in joint-custody arrangements compared to sole-custody arrangements were re-examined. The author reports better outcomes for children living in joint custody compared to those in sole custody. According to the results children living in joint custody regime show better adjustment:

> "This finding is consistent with the hypothesis that joint custody can be beneficial to children in a wide range of family, emotional, behavioural, and academic domains. (...) Joint-custody children showed better adjustment in parental relations and spent significant amounts of time with the father, allowing more opportunity for authoritative parenting. The findings for joint legal custody samples indicate that children do not actually need to be in joint *physical* custody to show better adjustment, but it is important to note that joint legal custody children typically spent a substantial amount of time with the father as well." (Bausermann 2002: 98)

There are several other studies that did not find significant differences when comparing joint to sole custody arrangements.[85] Interesting outcomes were provided by Buchanan et al.[86] who analyzed adolescents' experiences in divorced homes by interviewing 522 adolescents from 365 families with different custody regulations 4.5 years after their parents' separation. Three groups of custody arrangements were examined: sole maternal custody (70%), sole father custody (19%), and joint custody with dual residence (10%). The authors' focus of interest was the feeling of being caught in the middle of parental dispute, that children and adolescents often have in the course of divorce. The outcome showed that the feeling of being caught in the middle diminished adolescents' well-being. The feeling occurred mostly in conflicting post-divorce families with dual residences and where adolescents had a close relationship to both parents. Conversely, the same circumstances, except with good inter-parental contact, did not create the feeling of being caught in the middle among adolescents.

In 1994, a book, written by Maccoby and Mnookin, titled "Dividing the Child" received much attention.[87] The aim of this book was to analyze the consequences of a law favouring joint custody arrangements established in California in 1979. This law authorized courts to grant joint custody to parents who preferred it and suggested, moreover, that in cases of disagreement, the court should support the parent who preferred the participation of both parents in a post-divorce parenting. The authors investigated the substantial sample of 1,124 families who filed for divorce in California within a period of 7 months in 1985 and observed them for 3.5 years. Their outcomes revealed that although the majority of joint custody parents showed a high amount of participation in child care, the relationship between parents and

[85] The studies of Johnston et al. and that of Kline et al. (1989) did not find such differences.

[86] See: Buchanan et al. (1991): 1008–1029.

[87] See: Maccoby and Mnookin (1994): 277ff.

children was strikingly changed by parental divorce. The authors underline that it takes a considerable amount of effort for parents to create an atmosphere where children wanted to live alternately with both parents. The authors state that:

> "...the co-parental relationship between divorced parents is something that needs to be constructed, not something that can simply be carried over from pre-separation patterns. It takes times and effort on the part of both parents to arrange their lives in such a way that the children can spend time in both parental households..." (Maccoby and Mnookin 1994: 276)

Their results also showed that less than one third of all parents with joint custody successfully managed to establish co-parenting. For those parents who had difficulties, parenting took place on a parallel basis with insufficient communication and coordination. About a quarter of parents ended in conflict until the end of the observation period. The authors are basically in favour of co-parenting and conclude that joint custody is likely to produce positive effects in children. However, in the case of conflicts, it may be harmful:

> "(...), the results of the follow-up study of the adolescents in our sample families, as well as the research of others, makes us confident that there are important effects. Children derive real benefits – psychological, social, and economic – when divorced parents can have cooperative co-parenting relationships. With conflicted co-parental relationships, on the other hand, children are more likely to be caught in the middle, with real adverse effects on the child." (Maccoby and Mnookin 1994: 277)

Parental conflict is seen as the main obstacle to a joint custody arrangement. Therefore, many governments have established public institutions that offer counselling to couples in dispute before, during and after divorce. The aim is to help couples develop conflict-solving strategies, which in turn protects children and adolescents from being drawn into the conflict. Therefore the European Committee of Ministers to Member States on Family Mediation has acknowledged the special characteristics of family disputes and that separation and divorce impact on all the members of the family, especially on children. In their Recommendation they referred especially to the European Convention on the Exercise of Children's Rights, and in particular to Article 13 of this convention, which deals with the provision of mediation or other processes to resolve disputes affecting children.[88]

Three factors are supposed to have an impact on children's relationship to their non-resident parent, the visitation frequency of the non-resident parent, the quality of the parent–child relationship before separation and the children's age. Convincing evidence for the positive effect of post-divorce father involvement in parenting comes from a longitudinal study carried out by Aquilino. He investigated the relationship quality between adolescents and their noncustodial fathers by inquiring how the relationship changed over time into adulthood (18–24 years old).[89]

[88]See: Recommendation No. R (98) 1 of the Committee of Ministers to Member States on Family Mediation adopted by the Committee of Ministers on 21 January 1998.

[89]The results of this study are representational because it includes a large sample (359 households) and lasted for 12 years. Long-term studies of this length are rarely carried out and their results are highly significant.

The interest concentrated on the question of whether a non-custodial father's involvement with his young children, in terms of contact and involvement in decision-taking, would have positive consequences, such as a good father-son or father–daughter relationship later in life.[90] The results of this study proved once more that a father's involvement in his child's life at an early age pays off in later life stages. These sons and daughters tended to maintain contact to their fathers later in life. The author explains this outcome as follows:

> "When noncustodial fathers invested in their relationships with their sons and daughters during childhood and adolescence, the investment paid off in closer relationships with their biological offspring in early adulthood. Fathers who did not maintain a high level of involvement with their younger children were unlikely to have close relationships with their adult sons and daughters. The earlier level of father–child contact during adolescence was the strongest predictor of children's contact with noncustodial fathers in early adulthood. Nonetheless, level of contact does not tell the whole story. After controlling for earlier contact, a father's involvement in making important decisions that affected his adolescent child made a significant contribution to the likelihood that his child, as an adult, would turn to him for support." (Aquilino 2006: 942)

The author has also given evidence that remarriage of the non-custodial father does not necessarily lead to a decrease in the father–child relationship. This result is a helpful sign for non-custodial and custodial but non-residential fathers intending to keep in touch with their biological children. The result is also consistent with the view that a cooperative relationship among ex-spouses is a prerequisite for co-parenting, which in the long run has positive consequences for the father–child relationship. The implications for politics are therefore to offer counselling to divorcing parents in order to solve conflicts effectively. A study by Ahrons and Tanner[91] highlighted a related aspect with their investigation on the relationship between adult children and their fathers 20 years after parental divorce. They found out that most father–adult child relationships tended to stabilize over the years, even if the parents had had conflicts during the post-divorce phase. The authors describe the parent–child relationship as a stable subsystem within the family that is flexible enough to adapt to the family transition. They summarize their results:

> "Overall, our findings show that the majority of adult children felt their relationships with their fathers improved over the 20 years since their parents' divorce. In contrast to most of the literature that calls attention to the weakening bond between fathers and their children, 62% of these adult children reported that relationships either improved or stayed the same. Although relationships with parents generally improve as children mature to adulthood, that the divorce did not interfere with this positive trend is an important finding." (Ahrons and Tanner 2003: 348)

---

[90]Supposedly, a non-custodial father would have to make more effort to stay in contact with his child and to keep involved in his child's life than a sole or joint-custodial father.

[91]See: Ahrons and Tanner (2003): 348.

These outcomes are not in accordance with other studies that have shown a decrease of father–child contact after divorce. The authors explain the surprisingly positive results by the selection of families and their social class background. They underline that the parents' effort and ability to establish regular post-divorce contact outside marriage will pay off for many years later in life. However, reality seems to draw a different picture. Many parent–child contacts diminish over the years for many reasons. Thus another study on the long-term effects of divorce carried out by Finley and Schwartz[92] revealed that the majority of adult children 20 years after parental divorce, reported later that they would have desired more contact to their non-resident fathers.[93] Additionally, the authors argued that courts should be aware of the consequences of father absences and its psychological implications:

> "In sum, the present results indicate that, in divorced families, desired father involvement is powerfully linked to reported levels of father involvement. The vast majority of participants from divorced families desired more father involvement than they had received. As a result, it appears that divorce leaves many children with unmet desires for paternal involvement – desires that remain salient for many years after the divorce is finalized. This pattern of results is consistent with what Warshak (. . .) has called "the collective voice of children" and has argued that this should be used more extensively when making custody and access decisions within the family court system."

Among the father functions, two are missed the most; the instrumental function and the expressive function.[94] Young adults reported that they would have liked more contact with their fathers including supervision and guidance. Children often seem surprisingly mature in what they consider beneficial for them. Thus the authors criticize that courts concentrate too often on avoiding post-divorce conflicts and are often reluctant to grant joint custody in order to prevent conflicts. Thus they run the risk of neglecting children's voices and ignoring possible long-term consequences. Finley and Schwartz draw the following conclusion:

> "As has been cogently argued in recent literature (. . .), children's perspectives on their own best interests, particularly in the long term, are critical for researchers and policy makers. Equitable joint physical custody appears to be the post-divorce arrangement most preferred by children of divorce in the long term (. . .). Our results appear to suggest that providing custody arrangements that increase paternal involvement following divorce will result in decreases in feelings of missed opportunities and emotional longing in children from divorced families." (Finley and Schwartz 2007: 583)

There is not only a rewarding effect of father involvement in parenting for children but also for fathers (and mothers) themselves. Not only do fathers shape

---

[92]See: Finley and Schwartz (2007): 582.

[93]The authors consider the fact that some children were affected by parental divorce do not even express the desire for more contact to the non-resident parent is a subliminal sign of divorce-related distress. See: Finley and Schwartz (2007): 573ff.

[94]Whereas the instrumental function includes such activities as monitoring school work, exerting disciple, granting support or providing protection, the expressive function refers to the emotions that are experienced and expressed within the relationship.

their children but also the reverse is true; fathers are shaped by what they experience in the interaction with their children. There is evidence that a good father–child relationship contributes to fathers' psychosocial health, especially in the midlife years. Tiedje and Darling Fisher (1996, 475)[95] explain this positive effect by viewing the parent–child relationship from a developmental perspective. They speak of "life trajectories" that both parent and child would jointly begin with the child's birth:

> "When children are born, men and women are launched into developmental trajectories. If locked into traditional parenting roles, these trajectories may be very different for men and women. Keeping both men and women involved with children may potentially lead to more developmental synchrony and, hence, more satisfying relationships. Darling-Fisher's (1987) findings support this synchronous generativity hypothesis (. . .). Darling-Fisher found both fathers' and mothers' developmental status, were predictors of satisfaction with parenting, confidence with parenting skills, and overall adaptation to parenthood."

This aspect of the mutual effect of the parent–child relationship underlines an important notion of fatherhood. It implies that parental satisfaction with the individual post-divorce situation plays a vital role also for the quality of the parent–child relationship.

3.7 Conclusion

This chapter was dedicated to the analysis of the impact that parental divorce has on children and adolescents. We presented the theoretical model of the Divorce-Stress-Adjustment Perspective which was used to describe and explain the effects of parental divorce on the well-being of children and adolescents. This model includes mediating factors that stand for the stressful changes associated with divorce such as economic shortcoming, restricted contact between children and non-resident parent and exposure to parental conflict. Several studies have proved the assumption that these changes tend to produce lower outcomes in school performance, cognitive development and social competence. However, there is also evidence that children and adolescents have a high capacity of recuperation from these stressors once the conflict is settled. The Emotional Security Hypothesis was used to explain the dynamism of parental conflict and its impact on the offspring. Thereby, the content, the style and the outcome of parental conflict are relevant predictors for child adjustment. The longer children are exposed to a conflict the more detrimental the consequences tend to be. Some other researchers point to the protective factors that are activated in the case of parental divorce if parents acquire new conflict-solving strategies and maintain contact to their sons and daughters. The parent– child relationship is a source of knowledge transfer on

[95]See: Tiedje and Darling Fisher (1996): 471–484.

the emotional and the cognitive level. As such, a positive post-divorce parent–child relationship is more important than questions of residence or available time and money.

Research has clearly revealed that the father–child relationship is of essential importance for a child's development. As a reaction to the tendency of attributing sole custody mainly to mothers after divorce, research on the father–child relationship has become more predominant since the 1970s. Scientific results have shown that the father role includes several important functions for the child, such as that of a breadwinner, a caregiver, an educator, husband of the child's mother, son of the father's own parents and that of a playfellow and companion for the child. In the case of divorce these functions would suddenly be reduced to a minimum which tends to produce gender role deficiencies, lower educational attainment and lack of social competence. A joint custody arrangement after the divorce is supposed to benefit children and adolescents if parents are willing to cooperate. Economic stability is not the only relevant criterion for post-divorce child well-being. Emotional stability appears to be equally relevant and undoubtedly the father–child relationship is an inseparable component of it.

Chapter 4
Characteristics and Problems of Custody Arrangements

4.1 Introduction

This chapter presents an analysis of Spanish divorce sentences of the year 2007. The aim is to find out which factors play a role in decisions on custody arrangements. We will introduce a model based on five groups of decisive factors that predict custody arrangements. These factors are likely to influence the negotiation process between divorcing spouses. The regulating agreement stipulates the type of custody arrangement that will dominate the post-divorce scenario of parents and children.

Special reference is made to the jurisdiction and the modification of Spanish Family Law in 2005.[1] In the investigation a sample of 135 sentences which were brought before Courts of Appeal (Audiencia Provincial) by way of revision (recurso de apelación) will be analyzed. The focus of interest lies on the issue of joint custody and how often parents opt for this arrangement in their regulating agreement. We want to know whether there is any relationship between the factors mentioned in the model and the probability of a joint custody decision. Special attention is given to the legal argumentation for a custody arrangement in the court sentences.

4.2 Predictors of Custody Decisions

We want to know which role certain socio-economic, psychological and legal circumstances play in the divorce process and how they influence custody decisions. For the investigation of this influence we apply a multi-disciplinary model that includes five significant factors that are supposed to predict parental custody decisions. These factors include the parents' resources, the pre-divorce family composition, quality of the former marital relationship, the legal context and

[1] In 2005 Law 15/2005 was introduced, whereby the Civil Code and the Law of Civil Procedure in the Field of Separation and Divorce were modified. See: Ley 15/2005, de 8 de julio, por la que se modifican el Código Civil y la Ley de Enjuiciamiento Civil en materia de separación y divorcio, (BOE, 163, 9. 7. 2005: 24458–24461).

M. Gaffal, *Psychosocial and Legal Perspectives of Marital Breakdown*,
DOI 10.1007/978-3-642-13896-6_4,

pre-matrimonial contracts. Special attention is given to the legal provisions of Spanish family law that underwent a reform by the Ley 15/2005. One of the novelties of this reform was that parents may opt for a joint custody regime in their regulating agreement. In the introduction to the law it is stated that the new law supports the parents' free choice of custody regime and that it emphasizes the principle of parental co-responsibility among parents:

> "Se pretende reforzar con esta ley la libertad de decisión de los padres respecto del ejercicio de la patria potestad. En este sentido, se prevé expresamente que puedan acordar en el convenio regulador que el ejercicio se atribuya exclusivamente a uno de ellos, o bien a ambos de forma compartida. (...) Consiguientemente, los padres deberán decidir si la guarda y custodia se ejercerá sólo por uno de ellos o bien por ambos de forma compartida. En todo caso, determinarán, en beneficio del menor, cómo éste se relacionará del mejor modo con el progenitor que no conviva con él, y procurarán la realización del principio de corresponsabilidad en el ejercicio de la potestad." (Ley 15/2005)

In this chapter we will analyze the legal conditions of joint custody and make reference to the international and European legislation. As a conceptual frame we will take the Model of Predictors of Custody Arrangements elaborated by Kelly et al. who assume that five economic, psychological and legal factors predict post-divorce settlements.[2] As these factors tend to vary according to state and society we will adapt the frame to the Spanish context by using average statistical data on the factors involved while considering the Spanish legislation on Family Law.[3]

Several studies have investigated the conditions that lead ex-spouses to make decisions on custody and child support. They have shown that aspects such as parents' economic resources, the family composition and the quality of the pre-divorce marital relationship, establish the frame in which decisions are made.[4] Each parent translates these conditions into his or her own bargaining position. These conditions form the starting position for the negotiations to reach a regulating agreement whereby, at best, the ex-spouses try to find a common denominator. Additionally, the outcome of the divorce process will also depend on the parents' attitude towards compromise.

Kelly et al. wanted to know whether the introduction of joint custody in court orders had contributed to more gender-neutrality and to the best interests of the child. They assumed that the parents' education, profession income, number and age of children had an impact on the divorce outcomes. They placed these issues under five categories: (1) the parents' resources (economic and educational), (2) the pre-divorce family composition, (3) the marital relationship and reasons for the separation, and (4) the legal context. A fifth element (5) was added for cases where the spouses had set up a prenuptial agreement. The diagram shows the decisive factors for custody arrangements: (Fig. 4.1).

---

[2]See: Kelly et al. (2005): 25 ff.

[3]These statistical data are taken from the INE (Instituto Nacional de Estadística, Madrid available on: http://www.ine.es).

[4]Aspects such as personal maturity or individual personality characteristics are left aside because they are difficult to measure.

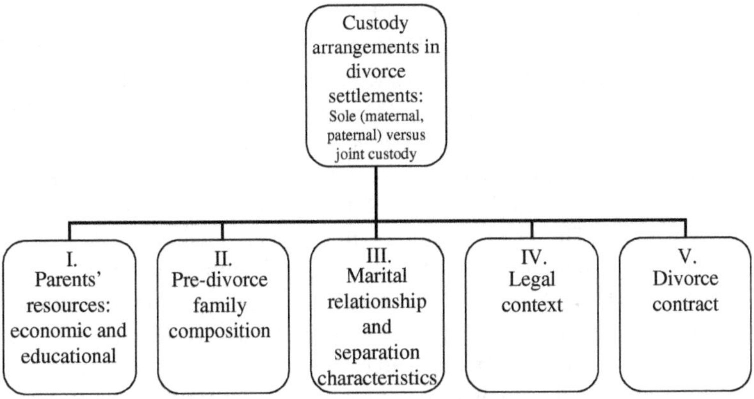

Fig. 4.1 Predictors of custody arrangements in divorce settlements[5]

By the first factor, the parents' economic and educational resources, the authors refer to monetary as well as non-monetary values.[6] A spouse's economic resources are supposed to increase his or her bargaining power in order to realize his or her post-divorce preferences. The authors view the negotiations as a process in which each spouse would intend to terminate the union at the most favorable individual conditions:

> "Such analyses view the divorce settlements involving minor children as resulting from parents' bargaining behaviors whose goals are to end the marriage at the lowest cost and to provide a framework for post-divorce relation in which monetary and non-monetary gains are maximized. (...)." (Kelly et al. 2005: 27)

As far as education and income are concerned, the authors hypothesized that if both parents had a higher total income and a higher education level they tended to choose more egalitarian or non-traditional custody arrangements such as joint or paternal custody. Therefore our research question is, whether higher resources increase the preference for joint custody.

The second factor, the pre-divorce family composition including the number, age and gender of children is assumed to have an impact on divorce outcomes. It affects the expected demand for financial resources and childcare after divorce. There seems to be a cultural preference in all societies to assume that younger children need their mothers more than their fathers.[7] From another standpoint,

---

[5]See: Kelly et al. 2005: 26.

[6]Whereas monetary values relate to income and property, non-monetary values concern education, formation and profession that represent a particular status in society.

[7]In the 1970s this argument was criticised as being gender-biased and was therefore rejected. As has been outlined in chapter three, an infant is capable of relating emotionally to any care-giving person, be it male or female, the biological or an adopting parent. In this context see also the principle of equal treatment of men and women in Article 3 of the Spanish Law on Gender Equality. (Ley Orgánica 3/2007, para la igualdad efectiva de mujeres y hombres).

several authors have pointed out that father presence is more important for older children, especially for boys.[8] For instance, Demo and Acock state that father absence is associated with a lack of socialization that cannot be substituted or compensated by the mother. They say that father absence affects especially boys because they lack a model of appropriate gender behaviour.[9]

Based on these data, parents and lawyers are often determined to seek maternal custody if young children are involved and prefer joint or paternal custody if older children are involved. This presupposition is reflected in the statistical data on Spanish couples and divorce settlements of the year 2006.[10] Within the group of divorced Spanish couples who had minor children (51.3%), child support was mainly paid by fathers (78.7%). Only in few cases both parents take took charge of the child support (3.6%) and child support was paid by mothers in only 2.5% of cases.

Although not all of the divorce sentences contain sufficient data on the family composition we are interested whether there is any relation between the children's age and the type of custody granted. A third factor when predicting custody arrangements is the pre-divorce quality of the marital relationship, its duration and the ground(s) for divorce. Relevant aspects in this context are: the level of conflict prior to divorce, marital misconduct and the time until the divorcing couple arrive at an agreement. A couple with a high level of conflict would not likely attempt a joint custody agreement because of the lack of sense of cooperation. On the contrary, a divorcing couple who has a low level of conflict would probably agree to joint custody. The authors expect high conflict couples to opt for sole custody and low conflict couples to opt for joint physical custody. Unfortunately, this aspect cannot be investigated because information on this issue is not mentioned in the divorce sentences.

Two further relevant criteria of divorce outcomes are the duration of marriage[11] and the distribution of family duties prior to divorce. Especially in marriages with a traditional role distribution, a divorce will most likely create an economic imbalance between the ex-spouses. As such, the woman will probably need substantial time and effort after the divorce to re-enter the labour market. Therefore spousal support is granted to the ex-spouse for whom divorce produces an economic disadvantage (Article 97 CC). The judge bases his decision on the amount of spousal support to be granted on the following criteria: agreements made among

---

[8]See: Yogman et al. (1995), 60, Pfiffner et al. (2001): 366, Messer 1989: 44ff.

[9]See: Demo and Acock (1988): 619–648.

[10]See: European Statistic Yearbook (2006): 9.

[11]According to the data provided by the Spanish National Institute of Statistics, the mean age of first marriage in Spain is 30.8 years for women and 33.8 years for men (data gained within the period 1980–2006). The mean age for a Spanish woman to give birth to her first child is 30.9 years (2006). The mean age among divorced women is 40.5 years and 42.8 years for men. The mean duration of marriage is 15.1 years (see: Movimiento Natural de la Población y Estadística de Nulidades, Separaciones y Divorcios, INE).

the spouses, spouse's age and state of health, formation and access to labour market, past and future dedication to family duties, the duration of marriage and others.[12] In his interpretation of Article 97 Marín López distinguishes spousal support from any other form of compensation or credit:

> "En cuanto a su naturaleza jurídica, la nueva redacción del artículo 97evidencia que no se trata de una indemnización por la ruptura del matrimonio, ni una prestación de alimentos, sino que tiende a ≪compensar≫ el desequilibrio económico sufrido por el cónyuge que la solicita. Su finalidad no es otra que la de colocar al cónyuge perjudicado por la ruptura del vínculo matrimonial en una situación de potencial igualdad de oportunidades – singularmente laboral y económicos – a la que habría tenido a no haber mediado tal matrimonio (. . .)." (Marín López 2009: 222)

In the present investigation we are interested in the amount and duration of spousal support payment ordered by judges to be given to the economically weaker part. The divorce contract forms the fifth element of the conceptual frame. Although a majority of couples does not normally set up a divorce contract, within the last decade, divorce contracts have become more popular in Spain as well as in other European countries.[13] Thus, a couple may set up conditions in advance and make decisions about the distribution of the property and assets gained during marriage for the hypothetical case of divorce in the future.

There are several reasons for this trend, such as: the increasing wealth of families, specifically of matrimonial property, a decline in marriage stability and an increasing responsibility for the social consequences of divorce. In fact, Ferrer i Riba, noticed a sharp increase in the number of couples who opted for a divorce contract between 1982 and 2001.[14] This trend started in 1982, 1 year after the reform of Spanish family, when divorce was introduced and private autonomy was supported.[15] During this time, the number of marriages declined and a rise in

---

[12]See: Art. 97.

El cónyuge al que la separación o divorcio produzca desequilibrio económico en relación con la posición del otro, que implique un empeoramiento en su situación anterior en el matrimonio, tiene derecho a una pensión que se fijará en la resolución judicial, teniendo en cuenta, entre otras, las siguientes circunstancias:

1°. Los acuerdos a que hubieren llegado los cónyuges. 2°. La edad y estado de salud. 3°. La cualificación profesional y las probabilidades de acceso a un empleo. 4°. La dedicación pasada y futura a la familia. 5°. La colaboración con su trabajo en las actividades mercantiles, industriales o profesionales del otro cónyuge. 6°. La duración del matrimonio y de la convivencia conyugal. 7°. La pérdida eventual de un derecho de pensión. 8°. El caudal y medios económicos y las necesidades de uno y otro cónyuge. En la resolución judicial se fijarán las bases para actualizar la pensión y las garantías para su efectividad." (Article 97, Spanish Civil Code).

[13]Ferrer i Riba distinguishes between the three types of contracts in his description of contracts in Spanish family law: contracts that regulate the organization of a present or future marriage, contracts that regulate the consequences of marriages in the process of breakdown and contracts that regulate the consequence of marriages breaking down in the future. (Hofer et. al. 2005: 275).

[14]See: Ferrer i Riba, quoted in: Hofer et al. (2005): 272.

[15]See: Ley 30/1981, de 7 de julio, por la que se modifica la regulación del matrimonio en el Código Civil y se determina el procedimiento a seguir en las causas de nulidad, separación y divorcio (BOE, 20. 7. 1981).

certified marriage contracts was reported. Whereas in 1982, a total of 15,000 contracts were signed, in 1992 the number increased to 29,000 and rose again in 2001, the total number of contracts peaked at 64,000. The author provides the following data:

> "(...) während die Eheschliessungsrate während der letzten zwanzig Jahre eher abgenommen hat, ist ein stetiger Anstieg von beurkundeten Ehevertägen zu verzeichnen: von 15,000 im Jahre 1982 (...) nahmen diese auf ca. 29,000 im Jahre 1992 und 64,000 im Jahre 2001 zu." (Hofer et al. 2005: 272)

Nevertheless, the Civil Code clearly distinguishes between personal assets ("bienes privativos") and joint assets ("bienes comunes or bienes ganaciales") within marriage. Personal assets include a spouse's property and rights acquired before the marriage, donations during the marriage, acquisitions made by a spouse's private property and those made by right of withdrawal, non-transferable patrimonial rights, compensation for injuries, clothes and personal belongings of minor value, necessary equipment for work purposes (Article 1346 CC).[16] Joint assets comprise all assets acquired by the spouses during the marriage, such as assets obtained by the work of either spouse, income or interests received form both, private and joint property, any acquisitions made by one or both spouses and businesses established during the marriage (Article 1347).[17]

In his chapter on agreements between spouses, Carrasco Perera, discusses Article 90 of the Civil Code and the validity of pre-divorce contracts to the regulating agreement.[18] According to the Spanish Civil Code, Article 1323, spouses

[16]See: "Artículo 1346.

Son privativos de cada uno de los cónyuges: 1. Los bienes y derechos que le pertenecieran al comenzar la sociedad. 2. Los que adquiera después por título gratuito. 3. Los adquiridos a costa o en sustitución de bienes privativos. 4. Los adquiridos por derecho de retracto perteneciente a uno solo de los cónyuges. 5. Los bienes y derechos patrimoniales inherentes a la persona y los no transmisibles inter vivos. 6. El resarcimiento por daños inferidos a la persona de uno de los cónyuges o a sus bienes privativos. 7. Las ropas y objetos de uso personal que no sean de extraordinario valor. 8. Los instrumentos necesarios para el ejercicio de la profesión u oficio, salvo cuando éstos sean parte integrante o pertenencias de un establecimiento o explotación de carácter común. Los bienes mencionados en los apartados 4. y 8. no perderán su carácter de privativos por el hecho de que su adquisición se haya realizado con fondos comunes; pero, en este caso, la sociedad será acreedora del cónyuge propietario por el valor satisfecho." (Código Civil, Art. 1346).

[17]See: "Artículo 1347.

Son bienes gananciales: 1. Los obtenidos por el trabajo o la industria de cualquiera de los cónyuges. 2. Los frutos, rentas o intereses que produzcan tanto los bienes privativos como los gananciales. 3. Los adquiridos a título oneroso a costa del caudal común, bien se haga la adquisición para la comunidad, bien para uno solo de los esposos. 4. Los adquiridos por derecho de retracto de carácter ganancial, aun cuando lo fueran con fondos privativos, en cuyo caso la sociedad será deudora del cónyuge por el valor satisfecho. 5. Las Empresas y establecimientos fundados durante la vigencia de la sociedad por uno cualquiera de los cónyuges a expensas de los bienes comunes. Si a la formación de la Empresa o establecimiento concurren capital privativo y capital común, se aplicará lo dispuesto en el artículo 1354." (Código Civil, Art. 1347).

[18]See: Carrasco Perera (2006): 52.

may transfer among each other any goods and rights and may make contracts of various kinds.[19] The author argues that transferable content is, however, limited by Spanish Civil Code (CC), Article 1328,[20] which voids any regulations that would either produce harm to the children or lead to inequalities among spouses. Accordingly, in her comment on Article 1328 Costas Rodal emphasizes that any stipulations of a divorce contract that are against imperative law are considered void. Such imperative norms include the spouses' equality and the protection of the children as well as customs and public order:

> "Son nulas las estipulaciones contrarias a las leyes imperativas: serían imperativas las normas de protección de terceros las que conforman el régimen matrimonial primario; a las buenas costumbres, como un pacto que impusiera a la mujer la licencia marital; o que no respeten la igualdad de derechos entre cónyuges: será nulo el pacto que instaura el régimen dotal entre los esposos o el pacto que conceda a uno solo de los cónyuges la administración o disposición de los bienes comunes (. . .)." (Costas Rodal quoted in Bercovitz Rodríguez-Cano 2006: 1574)

Generally, Carrasco Perera lists five reasons for a doctrine aimed at restricting the freedom to negotiate a matrimonial contract. The first reason is that spouses usually set up the conditions and details of the contract long before they can realistically anticipate and imagine a divorce. Second, after the divorce, one of the ex-spouses is usually economically disadvantaged which impedes his or her negotiation power. However, exactly this is a crucial phase when the disadvantaged spouse would need a stable position for the negotiations. Fourth, the conditions established in a pre-divorce contract often turn out to be against the best interests of the child and would therefore not be approved of. The author argues that the circumstances surrounding the actual separation are of higher relevance than those set long before it:

> "No solo por la intervención judicial sobre este tipo de acuerdos, sino porque, principalmente, este acuerdo sólo puede tener consistencia en la medida en que refleje la voluntad concorde de las partes en el momento de la ruptura. No puede seriamente pretenderse que el cónyuge que se obligó a renunciar a la custodia no pueda revocar este acuerdo." (Carrasco Perera 2006: 52f.)

A fifth objection is that matrimony as a long-term contract may be endangered by a change of conditions according to the rule of *rebus sic stantibus*. And fifth, the author considers it very unlikely that the spouses would modify their conduct according to rules prescribed for the hypothetical event of a divorce in the future divorce. After a description of the predictor for divorce decisions we shall now examine the legal frame within which such decisions are taken.

---

[19]See Article 1323 CC: "Los cónyuges podrán transmitirse por cualquier título bienes y derechos y celebrar entre sí toda clase de contratos." (Article 1323, Spanish Civil Code).

[20]See: "Art. 1.328.

Será nula cualquier estipulación contraria a las leyes o a las buenas costumbres o limitativa de la igualdad de derechos que corresponda a cada cónyuge." (Article 1328, Spanish Civil Code).

4.3 The Legal Context

A number of supranational legal instruments were designed to guarantee the fundamental rights of the family. These include the Universal Declaration of Human Rights (1948) which states that nobody is allowed to interfere in a person's private life, family or home (Article 12), that husband and wife are entitled to equal rights within marriage as well as after its dissolution (Article 16.1), and that the "family is the natural and fundamental group unit of society and is entitled to protection by society and the State" (Article 16.3.).[21]

The preamble of the United Nations Convention on the Rights of the Child underlines that the family environment provides the best conditions for child well-being and development.[22] According to the Convention a child's right to maintain family relations shall be guaranteed by the states (Article 8). Children shall not be separated from their parents against their will, except for cases in which parental contact would be against the best interests of the child. If the child is separated from his or her parents the child has the right to stay in contact with both parents on a regular basis (Article 9). The state has to provide alternative care for the child if remaining in the family environment would be harmful to the child (Article 20). Thereby, the Convention acknowledges the child's right of contact to both parents and views the parent–child relationship of vital importance.

However, if a parent's right to maintain contact to his or her child is grossly neglected he or she may draw on supranational principles. This applies to cases in which one parent denies the other parent to see the children, such as in the Parental Alienation Syndrome.[23] According to Article 8 of the Convention for the Protection of Human Rights and Fundamental Freedoms family life and privacy are especially protected against state interference.[24] In practice, parents are asked to opt for the parenting regime that best suits them and the family judge assesses the individual case if the custody agreement is in the best interest of the child (Articles 90, 91). This normative ascertainment includes rights on both sides; the child's right to

[21]See: The Universal Declaration of Human Rights (1948).

[22]See: United Nations Convention on the Rights of the Child (1990). Its aim is to protect children and support their well-being, prevent discrimination and respect their right to be heard in all matters that are of relevance to them.

[23]See the following sentences, in which judges recognized the Parental Alienation Syndrome as a reason for sanctions: SAP Vizcaya (JUR\2008\130045), SAP Murcia (JUR\2006\240424), SAP Madrid (JUR\2002\111924). See: Segura et al. (2006): 117–128, Baker 2005: 289–302, Vassiliou and Cartwright (2001): 181–191, Gómez Magán (2008): 63–78.

[24]The Convention came into force on 3 September 1953 and its aim is to protect rights and freedoms such as the right to liberty and security, the right to respect for private and family life, freedom of thought, conscience and religion etc. Article 8 of the Convention says:

maintain a relationship with both parents and the parent's right to keep in contact with the child.[25]

The Convention for the Protection of Human Rights and Fundamental Freedoms contains the principle of equality between ex-spouses. Its provisions point to each parent's equal right to maintain a (separate) parent–child relationship after divorce. Similarly, the Charter on Fundamental Rights of the European Union says that the right of each child to have contact to both parents must be respected (Article 24).[26] Thus it aims to guarantee a person's rights not to be discriminated on any ground, such as gender, race, colour, language, religion, political or other opinion, national or social origin (Article 14).

The process of European integration based on the free movement of goods, services and capital has created an interest in harmonizing European private law. The fact that there has been a growing number of bi-national families has generated a demand to harmonize family law in Europe. This would provide legal instruments especially for divorce cases in which the difference in national legislations causes difficulties, postpones or impedes a judicial solution. Therefore an international group of scholars founded the Commission on European Family Law (CEFL) in 2001.[27] Their aim is to promote comparative research in family law, to examine the possibility of a common core in legal solutions and to study the role of new member states for the harmonization process. The Commission has set up principles in the fields of divorce and maintenance, parental responsibilities and property relations. For the analysis of the divorce sentences we will now turn to the characteristic

---

[25]Several cases of fathers have been reported who took court proceedings at national courts of appeal or at the European Court of Human Rights against their ex-wives or earlier cohabitating partners because they refused them contact to their children. Court reactions were diverse and ranged from a reduction of child support payments, transfer of custody to the alienated parent, withdrawal of legal authority from the alienating parent to severe cases where the alienating parent was forewarned to be sanctioned with coercive detention. See the following cases in Germany and Austria: OLG Bamberg, 23.7.1985 - 7 UF 42/85; OLG Frankfurt, 29.1.1993 - 6 UF 125/92; OLG München, 12.4.91 - 26 UF 1464/89; OLG Celle, 25.10.1993 - 19 UF 208/93; OLG Bamberg, 28.3.1996, 7 WF 49/96; OLG München, 8.5.1996 - 12 WF 712/96; OLG Karlsruhe, 21.1.2000 - 16 WF 102/99; OLG Frankfurt, 4.5.2000 - 3 UF 146/99; OLG Frankfurt am Main, 3.9.2002 - 1 UF 103/00; Sahin *v*. Deutschland & Sommerfeld *v*. Deutschland, EGMR, 08.07.2003, Beschwerdenr./Aktenzahl: 30943/96 und 31871/96; Andrzej Cernecki *v*. Österreich, EGMR, 11.07.2000, Beschwerdenr./Aktenzahl: 31061/96; Elsholz *v*. Deutschland, EGMR, 13.07.2000, Beschwerdenr./Aktenzahl: 25735/94; P. E. *v*. Österreich, EKMR, 03.12.1997, Beschwerdenr./Aktenzahl: 31179/96.

[26]The Charter on Fundamental Rights of the European Union makes reference at children's rights in Article 24: "Article 24. The rights of the child: 1. Children shall have the right to such protection and care as is necessary for their well-being. They may express their views freely. Such views shall be taken into consideration on matters which concern them in accordance with their age and maturity. 2. In all actions relating to children, whether taken by public authorities or private institutions, the child's best interests must be a primary consideration. 3. Every child shall have the right to maintain on a regular basis a personal relationship and direct contact with both his or her parents, unless that is contrary to his or her interests." (Official Journal of the European Communities C 364/13, 18.12.2000, see http://www.europarl.europa.eu/charter/pdf/text_en.pdf).

[27]See: Commission of European Family Law (http://www2.law.uu.nl/priv/cefl/).

features of Spanish family law, describe the relevant statutes and enactments and analyse the legal doctrine to be applied.

4.4 Spanish Family Law

Although we base our analysis on the family law rules of the *Código Civil*, it is not valid throughout the territory of Spain but several of the 17 Spanish Autonomous Communities have their own legislations.[28] These are called foral laws ("derechos especiales o forales") and they contain specific rules for most matters that have principal validity over the Spanish Civil Code.[29] According to the Civil Code (Articles 13–15) foral laws are valid for citizens who possess the citizenship of the respective Autonomous Community.[30] The following Autonomous Communities have foral laws: Catalonia,[31] Navarra,[32] Balearic Islands,[33] the Basque Country,[34] Galicia,[35] and Aragon.[36] As a description of the different foral laws of these Autonomous Communities would go beyond the scope of this book this section deals mainly with the family law stated in the Civil Code.

In 2005 Spanish Family Law was reformed by the Ley 15/2005, de 8 de Julio in the field of separation and divorce and civil procedure.[37] In this reform the following articles of Book I, Title IV concerning spousal duties (Chap. V),

---

[28]There are presently 17 Autonumous Communities (Andalucía, Cataluña, Madrid, Valencia, Galicia, Castilla y León, País Vasco, Canarias, Castilla-La Mancha, Murcia, Aragón, Extremadura, Baleares, Asturias, Navarra, Cantabria, La Rioja) and two Autonumous Cities (Ceuta and Melilla). An Autonomous Community is a territorial entity within the constitutional system of Spain, which is equipped with autonomous legislative and executive powers and its own representatives. The structure of the Autonomous Communities of Spain is reflected in Article 2 of the Spanish Constitution of 1978 which recognizes and guarantees the right to autonomy of the Communities that form the State.

[29]See: Hofer et al. (2005): 273.

[30]Citizenship of an Autonumous Community ("vecindad civil") is acquired by birth from parents who hold regional citizenship (Article 14.2. CC). If parents hold different citizenships they may decide for their child which citizenship he or she should take. Citizenship may also be acquired after two years of uninterrupted residence in the corresponding Autonomous Community upon application (Article 14.5.1. CC) and is given automatically after an uninterrupted residence of ten years, unless the citizen declares otherwise (Article 14.5.2. CC).

[31]See: Catalan Law 9/1998 of 15.7.1998, del Codí de familia. See also: Martín Casals, (1999): 283–289.

[32]See: Navarra Foral Law 1/1973 of 1.3.1973, Compilación de Derecho Civil Foral de Navarra.

[33]See: Balearic Islands, decree 79/1990 of 6.9.1990, Compilación de Derecho Civil de Baleares.

[34]See: Law of the Basque Country 3/1992, del Derecho Civil Foral del País Vasco.

[35]See: Galicia Law 4/1995, de Derecho Civil de Galicia.

[36]See: Aragon Law 3/1985 Compilación de Derecho Civil de Aragón.

[37]See: Ley 15/2005, de 8 de julio, por la que se modifican el Código Civil y la Ley de Enjuiciamiento Civil en materia de separación y divorcio (BOE, núm. 163, de 09-07-2005, pp. 24458-24461). See: Appendix, Spanish Civil Code 1889 (CC), Ley 15/2005.

separation (Chap. VI) and divorce (Chap. VII) were modified: 68, 81, 84, 86, 90, 92, 97, Article 82 was cancelled.[38] Taking into account the rule of gender equity the legislator introduced the principle of co-responsibility with the aim of facilitating a smooth marital coexistence and promote cooperation among dual earner couples. Accordingly, Article 68 contains the rule of co-responsibility stating that the spouses should share their domestic responsibilities and the care for family members.

One major motive for the reform was to support the spouses' freedom to file for separation (Article 81) and divorce (Article 86) unilaterally.[39] For cases in which a marriage has broken down irretrievably and the spouses want to end it the law stipulates clearly that the spouses are no longer forced to sacrifice their personal freedom for incomprehensible reasons.[40] As such, they do not need to give any ground for their decision to divorce, a condition that had been required before the reform. The fault-regime that had governed divorce prior to the reform was changed to a no-fault regime and Article 82 was annulled.[41] As such, the legislator has established the basis for the spouses to exercise their personal freedom and enhance their private autonomy.[42]

---

[38]For a detailed study on the modifications see: Martín-Casals and Ribot (2006): 1331–1336, Martínez de Aguirre, (2008): 16ff.

[39]In the introduction to the law reference is made to Article 10.1. of the Spanish Constitution which guarantees the personal right to a free development of one's personality: "De acuerdo con ellos, esta ley persigue ampliar el ámbito de libertad de los cónyuges en lo relativo al ejercicio de la facultad de solicitar la disolución de la relación matrimonial. Con este propósito, se estima que el respeto al libre desarrollo de la personalidad, garantizado por el artículo 10.1 de la Constitución, justifica reconocer mayor trascendencia a la voluntad de la persona cuando ya no desea seguir vinculado con su cónyuge." (Ley 15/2005).

[40]In this context Law 15/2005 states that it is the aim of law courts to avoid a prolongation of marital conflicts especially when the marraige has broken down irretrievably: "Los tribunales de justicia, sensibles a esta evolución, han aplicado en muchos casos la ley y han evitado, de un lado, la inconveniencia de perpetuar el conflicto entre los cónyuges, cuando en el curso del proceso se hacía patente tanto la quiebra de la convivencia como la voluntad de ambos de no continuar su matrimonio, y de otro, la inutilidad de sacrificar la voluntad de los individuos demorando la disolución de la relación jurídica por razones inaprensibles a las personas por ella vinculadas." (Ley 15/2005).

[41]Ley 15/2005 expressly states that the spouses are not obliged to give any reasons for their decision to separate: "Así, el ejercicio de su derecho a no continuar casado no puede hacerse depender de la demostración de la concurrencia de causa alguna, pues la causa determinante no es más que el fin de esa voluntad expresada en su solicitud, ni, desde luego, de una previa e ineludible situación de separación." (Ley 15/2005).

[42]This is emphasized in the outline of the inspiring motives for the reform: "La reforma que se acomete pretende que la libertad, como valor superior de nuestro ordenamiento jurídico, tenga su más adecuado reflejo en el matrimonio. El reconocimiento por la Constitución de esta institución jurídica posee una innegable trascendencia, en tanto que contribuye al orden político y la paz social, y es cauce a través del cual los ciudadanos pueden desarrollar su personalidad." (Ley 15/2005) See also a person's right to develop his or her personality freely as stated in the Spanish Constitution (Article 10.1.).

Personal freedom is always situated within a certain socio-political and economic context. In other words, a spouse's preferences expressed in a regulating agreement will largely depend on his or her socio-economic conditions.[43] There are relevant factors, such as access to the labor market for the divorced parent and availability of affordable accommodation that will determine to what extent an ex-spouse is actually able to pursue his or her personal interests. In their article on the labour market conditions and family policy and their impact on young Spaniards' life trajectories Baizán, Michielin and Billari argue, however, that the extended family model in Spain does not particularly favour the process of personal individualization. They see the reason for this trend in the fact that the present welfare state promotes a traditional family model:

> "(...) the powerful internalization of welfare within the family implies that it would be much more difficult for young Spaniards to cultivate unorthodox living arrangements. Instead, they have positive incentives to count on family solidarity. New living arrangements such as living alone or in a consensual union, as well as divorces, and lone parenthood are penalized for powerful reasons. As shown above, the welfare state and its social policies do not support these "individualistic" living arrangements." (Baizán et al. 2002: 199)

In the Law on Gender Equality the legislator has especially taken into consideration the difficulties that mothers with dependent children may face and has taken measures to facilitate access to affordable accommodation.[44] Another novelty of Law 15/2005 concerns procedural aspects of the divorce which enables spouses to file for divorce directly without submitting an application for separation (Article 81) beforehand.[45] Separation may proceed in a consensual (*separación de mutuo acuerdo*) or non-consensual way (*separación contenciosa*), whereby in the first case a proposal for a regulating agreement is to be presented at the family court.[46]

---

[43]These conditions comprise age, level of formation, status in society and property held. Moreover personal autonomy is also influenced by the family policy pursued by the state, such as for instance benefits for the economically disadvantaged spouse to balance his or her living standard (e.g. child and housing benefit, single parent tax reduction, access to accommodation, legal support and mediation at affordable cost). For a comparison of different family law policies in European Members States see Chapter 2 and studies by Andreß et al. (2006): 533–560, Velarde (2006): 38–54.

[44]On accommodation see especially the Spanish Law on Gender Equality which contains provisions on urban policy, territorial organisation and housing (Article 31.2.). It states that the government aims at providing access to accommodation for custodial mothers who find themselves in a precarious situation or at risk of social exclusion. For more details see Chapter 2 (Ley Orgánica para la igualdad efectiva de mujeres y hombres, 2007: 12618).

[45]See the exposition of the motives for the Ley 15/2005, in which separation and divorce are described as two ways by which intractable marital conflicts may be ended: "En suma, la separación y el divorcio se concibe como dos opciones, a las que las partes pueden acudir para solucionar las vicisitudes de su vida en común." (Ley 15/2005, de 8 de julio, por la que se modifican el Código Civil y la Ley de Enjuiciamiento Civil en materia de separación y divorcio, BOE, 163, 2005: 24458–24461).

[46]Equally, the separation may start in a non-consensual way and the spouses may eventually reach an agreement during the separation process.

If parents do not present a regulating agreement, the judge will make decisions on all respective issues (Articles 91, 96). These decisions may, however, been altered as circumstances demand (Article 91).

The legislator has adapted the Law of Civil Procedure in the Field of Separation and Divorce to these changes and Articles 770, 771, 775 and 777 of the Law of Civil Procedure of Chap. IV on Processes referring Matrimony and Minor Children were modified.[47] In Article 771.2 on the Provisional Measures taken prior to Nullity, Separation and Divorce a legal rule was added which gives the parties the opportunity to reach an agreement at the court hearing.[48] Likewise, the parties may reach and agreement through family mediation as indicated in Article 777.2.[49]

In the following section we will deal with the legal nature of the regulating agreement (convenio regulador) and discuss its requirements.

4.4.1 Regulating Agreement

According to Article 90 of the Spanish Civil Code, the spouses are requested to set up a proposal on the following issues: legal authority and custody including visiting plans for the non-resident parent and grandparents (Article 90.1), attribution of the family accommodation and household equipment (Article 90.3), contribution to matrimonial expenses and child payment (Article 90.4), liquidation of the economic matrimonial union (Article 90.5), and spousal support (Article 90.6).[50] Parents may

---

[47]See: Ley 1/2000, de 7 de enero, de Enjuiciamiento Civil, documented in BOE núm. 7, de 8 de enero del 2000, pp. 575–728.

[48]See: "Articlulo 771.2: Artículo 771. Medidas provisionales previas a la demanda de nulidad, separación o divorcio. Solicitud, comparecencia y resolución.

2. A la vista de la solicitud, el Tribunal mandará citar a los cónyuges y, si hubiere hijos menores o incapacitados, al Ministerio Fiscal, a una comparecencia, en la que se intentará un acuerdo de las partes y que se celebrará en los diez días siguientes. A dicha comparecencia deberá acudir el cónyuge demandado asistido por su abogado y representado por su Procurador." (This paragraph was modified in accordance with Law 15/2005 and the Law of Civil Procedure, documented in BOE, 163: 24458–24461.).

[49]See: "Artículo 777. Separación o divorcio solicitados de mutuo acuerdo o por uno de los cónyuges con el consentimiento del otro. (...) 2. Al escrito por el que se promueva el procedimiento deberá acompañarse la certificación de la inscripción del matrimonio y, en su caso, las de inscripción de nacimiento de los hijos en el Registro Civil, así como la propuesta de convenio regulador conforme a lo establecido en la legislación civil y el documento o documentos en que el cónyuge o cónyuges funden su derecho, incluyendo, en su caso, el acuerdo final alcanzado en el procedimiento de mediación familiar. Si algún hecho relevante no pudiera ser probado mediante documentos, en el mismo escrito se propondrá la prueba de que los cónyuges quieran valerse para acreditarlo".

[50]See Article 90 of the Spanish Civil Code: "El convenio regulador a que se refieren los artículos 81 y 86 de este Código deberá contener, al menos, a los siguientes extremos:

A) El cuidado de los hijos sujetos a la patria potestad de ambos, el ejercicio de esta y, en su caso, el régimen de comunicación y estancia de los hijos con el progenitor que lo viva habitualmente con ellos. B) Si se considera necesario, el régimen de visitas y comunicación de los nietos con sus abuelos, teniendo en cuenta, siempre, el interés de aquéllos. C) La atribución del uso de la vivienda

also include a proposal for a visiting regime between children and grandparents (Article 90.B).[51]

Concerning the legal nature of the regulating agreement Montero Aroca points out that it is not an optional document containing partial agreements over specific economic questions of joint interests. On the contrary, it is a statute with legally binding character that regulates all the economic questions concerning the divorcing spouses and all questions affecting the children. The author gives the following description:

> "El convenio regulador no es, pues, un documento en el que se plasman los acuerdos parciales a que los cónyuges lleguen para conformar algunas de as cuestiones económicas entre ellos o de las cuestiones que afectan a los hijos menores, sino que es un verdadero estatuto ordenador de todas las cuestiones económicas relativas a los cónyuges (o ex cónyuges) y de todas las cuestiones propias de los hijos." (Montero Aroca 2002: 17)

The regulating agreement is considered both, a marital statute and a family negotiation that has legal character. Accordingly, Marín López views it a legal institute in which a spousal contract is combined with judicial authority, whereby the spouses take up the function that a judge would have had if the agreement would no have existed.[52] He says:

> "El convenio regulador puede definirse como el negocio jurídico familiar, que tiene carácter mixto, por intervenir los cónyuges y la autoridad judicial (...), que contiene las medidas definitivas que se aplicarán tras la sentencia definitiva de nulidad, separación o divorcio, supliendo de este modo la función que debería realizar el juez *ex* artículo 91 de no existir tal convenio regulador (...)." (Bercovitz Rodríguez-Cano 2006: 210)

However, this dual character does not seem free of inconsistencies. Various scholars have commented on the legal nature of the regulating agreement, for instance, Montero Aroca criticizes that neither the legal doctrine nor jurisprudence

---

y ajuar familiar. D) La contribución a las cargas del matrimonio y alimentos, así como sus bases de actualización y garantías en su caso. E) La liquidación, cuando proceda, del régimen económico del matrimonio. F) La pensión que conforme al artículo 97 correspondiere satisfacer, en su caso, a uno de los cónyuges. Los acuerdos de los cónyuges, adoptados para regular las consecuencias de la nulidad, separación o divorcio serán aprobados por el juez, salvo si son dañosos para los hijos o gravemente perjudiciales para uno de los cónyuges. Si las partes proponen un régimen de visitas y comunicación de los nietos con los abuelos, el juez podrá aprobarlo previa audiencia de los abuelos en la que éstos presten su consentimiento. La denegación de los acuerdos habrá de hacerse mediante resolución motivada y en este caso los cónyuges deben someter a la consideración del juez nueva propuesta para su aprobación, si procede. Desde la aprobación judicial, podrán hacerse efectivos por la vía de apremio. Las medidas que el Juez adopte en defecto de acuerdo, o las convenidas por los cónyuges, podrán ser modificadas judicialmente o por nuevo convenio cuando se alteren sustancialmente las circunstancias. El Juez podrá establecer las garantías reales o personales que requiera el cumplimiento del convenio." (Article 90, Spanish Civil Code).

[51]Grandparents may be received in audience by the judge. The right of contact between grandparents and grandchildren was included by Ley 42/2003.

[52]See: Marín López in Bercovitz Rodríguez-Cano 2006: 210.

have presented a clear definition of the exact legal nature of the regulating agreement.[53] As a result, the whole concept remained indistinct. He speaks of a double nature of the regulating agreement whereby its contractual dimension, depending on the actual situation, is sometimes affirmed and on other occasions negated. He says:

> "La jurisprudencia ha mantenido una cierta vacilación, en ocasiones negando su carácter contractual y luego afirmándolo, para llegar a dos posiciones: a) La autonomía de voluntad, en general (y) b) (su) Transacción sometida a condición". (Montero Aroca 2002: 69 f.)

Generally, the spouses' freedom to negotiate their preferred post-divorce conditions for the regulating agreement is limited by the following three constraints: the provisions must be in accordance with the general provisions on contracts (Article 1255, 1275, 1116), they must not be contrary to law (Article 7) and they must never be harmful to children or cause disadvantages to the ex-spouse (Article 90).

The concept of 'the best interests of the child', in Spanish 'el interés del menor' or 'interés del hijo', is a central issue in all legal orders and a decisive criterion for divorce sentences. The concept is not related to the moment or a short period in a child's life but refers to the whole childhood and teenage period until the age of majority. Most national civil codes contain the doctrine of the "best interests" of the child in order to address children's rights in the context of divorce.[54] Rivero Hernández points out that within Spanish family law reference to the best interest of the child is made in explicit and implicit ways.[55] Several legal rules explicitly refer to a child's best interests, such as, for instance, in the legislation concerning matrimonial crisis (Articles 90, 92, 94, 103), child support (Article 149), legal authority (Articles 154, 156, 159, 161, 170), recognition of filiation (Articles 121, 124 and 125), adoption (Articles 176, 180), and guardianship (Articles 216, 234, 235, 239, 245, 246).[56]

The best interest of the child is particularly recognized in Article 92, which states that the child has to be heard by the court on custody related questions. Paragraph four of the same Article stipulates that legal authority is to be arranged in such a way that it benefits the child. The judge may even decree joint custody if this is the only way of achieving a child's best interests (Article 92.8. CC and Article 39 CE). In this case the judge has to ground his decision on a favourable report of the Public

---

[53]See: Montero Aroca (2002): 69 f.

[54]The doctrine has its roots in the principle of "parens patriae" which is part of the Common Law tradition and is grounded on the rule of "favor filii" or "favor minoris". The condition for the overall protection of the family, and in particular, of underage children, is also established in Article 39 of the Spanish Constitution.

[55]See: Rivero Hernández (2007): 64.ff., see also Zarraluqui (2006): 50ff. on the explicit and implicit consideration of a child's best interests.

[56]The principle of the best interest of the child are also reflected in the Law of Civil Procedure of 1/2000 of 7 January (Ley de Enjuiciamiento Civil). See in particular the Articles 769 to 778 in Chapter IV on Procedure of Matrimony and Minor Children (De los procesos matrimoniales y de menores), BOE, 7, 2000: 575–728.

Prosecution. The family judge may also ask for an expert opinion of a specialist ascribed to the family court (Article 92.9).

Article 90.5 stipulates that the judge consents the parental agreement, unless it is considered it harmful to the child or detrimental to one parent. Only if it disregards a child's best interests or a parent's integrity is the judge obliged to reject the regulating agreement. The judicial prevention of any adverse effects on children or ex-spouse is an example for an implicit consideration of the best interest-principle.[57]

Although the legal doctrine is part of most civil codes and judges refer to it as an acknowledged legal concept, it lacks a precise definition. As an indefinite legal term a child's best interest is interpreted once it is applied to a specific case.[58] The complexity of the concept is due to the psychological, legal and socio-economic criteria that are part of it and have to be taken into consideration. It encodes a general conception of individual child well-being but the doctrine obtains its exact meaning only when it is applied to a particular context. As such, the "best interests" imply that overall child well-being corresponds to a positive development on a child's physical, intellectual, emotional and social level.[59] We may speak of a contended childhood if it enables the child to care for his or her own well-being later in life.

Relevant determinants for the application of the concept are a child's age (physical and cognitive development) and the socio-economic and cultural circumstances of the family. Three levels of types of hierarchically structured interests seem to be relevant in minor children, such as basic interests, developmental and autonomy interests. Once these needs such as physical care and emotional attention are satisfied the child usually develops own preferences and likes. The autonomy interest stands for a child's urge to act sometimes freely without parental supervision.[60] The cultivation of these three types of interests contributes to the child's integral development.

Within the Spanish Civil Code the principle of the best interests of a child is acknowledged in the statute on a parent's rights and duties associated with legal authority, 'patria potestad' (Articles 110, 154, 156, 160, 162, 164, 168). Two

[57]For a discussion of role and function of the report of the Public Prosection in the attribution of joint custody and whether the new legislation delimits the judge's competence, see Hernando Ramos (2009): 7–9 and Campo Izquierdo (2009): 10–12.

[58]Every legal system makes use of indefinite legal concepts because there is a need for legal rules that cover cases of similar characteristics but with different circumstances. Such concepts are described as consisting of a core meaning and a general meaning. In the case of a child's best interests, Kühne underlines that the interpretation of such concepts often depends on the perspective that is applied by experts of distinct professions. She points to the different significance that experts tend to ascribe to a child's best interests depending on the special field to which they belong. (Kühne 2006: 189).

[59]The right of physical well-being entitles a child to be cared for in the best possible way and to experience beneficial circumstances that provide comfort and security. Intellectual well-being implies the development of cognitive and social skills which is conditional for the ability to establish relationships. Equal importance has the right of social well-being which is the ability to establish ties within the peer group, to develop a sense of community.

[60]See: Rivero Hernández (2007): 101.

essential elements form part of legal authority, such as the duty to bestow guardianship and the obligation to guarantee custody. These duties contribute to the satisfaction of both, a child's material and non-material needs. The physical or material needs stand for custody and alimentation whereas the non-material or spiritual needs stand for psychological, intellectual, emotional, social needs. In his exploration of the concept of the best interest of the child, Rivero Hernández names a parent's most relevant obligations inherent in legal authority, such as education and legal representation. A parent has the duty to educate his or her child in a broad sense and is obliged to take legal decisions on behalf of the offspring. These two obligations cover a child's personal interests:

> "Los aspectos más relevantes de esa función y competencia (dirigir la vida del menor), por lo que aquí interesa, afectan eminentemente a la educación (en sentido muy amplio) y representación (adopción d decisiones jurídicas) del hijo menor de edad, porque el interés de éste, en el sentido en que es contemplado por las normas tantas veces invocadas que aluden a él, se refiere sobre todo al aspecto personal e intereses personales (espirituales más que materiales) del menor." (Rivero Hernández 2007: 214)

All these aspects form the basis for a child's ability to become gradually independent from the care-giving person. The view of children as autonomous human beings is especially outlined in the provisions of the Law on the Juristic Protection of Minor Children.[61] Likewise, children have the right to stay free of any accusations or allegations in the context of their parents' divorce.[62] Children are no longer considered as passive recipients of their environment but rather as active social beings interrelating dynamically with family, relatives and friends. Not only are they capable of creating their own personal space by identifying and satisfying their needs but they also learn to meet the needs of others during socialization. This view of children as participating and creative beings is also reflected in the Law on the Legal Protection of Minors, which states in its introduction:

> "El ordenamiento jurídico, y esta Ley en particular, va reflejando progresivamente una concepción de las personas menores de edad como sujetos activos, participativos y creativos, con capacidad de modificar su propio medio personal y social; de participar en la búsqueda y satisfacción de sus necesidades y en la satisfacción de las necesidades de los demás." (Ley Orgánica 1/1996)[63]

[61]See the provisions of the Ley Orgánica de Protección Jurídica del Menor in which the protection of children's autonomy is considered one of the pillars of judicial systems. The law conatins the following considerations: "El conocimiento científico actual nos permite concluir que no exciste una diferencia tajante entre las necesidades de protección y las necesidades relacionadas con la autonomía del sujeto, sino que la mejor forma de garantizar social y jurídicamente la protección a la infancia es promover su autonomía como sujetos. (...) Y, por lo tanto, es el reto para todos los ordenamientos jurídicos y los dispositivos de promoción y protección de las personas menores de edad. (Ley Orgánica de Protección Jurídica del Menor 1/1996: 3).

[62]See: Article 92.2 of Spanish Civil Code which states that the judge will procure that the child's right to be heard on any decisions referring custody and education is maintained.

[63]See: Ley Orgánica 1/1996, de 15 de enero, de Protección Jurídica del Menor, de modificación parcial del Código Civil y de la Ley de Enjuiciamiento Civil.

Coester gives a comprehensive overview of the decisive factors for judicial decisions concerning the best interests of the child.[64] The author lists the following criteria to elicit child well-being, such as the continuity and stability of educational conditions, the internal bonds of the child, the positive relationship with both parents, the attitude of parents and children to organize the post-divorce relationship and the child's intention as an expression of the self and as a measure for attachment. The determination of a child's best interest depends also on the specific educational goals that exist in a society.

According to Spanish family law a child's best interests in the post-divorce context are established in the concept of legal authority which shall be dealt with in the following section.

4.4.2 Legal Authority

The rights and duties associated with legal authority or '*patria potestad*' are regulated in Title VII of the Spanish Civil Code on the relations between parents and their children. The '*patria potestad*' is a right of dual character as it is held by both parents. The provisions of Article 154 include the following parental rights and faculties: to have the children in one's company and take care of them, to represent them and administrate their goods. The children have the right to be heard before custody decisions are taken that affect them.[65]

Although both parents are entitled to hold legal authority[66] they may however decide that one parent mainly exercises it (Article 156).[67] However, the other parent does not loose the right to have contact to the children (Article 160). If parents live separately legal authority is exercised by the one parent with whom the child resides

---

[64]See: Coester (1983): 176–203.

[65]See Article 154 CC: "Los hijos no emancipados están bajo la potestad de los padres. La patria potestad se ejercerá siempre en beneficio de los hijos, de acuerdo con su personalidad, y con respeto a su integridad física y psicológica. Esta potestad comprende los siguientes deberes y facultades: 1.° Velar por ellos, tenerlos en su compañía, alimentarlos, educarlos y procurarles una formación integral. 2.° Representarlos y administrar sus bienes. Si los hijos tuvieren suficiente juicio deberán ser oídos siempre antes de adoptar decisiones que les afecten. Los padres podrán, en el ejercicio de su potestad, recabar el auxilio de la autoridad." (Spanish Civil Code, Article 154).

[66]The legal authority is a fundamental parental right and can only be withdrawn through a court decision as stipulated in Article 111 CC: "Artículo 111 Quedará excluido de la patria potestad y demás funciones tuitivas y no ostentará derechos por ministerio de la Ley respecto del hijo o de sus descendientes, o en sus herencias el progenitor: 1. Cuando haya sido condenado a causa de las relaciones a que obedezca la generación, según sentencia penal firme. 2. Cuando la filiación haya sido judicialmente determinada contra su oposición. (. . .)." (Spanish Civil Code (CC), Article 111).

[67]See: "Artículo 156.

(. . .) Si los padres viven separados, la patria potestad se ejercerá por aquel con quien el hijo conviva. Sin embargo, el Juez, a solicitud fundada del otro progenitor, podrá, en interés del hijo, atribuir al solicitante la patria potestad para que la ejerza conjuntamente con el otro progenitor o distribuir entre el padre y la madre las funciones inherentes a su ejercicio." (Spanish Civil Code, Article 156).

(Article 156). If separated parents do not reach an agreement on the exercise of legal authority the judge bestows custody to one parent (Article 159). In this context, Montero Aroca distinguishes between entitlement to legal authority (‘*titularidad*’) and the actual rights and duties that are associated with its exercise (‘*ejercicio*’) thereof, by the custodial parent.[68] He gives the following explanation:

> “Si en principio la patria potestad se ejerce conjuntamente por ambos progenitores (Article 156, I, CC), cuando éstos viven separados aquella se ejercerá por el progenitor con quien el hijo conviva (Article 156, V), lo que supone que el acuerdo de los padres respecto de la guarda del hijo menor implica la atribución del ejercicio de la patria potestad. Estamos ante la distinción de la titularidad de la potestad (que es conjunta) y ejercicio de la misma (atribuido al progenitor que conviva con el hijo menor).” (Montero Aroca 2002: 107 f.)

This distinction is not always clearly understood. The reason is that some court sentences literally state that legal authority has been withdrawn from a non-custodial parent whereas in fact it was the exercise of legal authority that had been withdrawn:

> “La distinción no siempre se ha comprendido rectamente, pues de más de una sentencia pareciera que se desprende literalmente que se ha privado al progenitor non guardador de la patria potestad, cuando realmente se trata sólo de del ejercicio de la misma.” (Montero Aroca 2002: 109)

Likewise, in their interpretation of Article 156 CC Díez-Picazo and Gullón name the parents’ separation as one of three reasons[69] for the impossibility of a joint exercise of legal authority. They point to the vagueness in the wording of Article 156, specifically when it states that legal authority is bestowed to the parent who requests it in order to jointly exercise it (“*atribuir al solicitante la patria potestad para que la ejerza conjuntamente*”), it should actually be the exercise of the legal authority is bestowed to the parent who requests it. The author underlines that one parent can never interfere into the other parent’s right to legal authority:

> “Lo único claro de la norma es su supuesto de hecho: la falta de la convivencia de los padres, sin calificar su origen (. . .). Después se torna oscura. Efectivamente, parece que el criterio general es que en aquella hipótesis lo que hay que resolver es un problema de ejercicio y no de titularidad de la patria potestad, que la tendrán padre y madre. Pero se habla de ≪*atribuir* la patria potestad al solicitante para que la ejerza conjuntamente (. . .)≫, en lugar de atribuir ≪el ejercicio» conjunto simplemente. Creemos que la norma se refiere al ejercicio, porque no puede privarse de la titularidad a un progenitor por la petición del otro.” (Díez-Picazo and Gullón 2004: 269)

Legal authority implies that parents keep their right and duty to maintain contact with their children. This right is also guaranteed by Article 39 of the Spanish Constitution. Guilarte Martín-Calero (2005, 128)[70] points out that even if a parent is excluded from legal authority (Article 111 CC) or deprived of it (Article 110) as a

---

[68]Montero Aroca (2002): 107f.

[69]The authors name two more reasons for the impossibility of joint exercise of legal authority, such as simple or repeated disagreement among the ex-spouses and cases of defect, absence, incapacity or impossibility (Díez-Picazo and Gullón 2004: 269).

[70]See: Guilarte Martín-Calero (2005): 113–179.

sanction, he or she would still not be free of obligation for the child, such as caring for the child and paying child support.[71] This is because a parent's obligations for his or her child are neither linked to the rule of legal authority nor to marriage. The author gives the following explanation:

> "La patria potestad sobre los hijos se atribuye, por el hecho de la filiación, al padre y a la madre, salvo en los supuestos previstos en el artículo 111 del Código Civil que contempla la exclusión de la patria potestad cuando el progenitor haya sido condenado a causa de las relaciones a que obedezca la generación, según sentencia penal firme o cuando la filiación haya sido judicialmente determinada contra su oposición. (. . .) Sólo en estos casos queda excluida, como efecto legal de la filiación, la atribución de la patria potestad, cuya titularidad ostentan el padre y la madre desde el nacimiento del hijo hasta su extinción que se produce, según lo dispuesto en su artículo 169 del Código Civil, (. . .) y siempre, claro está, ninguno de ellos se vea privado de ella por sentencia fundada en el incumplimiento de los deberes inherentes a la misma o dictada en causa criminal o matrimonial/ artículo 170 del Código Civil)." (Guilarte Martín-Calero 2005: 135)

In cases where one or both parents are unable to provide for the child support stipulated by the judge, the Spanish State provides a necessary financial aid according to Royal Decree 1618/2007.[72] The aim of these provisions is to avoid any harm that children would suffer in a precarious family situation:

> "En nuestra sociedad actual se ha detectado un problema social derivado de los incumplimientos del pago de alimentos establecidos a favor de los hijos menores de edad en los supuestos de divorcio, separación, declaración de nulidad del matrimonio, o en procesos de filiación o de alimentos. (...) En ambos supuestos, el resultado es que se producen numerosas situaciones de precariedad para los hijos menores y, con ello, para la unidad familiar en que se integran junto con la persona que los tiene bajo su guarda y custodia." (Real Decreto 1618/2007: 51371)

In cases where the maintenance claim against the defendant party does not lead to payment the state stands in and provides the necessary financial aid thereby guaranteeing the child's best interest:

> "El Estado, ante el fracaso de la ejecución judicial del título que reconoció el derecho a alimentos, debe garantizar ante todo el superior interés del menor, sufragando con cargo a los fondos públicos las cantidades mínimas necesarias para que la unidad familiar en que se integra pueda atender a las necesidades del menor." (Real Decreto 1618/2007: 51371)

Parents who neglect their parental responsibilities of providing child support as stated in the regulating agreement approved by the judge trespass against Penal

[71]See STS de 24 de junio de 2004 que establece: "Excluir de la patria potestad a quien no la ejerció al no ser padre declarado del menor, no equivale al privarle a la patria potestad, concepto que comporta haberla ejercitado incurriendo en cause suficiente. La exclusión de la patria potestad se impone por ministerio de la Ley no por sentencia y se produce cuando el padre biológico no acepta su paternidad (. . .) la exclusión de la patria potestad constituye un imperativo para el juzgador, incluso aún cuando no hubiera sido formalmente solicitada." (STS de 24 de junio de 2004).

[72]On 17 December 2007 the Spanish Parliament passed an Act, the Real Decreto 1618/2007 that entered into force on 1 January 2008 with the aim of guaranteeing the payment of child support. (See: Real Decreto 1618/2007, de 7 de diciembre, sobre organización y funcionamiento del Fondo de Garantía del Pago de Alimentos BOE, 299: 51371–51376.).

Law, Article 618.2,[73] which sanctions such negligence by a fine or condemnation to community work. Similarly, Article 226 of the Criminal Law states that non-compliance with the duties inherent in legal authority will be punished with arrest from 8 to 20 weekends.[74] Additionally the judge may withdraw legal authority from a parent for a period of 4–10 years. In order to secure child support payment a parent's employer retains the amount of the salary corresponding to child support.

In his analysis of the concept of legal authority, Carrasco Perera concludes however, that the whole concept of legal authority seems to have lost its significance because it does not add any definite connotation to the legal parent–child relationship. More specifically, there are cases in which a non-custodial parent may have legal authority but can hardly exercise it. Conversely, a parent who is deprived of legal authority may still keep the right to have contact to his or her child. The author explains this in the following way:

> "Yo creo que ≪patria potestad≫ es un concepto que hoy ha perdido todo poder significativo, al no comportar ninguna connotación específica respecto del tipo de relación jurídica que existe entre padres e hijos. (. . .) Es inútil seguir estirando el concepto de patria potestad con objeto de dar cabida a todas las situaciones posibles en que pueden manifestarse las relaciones nacidas de la relación biológica de filiación." (Carrasco Perera 2006: 351)

In practice, the parent–child relationship may be coordinated in such a variety of ways such that one cannot make out legal authority as a leading principle behind all these different arrangements. The following section deals with the exercise of legal authority and possible forms of custody arrangements.

4.4.3 Custody

The concept of legal custody ('*guarda y custodia*') is inseparably linked to that of legal authority. The parents may agree on sole or joint exercise of their legal

---

[73]See: Ley Orgánica 10/1995, de 23 de noviembre, del Código Penal, Libro III., Faltas y Sus Penas, Título I. Faltas contra las Personas: "Artículo 618.

2. El que incumpliere obligaciones familiares establecidas en convenio judicialmente aprobado o resolución judicial en los supuestos de separación legal, divorcio, declaración de nulidad del matrimonio, proceso de filiación o proceso de alimentos a favor de sus hijos, que no constituya delito, será castigado con la pena de multa de 10 días a dos meses o trabajos en beneficio de la comunidad de uno a 30 días". (Spanish Penal Code, Article 618.2,)

[74]See: "Art 226 Abandono de familia.

1. El que dejare de cumplir los deberes legales de asistencia inherentes a la patria potestad, tutela, guarda o acogimiento familiar o de prestar la asistencia necesaria legalmente establecida para el sustento de sus descendientes, ascendientes o cónyuge, que se hallen necesitados, será castigado con la pena de prisión de tres a seis meses o multa de seis a 12 meses. 2. El Juez o Tribunal podrá imponer, motivadamente, al reo la pena de inhabilitación especial para el ejercicio del derecho de patria potestad, tutela, guarda o acogimiento familiar por tiempo de cuatro a diez años." (Spanish Criminal Law, Article 226).

authority in their regulating agreement taking into account the best interest of the child (Article 92.4.). Joint custody is granted if both parents agree on it or reach such agreement during the legal procedure (Article 92.5.). The judge has to ground the judicial decision on three conditions, a favourable report from the Public Prosecution, on a judicial hearing of the children if they have sufficient competence to judge, and on a report from a specialist ascribed to the Family Court (Article 92.6). Joint custody is not awarded if one parent is in criminal proceedings because of threatening or having harmed the physical or psychological integrity of the ex-spouse or the child (Article 92.7). Exceptionally, the judge may bestow joint custody, irrespective of parental agreement, if this is the only way of guaranteeing the best interest of the child (Article 92.8.). Guilarte Martín-Calero gives a general definition of custody and names the parental obligations towards their children such as alimentation, care, attention and education, formation and supervision as well as parental liability for any illegal acts caused by the children:

> "Puede definirse la guarda como aquella potestad que atribuye el derecho de convivir de forma habitual con los hijos menores o incapacitados, bien de forma permanente hasta que recaiga nuevo acuerdo o decisión judicial (atribución unilateral a un progenitor), bien de forma alterna en los periodos prefijados convencional o judicialmente (guarda compartida o alterna) y abarca todas las obligaciones que se originan en la vida diaria y ordinaria de los menores: la alimentación, el cuidado, la atención, educación en valores, formación, vigilancia y, desde luego, la responsabilidad por los hechos ilícitos provocados por los menores interviniendo su culpa o negligencia." (Guilarte Martín-Calero 2005: 136)

A review of the research literature shows a distinction between legal and physical custody in both, the Anglo-American and the Spanish legal systems. The table shows the corresponding terminology used to describe legal authority and custody in both systems (Fig. 4.2).

Joint physical custody refers to a parent-chosen and court-ordered system where the child stays with both parents at alternating intervals of days, weeks, months or even whole terms. The terminology plays a relevant role in the description of custody regulations. In his reflections on the expressions used in the recent reform of Spanish family law, the Ley 15/2006, Ivars Ruiz criticizes that the legal terms have not been sufficiently adjusted to the requirements of modern life.[75] The author refers particularly to Article 156.5, which states that if parents live separately the legal authority is naturally exercised by the one with whom the child resides.[76] He argues, that the expression "joint custody" does not add any new contents to what is already implied in the concept of legal authority:

> "Pero también lo es, que el párrafo quinto del mismo precepto señala que si los padres viven separados, la patria potestad se ejercerá por aquel con quien el hijo conviva. De manera que,

[75] Ivars Ruiz (2008): 35 f.

[76] See: Spanish Civil Code, Article 156, paragraph 5: "Si los padres viven separados, la patria potestad se ejercerá por aquel con quien el hijo conviva. Sin embargo, el Juez, a solicitud fundada del otro progenitor, podrá, en interés del hijo, atribuir al solicitante la patria potestad para que la ejerza conjuntamente con el otro progenitor o distribuir entre el padre y la madre las funciones inherentes a su ejercicio." (Article 156, Spanish Civil Code).

Anglo-American system	Spanish system
I. Legal authority/custody	I. Patria Potestad
II. Physical custody/guardianship	II. Guarda y custodia
1. Exclusive/sole physical custody	1. Custodia exclusive/unilateral
2. Joint physical custody/care	2. Custodia compartida
3. Split custody[77]	3. Custodia repartida

Fig. 4.2 Anglo-American and Spanish system

la custodia no tiene contenido en la adopción de medidas de tanta transcendencia, sin que ello suponga restarle valor a tan importante función, sino que la misma se desenvuelve en un quehacer más próximo y cotidiano, que sin lugar a dudas también contribuirá a la formación integral de los hijos y que difícilmente se puede compartir al mismo tiempo, precisamente por quienes no viven juntos." (Ivars Ruiz 2008: 35)

This critical evaluation is in accordance with the comment to Article 156 made by Ballesteros de los Ríos, who argues that the last paragraph of the article appears rather confusing. The legal norm states that if parents live separately, the legal authority is exercised by the one parent with whom the child lives. Nevertheless, on request of one parent the judge may concede that legal authority is exercised jointly by both parents or may distribute the functions implied in its exercise among both parents. The author points to the redundancy of the norm because the other parent keeps the right to maintain contact to the child (Article 160).[78]

Concerning the expression *'custodia compartida'* in Article 90, the author argues that because custody cannot be exercised simultaneously by both parents it needs to be distributed according to the circumstances in which parenting takes place. He sees a contradiction in the linguistic compound '*custodia compartida*' and pleads for more exactness in the choice of terminology. It would actually be more adequate to speak of 'joint-alternating custody' or '*custodia compartida en alternancia*'. The author gives the following explanation:

"Así, aún estableciéndose un régimen de custodia compartida consensuada o excepcional solicitada por un solo de los padres de conformidad con el actual artículo 92 del Código Civil, las tareas que comparten los progenitores en materia de custodia se ceñirán inevitablemente, en la práctica a los tiempos de estancia con los hijos. De hay que se deba hablar más correctamente de custodia compartida en alternancia." (Ivars Ruiz 2008: 35 f.)

[77]A split custody arrangement applies to families with more than one child and corresponds to the Spanish option of "custodia repartida", whereby one child resides with one parent and the other child with the other parent. As Article 92.5 of the Spanish Civil Code states that when judges reach a decision on custody they should take care that brothers and sisters are not separated. Therefore the split custody regime or 'custodia repartida' is not a recognized legal concept within Spanish family law, although it is legally allowed and there are cases in which such regime is preferred and exercised by the former family (e.g. SAP Cordoba 132/2006 de 12 junio, JUR\2007\78867).

[78]See: Ballesteros de los Ríos quoted in Bercovitz Rodríguez-Cano (2006): 291.

As outlined in chapter one on custody decisions there seems to be a preference in most societies that mothers act as primary caregivers especially with young children. Not surprisingly, the same is true for post-divorce parenting when mothers are more available in the majority of cases. Therefore the preferred post-divorce parenting regime is that legal authority is primarily exercised by mothers.[79] This is in accordance with the preferences that exist in other European countries where the majority of ex-spouses seem to opt for sole custody with the non-custodial parent being given the right of contact to the child at certain intervals. Although sole custody may be carried out by either of the parent, the legal practice shows that the majority of family judges grant sole custody to mothers. Spain is no exception to this trend. The most common custody regime after divorce is that the mother mainly exercises legal authority and the father has the right to visit the child at alternating weekends. Pérez Galán criticizes that the modifications made by Law 15/2005 and the intention to promote joint post-divorce parenting have had little or no effect in reality. The family lawyer argues that the father has still only visiting rights under a standard visiting regime:

> "en nuestro país lo más habitual es que la guarda y custodia de los hijos tras la ruptura de los padres, se atribuya de forma exclusiva a la madre, otorgándose el padre un régimen de comunicación y estancia (mal denominada visita). La relación padre-hijo ha pasado en estos años del primitivo de sábados y/o domingos, al de fines de semanas alternos desde el viernes a la salida del colegio, hasta el lunes por la mañana y una o dos tardes a la semana con pernoctas, más la mitad de todas las vacaciones escolares de Navidad, Semana Santa, feria y/o fiestas locales y verano (…)." (Pérez Galván 2009: 19)

It is often argued that a joint custody regime is more prone to conflicts and judges are reluctant to bestow it because they do not want to be confronted with appeals against divorce sentences. In this context the investigation of Marín García de Leonardo is interesting because she analyses the problems associated with the attribution of joint custody in litigious cases. If there is no agreement among ex-spouses joint custody may still be granted on the petition of one parent (Article 92.8.). In such cases the judge has to ask for a report of the Public Prosecution and may solicit a report from a psychologist ascribed to the family court in order to evaluate the best interest of the child. The author critically evaluates the role of the specialist report in order to assess the best interest of the child. She points out that although such report is not obligatory it has a crucial role in custody decisions. However, in practice there is often a lack of protocol on the procedure of such reports. In many cases the only decisive criterion for the attribution of custody is the availability of the non-working mother. Even in cases in which the father has the role of the main caregiver there is a preference to attribute sole custody to the mother.[80]

A sole custody regime may equally turn into a source of conflicts especially if parents do not have a good communication level. Several authors and in particular representatives of non-custodial father groups have pointed to the numerous kinds of problems that are associated with this regime. These include difficulties arising

---

[79]See: Arch Marin and Jarne Esparcia (2008): 28.

[80]See: Castillo Martinez (2007): 2.

from limited time for father–child contact, unilateral decisions made by mothers concerning change of residence or school, child health or coverage of additional costs, or even non-compliance of visiting times, to name but a few. This is highlighted by Hernando Ramos who is confronted with such difficulties in her work as a Public Prosecutor. She tells the following from her experience:

> "Si analizamos la realidad judicial actual llegamos a la conclusión, por un lado, que las guardas y custodias se otorgan, en la mayoría de los casos a las madres y que los regímenes de comunicación y estancias a favor del padre son más bien limitadas, lo que supone, por un parte una numerosa conflictividad judicial llena de demandas pos cambios de colegio sin previo consentimiento, cambios de domicilio a otra localidad distinta a la de donde ambos conviven, decisiones importantes en temas de salud, gastos extraordinarios no consensuados, obstaculización y/o incumplimiento en el régimen de visitas y comunicación de los hijos, perdida del seguimiento cotidiano del hijo en el progenitor no custodio. . .(lo que suele desembocar, bien en demandas ejecutivas en vía civil, o bien en juicios de faltas (. . .) en vía penal." (Hernando Ramos 2009: 7)

For a more detailed evaluation of the advantages and disadvantages of the joint custody regime, we shall therefore take psychological and sociological criteria into account. Guilarte Martín-Calero summarizes the arguments that support joint physical custody and lists altogether 11 advantages that are associated with this arrangement.[81] The first advantage (1) she sees in the *parents' equality* when it comes to duties and responsibilities in raising their child(ren). Such equality includes equal rights in both respects, in experiencing the child's development and exercising the duties of child care. This view is also supported by García Rubio who underlines the child's right of contact to both parents which helps to preserve the child's integrity. Joint or alternating custody allows both parents to maintain contact to their child which is to be preferred instead of favouring only one parent. She says the following:

> "Con carácter general, lo mejor para el desarrollo integral de los hijos es el mantenimiento de las relaciones con ambos progenitores (o padres adoptivos) de la manera más plena e intensa posible; así lo reconocen los estudios psicológicos más avanzados y recientes, y así lo han consagrado tanto los textos internacionales destinados a la salvaguarda de los derechos de los niños como los ordenamientos jurídicos de los países de nuestro entorno jurídico. Desde esta perspectiva, un régimen de guarda que garantiza el contacto con los dos padres en forma conjunta o alterna es, en los casos en los que sea posible (. . .), más conveniente que otro que privilegie el contacto con uno de ellos en detrimento del otro (. . .)."(García Rubio 2006: 95)

A second advantage (2) is the child's right to maintain a stable and uninterrupted relation to both parents whereby the offspring receives the affection, education and values that are characteristic for each parent. According to Article 154 co-parenting with a joint physical custody arrangement is considered the least harmful way of education for children for whom both parents have legal authority.[82] Thus the

[81]See: Guilarte Martín-Calero (2005): 14f.

[82]This is the normal case as stated in Article 154. CC: "Art. 154. Los hijos no emancipados están bajo la potestad de los padres. La patria potestad se ejercerá siempre en beneficio de los hijos, de acuerdo con su personalidad, y con respeto a su integridad física y psicológica. (. . .)" (Bercovitz-Ridríguez Cano 2006: 292).

parents' duties include "1.° Velar por ellos, tenerlos en su compañía, alimentarlos, educarlos y procurarles una formación integral. 2.° Representarlos y administrar sus bienes."[83] These responsibilities can best be assumed in a joint physical custody setting (3). The positive effect of an equal distribution of parental duties is also underlined by Marín García de Leonardo. She argues that the inconvenience of a child's continuous change from one parental home to the other is still outweighed by the advantage that is created by a joint exercise of parental rights and duties in the long run. She puts it like this:

> "En la guarda y custodia compartida ≪ambos progenitors contribuyen a la realización de una obra educativa eficaz y equilibrada y a instaurar con la prole una relación estable y responsable≫. La guarda unilateral impregna el proceso de lo lógica de vencedores y vencidos, en la que el menor es visto como un premio o un castigo." (Marín López and Lorente Acosta 2008: 5)

A fourth advantage (4) of joint custody is that it helps to prevent possible tendencies of alienation between the non-residential parent and the child.[84] As such, joint custody may be a protection against a possible detrimental development and act as anticipatory remedy. A further advantage (5) concerns the child's psychological development and the experience that the child comes into contact with two different ways of life. This is considered to be beneficial for the child as it broadens the mind rather than it would destabilize the child's emotional state. The author points to the necessity of supporting the emotional rather than the residential-related stability. She gives the following explanation:

> "Enriquece el mundo social, afectivo y familiar del menor que tendrá oportunidad de adaptarse a dos formas de ver la vida y de ello, más que inestabilidad pueden derivarse beneficios para el menor que adquiriría una visión más amplia y constructiva de su propia personalidad. La estabilidad de los hijos no está ligada a un domicilio estable o permanente, lo que ellos precisan es la estabilidad emocional que les proporciona sentirse queridos, educados y compartidos por quienes son sus padres." (Guilarte Martín-Calero 2005: 14)

Another strategic advantage is seen in the fact that joint custody allows both parents to understand the position of the other when it comes to custody, communication and stay. As both parents are confronted with the same responsibilities it enhances the chance that the commonalities prevail over adverse behaviour. This prevents the child of becoming a mere visitor of the non-residential parent, who knows little about the every-day reality of his or her parent.

This aspect seems a crucial issue because it implies that the divorced parents are basically willing to cooperate in child-related matters. But apart from high conflict post-divorce situations such willingness and business-like approach to the management of child-upbringing is relatively rare in divorced couples. This aspect is

---

[83]See: Bercovitz-Ridríguez Cano (2006): 292.

[84]See: Baker (2005): 289–302, Vassiliou and Cartwright (2001): 181–191, Campbell (2005): 365–377.

discussed by Carrasco and Perera [85] who doubts whether the new legislation can ever increase the chance of leading to joint legal custody arrangement. He points to the contradiction inherent in the assumption that joint custody is only feasible if the divorced parents are able and willing to cooperate similar as prior to divorce. But how can ever be reasonably assumed that this sense of cooperation has remained unaffected by the divorce. The following objection is put forward by the author:

> "Pero tal constructo es una pretensión que no se encuentra al alcance del legislador. Para que exista una custodia compartida, las partes tendrían que ser capaces de reproducir después de la ruptura una situación colaborativa similar a la existente antes de aquélla. Pero esta pretensión comporta desconocer el hecho mismo de la ruptura y de las causas que llevaron a ella, y presupone la necesidad de mantener los canales de comunicación de la pareja en una integridad tal que, de existir, seguramente habría impedido la ruptura. La custodia compartida pretende reproducir la situación familiar prerruptura, haciendo enormemente peligroso el incremento de intensidad de la vieja relación, que se quería dejar atrás, y profundamente decepcionante la expectativa de construir una nueva vida sin la presencia del ex. Por lo demás, si entre los padres existe este nivel de comprensión, empatía y solidaridad necesarias para construir una custodia compartida, ya se cuidarán de hacerlo, al margen de las previsiones legales." Carrasco Perera (2005a, b): 3

According to this argument, a court-ordered joint custody arrangement as a possible solution intended in Article 92.8 would hardly be successful because of lacking understanding, empathy and solidarity among the ex-spouses. The notion of high-conflict divorces is discussed by Kelly et al. who expect high levels of pre-separation conflict to be negatively related to joint custody.[86] However, the authors also point to an alternative scenario, in which a joint custody solution might be a way of dividing the responsibilities as an attempt of mediation:

> "Under such circumstances, a shared custodial arrangement might appear attractive as a way of splitting the difference on an important issue and thereby moving toward a final agreement." (Kelly et al. 2005: 28)

This view is supported by Guilarte Martín-Calero, who argues that joint custody compels the ex-spouses to share parenting responsibilities and obliges them to adopt a respectful position for the sake of the child's development. And she adds that such sense of cooperation could put an end to litigation and custody-related conflicts (8). Nevertheless, Carrasco Perera anticipates quite the opposite effect arguing that the introduction of joint custody as an option might turn into a powerful weapon against divorcing mothers. He assumes that mothers nearly always wish to gain sole custody because they tend to value it higher than fathers. However, in the negotiation process on the regulating agreement ex-husbands might turn their ex-wives' desire into their own strategic advantage. Fathers might achieve this advantage by demanding joint custody and thereby threatening their ex-wives to withdraw it from them. As a consequence a mother's negotiation power may

---

[85]See: Carrasco Perera (2005a): 3.

[86]See: Kelly quoted in Amato (1994): 154.

become weaker because she would be prepared to make unreasonable concessions for the sake of gaining sole custody. The author explains his point of view:

> "A todo esto hay que añadir que es sistema se convertirá en una poderosa arma contra las mujeres. Los maridos o ex maridos podrán amenazarlas más creíblemente con luchar por la (co)custodia de los hijos, erosionando una posesión que antes se aseguraba la madre la merced a la certeza de que el asunto de la custodia no podía ser usado creíblemente como una amenaza a su fuente real de poder sobre los aspectos domésticos de la relación de pareja (especialmente de los hijos), que le garantizaba su especialización histórica como gestora del hogar. Como la madre valora casi siempre mucho más que el padre la custodia de los hijos, acabará estando dispuesta a renunciar todo (pensión, alimentos, bienes matrimoniales) antes que perder el hijo, hundiendo con ello su posición negociadora." (Carrasco Perera 2005a, b 3)

In fact, there seem to be few couples who manage to consider their relationship after divorce in business-like terms intending to discuss matters in the most neutral way possible. Ex-spouses find it usually difficult or even impossible to communicate, which is a cause of divorce rather than its effect. Especially in the case of non-consensual divorces there is a certain danger of vindication among the ex-spouses. If the conflict deteriorates it may also be projected on the child or children and result in accusing a child of taking a parent's side. In such cases joint custody is considered as advantage as it may help to prevent possible processes of alienation that are initiated by one parent against the other. And even if there are first signs of alienation, joint custody ordered by the judge is viewed as the best remedy against it because it signals a limit to this misbehaviour (9).

Divorced parents may want to find a new partner after the family transition but this requires considerable adaptation skills from all people involved. The new relationship may be affected by adjustment difficulties between children and new partner. In this context the custodial setting is highly relevant. A sole custody arrangement may make it more difficult for children to accept a possible new partner. In general, one may conclude that joint custody puts both parents in a more egalitarian position when it comes to re-partnering after divorce (10).

A last advantage is seen in the economic aspects that are associated with joint custody. The fact that both parents pay child support and share the costs of child rearing according to their financial standards has advantages. It increases the parents' satisfaction to be able to contribute and helps to avoid conflicts resulting from non-payment of child support.

4.4.4 Liquidation of Matrimonial Property Regime, Family Accommodation and Spousal Support

The effects produced by annulment, separation and divorce include the liquidation of the matrimonial property regime (Article 95), the allocation of the family accommodation[87] and household equipment (Article 96), the coverage of matrimonial expenses and child payment (Article 93) and, if necessary, concession of compensatory payment to the ex-spouse (Article 97). The spouses are asked to find an agreement on the regulation of these issues in the regulating agreement. If they do not reach such agreement the judge will decide. In respect of the best interest of the child the family accommodation is always assigned to the children and the parent with whom they stay (Article 96). As such, González de Pozo underlines the importance of the accommodation as a primary pre-requisite for child well-being:

> "Ante todo, la satisfacción de ese superior interés del menor exige, en primer lugar, garantizar al mismo su derecho de habitación o posibilidad real de alojarse en una vivienda digna que les sirve de sede física en que vivir, crecer y desarrollarse en todos los órdenes: personal, familiar, educativo, relacional, afectivo, etc." (González de Pozo 2009: 16f.)

Taking this legal rule into account both ex-spouses have different starting positions from where they reorganize their post-divorce lives. As the children have the right to use the family home the primary custodial parent has the advantage of remaining in the family accommodation which may create an impression of safety and continuity in a time of emotional turmoil. The non-custodial parent, on the other hand, has to establish a new residence for his own use. In fact, the attribution of the family accommodation to the children often translates as an implicit form of spousal support to the custodial parent. González del Pozo points to the heavy financial burden that non-residential parents usually face in the post-divorce household formation:

> "el progenitor obligado a abandoner el domicilio conyugal viene obligado a procurarse un nuevo inmueble en que alojarse, y a asumir una carga económica adicional antes inexistente, al tiempo que debe que continuar abonando la mitad de la hipoteca del inmueble que constituyó del domicilio conyugal, todo lo cual le coloca en una situación de extraordinaria precariedad económica." (González de Pozo 2009: 16)

At the same time if both spouses jointly own the family accommodation the non-custodial may demand the division of the joint property according to Article 400 CC.[88] However, the division of the property does not affect the judicial decision on the attribution of the accommodation established in the regulating

---

[87] If the spouses own more than one accommodation the law applies only to the particular accommodation that the family *de facto* used as ordinary family residence on an every day basis. Marín Lopez explains this in his comment on Article 96: "El artìculo 96 se refriere a la atribución del uso de la ≪vivienda familiar y de los objetos de uso ordinario en ella≫. Por vivienda familia hay que entender la vivienda en la que los cónyuges cumplen su obligación d vivir juntos (art. 68), inaplicándose el artículo 96, por tanto, a otras viviendas privativas o adquiridas conjuntamente por los dos cónyuges." (Marín López in Bercovitz Roriguez-Cano 2006: 220).

[88] See Article 400 which states that each co-proprietor may ask for a division of the joint property: "Ningún copropietario estará obligado a permanecer en la comunidad. Cada uno de ellos podrá pedir en cualquier tiempo que se divida la cosa común. Esto no obstante, será válido el pacto de conservar la cosa indivisa por tiempo determinado, que no exceda de diez años. Este plazo podrá prorrogarse por nueva convención." (Article 400, Spanish Civil Code).

agreement. In such cases Article 405 applies establishing that the division of joint property must not place third persons at a disadvantage, they maintain the right to this property.[89] Consequently a property owned by both spouses may be divided in the course of divorce but the right to use this property is still attributed to the child. As such, Fernández Campos comments on a divorce sentence according to which a jointly owned property is legally divided but the child's right to use this property is preserved. The author underlines that both legal rules are equally valid, the owner's right to have a joint property divided (Article 400) and the provision that such division must not place a third person at a disadvantage (Article 405). Therefore both provisions are perfectly compatible and legally binding. He gives the following explanation:

> "Por consiguiente, la atribución del derecho de uso a uno de los cónyuges, sea o no uno de los cotitulares de la propiedad sobre la vivienda, no constituye un impedimento contra el ejercicio de la acción de división, y no por razón de una eventual jerarquía entre estos derechos sino porque los derechos del Article 400 y del Article 96 son combatibles si la división respeta ≪la ocupación judicial decretada y mantenida≫ (STS 28 de marzo de 2003)." (Fernández Campos 2008: 2042)

In cases of joint ownership of property the legal doctrine applied by the Supreme Court (Tribunal Supreme) in various sentences is unequivocal. Although the division of the property may be initiated unilaterally by one ex-spouse, the children's right to use the accommodation prevails. Neither the division nor the subsequent sale of the property eliminate the right to use.[90] Any changes of the right to use can only be achieved either by a change of the regulating agreement or by judicial decision in a non-consensual case. However, if the co-proprietors sell the property the custodial parent can never translate such right into an additional profit.[91]

Several authors view the question of the family accommodation as one of the most controversial among the divorcing spouses. For instance, García Rubio and

[89]See Article 405 of the Spanish Civil Code: "La división de una cosa común no perjudicará a tercero, el cual conservará los derechos de hipoteca, servidumbre u otros derechos reales que le pertenecieran antes de hacer la partición. Conservarán igualmente su fuerza, no obstante la división, los derechos personales que pertenezcan a un tercero contra la comunidad." (Article 405, Spanish Civil Code).

[90]See: Fernández Campos (2008): 588 f., who quotes for instance STS 8 mayo 2006 (RJ, 2006, 2342) and particularly STS 27 junio 2007, which contains the following clarification: "si bien el cotitular dominical puede pedir la division de la cosa común mediante el ejercicio de la acción procesal, la cesación de la comunidad no afecta a la subsistencia el derecho de uso (...) que corresponde al otro cotitular, ex-cónyuge, en virtud de la sentencia de divorcio. Por lo tanto, el derecho de uso se mantiene indemne." (STS, 27 junio 2007).

[91]For instance, Fernández Campos reports of a case in which a custodial parent justifies her claim to receive two thirds of the sales revenue of the joint property because she has the right to use in contrast to the other co-proprietor who is supposed to receive only one third. This claim was rejected by the judge who argued that an eventual reduction of the sales revenue due to the right to use goes to the expense of both ex-spouses and not just to one of the two. (Fernández Campos 2008: 593).

Otero Crespo criticise that the legislator has failed to carry out a profound reform of Article 96 CC and underline that the existing legal provisions would lead to unjust situations especially in cases where the former family accommodation is owned by the non-custodial parent. As the accommodation is always allocated to the children, the actual proprietor is deprived of both, using the immobile directly and making use of its market value. The authors state the following:

> "Confirma esta primera idea sobre la falta de decisión del legislador de 2005 la incomprensible omisión por su parte de cualquier referencia al Article 96 del CC, destinado a regular uno de los temas más polémicos en cualquier procedimiento de separación o divorcio: la vivienda familiar. Por razones difíciles de explicar y fáciles de adivinar, este precepto ha sido totalmente soslayado en la reforma de la separación y el divorcio, manteniendo un tenor literal que, con aparente fin protector del miembro más débil de la pareja, contiene una norma absolutamente obsoleta en el ámbito comparado, y muchas veces profundamente injusta: la de otorgar el uso de la vivienda familiar tras la crisis, no a su titular, sino a los hijos y a aquel de los cónyuges en cuya compañía queden (...). Se sigue pensando, pues, que la convivencia será las más de las veces con uno y no con el otro." (García Rubio and Otero Crespo 2006: 96)

The authors argue that once the accommodation has ceased to be one of the original family, it could as well be attributed to its owner, except for cases in which this would lead to economic hardship of the other ex-spouse. In order to avoid such inconvenience they plead for a distinction between two matters, the use of the family accommodation on the one hand and a parent's exercise of his or her legal authority. They are of the opinion that the owner of the property should have a principal right over it, unless the exercise of this right would put the other ex-spouse in a precarious situation.[92]

Likewise, the Principles of European Family Law Regarding Divorce and Maintenance between Former Spouses, contain the rule of self-sufficiency concerning the maintenance between ex-spouses (Principle 2.2.). According to this principle each spouse shall tend to become economically independent from the respective other.[93] After the divorce a custodial parent may want to cohabitate with a new partner together with the child for which he or she has custody. Such constellations may lead to tensions especially if we take into account that an ex-spouse cohabitates with a new partner in the accommodation for which the other ex-spouse still pays mortgage rates. As the right to use is granted primarily to the children an ex-spouse's remarriage or cohabitation with a new partner does not affect his or her right to remain in the former family accommodation. This is explicitly explained by Marìn Lopez in his interpretation of Article 96 CC:

[92]See: García Rubio and Otero Crespo (2006): 96.

[93]See: "Principle 2:2 Self sufficiency.
Subject to the following Principles, each spouse should provide for his or her own support after divorce." (Principles of European Family Law Regarding Divorce and Maintenance between Former Spouses).

> "No se extingue, en cambio, por el hecho de que el cónyuge contraiga nuevo matrimonio o viva maritalmente con otra persona, salvo que se considere que el nuevo matrimonio o la convivencia con esa otra persona resulte perjudicial para los hijos (. . .)." (Marín López in Bercovitz Rodríguez-Cano 2006: 220)

The economically disadvantaged ex-spouse is entitled to receive compensatory payment or spousal support according to Article 97 CC. It stipulates that in cases where a divorce produces economic inequality among ex-spouses or would imply a considerable deterioration of the economic status for one, he or she is entitled to receive temporary or even indefinite spousal support. The following criteria are relevant for the attribution of spousal support: agreements made between the spouses, age and state of health of economically weaker spouse, professional qualifications, pre-divorce family organisation and duration of marriage, collaboration in ex-spouse's business and special necessities. In the following section the study, its purpose and methodology and the technique of data selection will be outlined.

4.5 The Study: Purpose, Methodology, Data Selection

The purpose of this study is to analyze a total number of 135 divorce sentences against which an appeal (recurso de apelación) was taken by one of the ex-spouses. We wanted to know more about the reasons why an appeal was made against the sentence of the first instance. A special focus of interest is on the issue of joint custody and the problems associated with it. Therefore, data were primarily selected if one of the controversial issues was that of the custody arrangement. With reference to the theoretic model we are particularly interested in three groups of parameters, such as (1) legal authority, custody and attribution of accommodation, (2) family composition (number of children, parents' labor market participation and income), and (3) the liquidation of the matrimonial property regime (child support, spousal support, mortgage). These parameters are expected to provide results on the following research questions:

1. Which are the preferred custody options?
2. Which contact options are granted to the non-residential parent?
3. Is there a relation between the family composition (number of children, parents' resources) and the type of custody?
4. What is the average amount of child support?
5. Which are the conditions under which spousal support is granted?

We expect to find answers to these questions by analyzing the information given in the divorce sentences. We use a quantitative statistical method in order to get an overview of the socio-economic characteristics and tendencies associated with the divorce sentences. The results are supposed to indicate whether the introduction of the joint custody has led to any significant increase in the choice of this regime as a preferred option for parenting. We use a descriptive and comparative method for the analysis of the data. Results will be visualized by diagrams. Outstanding findings shall be discussed in detail whereby we apply a qualitative approach. Whereas the quantitative method shows general tendencies the qualitative method provides in-depth information on hidden parameters.

The selected cases were all brought to Spanish Provincial Courts (Audiencia Provincial) throughout the country in the year 2007. The first divorce sentences had been decided one or more years before the appeal, depending on the duration of the legal procedure. The criterion for selecting the sentences was "joint custody". More specifically, the database on jurisdiction[94] was searched through according to whether a divorce sentence of the Courts of Appeal contained the expression "guarda y custodia compartida".

From the statistic point of view, we use a characteristic element for the extraction of classes and frequencies from a total amount of data. A characteristic element divides a total class into sub-classes, within which the characteristic element is equally distributed.[95] More specifically we started from a total class of divorce sentences of the year 2007.[96] According to the characteristic element 1, ("court of appeal") we selected all those sentences that were brought to Courts of Appeal and as a result we obtained a class 1. We applied the characteristic element 2 ("joint custody") for a further selection and thereby received class 2. From this class we took a random sample[97] of divorce appeals and received a class 3. With respect to statistical validity the data must be organized in a way that we can correctly infer from the random sample. Therefore the sample should contain sufficient divorce appeals from every Autonomous Community. The number of inhabitants in each Autonomous Community was taken as a further criterion for selection and we finally received class 4. The process of data selection is depicted in the diagram (Fig. 4.3).

The number of sentences corresponds to the number of inhabitants in each Autonomous Community. Data were selected according to the relative amount of the population in every Autonomous Community.[98] The aim was to present an

---

[94]See database available on: http://www.westlaw.es.

[95]Sixtl introduces the following mathematical formula: "Wir betrachten ein Merkmal, das aus r Ausprägung besteht: $A = \{A_1, ..., A_i, ..., A_r\}$.

Die Menge der Objekte, welche die gleiche Ausprägung A_i aufweisen, heisst Klasse i. Die Anzahl der Objekte dieser *Klasse*, ihre Kardinalzahl, heisst *Häufigkeit* von i. Wir bezeichnen sie mit h_i, $i = 1,...r$. Wenn wir alle Häufigkeiten adieren:

$$\sum_{i=1}^{r} hi = h1 + \cdots + hr,$$

So zählen wir jedes Objekt einmal und nur einmal mit." (Sixtl 1996: 8f).

[96]See: Divorce Sentences in Autonomous Communities (2007) in Appendix. The abbreviation SAP stands for 'sentencia de la Audiencia Provincial'.

[97]A random sample contains a number of items, whereby every item has an equal chance of being selected. Random samples are used in statistics in order to test hypotheses about the population.

[98]For a comprehensive overview of the ratio between the amount of data and the inhabitants per autonomous Community see the Appendix.

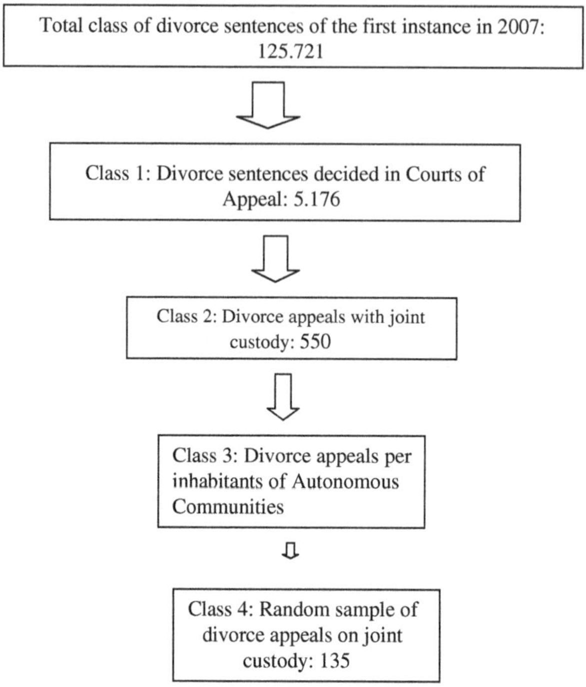

Fig. 4.3 Process of data selection

equivalent distribution of divorce sentences analogous to the number of inhabitants in the respective Autonomous Communities. In that way an equal ratio between data and population in each Autonomous Community should be guaranteed. Following this practice, we obtained most of the data for Catalonia (33 sentences),[99] followed

[99]See: SAP Barcelona 20-7-2007 (JUR\2007\284258), SAP Barcelona 19-7-2007 (JUR\2007\316774), SAP Barcelona 17-7-2007 (JUR\2007\284499), SAP Barcelona 19-7-2007 (JUR\2007\284371), SAP Barcelona 18-7-2007 (JUR\2007\284433), SAP Barcelona 17-7-2007 (JUR\2007\341881), SAP Barcelona 25-9-2007 (JUR\2007\329627), SAP Barcelona 12-9-2007 (JUR\2007\330479), SAP Barcelona 20-7-2007 (JUR\2007\284277), SAP Barcelona 20-7-2007 (JUR\2007\284309), SAP Barcelona 25-7-2007 (JUR\2007\284101), SAP Barcelona 25-7-2007 (JUR\2007\284103), SAP Barcelona 14-6-2007 (JUR\2007\72181), SAP Barcelona 20-9-2007 (JUR\2007\329851), SAP Barcelona 13-9-2007 (JUR\2007\330384), SAP Barcelona 15-6-2007 (JUR\2007\65225), SAP Barcelona 28-9-2007 (JUR\2007\334918), SAP Barcelona 25-9-2007 (JUR\2007\329641), SAP Barcelona 28-9-2007 (JUR\2007\329460), SAP Barcelona 15-6-2006 (JUR\2007\65213), SAP Barcelona 14-6-2006 (JUR\2007\18852), SAP Barcelona 12-6-2006 (JUR\2007\18969), SAP Barcelona 9-6-2006 (JUR\2007\11058), SAP Girona 24-5-2006 (JUR\2007\12010), SAP Girona 26-5-2006 (JUR\2007\65509), SAP Girona 8-6-2006 (JUR\2007\11132), SAP Tarragona 23-5-2006 (JUR\2007\19825), SAP Tarragona 24-5-2006 (JUR\2007\19791), SAP Tarragona 31-5-2006 (JUR\2007\65469), SAP Tarragona 12-7-2007 (JUR\2007\336713), SAP Tarragona 25-7-2007 (JUR\2007\292342), SAP Tarragona 25-7-2007 (JUR\2007\292348), SAP Tarragona 31-7-2007 (JUR\2007\364429).

by Andalusia (17),[100] Valencia (16),[101] Madrid (15),[102] Castilla and León (8),[103] Castilla-La Mancha (5),[104] Las Palmas (5),[105] Islas Baleares (5),[106] Galicia (6),[107]

---

[100]See: SAP Almería a 28-7-2006 (JUR\2007\47227), SAP Córdoba a 12-6-2007 (JUR\2007\78867), SAP Granada a 9-6-2006 (JUR\2007\48774), SAP Granada a 29-9-2006 (JUR\2007\129153), SAP Córdoba a 10-7-2006 (JUR\2007\185823), SAP Jaén a 7-5-2007 (JUR\2007\359838), SAP Jaén a 8-6-2006 (JUR\2007\41959), SAP Cádiz a 23-5-2007 (JUR\2007\359197), SAP Cádiz a 23-5-2007 (JUR\2007\359197), SAP Cádiz a 23-5-2007 (JUR\2007\359197), SAP Sevilla a 12-6-2007 (JUR\2007\78867), SAP Sevilla a 23-11-2006 (JUR\2007\181805), SAP Sevilla a 23-11-2006 (JUR\2007\181814), SAP Sevilla a 8-11-2006 (JUR\2007\182538), SAP Málaga a 24-5-2006 (JUR\2007\27758), SAP Málaga a 30-11-2006 (JUR\2007\163774), SAP Málaga a 3-5-2007 (JUR\2007\359929).

[101]SAP Valencia 25-7-2007 (JUR\2007\341234), SAP Valencia 24-7-2007 (JUR\2007\316313), SAP Valencia 12-9-2007 (JUR\2007\340148), SAP Valencia 6-9-2007 (JUR\2007\340308), SAP Valencia 5-9-2007(JUR\2007\340356), SAP Valencia 5-9-2007 (JUR\2007\340349), SAP Valencia 16-7-2007 (JUR\2007\317375), SAP Valencia 17-7-2007 (JUR\2007\317134), SAP Valencia 27-3-2007 (JUR\2007\213572), SAP Valencia 18-9-2007 (JUR\2007\340034), SAP Valencia 20-9-2007 (JUR\2007\339999), SAP Valencia 20-9-2007 (JUR\2007\339980), SAP Castellón 7-9-2007 (JUR\2007\340230), SAP Alicante 20-9-2006 (JUR\2008\140754), SAP Alicante 20-9-2006 (JUR\2008\118681), SAP Alicante 9-5-2007 (JUR\2007\261473).

[102]SAP Madrid 26-7-2007 (JUR\2007\336153), SAP Madrid 16-10-2007 (AC\2007\2324), SAP Madrid 13-9-2007 (JUR\2007\346268), SAP Madrid 16-7-2007 (JUR\2007\336589), SAP Madrid 27-3-2007 (JUR\2007\313894), SAP Madrid 21-9-2007 (JUR\2007\329739), SAP Madrid 7-7-2007 (JUR\2007\25887), SAP Madrid 19-7-2006 (JUR\2007\32432), SAP Madrid 20-7-2006 (JUR\2007\32345), SAP Madrid 19-4-2007 (JUR\2007\313629), SAP Madrid 14-7-2006 (JUR\2007\25424), SAP Madrid 13-7-2006 (JUR\2007\167719), SAP Madrid 14-7-2006 (JUR\2007\25374), SAP Madrid 13-7-2006 (JUR\2007\266461), SAP Madrid 19-7-2006 (JUR\2007\32431).

[103]SAP Valladolid a 12-7-2007 (JUR\2007\307507), SAP Valladolid a 12-7-2007 (JUR\2007\307507), SAP Valladolid a 28-7-2007 (JUR\2007\309909), SAP Burgos a 9-4-2007 (JUR\2007\282062), SAP Burgos a 27-2-2007 (JUR\2007\282623), SAP León a 26-2-2007 (JUR\2007\249673), SAP León a 26-2-2006 (JUR\2007\60650), SAP Salamanca a 30-11-2006 (JUR\2007\144094).

[104]SAP Toledo a 8-6-2007 (JUR\2007\301561), SAP Toledo a 25-4-2007 (JUR\2007\262101), SAP Ciudad Real a 12-6-2007 (JUR\2007\312105), SAP Albacete a 8-11-2007 (JUR\2007\46117), SAP Guadalajara a 16-10-2007 (JUR\2007\314485).

[105]SAP Las Palmas 24-9-2007 (JUR\2007\353964), SAP Santa Cruz de Tenerife 5-6-2007 (JUR\2007\337915), SAP Las Palmas 28-5-2007 (JUR\2007\344134), SAP Las Palmas 17-5-2007 (JUR\2007\288195), SAP Las Palmas 23-2-2007 (JUR\2007\151664).

[106]SAP Islas Baleares 29-5-2007 (JUR\2007\321875), SAP Islas Baleares 19-4-2007 (JUR\2007\296931), SAP Islas Baleares 27-2-2007 (JUR\2007\254010), SAP Islas Baleares 6-3-2007 (JUR\2007\282547), SAP Islas Baleares 13-3-2007 (JUR\2007\273221).

[107]SAP Lugo 27-4-2007 (JUR\2007\252972), SAP A Coruña 7-5-2007 (JUR\2007\279653), SAP A Coruña 13-7-2006 (JUR\2007\134868), SAP A Coruña 31-7-2006 (JUR\2007\297896), SAP A Ourense 14-7-2006 (JUR\2007\40301), SAP Pontevedra 6-3-2007 (JUR\2007\265018).

Asturias (2),[108] La Rioja (2),[109] The Basque Country (6),[110] Murcia (4),[111] Aragón (4),[112] Cantabria (2),[113] Navarra (2),[114] and Extremadura (3).[115]

The data were coded in a list containing all the relevant criteria mentioned, such as custody regime, attribution of family accommodation, number of family members and age of children, parents' profession and income level, amount of child support and spousal support and type of conflict as a reason for appeal. In the following section the results will be presented.

4.6 Results

The results are subsumed under the following three categories: (1) legal authority, custody and attribution of accommodation, (2) pre-divorce family composition and parents' resources, and (3) the liquidation of the matrimonial property regime (child support, spousal support and mortgage). In the following sections we present the findings gained by the analysis of the data.

4.6.1 Legal Authority, Custody and Family Accommodation

In a predominant majority of cases (94%) legal authority was exercised mainly by one parent, who remained with the children in the former family accommodation. The non-residential parent had visitation rights. We called this parenting option sole custody. Only in 3% of the cases had parents opted for joint custody.[116] A split

[108] SAP Asturias 31-5-2007 (JUR\2007\302934), SAP Asturias 20-6-2007 (JUR\2007\306985).

[109] SAP La Rioja 12-2-2003 (JUR\2003\93756), SAP La Rioja 18-2-2008 (JUR\2008\217672).

[110] SAP Guipúzcoa 19-12-2006 (JUR\2007\102814), SAP Guipúzcoa 21-12-2007 (JUR\2007\117075), SAP Álava a 27-4-2007 (JUR\2007\226393), SAP Vizcaya a 22-9-2006 (JUR\2007\100066), SAP Vizcaya a 27-7-2006 (JUR\2007\95898), SAP Vizcaya a 26-7-2006 (JUR\2007\95901).

[111] SAP Murcia a 23-5-2007 (JUR\2007\344200), SAP Murcia a 30-4-2007 (JUR\2007\313484), SAP Murcia a 6-3-2007 (JUR\2007\265019), SAP Murcia a 21-6-2007 (JUR\2007\320524).

[112] SAP Zaragoza a 24-7-2007 (JUR\2007\306816), SAP Zaragoza a 24-7-2007 (JUR\2007\336334), SAP Zaragoza a 27-3-2007 (JUR\2007\263758), SAP Huesca a 14-6-2007 (JUR\2007\311867).

[113] SAP Cantabria a 16-3-2007 (JUR\2007\125849), SAP Cantabria a 19-6-2007 (AC\2007\2242).

[114] SAP Navarra a 8-11-2007 (JUR\2008\127839), SAP Navarra a 27-8-2007 (JUR\2008\7079).

[115] SAP Cáceres a 11-4-2007 (JUR\2007\262787), SAP Cáceres a 5-3-2007 (JUR\2007\265115), SAP Badajoz a 21-11-2006 (JUR\2007\14327).

[116] See the cases: SAP Islas Baleares 29-5-2007 (JUR\2007\321875), SAP Islas Baleares 27-2-2007 (JUR\2007\254010), SAP Asturias 29-11-2006 (JUR\2007\23523), SAP Castellón 7-9-2007 (JUR\2007\340230).

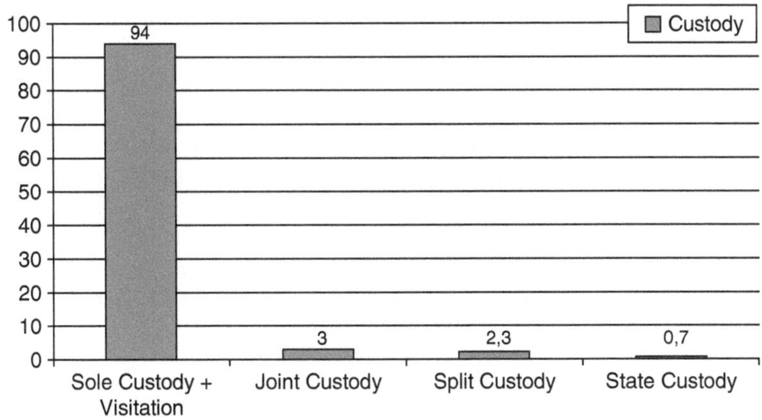

Fig. 4.4 Types of custody and their relative distribution

custody arrangement occurred in only 2.3% of cases.[117] In one case the state had taken custody for the children.[118] The diagram shows the distribution of the four types of custody (Fig. 4.4).

It may be concluded that there does not appear to be a considerable increase of joint custody as a result of the introduction of this regime by Law 12/2005. There are a number of reasons for this outcome, one may be that joint custody requires more organization and communication at least in the first post-divorce phase until parents get accustomed to it and it becomes routine. However, a precondition for its exercise is a sense of cooperation and teamwork among ex-spouses, which is in fact rarely the case. This argument is underlined by Carrasco Perera who points to the inherent contradiction according to which the legislator starts from the assumption that this sense of cooperation would still be intact despite of divorce.[119] Ex-spouses would have to reestablish a sense of cooperation that had existed before the divorce for joint custody to function effectively. On the other hand, the legislator can neither order such collaboration nor claim in the skills for its exercise.

Another reason is that joint custody seems less feasible to parents, at least at first sight, because the scheme differs substantially from traditional parent roles and requires flexibility, confidence and the conviction that it will work from the start. From the perspective of jurisdiction the lack of popularity has probably to do with judges being concerned that it might not work and they may again be confronted with the case at court. Thus, traditional views and preventive concerns seem to prevail over its expected beneficial effects on the relationship between children and parents.

[117]See the cases: SAP Asturias 31-5-2007 (JUR\2007\302934), SAP Córdoba a 10-7-2006 (JUR \2007\185823).

[118]See the cases: SAP Toledo a 8-6-2007 (JUR\2007\301561).

[119]See: Carrasco Perera (2005a, b).

Concerning the gender-specific aspect, sole custody was mostly bestowed to mothers and fathers kept their right of contact. A predominant majority of mothers (83.1%) was granted sole custody, whereby the children remained together with the mother in the family accommodation. Only rarely did fathers receive sole custody (11%) and mothers had visitation rights.[120] Joint custody was preferred in six cases (2.9%)[121] and was nearly as uncommon as the split custody arrangement (2.3%).[122] The chart shows the relative amount of each type of custody (Fig. 4.5).

In the conceptual frame the authors hypothesized that fathers would be more likely to be given sole custody if older children are involved. The results confirm this hypothesis because in 6 out of 7 cases in which fathers were bestowed sole

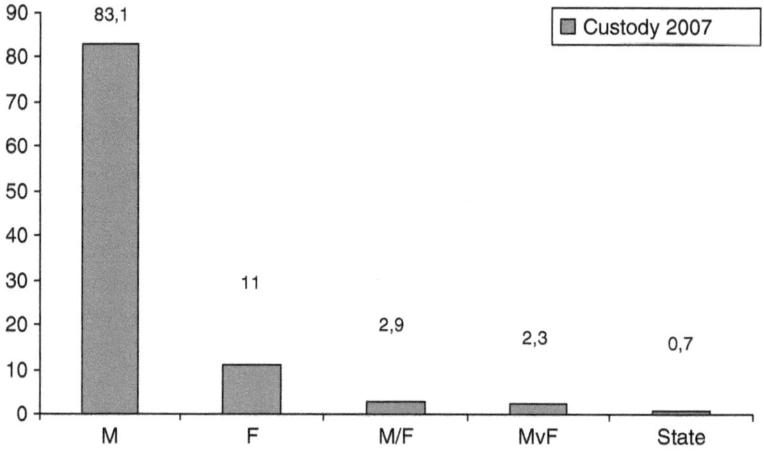

Fig. 4.5 Diagram showing the distribution of custody options among mothers and fathers[123]

[120]See the cases: SAP Barcelona 19-7-2007 (JUR\2007\284371), SAP Barcelona 12-9-2007 (JUR \2007\330479), SAP Barcelona 28-9-2007 (JUR\2007\334918), SAP Girona 26-5-2006 (JUR \2007\65509), SAP Tarragona 24-5-2006 (JUR\2007\19791), SAP Tarragona 25-7-2007 (JUR \2007\292348), SAP Tarragona 31-7-2007 (JUR\2007\364429), SAP A Coruña 13-7-2006 (JUR \2007\134868), SAP Asturias 20-6-2007 (JUR\2007\306985), SAP Castellón 7-9-2007 (JUR\2007 \340230), SAP Alicante 20-9-2006 (JUR\2008\140754), SAP Guipúzcoa 19-12-2006 (JUR\2007 \102814), SAP Burgos a 9-4-2007 (JUR\2007\282062), SAP Burgos a 27-2-2007 (JUR\2007 \282623), SAP Guadalajara a 16-10-2007 (JUR\2007\314485).

[121]See the cases: SAP Islas Baleares 29-5-2007 (JUR\2007\321875), SAP Islas Baleares 27-2-2007 (JUR\2007\254010), SAP Asturias 29-11-2006 (JUR\2007\23523), SAP Castellón 7-9-2007 (JUR\2007\340230), SAP Guipúzcoa 19-12-2006 (JUR\2007\102814), SAP León a 26-2-2007 (JUR\2007\249673).

[122]See the cases: SAP La Rioja 18-2-2008 (JUR\2008\217672), SAP Córdoba a 12-6-2007 (JUR \2007\78867).

[123]M, F = sole custody + visitation, M/F = joint custody, MvF = split custody, S = State custody

custody the children's age ranged between 11 and 17 years.[124] When mothers exercised sole custody the right to child-contact was always granted to fathers (82.2%). Except for one case in which the mother had sole custody and their teenage children refused contact to their father and the judge did not decide otherwise.[125] The same is true for the reverse case, if fathers have sole custody mothers receive visitations rights, except for one case where the offspring has reached the age of majority and no legal order on visitation is required.[126] The chart shows the attribution of visitation rights to parents (Fig. 4.6).

The visiting scheme most frequently ordered within sole custody is that the non-custodial parent sees his or her child on alternating weekends, the visit starting on Friday evening and ending on Sunday evening, including half of the school holidays. As legal authority always implies a right to contact, sole custody entails non-custodial parent–child contact. This may lead to the impression that – in practice – the dividing line between sole and joint custody is blurred. In one sentence a judge addresses this issue and states that although the two concepts appear similar they should be clearly kept apart. He points to the legal provision according to which the parents' agreement to opt for joint custody is a precondition for it to be granted. The judge gives the following explanation:

> "El tema planteado ha sido objeto de análisis en la reciente sentencia de esta Sala de fecha 26-9-06 en la que se declaraba "Ciertamente, desde un plano material, la línea de separación entre la figura de la guarda y custodia compartida y el régimen de comunicación y

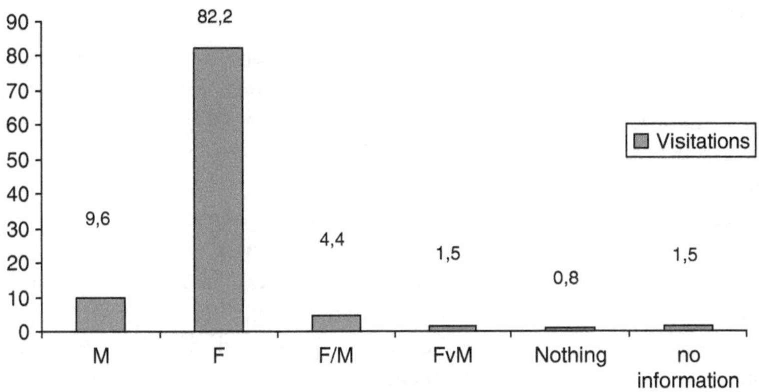

Fig. 4.6 Attribution of visitation rights[127]

---

[124]See cases: SAP Barcelona 19-7-2007 (JUR\2007\284371), SAP Barcelona 28-9-2007 (JUR \2007\334918), SAP Girona 26-5-2006 (JUR\2007\65509), SAP Tarragona 25-7-2007 (JUR\2007 \292348), SAP Burgos a 27-2-2007 (JUR\2007\282623), SAP Guadalajara a 16-10-2007 (JUR \2007\314485).

[125]See SAP Barcelona 17-7-2007 (JUR\2007\341881).

[126]See e.g.: SAP Tarragona 25-7-2007 (JUR\2007\292348).

[127]M = mother, F = father, F/M = joint custody, Fvm = split custody

visitas del Article 94 del CC es más difusa cuanto más amplio sea el régimen de comunicación y visitas, pero desde el plano técnico ello no autoriza a igualar uno y otro, en cuanto que el otorgamiento de la guarda y custodia confiere a su titular el derecho-deber de decidir sobre la adecuada atención ordinaria de los menores bajo su custodia en un plano superior al progenitor que los recibe en razón del régimen de visitas establecido, quien no por ello no deja, como es lógico, de constituirse en garante de su cuidado mientras están con él, careciendo de sentido, por el contrario, el establecimiento de un régimen de visitas si lo acordado y decretado es la guarda compartida" y se añade que "Ahora bien, en la actual regulación de la guarda y custodia compartida se requiere el consenso de ambos progenitores o la propuesta de uno con informe favorable del M.F."[128]

The results show that family judges do not always strictly adhere to a standard visiting scheme in sole custody arrangements as mentioned above but rather give parents the possibility of making changes in the contact scheme upon mutual agreement.[129] Sometimes judges propose an elaborate age-specific parenting plan, especially if young children are involved, such as in the following case:

"2.– Se atribuye a D. Ismael el régimen de visitas siguiente bajo los principios de flexibilidad y adaptabilidad que el bien de la hija imponga: Hasta que la menor cumpla tres años podrá tenerle en su compañía todos los martes y jueves desde las diecisiete hasta las diecinueve horas, debiendo recoger y reintegrar a la menor en el domicilio materno. Cuando la menor cumpla tres años podrá tenerla en su compañía en fines de semanas alternos desde las diez hasta las veinte horas del sábado y del domingo, así como todos los miércoles desde las diecisiete hasta las diecinueve horas, (...). Cuando la menor cumpla cinco años podrá el padre tenerla en su compañía en fines de semanas alternos desde las dieciocho horas del viernes diez hasta las diecinueve horas del domingo, (...), y podrá además, tener en su compañía a la hija la mitad de las vacaciones escolares de Navidad y Semana Santa, y el mes de julio y el de agosto."[130]

Judges use the following expressions in cases where parents opted for joint custody and the court approved it: "- se atribuye a ambos progenitores LA PATRIA POTESTAD Y LA GUARDA Y CUSTODIA DE LA HIJA MENOR (...), QUE DEBERAN EJERCER CONJUNTAMENTE; en los siguientes términos",[131] "Se establece un sistema de patria potestad y custodia compartida",[132] or "Los hijos del matrimonio menores de edad M. y J. quedarán bajo la guarda y custodia de su padre, siendo ejercida la patria potestad por ambos progenitores".[133]

In a joint custody arrangement child residence takes usually place in one of the following ways: child residence with one parent for full alternating weeks including half of school holidays,[134] on specific consecutive days during the week according to a biannual pre-arranged visiting plan,[135] on two specific consecutive days in 1

---

[128]See: SAP Asturias 29-11-2006 (JUR\2007\23523).

[129]See: for example the case SAP Las Palmas 17-5-2007 (JUR\2007\288195).

[130]See: SAP Las Palmas, JUR\2007\353964.

[131]See: SAP Asturias 29-11-2006 (JUR\2007\23523).

[132]See: SAP León a 26-2-2007 (JUR\2007\249673).

[133]See: SAP Guipúzcoa 19-12-2006 (JUR\2007\102814).

[134]See: for example SAP Islas Baleares 29-5-2007 (JUR\2007\321875).

[135]See: SAP Islas Baleares 27-2-2007 (JUR\2007\254010).

week and two other days in the following week including alternating weekends,[136] or even whole months under the condition that the non-resident parent may see the child every fortnight and additionally on certain days.[137] In most of the joint custody orders judges give parents the possibility of mutually agreeing on changes to the visiting plan if necessary and also name measures for the case of disagreement.

In two sentences, judges gave arguments against joint custody.[138] In one sentence custody is considered to be responsible for creating two main problems, such as a constant intrusion of one ex-spouse into the private sphere of the respective other and inverse and for the children a continuous "pilgrimage" from one residence to the other within a limited amount of time. Additionally, it is argued that the matrimonial crisis would find its reflection in the joint custody arrangement which may provoke disadvantage and exclusion to one of the people involved. The legal provisions stated in Article 39 of the Spanish Constitution together with the Spanish Civil Code (CC), Article 92 are designed to prevent such problems. The judge describes the problems associated with the joint custody arrangement:

> "Mas la guarda y custodia no tiene su contenido en la adopción de medidas de tanta trascendencia, sin que ello suponga restarle valor tan importante función, sino que la misma se desenvuelve en un quehacer más cotidiano y doméstico, que sin lugar a dudas también contribuiría a la formación integral del hijo y que difícilmente podrían compartirse por quienes no viven juntos, lo que supondría de admitirse otra tesis, una invasión de la esfera privada de un progenitor en la del otro, o en otro caso un continúo peregrinaje de los hijos de un hogar al otro, siendo, entonces, más correctamente denominarla en este supuesto, custodia periódicamente alternativa."[139]

A similar reason against joint custody is given in another sentence where the judge points to the inconvenience and discord caused in the children if they are supposed to move from one residence to the other within a limited amount of time. The judge emphasizes that children do not profit from a constant change of places and time schedules, different ways of lives and habits. The following objection is given:

> "En otro sentido la guarda y custodia conjunta en puridad terminológica y jurídica es inviable con las medidas nucleares de la separación y divorcio que implica una separación física de cuerpos; y la alternativa está mirada con disfavor por la doctrina jurisprudencial desde diciembre de 1985; pues ha de evitarse, por ser perjudicial para los hijos, el que éstos, cada poco tiempo, tengan que mudarse de domicilio o, en otro caso, ver en su domicilio cada poco a uno y otro progenitor con el cambio de estilos, modos y costumbres, horarios, exigencias etc."[140]

[136]See: SAP León a 26-2-2007 (JUR\2007\249673).

[137]See: SAP Asturias 29-11-2006 (JUR\2007\23523).

[138]See: SAP Valencia 20-9-2007 (JUR\2007\339980), SAP Madrid 13-9-2007 (JUR\2007\346268).

[139]See: SAP Madrid 31-10-1995 cit. in: SAP Valencia 20-9-2007 (JUR\2007\339980).

[140]See: SAP Madrid 13-9-2007 (JUR\2007\346268).

In just three cases do we find a split custody arrangement, whereby usually one or two children reside with one parent and a further child lives in the other parent's residence.[141] Both parents have the right to contact to the respective other child or children. No child support is paid in cases where each parent resides with one child because both parents contribute equally.[142]

Although we received only limited data on the attribution of the family accommodation (50%), in almost half of the cases (45.9%) that provided information custodial mothers remained in the family accommodation together with their children. Fathers remained in the accommodation only in four cases (6.7%) with exceptional circumstances.[143] In no more than 1.5% of the cases the family accommodation was suspended. The fact that relatively few family accommodations are liquidated suggests that the most important consideration seems to be to maintain continuity for the children. This thought appears to prevail over economic calculations on the affordability of the accommodation under such changed circumstances. The chart shows the comparative attribution of the accommodation in the divorce sentences (Fig. 4.7).

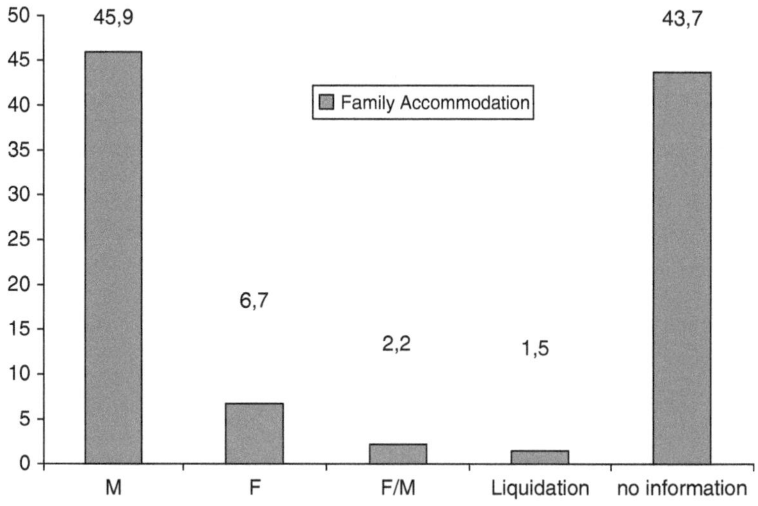

Fig. 4.7 Attribution of family accommodation[144]

---

[141]See: SAP Asturias 31-5-2007 (JUR\2007\302934), SAP La Rioja 18-2-2008 (JUR\2008\217672), SAP Córdoba a 12-6-2007 (JUR\2007\78867).

[142]See for example the explanation of the judge in SAP La Rioja 18-2-2008 (JUR\2008\217672).

[143]See: SAP Islas Baleares 13-3-2007 (JUR\2007\273221), SAP Barcelona 17-7-2007 (JUR\2007\341881), SAP Barcelona 25-7-2007 (JUR\2007\284101), SAP Barcelona 28-9-2007 (JUR\2007\334918), SAP Tarragona 24-5-2006 (JUR\2007\19791), SAP Tarragona 25-7-2007 (JUR\2007\292348), SAP Madrid 19-4-2007 (JUR\2007\313629), SAP Guipúzcoa 19-12-2006 (JUR\2007\102814), SAP Córdoba a 12-6-2007 (JUR\2007\78867).

[144]M = mother remains in fam.acc., F = father remains in fam.acc., F/M = family owns two accommodations, Liquidation of family accomm.

In the research literature the liquidation of the family accommodation due to divorce and its consequences on children is a controversial issue.[145] Because of economic considerations it seems to be more common practice in some countries to sell the house or flat after divorce and divide the proceeds according to earlier contributions. From the economic point of view, the new start made by each ex-spouse after divorce would then be determined by both, their respective profit share gained through the sale and on their labour market participation. In societies with marked social classes children's change of residence is characterized by certain socio-economic conditions such as income level, social prestige, way and standard of life, location and type of residence, choice of school, spare time activities, etc. As custodial mothers tend to be economically disadvantaged after divorce several authors have pointed to the detrimental consequences that a change of residence usually entails for children of divorced parents.

Nevertheless, in the analysis of the notion of a change of residence it is equally imaginable that a change of a parent's status within the same environment may produce some sort of discrimination within the child's peer-group, because the information about parental divorce is difficult to hide from relatives and peers. Therefore a certain advantage may also be seen in a change of environment with the chance for both, children and custodial parent to venture a new start.

4.6.2 Family Composition and Resources

According to the conceptual frame such aspects as the number of children, the parents' labor market participation and income have an influence on custody outcomes. The findings show that over 80% of the divorced families have either one or two children, whereas only around 10% have three or four children. There is an obvious tendency towards smaller families compared to the extended family model of earlier generations. The chart displays the amount of children per family (Fig. 4.8):

Concerning the labour market participation of parents there were insufficient results, no information was given in half of all cases. For the other half both models, the dual and the single earner model, were equally present. For dual earner parents there is a slight tendency to share mortgage rate payments on a 50% base.[146] This is shown in the diagram (Fig. 4.9).

---

[145]See: Andreß et al. (2006): 539, Amato (2000): 1272, Hawkins et al. (2006): 125.

[146]See the cases: SAP Las Palmas 24-9-2007 (JUR\2007\353964), SAP Las Palmas 17-5-2007 (JUR\2007\288195), SAP Las Palmas 23-2-2007 (JUR\2007\151664), SAP Islas Baleares 19-4-2007 (JUR\2007\296931), SAP Barcelona 20-7-2007 (JUR\2007\284258), SAP Barcelona 17-7-2007 (JUR\2007\341881), SAP Barcelona 12-9-2007 (JUR\2007\330479), SAP Barcelona 25-7-2007 (JUR\2007\284103), SAP Barcelona 15-6-2006 (JUR\2007\65213), SAP Barcelona 14-6-2006 (JUR\2007\18852), SAP Tarragona 23-5-2006 (JUR\2007\19825), SAP Tarragona 31-5-2006 (JUR\2007\65469), SAP Valencia 24-7-2007 (JUR\2007\316313), SAP Valencia 5-9-2007 (JUR\2007\340356), SAP Valencia 5-9-2007 (JUR\2007\340349), SAP Valencia 17-7-2007 (JUR

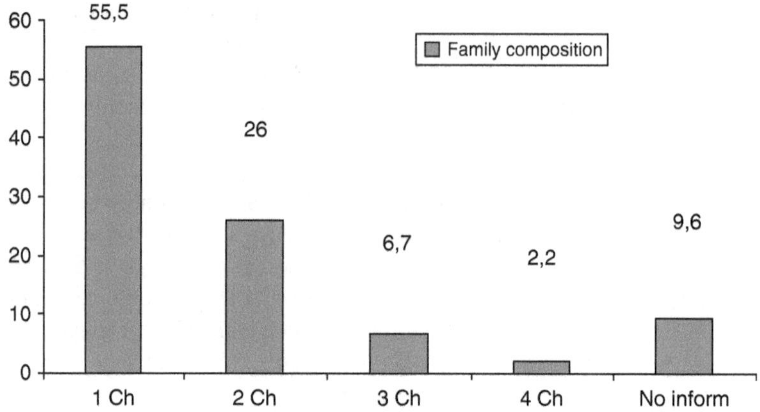

Fig. 4.8 Number of children per family

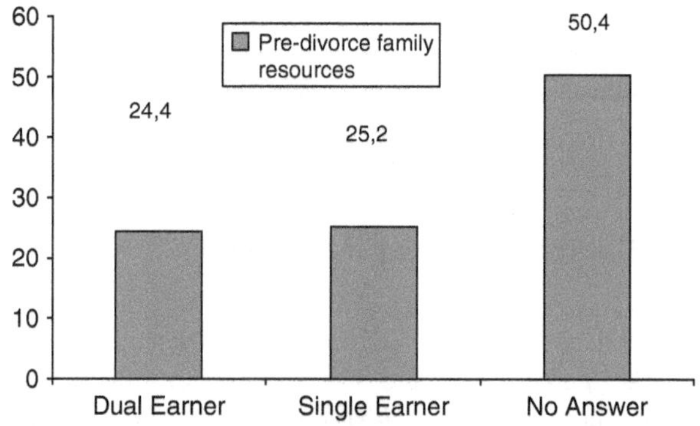

Fig. 4.9 Pre-divorce family resources: dual-earner or single-earner couple

We received an insufficient amount of data on the income level of parents, only half of the cases (67) contained information on this issue. For the other half the following classification can be noticed: generally more fathers (61) than mothers (31) participate in the labour market. A majority of the fathers (40) and mothers (24) earned between 500 and 1,499 Euros. Fathers earned generally more than mothers which is displayed by the two graphs in the following diagram. Within the

\2007\317134), SAP Valencia 18-9-2007 (JUR\2007\340034), SAP Madrid 16-10-2007 (AC\2007 \2324), SAP Madrid 13-9-2007 (JUR\2007\346268), SAP Madrid 16-7-2007 (JUR\2007\336589), SAP Madrid 19-7-2006 (JUR\2007\32432), SAP Guipúzcoa 21-12-2007 (JUR\2007\117075), SAP Álava a 27-4-2007 (JUR\2007\226393), SAP Navarra a 27-8-2007 (JUR\2008\7079), SAP Valladolid a 12-7-2007 (JUR\2007\307507), SAP Valladolid a 12-7-2007 (JUR\2007\307507), SAP Burgos a 9-4-2007 (JUR\2007\282062), SAP León a 26-2-2007 (JUR\2007\249673), SAP Salamanca a 30-11-2006 (JUR\2007\144094), SAP Toledo a 25-4-2007 (JUR\2007\262101), SAP Albacete a 8-11-2007 (JUR\2007\46117).

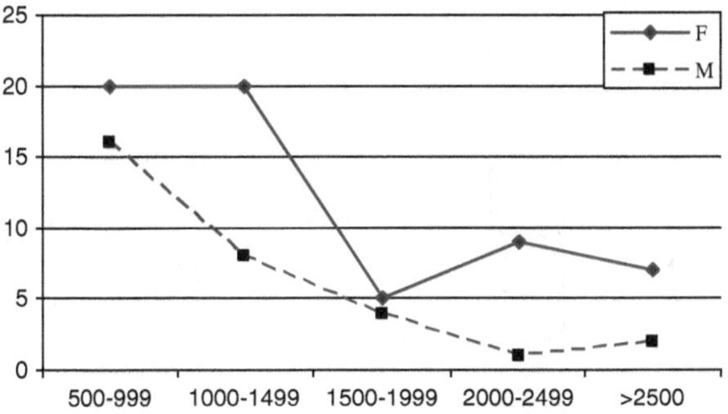

Fig. 4.10 Parental income

group with higher incomes (>2,000 Euros) there were only 3 mothers but 16 fathers (Fig. 4.10).

Within the higher income group parents either held joint custody with higher child support payments (1,000 Euros for two children) that is partly paid by father (60%) an the mother (40%).[147] In other cases where the ex-husband earned considerably more than his ex-wife he would fully cover the mortgage rates.[148]

4.6.3 *Liquidation of Matrimonial Property Regime*

In this category we received results on the amount of child support payment, the number of cases where spousal support payments were ordered and how the costs of the family accommodation is covered. The amount of monthly child support ranged between a minimum of 120 Euros and a maximum of 1,200 Euros per child. According to the chart below, one-third of the parents (28.2%) pay between 200 and 300 Euros per child. Almost a quarter of the parents (22.8%) pay between 300 and 400 Euros and another third (29.2%) pays over 400 Euros (Fig. 4.11).

The following two diagrams show the distribution of the different amounts and deviations from the average amount of child support (Fig. 4.12a).

Whereas the previous figure shows the amount of child support payment in a bar diagram, the next figure shows deviations from the average child support payment (Fig. 4.12b).

Not surprisingly, the amount of child support payment depends in part on the type of custody. In a joint custody arrangement, both parents share child support on a more or less equal base, whereas in a sole custody order the custodial parent receives and administrates the incoming child support. One motive for a parent to

[147]See: SAP Islas Baleares 29-5-2007 (JUR\2007\321875).

[148]See: SAP Barcelona 18-7-2007 (JUR\2007\284433) and SAP Barcelona 25-7-2007 (JUR\2007 \284101).

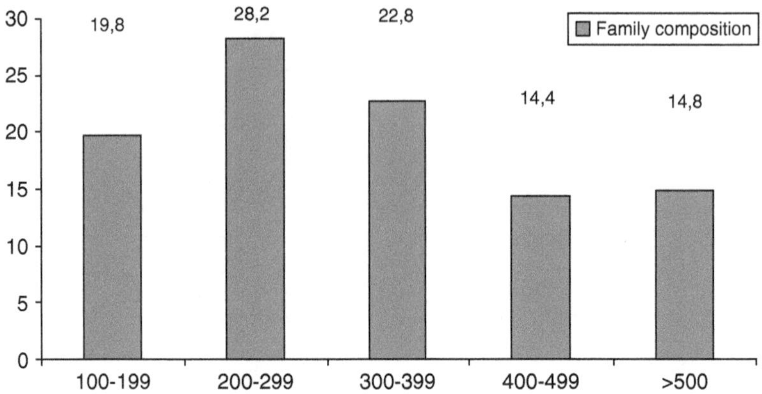

Fig. 4.11 Amount of child support

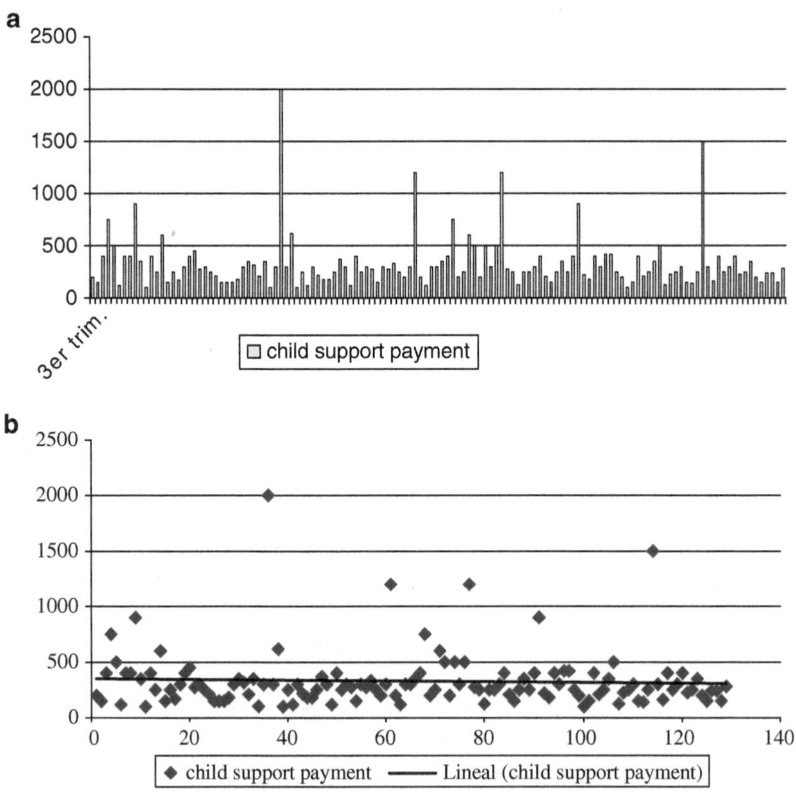

Fig. 4.12 (**a**) Diagram showing the amount of child support payment. (**b**) Deviations from the average child support payment

appeal against a divorce sentence may therefore be the reduction of child support payment by claiming joint custody. It will largely depend on a judge's knowledge of human nature to identify such motives and take the appropriate measures.[149]

The following diagram shows the number of cases in which the economically advantaged ex-spouse was ordered to pay spousal support. Although there were few cases where the ex-wife's income was higher than that of her ex-husband,[150] if spousal support had to be paid it was always the ex-husband. Our analysis showed that the majority of mothers (55.6%) did not receive any compensatory payment in the form of spousal support. In some cases the ex-spouse made an appeal in order to claim spousal support but this was refused by the judge.[151] In this context we have to distinguish between direct and indirect support that goes to an ex-spouse, of which the former corresponds to the spousal support (SS) payment and the latter includes payments made by the ex-husband to cover the mortgage rates. The chart shows the distribution of financial support payments (Fig. 4.13).

A minority of ex-wives (16.3%) received a direct payment in the form of spousal support. In 4.4% of the cases investigated, ex-husbands cover the whole amount of mortgage rates (100%), which in fact functions as an indirect support to ex-wives. In 18.5% of the cases, the ex-husbands pay half of the mortgage rates. In a minor

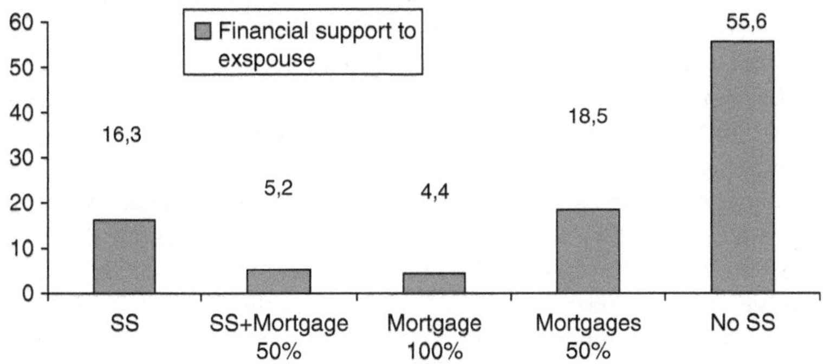

Fig. 4.13 Diagram showing direct and indirect financial support to ex-spouse[152]

[149]See for example the case in which a mother claims higher child support payments and a reduction of contact between father and child. The non-custodial father, on the other hand, pleads for a change from sole to joint custody. See: SAP Islas Baleares 6-3-2007 (JUR\2007\282547).

[150]See cases: SAP Las Palmas 23-2-2007 (JUR\2007\151664), SAP Barcelona 25-9-2007 (JUR \2007\329627), SAP Barcelona 15-6-2007 (JUR\2007\65225), SAP Valencia 17-7-2007 (JUR \2007\317134), SAP Córdoba a 10-7-2006 (JUR\2007\185823). SAP Sevilla a 12-6-2007 (JUR \2007\78867).

[151]See the cases: SAP Valencia 24-7-2007 (JUR\2007\316313) and SAP Valencia 12-9-2007 (JUR \2007\340148). The judge argued that "... no se da el desequilibrio que justificaría el reconocimiento de una pensión compensatoria".

[152]SS = spousal support, SS+Mortgage 50% = ex-spouse pays spousal support and half of the mortgage rate, Mortgage 100% = ex-spouse pays the total amount of mortgage rate, Mortgage 50% = ex-spouse pays half of the mortgage rate, No SS = no spousal support granted.

group that represents 5.2% of cases the ex-spouses receive direct and indirect payment in the form of spousal support and incoming mortgage rates. If we sum up the three groups who receive direct or indirect support, we obtain the remarkable result that nearly a third of all divorced ex-spouses (28.1%) profit from such financial assistance. Although the primary aim of attributing the family accommodation to the children is to guarantee their best interests, the mortgage rate paid by the non-residential ex-husband is an essential financial backing for his ex-wife.

If we take into account that such financial assistance to the children and the ex-spouse is legally justified, it is equally pertinent to ask for the consequences of such regulation for the respective other. In fact, this means that paying ex-spouses have to cover up to four expenditure items.[153] A new start after divorce is therefore often characterized by substantial financial limitations, unless ex-husbands mostly had higher incomes.[154]

In his article on the right to use the family accommodation in cases of joint custody, González del Pozo argues that the criterion of the best interest of the child may only be viewed in relative terms because custody is held by both parents.[155] As an alternative to the standard rule applied in the majority of cases the author proposes six different modes in which the provisions on the use of the family accommodation may be combined with a joint custody regime. The first mode of joint custody with children living in a permanent residence (*modalidad de custodia conjunta con domicilio fijo de los hijos, denominado tipo* "*nido*"), is only feasible if there are three residences available, one for the children and one for the each of the parents. Each parent exercises custody alternately in the children's residence at fixed intervals. This regime requires a good level of communication among parents and involves high costs of maintaining three residences.

A second possibility is joint custody with rotating residence, whereby the children reside alternately at each parent's flat at certain intervals. This regime requires from the children a high ability of adaptation to two parental homes and is only feasible if both residences are close enough. A third option is joint custody with an exclusive but temporal attribution of the family accommodation to the ex-spouse who is not the owner of the residence. This is a direct application of Article 92.3. and is used if the non-owner of the residence is in special need of protection.

A fourth option is joint custody with an exclusive but temporal attribution of a jointly owned family accommodation to one ex-spouse. This is applied in cases in which one ex-spouse is in special need of protection. A fifth option is joint custody with exclusive attribution of the residence to the one parent who owns the residence for cases in which the other parent can afford and guarantee to maintain his or her

---

[153]These expenditure items include child payment, spousal support, mortgage rates and the cost for renting or buying accommodation for personal use.

[154]See the following cases for the relation between income and financial support payments, eg: SAP Las Palmas 17-5-2007 (JUR\2007\288195); SAP Valencia 20-9-2007 (JUR\2007\339999), SAP Castellón 7-9-2007 (JUR\2007\340230), SAP Madrid 7-7-2007 (JUR\2007\25887), SAP La Rioja 18-2-2008 (JUR\2008\217672).

[155]See: González del Pozo (2009): 17f.

own residence. The sixth option is joint custody without attribution of the family residence to none of the parents for cases in which the ex-spouses have agreed on the sale of the property with the aim of avoiding conflicts.

4.7 Conclusion

The outcomes of the study have highlighted some interesting aspects. The first economic aspect is the answer to the research question initially posed, whether there is a relation between the family composition (number of children, parents' resources) and the type of custody? It is striking how many divorces occur in families with lower income levels. Although a divorce tends to have detrimental economic consequences for all family members involved they appear especially disadvantageous for lower income groups with just a single earner. For single earner families this leads to a post-divorce scenario in which the non-residential parent, mostly the father, has to cover the costs for two households and additionally pay child support. In some cases this puts fathers in danger of becoming insolvent.

Concerning the group of dual earner couples two thirds of the non-residential parents pay a part or the full amount of the mortgage rates for the family accommodation. Accordingly, one third of the residential parents continue to cover part of the mortgage rates of the family accommodation. Only in a minority of cases the accommodation was liquidated and subsequently sold. As a conclusion one third of the ex-spouses remain linked by a long-term contract of sharing the costs of the family accommodation. The question remains if such constellation is beneficial for all the people involved in the long run. As more and more women tend to have a job formation equal to men, women are in the position of becoming financially independent and make a new start after divorce.

Referring the preferred custody options, the results show that in the majority of cases mothers function as primary custodial parent with the fathers maintaining their right to have contact to their child(ren). Parents rarely opted for joint custody as a post-divorce parenting arrangement. The following reasons are responsible for this trend: its feasibility is restricted because of a limited amount of time available for its exercise. Parents' working hours, children's school hours and traveling times leave little space for shared parenting. Joint custody is also associated with higher expenses (traveling, equal standards and equipment in both households, etc.) The functioning of joint custody is often impaired by a lack of cooperation and communication among ex-spouses. On the other hand, joint custody is based on the idea of equal rights and obligations among parents. As an in-depth analysis of cases has shown, joint custody runs the risk of becoming an implicit means to achieve a modification of child support payments. Thus, one parent may want to achieve higher child support payments by impeding joint custody and claiming sole custody. Or in the reverse case, a parent's motive for preferring joint custody may be the implicit intention to reduce payments. As a consequence children might be torn into the problems and inconveniences associated with the joint custody regime.

Joint custody seems difficult to manage and requires a high sense of cooperation as well as an unemotional attitude among ex-spouses. From the psychological point of view this poses a kind of inherent contradiction because the ex-spouses intend to distance themselves from one another whereas at the same time they are expected to cooperate. It is questionable whether the introduction of the joint custody regime by the legislator has increased parents' readiness to opt for it as a practicable solution. It is not yet clear whether this custody arrangement will function as a model example for divorced parents in the future.

Chapter 5
Divorce Mediation

5.1 Introduction

In the first part of this chapter a definition of mediation is proposed and mediation is distinguished from other forms of therapeutic family interventions. We will give an overview of the advantages of mediation in non-consensual divorces in contrast to court ordered dispute resolutions. In Spain the Law on Family Mediation was introduced in all Autonomous Communities within the years 2001 and 2009. The need for mediation is obvious if we consider that family conflicts can have the following serious consequences: they have an impact on the mental and physical health of the divorced including higher rates of mental and psychosomatic disorders and medical treatments, and they have an economic impact on families and the state, for instance economic shortcomings after divorce, job loss and socialisation deficits in children and adolescents. Therefore it seems worthwhile to make efforts in order to reduce family conflicts.

The possible outcomes of mediation will be discussed in the context of the divorce cases brought to Spanish Courts of Appeal in 2007. This is followed by an analysis of the suitability of mediation for divorcing couples. The second part of this chapter deals with procedural aspects of mediation. In order to gain a deeper insight into the dynamics of mediation the characteristic elements of conflicts are described. This is followed by a detailed overview of the different concepts and models of mediation. These concepts include the three approaches to mediation, such as facilitative, transformative and evaluative mediation. Lastly, we will present the successful model of the Harvard Negotiation Project as a special form of alternative dispute resolution.

5.2 Defining Divorce Mediation

Mediation is a family-oriented process in which an unbiased intermediary meets with a divorcing couple to help them reach a mutual agreement for their separation, divorce, or post-divorce conflict. The motivation for mediation as an alternative is that conflicts are mentally and emotionally demanding for the individuals involved.

M. Gaffal, *Psychosocial and Legal Perspectives of Marital Breakdown*,
DOI 10.1007/978-3-642-13896-6_5,

Therefore one of the inspiring motives for the Law 15/2005 was to reduce the level of conflict in the post-divorce family. In the introduction to the law mediation is characterized as a voluntary form of alternative conflict resolution which seeks to facilitate the dialogue among all family members and thus helps to protect the interests of minor children in the post-divorce phase:

> "Con el fin de reducir las consecuencias derivadas de una separación y divorcio para todos los miembros de la familia, mantener la comunicación y el diálogo, y en especial garantizar la protección del interés superior del menor, se establece la mediación como un recurso voluntario alternativo de solución de los litigios familiares por vía de mutuo acuerdo con la intervención de un mediador, imparcial y neutral." (Ley 15/2005)

Mediation is an alternative dispute resolution (ADR)[1] in order to reach settlements in court. It is basically voluntary, confidential, and collaborative. There are binding and non-binding forms of ADR. Negotiation and mediation are generally non-binding as they depend on the willingness of the parties to reach an agreement. Arbitration may be either binding or non-binding, the former option implying that a third party produces a decision that the parties have to follow and in the latter the parties may reject the decision.[2] Likewise, the European Parliament has emphasized the advantages of mediation in its Directive on Certain Aspects of Mediation in Civil and Commercial Matters.[3] The Directive provides the following definition of mediation:

> "(a) 'Mediation' means a structured process, however named or referred to, whereby two or more parties to a dispute attempt by themselves, on a voluntary basis, to reach an agreement on the settlement of their dispute with the assistance of a mediator. This process may be initiated by the parties or suggested or ordered by a court or prescribed by the law of a Member State." (Directive 2008/52/EC)

Alternative dispute resolution (ADR) has become an approved method of conflict resolution in many areas of life.[4] It denotes any means of settling disputes outside of the courtroom and includes arbitration, mediation, neutral evaluation,

[1]The ADR movement in the United States came into being in the 1970s and started as a social movement to resolve community-wide civil rights disputes through mediation. As a legal movement it emerged because of the increasing loss of time and financial resources in litigations and an overloaded court system. This has produced a number of innovations in ADR models and has led to an increase of government-mandated and court-based ADR in state and federal systems.

[2]Arbitration is a sort of alternative dispute resolution (ADR) in order to solve disputes outside the courts. It is a special method in which a third party reassesses case and orders a legally binding decision.

[3]See: Directive 2008/52/EC of the European Parliament and of the Council of 21 May 2008 on certain aspects of mediation in civil and commercial matters. The directive was published in the Official Journal on 24 May 2008, entered into force on the 20th day thereafter, and must be implemented into national law by the 21 May 2011.

[4]In commercial disputes arbitrators function as impartial third parties who hear the case, consider the evidence and subsequently decide. ADR finds its application in many fields and may involve individuals, companies, organisations or even whole nations.

and conciliation. From a cultural point of view it may be considered a refined skill of conflict resolution that is an improvement to the controversial court settlement. Mediation is democratic in the sense that it involves an ongoing discourse in order to reach a consensual agreement.[5]

In family conflicts, mediated settlements are more suitable than litigated outcomes as they are built on cooperation and a view of the family in transition. Mediation originated in the United States in the 1970s and became a successful method of dispute resolution in divorce cases. Thus it spread rapidly to Canada where it was installed free of cost at the beginning of the 1980s. In the Latin American Countries it was first introduced in Argentine in 1992 as a mandatory instance before going to court. In 1998 the European Council published the Recommendation No. R (98) 1 on Family Mediation,[6] in which it recognized the growing number of family disputes resulting from separation or divorce. The Council pointed to the detrimental consequences of conflict for families and the high social and economic cost to status in the case of litigation. In the Recommendation the Council pointed to the detrimental consequences of family conflicts and stated that these are particularly detrimental to the children:

> "5. Acknowledging the special characteristics of family disputes, namely:
> - the fact that family disputes involve persons who, by definition, will have interdependent and continued relationships
> - the fact that family disputes arise in a context of distressing emotions and increase them
> - the fact that separation and divorce impact on all the members of the family, especially children;" (Recommendation No. R (98))

Following the Recommendation to introduce and promote family mediation, the Member States were asked to take measures in order to implement the use of family mediation as an appropriate means of resolving family disputes. If we consider that family mediation has existed since the 1970 it has a comparatively short history in Spain. Therefore there are relatively few studies available that address the problems and functioning of family mediation in Spain. The first reference to consensual conflict resolution was made in Law 30/1981 of 7 July according to which the divorcing spouses were asked to propose a regulating agreement on all relevant divorce-related issues. Mediation as method of conflict resolution was later established in the legal system by Law 15/2005 of 8 July. Following the recommendation of the European Council the following Autonomous Communities in Spain implemented autonomous legislations in family mediation within the years 2001 and

[5]In fact, in many countries mediation is being widely practiced in family disputes and courts, social services departments. It is also applied in public and private organizations to deal with interpersonal or institutional conflicts. These include for example commercial disputes between companies, interdepartmental conflicts, cases concerning discrimination (e.g. ethnic, gender, disabled) in the public as well as in the private sector. For a detailed description of the areas in which mediation is applied. See: Moore (2003): 27f.

[6]See: Council of Europe Committee of Ministers, Recommendation No. R (98) 1 of the Committee of Ministers to Member States on Family Mediation, adopted by the Committee of Ministers on 21 January 1998 at the 616th meeting of the Ministers' Deputies.

2009:[7] País Vasco,[8] Cataluña,[9] Galicia,[10] Asturias,[11] La Rioja,[12] Comunidad Valenciana,[13] Aragón,[14] Castilla-La Mancha,[15] Canarias,[16] Navarra,[17] Islas Baleares,[18] Madrid[19] and Castilla y Leon.[20]

---

[7]See: Marín López (2008).

[8]Ley 1/2008, de 8 de febrero, de Mediación Familiar (BOPV n. 34, de 18 febrero de 2008.).

[9]Ley 9/1998, de 15 de julio, del Código de Familia de Cataluña (DOGC n.° 2.687, de 23 de julio de 1998; BOE n.° 198, de 19 de agosto). Ley 1/2001, de 15 de marzo, de Mediación Familiar (DOGC n.° 3.355, de 26 de marzo de 2001, con corrección de errores en DOGC n.° 3.548, de 8 de enero de 2002; BOE n.° 91, de 16 de abril de 2001). Decreto 139/2002, de 14 de mayo, por el que se aprueba el Reglamento de la Ley 1/2001, de 15 de marzo, de Mediación Familiar de Cataluña (DOGC n. 3641, de 23 de mayo de 2002; correcciones de errores en DOGC n.° 3867, de 17 de abril de 2003, y n.° 3898, de 4 de junio).

[10]Ley 4/2001, de 31 de mayo, reguladora de la Medición Familiar (DOG n.° 117, de 18 de junio de 2001; BOE n.° 157, de 2 de julio). Decreto 159/2003, de 31 de enero, por el que se regulan la figura del mediador familiar, el Registro de Mediadores Familiares de Galicia y el reconocimiento de la mediación gratuita (DOG n.°34, de 18 de febrero de 2003; corrección de errores en DOG n. 44, de 4 de marzo).

[11]Ley 3/2007, de 23 de marzo, de Mediación Familiar (BOPA n.° 81, de 9 de abril de 2007; BOE n.° 170, de 17 de julio). Decreto 93/2005, de 2 de septiembre, por el que se regulan los Puntos de Encuentro Familiar (BOPA n.° 214, de 15 de septiembre de 2005).

[12]Decreto 2/2007, de 26 de enero, por el que se regulan los Puntos de Encuentro Familiar (BOR n. 14, de 30 de enero de 2007).

[13]Ley 7/2001, de 26 de noviembre, reguladora de la Mediación Familiar en el ámbito de la Comunidad Valenciana (DOGV n.° 4.138, de 29 de noviembre de 2001; BOE n.° 303, de 19 de diciembre). Decreto 41/2007, de 13 de abril, por el que se desarrolla la Ley 7/2001, de 26 de noviembre, reguladora de la Mediación Familiar en el ámbito de la Comunidad Valenciana (DOGV n.° 5.492, de 18 de abril de 2007).

[14]Ley 4/2007, de 22 de marzo, de prevencion y protección integral de las mujeres víctimas de violencia en Aragón (BOA n. 41, de 9 abril de 2007; BOE n. 141, de 13 de junio).

[15]Ley 4/2005, de 24 de mayo, del Servicio Social Especializado de Mediación Familiar (DOCM n.° 111, de 3 de junio de 2005; BOE n.° 203, de 25 de agosto).

[16]Ley 15/2003, de 8 de abril, de la Mediación Familiar (BOC n.° 85, de 6 de mayo de 2003; BOE n.° 134, de 5 de junio). Decreto 144/2007, de 24 de mayo, por el que se aprueba el Reglamento de la Ley de la Mediación Familiar (BOC n.° 114, de 8 de junio de 2007).

[17]Ley Foral 22/2002, de 2 de julio, para la adopción de medidas integrales contra la violencia sexista de Navarra (BON n.° 84, de 12 de julio de 2002; BOE n.°199, de 20 de agosto).

[18]Ley 18/2006, de 22 de noviembre, de Mediación Familiar (BOIB n.° 169, de 30 de noviembre de 2006; BOE n.° 303, de 20 de diciembre).

[19]Ley 1/2007, de 21 de febrero, de Mediación Familiar (BOCM n.° 54, de 5 de marzo de 2007; BOE n.° 153, de 27 de junio).

[20]Ley 1/2006, de 6 de abril, de Mediación Familiar (BOCL n.° 75, suplemento, de 18 de abril de 2006; BOE n.° 105, de 3 de mayo, con corrección de errores en BOE n.° 135, de 7 de junio). Decreto 50/2007, de 17 de mayo, por el que se aprueba el Reglamento de desarrollo de la Ley 1/2006, de 6 de abril, de Mediación Familiar (BOCL n.° 99, de 23 de mayo de 2007).

Fig. 5.1 The mediation triangle

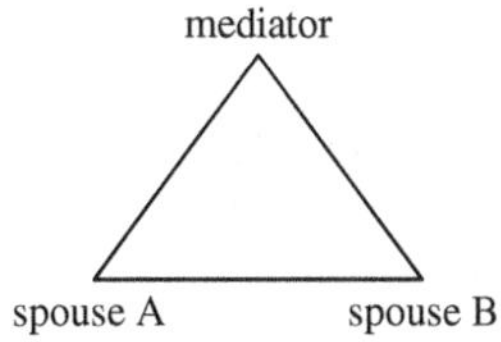

Mediation should not be confused with family or couples therapy because it is not a therapy that aims to restore the family life.[21] It is part of the mediation concept to accept that there will not be reconciliation. Whereas the aim of psychotherapy may be to understand why something went wrong and how a relationship or event can be more fully understood mediation is always goal-oriented. Parties shall reach a decision that can be translated into a legal document. The past is only relevant to find a solution and not to provide an in-depth analysis.[22]

Although the children play a predominant role in the process of mediation, they do not normally take part in the sessions.[23] Once the divorcing spouses have failed to reach an agreement they attend sessions with the mediator to discuss issues such as custody, visitation rights, child support, spousal support, and the liquidation of assets. García-Longoria Serrano et al. summarize the function of mediation in the areas of separation and divorce:

> "La mediación familiar en la separación y divorcio. Se trata de la intervención de una persona neutral para apoyar la toma de decisiones respecto al proceso de separación y divorcio. Las cuestiones generales se relacionan con la forma de comunicar a los hijos la separación, decidir quien debe tener la custodia de los hijos, pactar el régimen de visitas, de alimentos o de pensión compensatoria, decidir de que forma se lleva a cabo la liquidación del régimen económico y revisar y actualizar los pactos hechos tiempo atrás." (García-Longoria Serrano 2004: 264)

Accordingly, Friedman views the relationship between the divorcing spouses and the mediator as 'mediation triangle', in which the mediator has the role of a neutral third party without becoming a decision maker or an advocate for any of the two divorcees. The scheme shows the actors in the mediation triangle (Fig. 5.1).[24]

---

[21]In family therapy one or more therapists help the family members to identify negative patterns of behaviour and to learn new forms of conduct. The therapeutic methods include discussion and problem-solving sessions with individuals in one-to-one settings and as a group. Its aim is to facilitate communication among the members and to restore the family system. The same aims and methods are applied in couples therapy.

[22]For further criteria of distinction between psychotherapy and mediation see Katz (2007): 96.

[23]There has nevertheless been an extensive discussion among experts over the question whether children should have the right to take part in mediation in order to follow and realize their interests. For a detailed overview of the arguments for and against children participating in mediation see: Soria et al. (2008): 37–44.

[24]See: Friedman (1993): 20.

In this process the law plays an important role although it is not considered more relevant than the spouses' personal sense of fairness or their mutual respect. The child may be considered as the physically absent but nevertheless substantially present fourth party as custody decisions are of major importance during the separation and divorce processes.

In this context we shall point to a characteristic feature within Spanish society that may pose an obstacle to viewing the mediator as a neutral third party offering help. One characteristic feature is the high social distance among people which means that relationships are basically distant, impersonal and relatively unemotional.[25] However, family relationships are more affective and close. Therefore it becomes obvious that for a couple to seek the advice of a mediator means that they have to overcome the barrier of the high social distance in order to communicate personal feelings to an unknown person. As conflicts are mostly emotional, subjective and highly contextualized people do not normally assume that a person from outside may be capable of resolving private conflicts. The parties may weigh the negative effects of a possible face loss higher than the help an expert might provide for the solution of the conflict. An aversion against mediation may also come from the misconception that a party may have when confronted with mediation. Lapasió Campos and Ramón Marqués underline the particular status of mediation by giving the following definition of family mediation:

> "La mediación familiar es el proceso de resolución de conflictos, no terapéutico ni jurídico, que permite a las parejas que desean separarse el disponer de un lugar (al margen del Juzgado) donde dialogar y llegar a soluciones satisfactorias respecto del futuro de sus hijos y del suyo propio. La mediación familiar, por tanto, no es jamás una terapia, sino un proceso con identidad propia." (Lapasió Campos, Ramón Marqués quoted in Soria et al. 2008: 141f)

Whereas in most civil court cases the dispute among parties is about money matters or monetary measurable issue, in family conflicts immaterial objects, such as the quality of parent–child relationship, are at stake. Therefore, McWinney argues that for parents in custody conflicts it is not so much the high costs of litigation or the indignity due to state interference in private matters that deters them, but rather, it is the fear of losing their relationship with their child. The danger lies in the ongoing divorce proceedings with an equal number of accusations and the reciprocal hurt of one parent against the other, which leads to a situation of competition. It appears that such competition ends in a victory for one party and a major loss of the other, depending on how custody is decided and assets are distributed. The actual loser in this battle is the child because he or she has lost the presence of one parent, and most probably, the certainty of continuing parental affection. This aspect is underlined by McWinney who speaks of the "winner–loser syndrome" in the determination of child custody and points to the detrimental consequences of conflicts of custody for the children:

[25]See: Padilla-Gálvez and Gaffal (2005): 35f.

"The majority of children regard the loss of a parent as the single most negative aspect of separation and divorce. Children also worry that if their parents can stop loving each other, they could surely stop loving them as well; and parental custody battles seldom persuade a child that he or she is greatly loved." (McWinney 1995: 101)

We will now approach mediation from the perspective of game-theory and analyze the possible options of outcomes.

5.3 Game-Theory and Factors that Influence Mediation

Once the family union has come to an end each family member follows his or her own interests with the state representing and guaranteeing the interests of minor children. In the context of divorce conflict stands for a diversity of interests and the belief that a satisfaction of the needs of all parties cannot be achieved simultaneously. In the intention to maximize personal gains each ex-spouse will tend to satisfy the most urgent personal needs.

As such, mediation may be viewed as a change of paradigm from the "win–lose" principle to a 'win–win solution' providing gain for all parties involved and avoiding the exclusion of any one party. A 'win–win strategy' is a form of conflict resolution in which the parties collaborate in order to accommodate all disputants. According to game theory[26] a win–win strategy is considered a cooperative group game in which the gain of the winner does not imply the loss of another player. In cooperative games the parties are willing to collaborate and the benefit of the group is thought of as more important than egoistic behaviour or domination of the one over the other. Two preconditions for a win–win game are that (1) there is no fundamental contradiction of interests and (2) the players are forthcoming with their interests. The table shows four possible options in an elementary win–win game between two players (Fig. 5.2).

Fig. 5.2 Options in a win–win game[27]

player 1/player 2	a	b
a	2 / 2	0 / 0
b	0 / 0	1 / 1

[26]Game theory according to their founders von Neumann and Morgenstern includes extensive games, normal form games and coalition games. In their recognized publication "Theory of Games and Economic Behavior" (1944) the authors developed a rationality concept for individual behaviour whereby one aims to maximise the objectively expected utility.

[27]a, b = strategies, 0/1/2 = amount of gain.

There are four possible outcomes in a win–win position: If both players choose the same strategy, strategy a, then both will receive the maximum gain of 2 (option 1).[28] This option stands for the cooperation between two players that produces a maximum gain for both. If player 1 chooses strategy *a* and player 2 chooses strategy *b*, cooperation has failed and, consequently, there is no gain for either of the two players (options 2 and 3). If both players choose strategy *b*, which stands for the cooperation under a condition of compromise, then there is a restricted pay-off of 1 for both players involved (option 4). This fourth option still produces winners, but with a reduced gain. Although human behaviour is much more complex than it is described in the elementary win–win game, it nevertheless follows a similar rationale. If the spouses decide on the same strategy the pay-off is maximized for both, but if their interests clash fundamentally then cooperation fails and the gains are reduced. If both still agree to make a compromise and arrive at the smallest common denominator, then they still feel as winners, despite of a reduced reward. Moreover, the chance of a counter-reaction is low.

The Harvard Negotiation Project (HNP) defines win–win negotiations as integrative and the win–lose negotiations as distributive types of bargaining. Integrative negotiations are those in which the parties try to find a solution with maximum mutual gains. If a party plans to have further negotiations in the future it seems wise to use this form of negotiation because it facilitates a successful working climate. On the contrary, distributive negotiations imply that one party entirely profits whereas the other gives something up. As this kind of negotiation benefits one party on the cost of the other it does not produce constructive long-term relationships.

For the sake of interest for the children, it is more rewarding for ex-spouses if they use a cooperative approach to the settlement of custody. García García sees a chance for integrative negotiations if both ex-spouses aim to avoid the distress associated with a court trail, such as the embarrassment of revealing details of family life at court. The author points out that even a difference in the spouses' priorities might turn into an advantage if the spouses are willing to exchange mutual gains in matters where there are different individual preferences for each:

> "Los intereses compartidos – el bienestar de los hijos, el deseo de evitar el litigio ante los tribunales y de que se divulguen determinados aspectos de la vida privada – pueden determinar una covariación de las ganancias y las posibles pérdidas de los implicados y convertir una negociación gana-pierde, en otra en la que ambos pueden ganar. Pero también las diferencias pueden dar lugar al mismo resultado; si se consigue identificar diferencias en la relevancia que las partes otorgan a distintos aspectos de la negociación, se pueden realizar intercambios que supongan beneficios para ambos." (García García 2003: 128)

In a zero-sum game what one party gains the other loses and it tends to produce exclusion and dominance as. Unfortunately win–lose games are unavoidable in our

---

[28]See: Rieck (1992): 50.

society and they seem to have a destructive effect when used in interpersonal relationships.[29] From the psychological point of view, win–lose games tend to produce a spirit of opposition and subsequent counterclaims, or they result in submission and capitulation.[30] This notion is also underlined by de Armas Hernández who says:

> "El gran aporte de la mediación al conflicto es la sustitución de la concepción tradicional de ≪ ganar–perder ≫ en las disputas, por ≪ ganar–ganar≫, pues este cambio de concepción no sólo afecta a los resultados, sino también al proceso mismo, ya que modifica la actitud de las partes." (de Armas Hernández 2003: 127)

In game-theoretic terms the intact family is a coordination game in which all players receive more or less mutual gains by making reciprocally consistent decisions.[31] This cooperative union is disbanded by divorce and the question remains of how much sense of cooperation among the parents will has remained after marital breakdown? The answer to this question will mostly affect the children because the quality of their post-divorce life will depend largely on the functioning of post-divorce parental cooperation.

These theoretical considerations shall be applied to some divorce sentences of the study presented in Chap. 4. The sentences contain examples of ex-spouses who either cooperated (2/2), made compromises (1/1) or did not cooperate (0/0) in certain aspects of the post-divorce regulation. Certain regularities may be noticed in the way people act or respond to specific typical circumstances.

In the majority of divorce cases investigated ex-spouses asked for changes to the regulating agreement. However, in some cases these claims appeared either unfeasible in practice, unreasonable, or legally impossible. One example for a 0/0-outcome is the case[32] in which an ex-husband asks for a change from a sole to a joint custody regime for his two children (strategy a). The reason for this change is obviously a reduction of child support payments for the two children. His ex-wife wants to maintain the existing agreement (strategy b). The judge refuses any such changes to the divorce agreement. The following explanation given by the judge is an example for the line that Courts of Appeal tend to follow in cases where the non-custodial parent intends to reduce child support payments:

---

[29]For instance the underlying principle in a job application is a zero-sum game because the chosen applicant receives the job on the cost of the other applicants not having been selected.

[30]From the psychoanalytic point of view this dynamism can be explained by Freud's theory of the urges ("*Triebtheorie*") and its further development to the theory of object-relations. Basically, in a winner–loser game the loser suffers the loss of an object, an event that provokes emotions. In this context ‚objects', that in a general sense include persons as well as inanimate objects, are recipients of urges (such as libido or aggression). If the object is withdrawn the individual reacts with emotions that range from frustration and sadness, to aggression or dependency and regression (Freud 1970: 280f.).

[31]In coordination games coalition among players supports cooperative behaviour.

[32]See: SAP Las Palmas JUR\2007\288195.

"El principal motivo de discordia entre los litigantes se refiere a la atribución de la guarda y custodia de las menores..., que en la sentencia de instancia se otorga a la madre, y que el padre recurrente insiste en reclamar de forma compartida."[33]

Another example for a 0/0-outcome is a similar case in which the judge made decisions for the regulating agreement because the ex-spouses were unable to reach an agreement. A mother was given sole custody of her children and remained together with the children in the former family home (strategy a). The judge ordered the father to pay child support (strategy b), but the father appealed against this order asking for a reduction of child support (strategy c). When the judge refused this claim, the father appealed again changing his strategy by soliciting sole custody for both children (strategy d). The judge refused this claim again and gave the following order:

"Al ser el principal motivo de disconformidad con la Sentencia de instancia la atribución a la madre de la guarda y custodia de la hija menor de edad de los litigantes y que el apelante solicita que se revoque y le sea atribuida a él."[34]

Once the father's strategy had turned out unsuccessful, he changed it again and asked for split custody in which the younger child would live with the mother and the older child with him (strategy e). He argued that if each of the parents paid child support reciprocally, the actual payments would cancel each other out. The judge refused and ordered the father to pay child support for both daughters:

"Se establezca una pensión de alimentos (...) a abonar por la madre a favor de Bianca por un valor de 150 euros, así como a Desiree por el mismo importe."[35]

If both parties choose strategy b, which calls for cooperation under the condition of compromise, then there is a restricted gain for both parties (1/1-outcome). This occurs, for instance, in the following case: a father asked for a joint custody arrangement (strategy a) and the mother wanted an increase in child support payment (strategy b). The father argued that his ex-wife made this claim because of her own problems. Consequently the judge rejected the mother's claim and accepted the father's request to spend more time with his children by ordering an extended visitation time. The judge gave the following order:

"Declarar que ha lugar a la siguiente modificación de medidas respecto de las acordadas en sentencia de fecha 16 de enero de 2003:

a) Que las visitas del progenitor no custodio para con su hijo y respecto de los martes, se regirán por el siguiente régimen: (...).
b) Que con respecto de las visitas del progenitor no custodio los jueves (...).
c) Las entregas del menor en el régimen de fin de semana se realizarán (...)."[36]

[33]See: SAP Las Palmas JUR\2007\288195.

[34]See: SAP Barcelona JUR\2007\329460.

[35]See: SAP Barcelona JUR\2007\329460.

[36]See: SAP Islas Baleares JUR\2007\282547.

If both parties choose the same strategy they receive a maximum gain ("2/2"-outcome). This option produces the highest pay-off for both. In one case, the father opposed the order of the first instance because the judge had forgotten to take into account the regulating agreement that the couple had reached before the divorce.[37] The judge acknowledged the intervention and declared the following:

> "Recurre el Sr. (...) el pronunciamiento de la sentencia relativo al régimen de visitas paterno-filial, alegando que llegaron a un acuerdo las partes sobre dicho extremo, tal como manifestaron como cuestión previa al inicio de la Vista, sin que se haya recogido en la sentencia."[38]

For a better understanding of the contents of divorce conflicts we have to offer an explanatory model that takes individuals' basic needs into account. In this context we proposed a hierarchy of needs described by Maslow, according to which a higher need only emerges once the hierarchically lower need is satisfied. After divorce the basic need for safety becomes virulent which includes such necessities as accommodation (property), security of body and employment. Whereas higher needs such as friendship, confidence or respect of others are required for the process of mediation it becomes evident that they can only be activated once questions of accommodation and income have been resolved. From the perspective of mediation the divorcing spouses are supposed to have all the skills available that are necessary to the solution of the conflict. However, this assumption is contrary to their actual state of needs.

If one takes Maslow's model into consideration it appears rather surprising that conflicting parties should be prepared to use skills of self-actualization that are situated at the top of the hierarchy. Such self-actualization includes a sense of problem solving and the willingness to accept facts or avoid prejudice. But these abilities are rather an outcome of mediation than a pre-requisite. In fact, some authors have pointed to the inherent contradiction that mediation poses for the ex-spouses. For instance, Bastine quotes the sociologists Cardia-Vonèche and Bastard who pointed to the relatively little response that mediation has received as a means of conflict resolution. They see the main reason for an eventual failure of mediation in the inherent paradox, that it grounds on the optimistic assumption that the parties act in good faith and have the desire to overcome the post-divorce the difficulties. They give the following explanation:

> "Wir meinen, dass die Mediation bei Trennung und Scheidung eher eine Randerscheinung bleiben muss, weil sie auf einer übertrieben optimistischen Annahme beruht, die Partner seien guten Willens und hätten das Bedürfnis, die Schwierigkeiten der Nachscheidung selber zu regeln." (Cardia-Vonèche, Bastard in Bastine (2005): 15)

On the one hand the parties aim to distance themselves from one another and on the other hand they are asked to cooperate. This is most unlikely for the following reasons: Why should an ex-spouse cooperate if the respective other has hurt his or

---

[37]See also SAP Valencia JUR\2007\340034.

[38]See: SAP Barcelona JUR\2006\65213.

her feelings beforehand? Why should one ex-spouse develop a conciliatory attitude towards the other if the respective other is living with a new partner? In other words, if the divorce was initiated by one spouse it is rather unlikely that the other will develop cooperative behaviour. How can an ex-spouse ever realistically develop an interest in reconciliation if he or she is confronted with vital problems such as economic survival, job search, household formation and organisation of child care? Why should an ex-spouse consider questions on joint custody or quick reconciliation more important than his or her own fear of losing the accommodation? Why should the concern for the children's well-being be stronger than feelings of uncertainty and distress associated with the post-divorce organisation of one's life?

Another complicating factor is addressed by Yahm's psychoanalytic investigation of divorce conflicts in which the author highlights the dynamics that underlie adversarial divorces and describes their consequences. He argues that the strategy that most lawyers apply during the negotiation process tends to make the client dependent on his lawyer. This procedure does not only exclude the client's resources but also leaves aside his emotions and, thereby, provokes regressive tendencies. Although this seems to be a complex issue, it is nevertheless a relevant objection. According to the view of conflict as an iceberg, where parts of it remain unseen, unsolved emotional problems tend to emerge again. The author explains this mechanism in the following quotation:

> "The adversarial divorce, with its emphasis on authority dependence, power tactics, winning as much as possible, and defeating the opponent, exacerbates regressive tendencies. By defining the best interests of clients in strictly monetary and legal terms, matrimonial attorneys ignore the emotional and developmental needs and interests of their clients and their clients' children and unintentionally join with the least mature or most underdeveloped aspects of their clients' personalities. By pursuing win–lose solutions and by viewing the spouse primarily or even exclusively in adversarial terms, attorneys intensify their clients' regressive experiences of separation and loss and of rivalrous sibling relationships. By promising to take care of everything and by assuming primary if not exclusive control of the negotiations, these professionals unwittingly encourage a regressive dependence that often leaves their client feeling betrayed and abandoned when everything proves not to have been taken care of." (Yahm, 1984: 60. ...)

On the contrary, win–win resolutions are considered to be a powerful tool for assisting those people who have suffered from emotional distress. This occurs because the win–win resolutions create an atmosphere of mutual esteem and equality. In theory, mediation has the same goals in that it aims to facilitate collaboration among the disputing parties and to encourage a win–win strategy. Litigation can be damaging to both parties in a dispute and may result in a zero-sum game after the rule of what one party gains the other loses. Mediation can help to reduce hostility between the parties and can lead to a win–win result. García García puts it like this:

> "Negociar supone reconocer al otro, es decir, aceptar su existencia. Cuando dos personas negocian, cada una de ellas espera obtener algo. La búsqueda de soluciones beneficiosas para ambas constituye la clave del éxito del proceso." (García García 2003: 126)

In an adversarial divorce case lawyers tend to concentrate on a maximization of the party's gain which leads to increasing tensions among the parties. In this context, Falco underlines that the parties do not only appear in the role of divorcing husband and wife, but they also have to be aware of their role as father and mother, who are asked to act in the best interests of their child. He criticizes the tactics of lawyers who use the court room as an arena for an escalation of the conflict and argues that lawyers would need special skills in order to be able to deal with family conflicts effectively. These skills are different from those used in other civil cases. In reference to the role of lawyers in divorce conflict, Falco states the following:

> "(Lawyers) favor the traditional view of litigation as the arena of winners and losers. They see themselves as guardians of zealous advocacy with the obligation to advance the client's agenda as if the client was the sole hero or heroine whose interests are at issue in his or her family's case. (...)
>
> Some parents and their advocates abuse the divorce and custody determination process (...) wasting valuable system resources, prolonging the conflict and cost of divorce, or undermining parenting arrangements" (Falco 2003: 171)

Furthermore, the author maintains that lawyers often lack an adequate formation in dealing with divorce conflicts that require alternative techniques of conflict resolution. Academic law studies do not normally cover relevant fields such as psychology or conflict resolution in their curriculum. This view is also supported by the results of a study carried out by Hedeen and Salem, who made a survey among legal professionals and law students inquiring about what types of knowledge family lawyers should have nowadays. The respondents underlined that apart from legal knowledge, additional know-how is required to meet the demands of the clients in a divorce crisis. Thus, legal experts should be familiar with various other techniques, such as close listening, psychological intervention, financial grounding, negotiation skills, and the potential effects of divorce on the children.

However, students' views were different from those of legal practitioners concerning the importance of the skills, with the latter putting more emphasis on practical know-how.[39] Hedeen and Salem sense a demand for an interdisciplinary approach to family law. The notion of practical know-how is also emphasized by Falco who argues that legal scholars do not usually function as practitioners and therefore they often lack practical experience in this field. Additionally, academic legal formation does not normally include tuition of psychological knowledge to students:

> "(...) legal education does not really prepare lawyers to handle the full range of issues, both legal and nonlegal, that can arise in any divorce case. The principal focus in law school is on the substantive law or legal procedures, and law professors, as nonpracticing lawyers, may be particularly unsuited to address the psychological elements that lawyers need to learn to handle divorce cases adequately." (Parley quoted in Falco 2003: 171)

Therefore, lawyers have acquired additional knowledge in divorce mediation and offer alternative conflict resolution. Whether or not an agreement is reached

---

[39] See: Hedeen and Salem (2006): 601 ff.

depends mainly on the two parties whereby the mediator would never impose any solution on the disputants. Mediators are supposed to facilitate the dialogue and to provide information to the parties. The following topics are objects of the mediation process, including the amount of child support to be paid by the non-custodial parent, the parenting scheme, child support payments, liquidation of the matrimonial property regime, the allocation of the family accommodation, and the allocation of outstanding debts.

Mediation rests on the principle of the parties' voluntary participation and the mediator avoids to impose a solution on the parties or to threaten the parties with a judgment. Resolutions achieved by mutual compromise tend to be more stable than solutions that have been forced on the parties. On the other hand authors, such as Moore, believe that couples should in some way be induced to at least try mediation. He argues that some sort of mainstream pressure coming from outside, such as from friends or legal practitioners, would be justified because they may induce the couple to make an attempt with mediation. He explains his view in the following way:

> "Voluntary participation does not, however, mean that there may not be pressure to try mediation. Other disputants or external figures, such as friends, colleagues at work, constituents, authoritative leaders, or judges, may put significant pressure on a party to make an attempt at negotiation with the assistance of a mediator. Some courts in family and civil cases in the United States have even gone so far as to rule that parties must make a good faith effort at mediation before the court will be willing to hear the case. Attempting mediation does not, however, mean that the participants are forced to reach agreements." (Moore 2003: 20)

On the whole, results have shown that mediation is a practical, less expensive, and less conflicting alternative to divorce procedures at court.[40] In fact, research has brought to light a number of convincing advantages that mediation has in contrast to court settled divorces. These advantages include more contentment of divorcing spouses with the process and its outcomes.[41] This is mainly due to the fact that they have taken part in the decision making process. Other gains concern lower costs of the whole procedure, fewer divorce cases for courts to deal with, higher levels of adjustment to divorce outcomes[42], fewer cases of re-litigation,[43] and better post-divorce cooperation of parents in child-related matters.[44] Research has also shown that mediated divorces are associated with better rates of children's adjustment in the post-divorce situation.[45] Accordingly, Cohen et al. summarize the benefits of

[40]See: Kelly (1991): 387f.

[41]See: Emery (1994) and Walker et al. (1994).

[42]See: Maxwell 1992: 353 ff. and Pearson and Thoennes (1984): 497–524.

[43]See: Irwin and Benjamin (1992): 35 ff.

[44]See: Dillon and Emery (1996): 131 ff.

[45]See: Stull and Kaplan (1987): 53–59.

divorce mediation and point to the risk of re-litigation in the case of court ordered divorce settlements:

> "(. . .) mediation remains a form of dispute resolution that allows divorcing spouses to make the decisions that will shape their own and their children's futures in an atmosphere which enables both parties to express their wants, feelings and concerns, to discuss and work towards joint post-divorce parenting, and to arrive at mutually acceptable arrangements without the time pressure of crowded court calendars and the financial pressure of sky-high legal fees, and with the facilitation of trained professionals, who can help each spouse see the other's point of view. At the very least, mediation is a potentially kinder method than adversarial legal proceedings, which certainly do not help and may, in fact, greatly exacerbate the enormous stress inherent in the break-up of a marriage." (Cohen 1999: 330)

Adversarial divorce is costly and demanding and tends to lead to further litigation whereas out-of court settlements benefit ex-spouses because they are the agents of their own decision making process. As mediation produces more advantages than adversarial settlements, governments in the United States and Europe offer pre-divorce mediation for couples. It enables parents to reach an agreement and avoid state interference. Studies on the outcomes of mediation show that in 40–70% of mediated divorce cases the parties reach an agreement.[46] For instance, Marcus et al. carried out a study in the United States in which they compared the outcomes of 199 privately mediated divorce cases to 201 adversarial divorces. They wanted to know whether there would be significant differences for one group in the amount of child support, the duration of alimony payments, and the custody option. Furthermore, they made reference to the previous research literature which suggested that men profited more from mediation than women. Firstly, their results showed that women were not disadvantaged in any of the areas mentioned. The authors summarize their results:

> "Our findings are contrary to predictions made about the results of mediation for women by those who argue that mediation favors men. Not only do women obtain similar percentages of family income and family liabilities in mediated versus adversarial cases, but they also obtain similar amounts of periodic alimony and similar percentages (. . .). In a non-financial arena, our study indicates there also is no difference in the number of days children spend with each parent neither in the differing formats nor in the type of custody arrangement most frequently chosen." (Marcus et al. 2007: 148)

However, their results showed that women in mediated divorces received higher child support payments and spousal support for a longer period of time than those in adversarial divorces. On the other hand, more men in mediated cases were bestowed joint custody of their children. The authors state the following:

> "Surprisingly, women in mediated cases obtain a higher percentage of family assets, receive periodic alimony for more years than their adversarial counterparts, and obtain greater amounts of child support. While women obtain superior outcomes via mediation in several financial areas, men who mediate were more likely than those using the adversarial process to obtain joint legal and joint physical custody." (Marcus et al. 2007: 148)

---

[46]See: Emery and Wyer (1987): 179–86, Koch and Lowery (1984): 109–120, Sprenkle and Storm (1983): 239–258.

Most significantly, the results showed that the post-divorce gains were higher for the family as a whole in the mediated cases because once the agreement had been reached fewer changes were made to the post-divorce arrangement. It turned out that mediation took less time, was less expensive, and was less disturbing with respect to post-divorce adjustment. The authors state the following:

> "Results in our study that suggest mediation is actually advantageous for not only women but couples are that mediation leads to significantly fewer post-judgment modifications, that mediation is a speedier process, and that children's college education is more likely to be included in the agreement when couples mediate. Reduction of post-judgment actions and faster process suggest mediation would be less costly to couples and less disruptive of their lives as well as advantageous to the court system." (Marcus et al. 2007: 149)

From the psychological perspective, it is relevant to take into account that a self-negotiated agreement does not normally produce feelings of inequality, unfairness, or revenge. The mediation setting provides a safe and confidential space in which parties can negotiate and make compromise. In contrast to court settlements, mediation does not only focus on a party's legal rights but allows them to express their emotions that would otherwise have remained tacit but would still have exercised their effect on the process. This is a relevant aspect because emotions play a decisive role in the development of conflicts. García García points out that although ex-spouses negotiate about divorce related facts the role of emotions must never be underestimated:

> "No obstante, nunca pueden olvidarse los sentimientos, que juegan un papel importante, a veces decisivo; la emotividad con la que se acude a la negociación constituye un elemento a tener muy en cuenta. Es necesario analizar las emociones y la sensibilidad de los partes, pues ello nos puede dar pautas para conocer de qué forma pueden estar condicionando los comportamientos y/o entorpeciendo el proceso." (García García 2003: 127)

Most significantly, mediation helps to improve communication and understanding among the ex-spouses which is especially helpful for the future relationship between the parties and for their success in parenting. We shall now deal with the question for whom mediation is a suitable method. The following section contains results of studies that investigated the indicators that predict whether a couple would profit from mediation or not.

5.4 Suitability of Couples for Mediation

Divorce mediation is not necessarily the best solution for every divorcing couple. It may only be successfully offered to couples who have certain characteristics. As such, Friedman names four interrelated criteria that are considered indispensable pre-conditions for the mediation process: (1) the motivation to mediation, (2) self-responsibility, (3) the ability to express the own point of view and (4) the ability to make compromise. If a divorcing couple expects mediation to be successful, both spouses should meet these criteria. Firstly, each spouse should be motivated to participate in mediation; secondly, the more sense of responsibility the spouses bring in the better; thirdly, they should be capable of disagreeing; and fourthly, they should have the ability to cooperate.

The first criterion starts from the assumption that if a dispute shall be resolved, the participants must negotiate a solution. A principle that applies to all types of conflicts is that if the parties want to avoid escalation, the solution can only be found in negotiations. The obstructive processes underlying family disputes show some commonalities with hostile processes that lead to political conflicts. As such, war may be defined as a state of unsolvable conflict that is followed by a mutual threat, a declaration of war, and subsequent fights. Such escalation can only be ended if the parties offer armistice. In order to maintain armistice the parties must send intermediaries and mediators to discuss solutions at the negotiation table. Should such peace negotiations be successful, a peace treaty is set up and measures are taken to maintain peace. The two opposing parties need a mediator who helps them solve their conflict. The aim is to find a solution at the negotiation table that is acceptable to both of the divorcing parties. For Haynes the mediator acts as a go-between who coordinates the bargaining process among the parties in dispute:

> "The process of mediation is the management of other people's negotiations, and the mediator is the manager of the negotiations who organizes the discussion of the issues to be resolved. The more coherent and organized the process, the easier it is for the participants to arrive at solutions that are mutual and appropriate for them." (Haynes 1994: 1)

An individual's motives for choosing mediation often remain tacit. Among such motives is a party's desire to avoid the potential negative consequences of a hostile legal battle, to save money, or to accelerate the whole divorce process. A party may also think altruistically and want to help the other to ease the pain of separation by reaching a mutual agreement. However, the author warns of hidden and less beneficial reasons for mediation that might put the whole process at risk, such as one's aim to minimize personal feelings of distress for having initiated the divorce. Friedman describes the dynamics of such motivation in the following way:

> "Not all the motivations are so helpful or beneficial. Some people choose mediation in the hope of getting a better deal than they think lawyers could get them, or out of a desire to perpetuate a power imbalance that favors them. Some enter the process seeking to assuage the bad feelings engendered by their decision to separate; in fat they are willing to throw in the towel, hoping to buy peace by leaving all the decision making to the other spouse. Such motivations, if left buried, can derail the process." (Friedman 1993: 21)

The second criterion of self-responsibility is a fundamental pre-condition in which individuals assume responsibility for their own well-being. This requires at least three skills: the attempt to understand one's situation; awareness of one's own priorities; and the willingness to express one's opinion and stand up for oneself. For any problem that may arise during the mediation process, it is the task of the mediator to facilitate self-responsibility by providing essential information on the economic, practical, emotional and legal dimensions of a problem. Friedman anticipates that becoming a self-responsible and independent person may turn into a difficult task because it is linked to fundamental questions, such as one's sense of life, personal needs and future plans. He speaks from his experience as a mediator:

> "Assuming responsibility for yourself can be a difficult task. If you enter the process wholeheartedly, you may discover that you are facing very basic questions, such as what you want to do with your life. This process of self-assessment can be daunting, particularly if you have had no experience in living on your own. But while experience with being responsible for yourself is useful, willingness to figure out your personal responsibilities is indispensible." (Friedman 1993: 23)

Self-responsibility is a precondition for private autonomy. Although it is a highly private matter and it is difficult to measure, it is nevertheless influenced by the conditions that exist in a society. Relevant questions in this context include the following: Do the economic and political circumstances either support or impede a person's attempt to become self-responsible and independent? Is affordable accommodation available and are there job opportunities? A related aspect concerns the social dimension, if it is socially accepted that adults live independently or share accommodation? What are the framing conditions for becoming an independent young adult in Spain?

As refers the availability of accommodation, a majority of people are home owners in contrast to a minority who lives in rented accommodation. Accordingly, the following statistics shows that Spain has the fourth highest number of home owners among 25 European countries. In particular over 75% of the population own their homes followed by a minority of tenants and people who rent accommodations at reduced prices or free of charge. This can be seen in the statistics (Fig. 5.3).

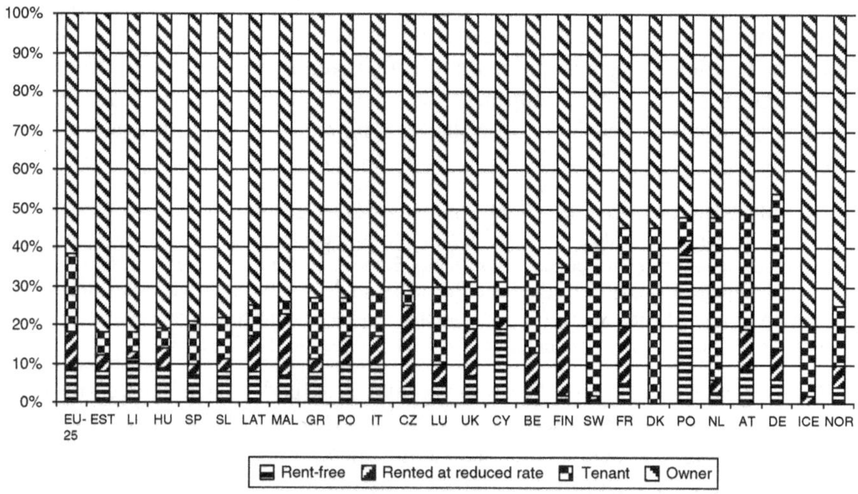

Fig. 5.3 Tenure status of households in 25 European countries[47]

[47]See: European Statistic Yearbook (2008): 234.

First household formation is more difficult for Spaniards because of a high-priced private housing market and few rented accommodation available. Additionally, it is neither common for adults to live alone in a rented accommodation nor does it seem highly accepted. In fact the Spanish family policy does not seem to support individualistic life experiences.

As such, the experience of economic independence as well as emotional self-sufficiency may be completely new for most of the divorced. This is supported by the following comparative statistics on the number of adults living in parental households in European Member States which shows that in Spain around 62% of young men and 49% of young women live in their parental home until their late 20s. More specifically, among the 25 countries of the European Union, Spain is situated among those nine countries where over 60% of young men aged live in their parent's home at an age of 25–29 years. This is displayed in the diagram (Fig. 5.4).

These statistics suggest furthermore that young adults who move out from their parental home in their late twenties are less likely to live on their own before they settle down with a partner. This is also confirmed by statistics on the mean age of the first marriage in Spain which is 30 for men and 28 for women.[48] As such a considerable amount of adults have never experienced a form of life that is characterized by economic independence and emotional self-sufficiency.[49] In fact,

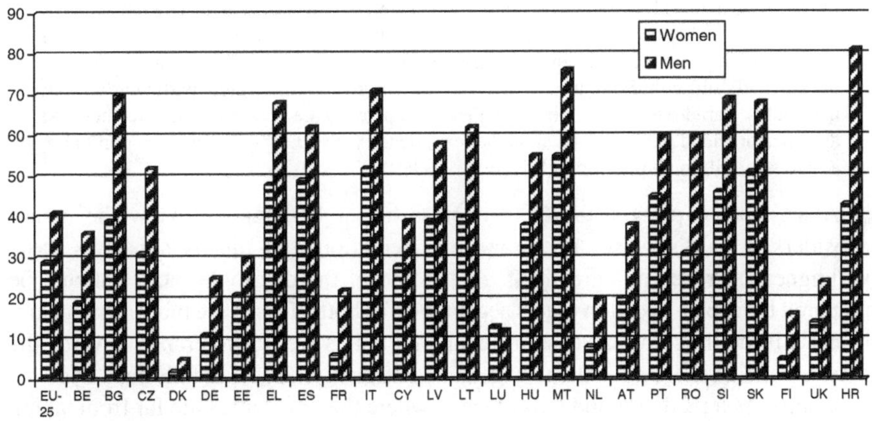

Fig. 5.4 Women and men aged 25–29 living in parental home, 2005[50]

[48]See: INE: http://www.ine.es/jaxi/tabla.do

[49]By 'self-sufficiency' we mean a person's ability to provide for his or her own needs without help from others. In this context we refer only to independence from self-chosen private relationships and leave aside lasting relationships to members of the family of origin and relatives or job-related relationships.

[50]See: European Statistic (2008): 24.

if adults in their early thirties get married they often move from their parental home directly to their marital home. If we take these preconditions into account, the experience of being single after divorce is new and may appear rather daunting. On the other hand, such a phase of individualization holds the chance of developing the valuable skills necessary in order to care for one's individual well-being (e.g. on the economic, physical, emotional and social level). Friedman considers a person's knowing and understanding of his or her own personality as important pre-condition for further development.

A third criterion that the author considers indispensable for mediation is a party's willingness to disagree or the ability to stand up for oneself. At first sight this appears contradictory to the idea of mediation. Nevertheless, it is a pre-condition for negotiations in the sense that each ex-spouse is asked to express his and her standpoint openly. The aim is to avoid any exclusion of issues that would subsequently inhibit the process of moving forward. This can be explained by the theory of suppressed contents according to which hidden objections that remain tacit in the subconscious tend to re-emerge again at a later time. They would come to light as opposition in any other related aspect of discussion and obstruct the process. The danger lies in the avoidance of conflict and a tendency of mediators to circumvent controversy and disagreement. The author explains why:

> "The greatest danger is not you and your spouse getting into a fight that leaves you unable to move forward. (...) It would be better to find yourselves in a stalemate than reach an unfair agreement favoring one of you over the other. In that case, the disadvantaged spouse winds up either living with a bad agreement or trying to convince a judge to overturn it, which can be extremely difficult. So in a sense it is safer to disagree than to agree, particularly if one has doubts. Paradoxically, the ability to disagree opens up the possibility of agreement. As an educator friend put it, talking about her experience with young children: You don't have a real yes until you have a no." (Friedman 1993: 25)

Apart from a party's ability to express his or her point of view the author considers a fourth aspect necessary for mediation and this is a party's basic willingness to reach an agreement. At the end of the day, both parties should be prepared to reach a decision that is acceptable for both. This is the most difficult aim because it requires both a sense of reconciliation as well as tolerance towards the other's position at a very critical stage in negotiation. The author falls back upon his experience as a mediator and tells of cases where the ex-spouses are far from taking a conciliatory position but rather refuse any goodwill:

> "Some people going through a divorce cannot bear the fact that their spouses are not going to be punished or that, quite simply, their spouses will be able to make their lives work." (Friedman 1993: 25)

A party's willingness to reach an agreement may be obstructed by overwhelming emotions of envy and vengeance. There are constellations where mediation is not recommended, such as if a party lacks control of will in the case of domestic violence. Domestic violence can include physical abuse, psychological abuse, threat or economic coercion.[51] In cases where it is impossible to build up reliability among the parties and to maintain continuity by sticking to agreements, mediation can hardly be successful.

Concerning the last two preconditions, the author has rather high demands on the parties because it is assumed that each spouse is in control of the situation and is conscious of his or her needs, wishes, and plans. However, this is rarely the case in the post-divorce phase when the process of overcoming the family transition has only just begun. People at this stage tend to be emotionally instable and irritated and hardly have the self-confidence necessary for the negotiation process. Another idealistic assumption is the view that each party has the best intentions and is completely free of egoistic or opportunistic aims. In reality, the opposite is often true because the separation has most likely produced emotional harm together with a range of deconstruction feelings.

However, García Tomé points also to the preventive function of mediation and reports from her experience when working with conflicting couples that four out of ten couples still decide to reconcile after some mediation sessions. This reconciliation is the consequence of a process in which the spouses are given time and space to express their frustrations, fears and anxieties and in which the mediator helps to introduce a structure in the communication between the parties. Both spouses are asked to put themselves in the position of the other and reconsider their own feelings and those of the respective other. The author describes the process in the following way:

> "La intervención del mediador va dirigida a trabajar con la pareja el conflicto y los sentimientos, miedos y percepciones erróneas que puedan tener; absorbiendo la cólera y la frustración que sienten, y estructurando la comunicación entre ellos de una manera constructiva para que puedan hablarse de lo que piensan y de lo que sienten. Pone a cada uno de ellos en el lugar del otro, para que puedan comprenderse y comprender los sentimientos por los que están pasando, y de esta manera puedan tomar una decisión acertada. Si se comprueba que la decisión de separarse no es una decisión clara y firme, debemos tener con ellos otras sesiones en mediación hasta que se verifique de manera clara su decisión. En este primer paso del proceso de mediación preventivo (...) 4 de cada 10 parejas, que en un principio van a mediación con la decisión de separarse, consideran su situación y deciden continuar su vida en común." (García Tomé 2008: 52)

From a cost-benefit perspective it is useful for the mediator and the related institution to identify possible complicating factors in advance that may impede the process. In fact, mediators with long years of practical experience seem to be able to detect whether a divorcing couple would profit from mediation or not. This is particularly true for Cohen[52] who has many years of experience as a divorce mediator and has summarized her knowledge in a typology of divorcing

---

[51]For a discussion on theoretic considerations and practical experience with mediating high conflict couples see Soria et al. (2008): 33ff.

[52]See: Cohen (1999), 329–344.

couples. By making reference to already existing typologies[53] she describes seven prototypical couples interested in mediation who have particular psychological and behavioral characteristics. Its aim is to offer orientation for mediators, judges and social workers with little experience who are asked to make rapid decisions about utility of divorce mediation for a particular couple.

The typology is based on five dimensions that are used to describe the current state of a couple prior to divorce. These dimensions include the commitment to divorce,[54] prior litigation,[55] spousal relationship,[56] ability to communicate[57] and commitment to children.[58] Although most couples would not totally fit into one of the categories proposed, the typology is a useful guide for decision-making. The author names seven different typologies including the following: 1. Semiseparated couples, 2. Emotionally withdrawn and non-communicative couples, 3. Couples in a power struggle, 4. Leaver-left couples, 5. Battling couples, 6. Enmeshed couples, and 7. Violent couples. Whereas the first four types are most likely to reach a full or partial agreement, success is less probable for the last three typologies. Therefore, we shall characterize the first four typologies in more detail and briefly describe the last three typologies. These latter typologies have in common that their conflicts either have the origin in the individual personality or have become too deep-rooted to be resolved within a reasonable time. The spouses may also be emotionally

[53]See for example the typology developed by Kressel et al. who carried out a comparative study in which they compared nine divorcing couples using mediation to a control group of five couples who took the traditional adversarial way. They based their investigation on recordings of the mediation sessions as well as on post-divorce interviews with the former couples. The results showed that couples with high levels of pre-divorce conflict and unilateral divorce had negative attitudes towards mediation. Relevant predictors for mediation to be effective are the level of ambivalence, communication style and the characteristics of the conflict. The authors found out that couples who were disenganged and direct had more success than those who were enmeshed, introvert or non-communicative (Kressel et al. 1980: 101f).

[54]This dimension describes the extent to which the spouses are really committed to divorce in terms of readiness to act. It is assumed that although a couple may expressly declare their wish to divorce they may show contradictory behaviour during the process due to a strong attachment to the other or an underlying fear of becoming lonely afterwards (Cohen 1999: 334).

[55]According to the scientific literature couples are distinguished according to whether they have had prior experience with litigation or not. This is because different characteristics are associated with both types. Whereas couples who join mediation are supposed to have good faith and are willing to reach compromise, a couple who had litigated before is assumed to have a higher level of anger, less functioning communication and hardened positions (Cohen 1999: 334).

[56]The higher the level of destructive behaviour the lower is the ability to compromise. The more problematic the individual psychological structure of a spouse is the more difficult will be mediation. This is where mediation comes up against the limiting factors such as psychopathological character or violent behaviour.

[57]A couple's ability to communicate includes the level of openness, clarity and directness as positive indicators on the one hand in contrast to ambiguity, manipulation and personal attacks as detrimental indicators on the other hand (Cohen 1999: 336).

[58]The dimension 'commitment to children' appears to be a relevant indicator because it denotes whether a couple has similar views on child up-bringing and has confidence in the respective other's parenting (Cohen 1999: 336).

entangled in a way that would require special therapeutic concepts, such as a combined approach of psychotherapy and mediation.

The following four typical characteristics of high conflict couples pose as obstacles to successful mediation. First, if there is too much tension between the spouses, mediation would be ineffective because their emotionality precludes listening to one another or focusing on an issue. Second, negative feelings inhibit the spouse's ability to relate and therefore they cannot agree on a solution with successful long-term consequences. Third, the communication among the spouses is affected by all kinds of negative associations, experiences, and emotions. Lastly, one or both spouses lack problem solving strategies and therefore tend to let the conflict escalate.

We will now describe those typologies for which mediation is most likely to be successful. The characteristics of semiseparated couples are that they have agreed to end their marriage, have low levels of emotionality at this stage and are in the process of rebuilding their lives. Their main concern is the organization of their parenting and their children's wellbeing. As communication functions well they favour an out-of-court solution. Cohen describes this type of couples as follows:

> "The desire and ability of semiseparated couples to resolve dispute make them excellent candidates for mediation. These couples need the mediator to provide information about such matters as divorce procedures, subjects on which decisions must be made, the social rights of single parent families, and so on, and a framework in which they can formulate their own divorce settlement." (Cohen 1999: 337)

As communication is an essential element of a relationship, things become difficult if a couple hardly communicates. Emotionally withdrawn and non-communicative couples are described as having introverted personalities and problems in expressing their opinions, wishes or plans. They may not have noticed the signs that indicated that their relationship had come to an end, but are still surprised and vulnerable because of the end of their relationship. The author describes the following emotional scenario:

> "They are turned inward, each into him- or herself, busy picking up the pieces of their lives. Otherwise, they are in a kind of temporary paralysis or deep freeze, so that outwardly, things are much the same as they had been prior to the decision." (Cohen 1999: 337)

A mediator could help in this case by encouraging the couple to express their points of view and talking openly about their wants and desires. As the conflict is mainly due to a lack of communication and not a personal aversion, a mediator can facilitate the dialogue among the spouses which often improves the situation.

The following typology has some similarities with the previous in that couples in a power struggle are often suspicious and distrustful of one another. However, in this case the spouses fear that the other may take advantage of any weakness and would therefore compete in every detail of divorce. Usually both are interested in their children's well-being and are dedicated to parenting. They use hostile communication, reproaches and tend to take extreme positions in order not to reveal any weak points. As each tends to draw the mediator on one side the mediator will have to clarify the rules of mediation by showing strictness rather than empathy. Although mediation seems much more difficult with this typology it may nevertheless lead to success if the mediator manages to help the spouses out of the vicious circle of power fight.

Whereas in the three preceding typologies both spouses want to divorce, it is one spouse who wants the divorce in leaver-left couples and the other one wants to prevent it with all means. The left spouse will often tend to make unjustified or impossible demands that may provoke the conflict to escalate. Conversely, the leaver may also be prepared to make considerable concessions in order to convince the leaving spouse to stay. The diverging views on the future of the relationship leads to an imbalance in the desire to communicate. Whereas the leaver avoids communication in order not to be trapped into relationship, the left part tends to take every subject as starting point for discussion. In this case the mediator is required to facilitate the transmission of messages among the spouses.

Mediation is a much more difficult task with battling couples because they have ended up in a downward spiral of conflict from which they cannot escape without help from outside. The spouses usually consult a mediator because they are either exhausted by the conflict. Although both spouses know that divorce is inevitable they are unable to reach an agreement because both feel emotionally harmed and/or use tactical reasons in order to achieve a better settlement. The spouses hardly communicate and there is a danger of the child(ren) being torn into the conflict.[59] Although the prospects of reaching an agreement are relatively low it is the task of the mediator to find common interest in both parties and establish a regular schedule of carrying out habitual parental duties.

Similar conditions apply to enmeshed couples whose divorce is unavoidable, but neither spouse takes responsibility for the breakdown, the decision to divorce or the procedure. Both are unaware of their personal problems but blame their partner for the situation. Children are mostly torn into the conflict and are used for transferring messages from one to the other. There is little chance for mediation to be successful and court proceedings usually last for years.

With violent couples[60] the situation is even worse because the spouses neither refrain from harming each other nor from harming themselves. The primary aim is to stop violence. There has been a controversial debate about the question whether mediation can be a successful means of conflict resolution. We will briefly give an overview of the arguments for and against accepting violent couples for mediation. Soria et al. summarized the factors that experts consider relevant before starting mediation with a violent couple.[61]

[59]There is a high risk in battling couples that one spouse might start to alienate the child from the other. This kind of conflicting relationships holds the conditions that are typical for the parental alienation syndrome.

[60]If we speak of violent couples we refer to relationship which is characterized by an imbalance of power whereby the abuser utilizes verbal and/or physical violence against the abused spouse.

[61]See: Soria et al. 2008: 34 ff.

The reasons against it include the endangered security of the abused spouse, domestic violence, and the cementing of detrimental relationship dynamics and power. Firstly, it is argued that abusers tend to take the mediation sessions as an opportunity to threaten the abused partner. Secondly, by offering mediation to a violent couple the institution makes violence appear harmless whereas it is factually a crime. As such, the criminalization of domestic violence is considered a success. It can only be combated if the issue is put on the political agenda and public awareness is increased. Opponents to mediation mention a third argument, which assumes that there is a fundamental power imbalance between men and women in our present societies. This discrepancy may result in gender violence.[62] As a full analysis of the phenomenon of gender violence would go beyond the scope of this study we shall now concentrate on the characteristic elements of conflicts.

5.5 Characteristic Elements of Conflicts

Before we present a theory of how agreements can be achieved in divorce conflicts, we need to know more about the structure and the dynamics of conflicts. Therefore, we will analyze the typical components of conflicts and then specify the characteristic features of family conflicts.

A conflict may be defined as a state of opposition and discord between two or more persons caused by their actual or perceived opposition of needs, values and interests. From the procedural point of view, conflict denotes a situation in which the parties have incompatible goals and seek to undermine each other's goal-seeking capability. Each conflict has its origin and the individual involved chooses the steps that lead to escalation of a conflict or prevent it from escalating. Conflict can be viewed as a crisis in human interaction. Thus, crisis is a decisive moment or turning point when an individual has to decide whether a course of action must continue, be modified or be terminated.

If we take these aspects into account we may view conflict as having similar characteristics as iceberg, where we can only see part of it and the remaining much bigger part is invisible. What becomes obvious of a conflict is just the peak of the iceberg, but the hidden basement plays a decisive role in the development of the conflict. This is depicted in the diagram (Fig. 5.5).

[62] Women in violent relationships often lack the confidence and the skills that are necessary for effective negotiation. Most of the experts who do not oppose to mediating violent couples accept the objection that in some severe cases it will not be successful. However, they argue that the alternative of the adversarial way usually tends to aggravate the problem and lead to an escalation of the conflict. If mediation is offered to violent couples the mediator needs an additional specific formation how to deal with such conflicts. In principle such offer should be voluntary and the process should guarantee safety for the abused spouse and fairness for the abuser.

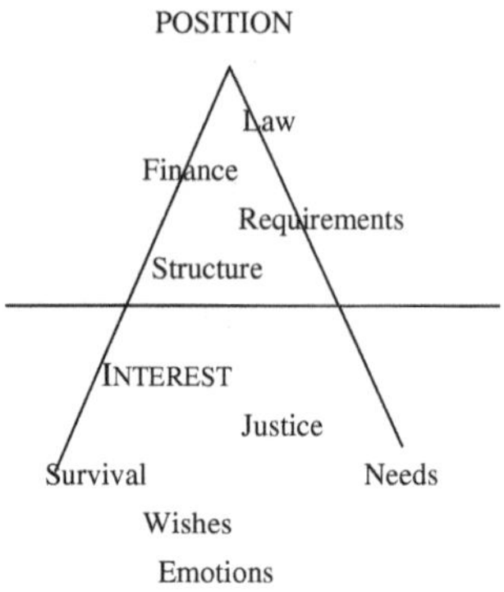

Fig. 5.5 Conflict and its elements viewed as an iceberg

According to Thomas and Kilman there are five possible ways in which people tend to react to conflicts, such as *accommodation*, *avoidance*, *collaboration*, *compromise* or *competition*.[63] A party may want to accommodate[64] the other party by capitulating and submitting his or own needs. He or she may as well avoid or postpone a conflict by ignoring it and thereby gain time to concentrate on minor, less important problems. Conflict avoidance may result in cease of communication or a point where one party breaks off.[65] In order for collaboration to be effective, the parties need to have a certain amount of respect, trust and functioning communication.[66] Compromise is achieved if the parties find a middle ground which partially satisfies both.[67]

[63]See: Thomas and Kilman (1976).

[64]A person who uses this style is basically willing to meet the needs of others at the expense of his or her own needs. The accommodator knows the point of surrender and can even be persuaded to give in if it is not clear that he or she would loose. People suing this style tend to be insecure and highly collaborative. It is not recommended in cases where the accommodator is not treated reciprocally and often runs the risk of giving up too early.

[65]People who use this style aim to escape the conflict or tend to accepting wrong decisions in order not to hurt other people's emotions. It may be useful if a gain is not expected or when the other party is in more favourable position to solve the problem. However in many situations this is a weak and less effective approach.

[66]People who use a collaborative style try to meet the needs of all people involved. These people can be highly assertive but unlike the competitor, they cooperate effectively and acknowledge that everyone is important. This style is useful when you need to bring together a variety of viewpoints to get the best solution; when there have been previous conflicts in the group; or when the situation is too important for a simple trade-off.

[67]People who prefer a compromising style try to find a solution that will at least partially satisfy everyone. Everyone is expected to give up something, and the compromiser him- or herself also expects to relinquish something. Compromise is useful when the cost of conflict is higher than the cost of losing ground, when equal strength opponents are at a standstill and when there is a deadline looming.

Conflict may also result in competition whereby one party asserts its interests at the potential expense of another.[68]

The question is at which point do the divergences among ex-spouses turn into a conflict? Which behaviour provokes a conflict to escalate and what conduct leads to de-escalation? The author and conflict mediator Glasl has presented a general model depicting the steps on the way to conflict intensification.[69] This model was designed to facilitate conflict analysis and enable the parties or a neutral third party to develop counter strategies. He gives the following definition of conflict:

> "Sozialer Konflikt ist eine Interaktion zwischen Akteuren (Individuen, Gruppen, Organisationen usw.), wobei wenigstens ein Akteur Unvereinbarkeiten im Denken, Vorstellen, Wahrnehmen und/oder Fühlen und/oder Wollen mit dem anderen Akteur (anderen Akteuren) in der Art erlebt, dass im Realisieren eine Beeinträchtigung durch einen anderen Akteur (die anderen Akteure) erfolgt." (Glasl 2004: 14)

His model shows three stages of human conduct that indicates conflict, starting with a "win–win" situation which turns into a "win–lose" position and finally deteriorates to a "lose–lose" situation if no intervention is taken. Each of the three stages subsumes three sub-steps of typical behaviour that make the conflict worse. The scheme shows all nine stages of conflict escalation (Fig. 5.6).

The first sign indicating a deterioration of a win–win position is the cementing of a problem (1). This is often followed by polarization and a controversial debate (2. Polarization and Debate). A further critical point is reached if communication is affected and the participants have ceased discussing a subject and began to act instead (3. Facts instead of Words). Phase three marks the first point of no return because it means that communication has failed as a means of conflict treatment. If words do not create an effect, the parties intend to create facts instead. Whereas, in the win–win constellation, (steps 1–3) the parties still prefer and aim to achieve a positive solution. In the following "win–lose" constellation (steps 4–6) the conflict has taken a negative turn pointing towards loss. At least from the end of phase 3 onwards, the parties tend to follow the principle "As I won't win neither should you win".

At the beginning of a "win–lose" position the participants have concerns about their image and the coalition that is at stake (4. Concern about Image and Coalition). The parties try to force one another into fixed roles and positions and create stereotypes, image campaigns and rumors. At the same time each of them intends to gain supporters for their perspective. If a compromise cannot be achieved the parties aim at harming the public image of the respective other, which as a reaction,

---

[68]People who tend towards a competitive style take a firm stand, and know what they want. They usually operate from a position of power, drawn from things like position, rank, expertise, or persuasive ability. This style can be useful when there is an emergency and a decision needs to be make fast; when the decision is unpopular; or when defending against someone who is trying to exploit the situation selfishly. However it can leave people feeling bruised, unsatisfied and resentful when used in less urgent situations.

[69]See: Glasl (2004): 236f.

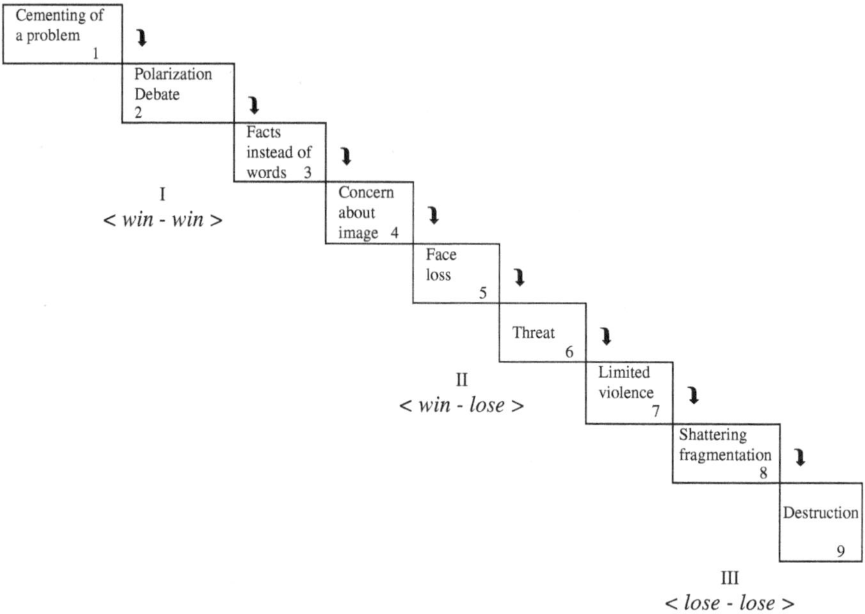

Fig. 5.6 The nine stages to conflict escalation (Glasl)

leads to fear of face-loss on both sides (5. Public Face-loss).[70] The parties would start public and direct attacks with the aim of demasking the other and thereby causing disappointment in the observer. The next phase is characterized by threat based on demanding conditions to be fulfilled and count-threats made by the respective other party (6. Strategies of Threat).

In the third stage of the "lose–lose" constellation, the conflict has taken momentum and the chance of a positive solution is rather low. The conflict has become more stressful and has increased in speed. In phase 7, the parties use limited violence with the aim of forcing the opposing party to either give in or make compromise. Strategically, the parties would present limited own damage as gain. In phase 8 one party seeks to destabilize the fundamentals, isolate particular groups from the centre, and subsequently destroy the other (Shattering). The parties attempt to destroy one another either in the physical-material sense and/or on the mental-social level. This phase changes into the last point of no return in which both parties accept self-damage if only the other party is destroyed (Destruction). The diagram shows the three stages and its constitutive features (Fig. 5.7).

[70]Face-loss denotes a person who suffers disgrace, humiliation, or embarrassment in public and which means loss of respect of others. It applies especially to the image of public figures. In collective societies (e.g. Spain) face loss is of higher relevance than in individualistic societies (e.g. Germany, Great Britain, etc.). This phenomenon is described in more detail in: Padilla-Gálvez and Gaffal (2005): 169 ff.

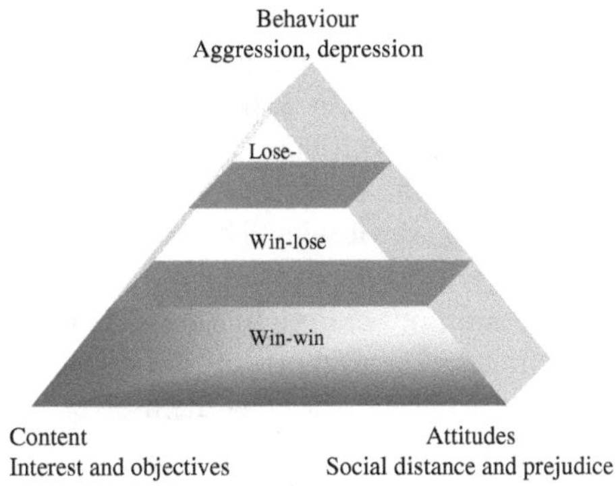

Fig. 5.7 Stages of conflict escalation

This model helps to detect the phases of a conflict and to develop strategies of de-escalation. It must be taken into account, however, that in practice conflicts are more complex and the phases are less linear, overlap, or some are non-existent. Although human behaviour never occurs in a standardized way, the expert is nevertheless able to make out regularities and recurring patterns of behaviour. As such, a mediator can help a couple to understand their conflict and to offer strategies of conflict solution. Thus, mediation can also be considered as a process during which the mediator guides the parties in conflict to undertake a series of constructive and well-founded steps. However, this is only possible if the divorcing spouses accept the thought that a third person knows more about their conflict than they themselves do.

Special reference shall be made to the Spanish context by naming two characteristic features of conflicts and its implications. According to Hofstede, Spain is a highly-contextualized culture, in which the non-verbal communication plays an important role.[71] If we distinguish between verbal and non-verbal communication, the first implies that information is transmitted mainly by words and the second implies that non-verbal signs such as gestures, facial expressions, eye-contact and intonation reveal essential information. In fact, in Spain the context of information is usually more important than its actual verbal content and information is primarily transmitted in implicit ways. This distinctive feature has important consequences for communication. The divorce mediator has to find out in which aspects the opposing parties implicitly agree or disagree in order to facilitate communication. In other words, the mediator has to detect the problems that underlie a conflict. It is the mediator's task to induce the parties to bring the underlying issue to light and to encourage them to deal with it.

Another characteristic feature within the Spanish culture is that conflicts tend to be personalized. This means that a problem is not viewed as an isolated single phenomenon but is rather closely associated with a particular person in a particular situation. Because of this constellation people generally aim to prevent being drawn

[71]See: Hofstede in Padilla-Galvez and Gaffal (2005): 187–191.

into a conflict and try to circumvent it. For the participants of family mediation it is therefore one central aim to develop a form of self-distance and emotional distance which allows them to deal with a conflict on a less subjective level.

At first sight conflicts tend to create feelings of instability and insecurity. It is, however, not the conflict that is either productive or destructive but rather the way in which it is dealt with. The constructive aspect of conflict and crisis is that they are a chance to balance out inequalities and to restructure one's personal, economic, and political relationships. This enables the actors of conflicts to adapt to new framing conditions and to make progress. A solution to conflict is only possible if the parties view themselves as conflict solving partners rather than as opponents.

5.6 Concepts and Models of Mediation

There are basically four different concepts of mediation, such as (1) facilitative mediation, (2) transformative mediation, (3) evaluative mediation, and (4) therapeutic mediation. We will only concentrate on the first three concepts and leave aside the therapeutic mediation because it is not considered mediation in a strict sense it applies mainly to high-conflict couples. Instead, we present the Harvard Negotiation Project and describe its concept of mediation. In practice mediators do not strictly adhere to one particular style but rather use a combination of these styles.

5.6.1 Facilitative Mediation

The mediator does not make any recommendations or give advice on what the parties should do. The mediator's function is rather to ask questions, find interests behind the party's positions, and help them find possible solutions. It is based on the belief that the people involved in the situation have the best understanding of what they need for themselves. Therefore, it is a non-directive method in which the mediator supports the parties to make their own decisions.[72] Zumeta describes the role that the mediator has in facilitative mediation:

> "(. . .) the mediator structures a process to assist the parties in reaching a mutually agreeable solution. The mediator asks questions, validates and normalizes parties' points of views; searches for interests underneath the decisions taken by parties; and assists the parties in finding and analyzing options for resolution. The facilitative mediator does not make recommendations to the parties, give his or her own advice or option as to the outcome of the case, or predict what a court would do in a case. The mediator is in charge of the process, while the parties are in charge of the outcome." (Zumeta 2000: 1)

[72]This style was developed in the 1970s, at a time when mediators were needed but formation in this field was not yet fully developed. Therefore, social workers or even interested laymen were in charge of mediation.

There are four characteristic elements of facilitative mediation, such as (1) it is process-oriented, (2) it is client centered, (3) it is communication focused, and (4) it is interest based. We will explain these four principles in more detail.

(1) Facilitative mediation is process-oriented.

Within the facilitative mode the mediator does not view himself or herself as an expert in any of the associated fields and refrains from making recommendations about the possible outcome. Rather, he or she gives the parties space to find their own solution and only interferes in aspects that concern the process of mediation.

(2) Facilitative mediation is client centered and
(3) Focused on Communication.

As the parties are fully in charge of the outcome and communication has a crucial role, it is the mediator's primary task to help them communicate effectively. He or she would ask a party to clarify his or her point of view, ask for the underlying interest or inquire the parties' preferred options. This method is based on the assumption that once communication is working the parties would reach an agreement. Folgerg et al. put it like this:

> "The focus often requires mediators to first establish effective communication between themselves and each of the parties. Occasionally it means restricting direct communication among the parties until they are ready to engage directly with each other in an effective way." (Folberg et al. 2004: 33)

(4) Facilitative mediation is interest based.

The most important goal of facilitative mediation is to find out the parties' interests and to encourage them to express these interests openly. It is assumed that joint understanding is a precondition for agreement and it is facilitated once a party comprehends the other party's interest and appreciates the underlying need. The mediator would use an integrative approach and focus on the most reasonable options when it comes to dividing limited resources etc.

5.6.2 Transformative Mediation

Transformative mediation is a technique that helps clients to increase autonomy and responsibility for themselves and at the same time to become more responsive and respectful towards others. Folberg, Milne and Salem give the following definition of transformative mediation:

> "Mediation is defined as a process in which a third party works with the parties to help them change the quality of their conflict interaction from negative and destructive to positive and constructive, as they explore and discuss issues and possibilities for resolution." (Folberg et al. 2004: 59)

According to Folger and Bush[73] *transformative mediation* has two main goals, such as recognition and empowerment. On the one hand the mediator aims to empower the disputing parties by helping them to analyze situations and to respond appropriately to them. The overall aim is to support the party's sense of responsibility and autonomy to make decisions independently. On the other hand, the mediator tries to enhance the parties' understanding and respect for the other by helping them to see the other's point of view. These two goals are valuable interpersonal skills that are useful for communication in general. This increases each party's recognition of the respective other. Folberg et al. describe the goals that mediators follow in transformative mediation:

> "The mediator's primary goals are (1) to foster empowerment shifts by supporting, but never supplanting, each party's deliberation and decision making, at every point in the session where choices arise (regarding either process or outcome); and (2) to foster recognition shifts by encouraging and supporting, but never forcing, each party's freely chosen efforts to achieve new understandings of the other's perspective." (Folberg et al. 2004: 59)

Supporters of transformative mediation assume that it is not just a method of dispute resolution, but may even bring about transformations in the character of the clients. This method is a tool for making clients more self-determined and more responsive to others. Mediators who use this method will also put special emphasis on the party's responsibility for the outcome produced through mediation. Accordingly, the mediator will basically tend to avoid any judgments about the parties' views or decisions taken. The mediator will rather take an optimistic view and aim to support the parties' capabilities and resources. Folberg et al. give the following description of a moderator's role:

> "The mediator's role is to help the parties make positive interactional shifts (i.e. empowerment and recognition shifts) by supporting the exercise of their capacities for strength and responsiveness through deliberation, perspective taking, communication, and decision making. (Folberg et al. 2004: 59)

In the sessions the mediator should give the parties room to express their concerns and emotions. As emotions sometimes reveal implicit beliefs, its verbalization may lead to a better understanding of the underlying motives. The mediator should also encourage the clients to speak about past events that created misunderstandings or confusion and aim to bring clarity to the matter. As past experiences are often the reason for a person's reactions in the present it is helpful if a party tries to explain the reason for his or her conduct. However, the mediator should be patient to let the party explain and analyze the reactions rather than give his or her own view. Clarified issues produce empowerment and recognition in the parties.

A mediator's careful listening is essential in order to understand the message behind a client's words. Rather than giving an overview of what the client is saying the mediator should concentrate on the statements that a party makes. Folberg et al.

---

[73]See: Folger and Busch (1996): 263–278.

give examples of how the mediator can learn to understand the message a client is giving:

> "For example, asking "What should I do?" shows that a party sees the mediator as the decision maker and feels dependent on his guidance. "I'm really confused "expresses lack of clarity and probably uncertainty. "I've had enough of this!" expresses strong emotions and feelings and shows a sense of helplessness or frustration. "What do you expect from someone like that?" indicates a negative view of the other party and hence self-absorption." (Folberg et al. 2004: 61)

How do mediators work in practise and how are these theoretical considerations translated into practical skills? Mediators use mainly three techniques to reach the goals of transformative mediation, such as *close listening*, *reflection* and *summary*. Close listening implies that the mediator must be aware of what the client says as well as what he or she hints at by indirect information, gestures, intonation or non-verbal signs. He should be able to detect implicit information or 'signifiers' behind the words that influence the process. Folberg et al. describe close listening as follows:

> "Close listening, combined with observation of what the parties are conveying through body language is thus a foundational skill that is used continuously throughout the mediation. Nuances in the language used by the parties as they move through the discussion are crucial indicators of shifts, and body language is as important as the actual words spoken." (Folberg et al. 2004: 62)

The technique of *reflection* means that the mediator reports what he or she hears the party is saying and thereby gives feedback to the party. Thereby the mediator encourages the party to explain a point of view or to clarify vague or indistinct statements in more detail. Folberg et al. give an example of a reflection by reporting the case of a couple who argue about concerning the division of assets whereby both felt entitled to receive their country house:

> "The husband, John, says, "Our house in the country is mine. I bought it before we got married. After we got married and spent more time there, I completely renovated it myself. I gutted the inside to open it up, put in windows and added a new room. Oh, and a new roof and cedar shingles on the outside walls. It's worth a lot more now, and there is no way she is going to share in the value."
>
> The mediator's reflection could be: "So, you feel strongly that the country house is entirely yours and that Lois [his wife] should not share in its value at all. You bought the house before you married, and after your marriage you spent more time there, and you did extensive renovations. You gutted the inside, put in windows, added a new room, a new roof and shingles. You are saying that it s worth a lot more now, and you put a lot of personal labour into making the value increase, and you see the house as yours." (Folberg et al. 2004: 63)

Whereas in the reflection technique the mediator speaks to one of the clients and enables the other to listen from some distance to what the respective other has said, in a *summary* the mediator speaks to both clients. By summarizing larger parts of a discussion or an argument between the two parties, the mediator enables the parties to rethink their positions. Additional techniques include checking in, questions and allowing silence.

Generally, in transformative mediation the emphasis is on the small steps taken by the clients. The mediator should share such success with his or her clients and consider it as a value of its own before it is actually applied to problem solving.

5.6.3 Evaluative Mediation

Evaluative mediation has the following characteristics, such as (1) mediator's evaluation is focused on the status of negotiations, (2) the mediator's evaluation is focused on the behaviour of parties, (3) mediator's evaluation is focused on the priorities of the parties, (4) mediator's evaluation is focused on specific plans for a conflict resolution, (5) mediator's evaluation is focused on the alternatives outside the mediated negotiation.

(1) The mediator's evaluation is focused on the status of negotiations.

Whereas in adversarial divorces the parties' lawyers fight for a maximum gain of the one party whom they represent, the clients invest in their lawyers to achieve an optimal result for themselves. However, this strategy implies always the risk of losing the process, which among other consequences affects the division of property. Evaluative mediation may produce a more beneficial solution. On the contrary, in a mediated case the spouses may find an agreement about how to divide the assets in a reasonable way thereby avoiding extensive loss.

(2) The mediator's evaluation is focused on the behaviour of parties.

Sometimes one party shows conduct that leads to break off in the negotiations. Here the mediator may give valuable feedback and show the party the consequences and possible alternatives to their conduct. Such feedback may be given in one-to-one sessions in order to prevent face loss. In fact, mediation may be the only forum in which the ex-spouses are willing to talk.

(3) The mediator's evaluation is focused on the priorities of the parties.

It is the aim of the mediator to find out about the parties' priorities as these are not always apparent from the beginning. If the party's primary interest becomes obvious the negotiations will be more effective. A first step would be that the mediator understands the priorities and then he or she would b able to evaluate it, always in the light of how would be the chances of achieving the intended objective.

(4) The mediator's evaluation is focused on specific plans for conflict resolution.

If a client has a particular plan the mediator can help to evaluate this plan in the most effective and beneficial way. Folberg et al. give an example of an ex-husband who has unrealistic ideas about his ex-wife. They describe a husband's difficulty of distancing himself from his wife who had left him several months ago. He still believes that his problem could be solved by his wife's returning home. In this case, the mediator has to intervene by concentrating on the facts and encourage the client to rethink his plans and reevaluate them:

> "At the end of the first 8 h of mediation, the husband asked the mediator, "Do you know what would solve these problems? My wife just needs to come home." That was a plan that would solve things in his mind, but there was no indication from his wife, who at that point had been living apart from him for months, that she wanted or intended "to come home". The husband thought that this suggestion was a solution, but it was not one that appeared to have any possibility of success. Deep into denial and caught up in wishful thinking, his lawyer could not move him to look at the future any different from what he wished it to be." (Folberg et al. 2004: 82)

(5) The mediator's evaluation is focused on the alternatives outside the mediated negotiation.

The success of this technique depends largely on the experience that the mediator has gathered and the amount of realistic estimation he or she can bring in. The parties tend to achieve a maximum of benefit in negotiations and this benefit is always set in relation to other alternatives outside negotiations. Not surprisingly, a spouse would certainly refrain from mediation if he or she had good chances to achieve a higher gain in an adversarial divorce process. Therefore, it is important that the mediator has experience and knowledge about tendencies in court decisions and can give a realistic picture of the probability of success. Folberg et al. give the following explanation:

> "The evaluation directs the mediator either to encourage the acceptance of the proposed agreement or to consider the dangers in accepting the terms proposed. The mediator's experience or expertise is most helpful in that evaluative moment, whether that experience is in child development, financial planning, real estate, or another subject in dispute." (Folberg et al. 2004: 83)

5.6.4 *The Harvard Negotiation Project*

In 1978 the *Harvard Negotiation Project* (HNP) was established as an interdisciplinary institute for research and tuition in negotiation techniques and conflict management at Harvard Law School. More specifically, the law professors Fisher[74] and Ury developed a result-oriented negotiation technique that became widely known as the "Harvard Negotiation Project". They worked out a number of concepts of successful negotiations and arbitration that could be utilized in many different areas, such as in business, politics, and many forms of out-of-court settlements. The method is based on a negotiation style that has brought several novel characteristics to the traditional negotiation culture. It was designed to help people to deal more effectively with different kinds of disputes.

---

[74]One of its founders Fisher had gained reputation not only as academic for international law but had also successfully functioned as mediator in international peace processes, hostage crises, diplomatic negotiations, commercial and legal negotiations. See: Fisher and Ury (1991).

The problem is that conflicting parties are too often focused on their winning strategies than on achieving a mutually acceptable and still profitable deal. This attitude poses an obstacle to effective negotiation because it cements the parties' positions and tends to provoke a stand-still. In such situations the parties should rather become flexible and willing to continue the negotiations.

If a failure of negotiations is in view it is advisable to aim at the "Best Alternative to a Negotiated Agreement" (BATNA), which stands for an agreement that may still be reached if the intended settlement was impossible to achieve. This best alternative plays a crucial role in the negotiation project. The idea is that a party should not accept any worse solution than the BATNA, although, in practice, it is often difficult to evaluate.[75] It is supposed that each party has determined his or her individual best alternative by considering the minimum acceptable result. García García defines BATNA (span. MAAN) as the space open for negotiations delimited by an outcome that is still acceptable:

> "La evaluación que hagan la partes acerca de su mejor alternativa a un acuerdo negociado (MAAN), determina el mínimo resultado aceptable por cada uno en la negociación, es decir, su punto de retiro (PR). Los respectivos puntos de retiro, a su vez, darán lugar o no a la existencia de una zona de acuerdo posible o, lo que es lo mismo, delimitan lo negociable." (García García 2003: 129)

The negotiation techniques used in the Harvard Project are principled negotiations, which concentrate on the management and resolution of conflicts. They are based on game theory and denote a win–win strategy in which the parties aim to mutually share the outcome. The method is mostly used in the United States and has become a constructive tool for mediation practitioners. Before we describe the different stages of the negotiation process we will first present the five basic principles of out-of-court settlements proposed by the HNP.

These include (1) flexibility and party autonomy, (2) confidentiality and consultation of experts,[76] (3) openness, (4) reconstruction of the relationship, and (5) avoidance of costs. The first principle of flexibility and party autonomy stands for the parties' freedom to choose the form of negotiation that suits them best and to lay down the results accordingly. Although this autonomy is limited by the national legal orders the parties still have considerable space for self-determined solutions. Whereas in legal solutions the party's individual interests are restricted to legal positions, out-of-court solutions allow individual interests to have preference over

---

[75]In order to detect the BATNA the parties must know their reservation point and should take into account elements, such as the time money invested in the relationship and the and estimated degree of the other party's reliability. If a party dedicates little time in analysing its real options and overrates its BATNA it may result in faulty decisions. However, all these consideration are difficult to measure and to quantify, which is the insecurity that is part of all negotiations.

[76]Confidentiality and the possibility of consulting an expert in any of the relevant issues addressed is another important principle. As mediated solutions are carried out confidentially, the mediator is bound to secrecy. However, the parties may seek advice from an expert referring issues such as taxes, psychological assistance, etc. under the condition that none of these experts consulted is allowed to give evidence in court.

legal formula. The authors of the recognized book called "Getting to Yes",[77] Fisher, Ury and Patton point to the advantage of remaining flexible in negotiations. They warn negotiating parties of falling into the trap of bargaining over positions. They describe the nonconstructive mechanism of positional bargaining in which the parties lock themselves into a position the more they aim to clarify and defend it against objections. If a party concentrates mainly on a certain position other possible solutions are left aside. The authors describe this process as follows:

> "The more you try to convince the other side of the impossibility of changing your opening position, the more difficult it becomes to do so. Your ego becomes identified with your position. You now have a new interest in "saving face" – in reconciling future action with past positions – making it less likely that any agreement will wisely reconcile the parties' original interests." (Fisher et al. 1991: 5)

Values, convictions and beliefs have an influence on the positions we take. Values are moral principles, beliefs, and convictions that can be defined as solid persuasions or stable belief in something without need for proof or evidence. These are acquired during socialization, via religion and customs and are mainly transferred within the family system. Once they are adopted they become anchored in the individual mind and are often resistant against experience or objective proof. Conflicts are nearly always linked to values and convictions, especially if they concern the family system. If a couple gets married under the conviction that a marriage shall last for life, the divorce is a shattering experience for the spouses. They may find it hard, though, to change their convictions as they appear resistant to experience. This rigidity of beliefs and convictions make mediation a difficult undertaking because they lead to positional bargaining. García García emphasizes the crucial role of values in conflicts and points to its obstructing effects in negotiations:

> "Gran parte de los conflictos a los que nos enfrentamos son conflictos de valores, y la dificultad de su maneja estriba, esencialmente, en la diferente percepción de la citación que tiene cada una de las personas implicadas. Cuando la discusión se centra en una cuestión de valores, las diferencias so prácticamente irreconciliables y crecerán, en lugar de disminuir, con la aportación de argumentos. Cuanto más se discuta, más dispares serán las posiciones de las partes enfrentadas." (García García 2003: 126)

In societies where the assumption of an objective reality is weak and beliefs and convictions are firmly attached in the mind, mediation appears a difficult task because conflicts tend to end up in positional bargaining. One characteristic and a further obstacle is that such convictions and beliefs are normally part of a person's implicit knowledge which creates a certain resistance to discuss them openly. In this context the mediator has the demanding tasks of making these convictions accessible to communication.

In fact, there are certain individual dispositions and cognitive skills that are considered a pre-requisite for successful mediation. Mediation depends on the knowledge and the resources that the parties have to find creative solutions to the needs of the

---

[77]See: Fisher et al. (1991).

family members. As such it is useful if the parties either have the following individual skills available or develop them during the mediation process. These include the abilities of self-distance and emotional distance, reflectivity and analytical capacity. Self-distance denotes the ability consider a conflict from an outside perspective without concentrating on the own self. It is closely linked to the ability of emotional distance that refers to a view of conflict with little emotional participation. Reflectivity means the ability to reflect on possible strategies in a conflict and analytical capacity means the ability to single out and examine specific aspects of a conflict.

In the Harvard Negotiation Project the authors have worked out an alternative method to positional bargaining called *principled negotiation*. There are four cornerstones on which this method rests and that include the following instructions: (1) separate the people from the problem, (2) focus on interests, not on positions, (3) create a variety of possibilities before making a decision, and (4) insist that the result shall be based on some objective criteria.

The first requirement of separating the people from the problem points to the danger that conflicts tend to increase in complexity if they are personalized. Therefore, it is recommendable that participants concentrate on the subject and avoid personal attacks. In order to do so the parties have to accept that people view things differently and treat conflicts in different ways. This is mainly due to how we were brought up, socio-cultural influences and individual experience. The parties should increase their mutual tolerance for the other's perspective. The parties should therefore not only separate the person from the problem but also concentrate on interests rather than on positions. The authors point out that everyone has an interest in the matter as well as in the relationship. They suggest that everyone who is involved in negotiations should try to get some distance to the conflict and try to analyze the other party's underlying interests. They say:

> "A negotiated position often obscures what you really want. Compromising between positions is not likely to produce an agreement which will effectively take care of the human needs that led people to adopt those positions." (Fisher et al. 1991: 11)

What is the relevance of these criteria in divorce mediation? Undoubtedly, it is not easy for a couple in the process of divorce to separate the person from the problem. A history of joint experiences and the proximity to the spouse make it difficult to take a distance. On the other hand, the process of digressing from the problem and becoming estranged is the first step to a new point of view.

Rather than asking the respective other what he or she wants, the questions should be *why* the other wants one thing or another. This is based on the assumption that everyone has a reason for a certain position and every interest points to a fundamental need. If we suppose that the other party does not act just arbitrarily or completely unreasonably, we can always detect a need behind a certain interest. These include needs such as for physical safety and security, economic well-being, a sense of love and belonging, recognition, and control over one's life.[78] If the

[78]See: Maslow's hierarchy of fundamental needs in Maslow (1943, 1954): 370 f.

underlying need is detected, the actual problem can be addressed openly. It is the task of the mediator to focus the parties' attention on these interests and to facilitate dialogue and communication over these issues. This can help them to understand each other better and to mutually respect their interests.

The third aspect concerns the invention of several possibilities before making a decision. The idea behind this requirement is the extent to which the individual flexibility exists when it comes to finding solutions that are also acceptable for the other. This requires a special effort because we tend to be convinced of our own position and are not normally creative in developing alternatives. In order to find alternatives we need to overcome at least three obstacles, such as avoid premature judgment, accept the view that there are several solutions to one problem, and the view that a solution depends entirely on one part only. The approach should rather be cooperative in that the parties should try to find common interests, such as to create a functional relationship as to facilitate post-divorce parenting.

The fourth advice refers to the claim that objective criteria shall be introduced in the search for problem solutions. In order to avoid any unreasonable tendencies it is recommended to make the parties agree on the objective criteria before starting the mediation. Fisher et al. highlight the advantages of introducing objective standards into negotiations:

> "Approaching agreement through discussion of objective criteria also reduces the number of commitments that each side must make and then unmake as they move toward agreement. In positional bargaining, negotiators spend much of the time defending their position and attacking the other side's. People using objective criteria tend to use time more efficiently talking about possible standards and solutions." (Fisher et al. 1991: 83)

Negotiations do not make sense if a party makes an unreasonable, immoral or illegal proposal. In the case of divorce, the mediator has the duty to inform the parties of the legal options.[79]

5.7 Conclusion

Mediation is a useful tool of conflict resolution in divorce crisis conflicts. It is different from family therapies or individual psychotherapy because it is goal oriented and intends to lay down the result in a legal contract. Mediation is Spain has a relatively short history as its origins date back to Law 30/1981 when the regulating agreement was introduced. Mediation as an option of conflict resolution in divorce disputes was implemented as part of Law 15/2005. Between 2001 and 2009 the Spanish Autonomous Communities introduced legislations on family mediation.

[79]See Sect. X. of the Recommendation on Family Mediation: "X. the mediator may give legal information but should not give legal advice. He or she should, in appropriate cases, inform the parties of the possibility for them to consult a lawyer or any other relevant professional person." (Recommendation No. R (98) 1)

We investigated mediation from the perspective of game theory and discussed the possible options of outcomes by making reference to the divorce cases that were brought to Spanish Courts of Appeal. The investigation showed that win–win solutions are considered as the most advantageous form of conflict resolution for the ex-spouses and, especially, for the children involved. This type of solution is not only the best form of conflict resolution but is also a helpful tool for the post-divorce adjustment of ex-spouses and children. Conflicts in Spain tend to be highly contextualized and personalized. Therefore mediation can help the parties to bring an implicit problem to light and to disentangle to problem from the emotions.

We analyzed the suitability of divorcing couples for mediation and presented a typology of seven prototypical couples with certain psychological and behavioural characteristics. In the second part of this chapter we concentrated on the process of mediation and described the characteristics of conflicts in general. Then we gave a detailed survey about different concepts and models of mediation which include the three approaches to mediation, such as facilitative, transformative and evaluative mediation. As a special form of alternative dispute resolution the Harvard Negotiation Project was presented.

The advantages of mediation include a number of practical as well as emotional benefits. The parties maintain a higher degree of privacy and are more in control of the divorce process and its outcome. It helps the parties to accept their own needs and the justifiable rights and needs of the other. A hard won agreement seems to be more durable and stable than a solution that has been inflicted on the parties.

Conclusions

This book has tried to answer the question why so many marriages end in divorce. As the family unit has been exposed to many changes of socio-economic conditions within the last decades, its size, function and the quality and organisation of internal relations have changed. Spanish couples tend to marry later and start their first household formation later than young adults in the rest of Europe. A demand for job flexibility, the low profile of the Spanish family policy and an over-priced private housing market put a heavy burden on young couples and do not particularly facilitate family formation. The number of family members has decreased, several aspects of the gender roles have lost their functions and new tasks needed to be incorporated. The resistance to adapt to these changes is likely to produce conflicts. Violence may be viewed as a consequence of the refusal to accept these changes and make necessary adjustments.

In Spain divorce has had a relatively short history. Due to the political and socio-economic conditions, industrialisation and all related consequences reached Spain approximately two decades later than other countries of Western Europe. At the same time the European integration process and globalization in general have accelerated the development of society. It is a heavy burden for the family to keep up with all these processes. A systemic approach to the explanation of marital stability and instability revealed that spouses use a multifaceted rationale to assess their marital satisfaction. In order to guarantee stability each spouse would invest time and attention and as a reward gain relational profit. In order to maintain a balance of mutual welfare spouses are supposed to tailor their respective gender roles to their own preferences and needs.

How does this view translate into the public and private sphere of individuals in Spain? The in-depth analysis revealed that Spanish couples do not extensively negotiate their gender roles but rather follow traditional role models. Dysfunctions occur if inappropriate models are applied to new circumstances. In fact, there seems to be a discrepancy between the requirements that individuals are expected to fulfil within an increasingly global society and the actual family policy that the state applies. Here are some examples of this discrepancy: Laws on gender equality have an important function. At the same time the Spanish family policy supports the internalisation of welfare functions in the family and thereby tacitly supports a traditional distribution of household tasks. Statistics have revealed that more women than men initiate divorce. Women take an active role in preparing and planning for divorce and are more consistent in carrying out their plans. In Spain women have enhanced their bargaining power by contributing to the household budget. Additionally, a woman's earning capacity creates and independence effect that allows her to end an unhappy marriage. Several studies have shown a significant correlation between women's employment and divorce rates.

Divorce has long been viewed as producing only deficits and negative effects. Nowadays it is more seen as a family transition, which develops over time and that may also benefit the family members. People with longer education and higher cognitive abilities have an advantage and adjust to divorce more easily. The economically weaker part, mostly the mothers, have more economic and financial disadvantages after divorce than their ex-husbands in most European countries. The contrary is true for Spain. The spouse who initiates divorce has a temporal and an emotional advantage which – consequently – supports adjustment. Several studies have investigated the economic impact of divorce on families and have shown that men and women have different economic consequences. Women usually face a decline in living standard and are even at risk of poverty. On the contrary, men experience fewer changes and sometimes even improve their economic status. There is a reverse effect in Spain, where more men suffer from economic difficulties because of the many financial concessions that they are obliged to make.

Children face a number of changes, before, during and after their parents' divorce, such as economic decline, parental dispute and less contact to the non-resident parent. If parents have ongoing disputes, children suffer from the unpredictable and incoherent behaviour that parents show. But it is also the content of the conflict and its style that affects them. The father has a number of sociological functions for a child. From a cultural point of view it may be considered a more refined technique of conflict resolution compared to litigation. In the case of divorce these father roles are dramatically reduced. In fact, a recent study on this issue has highlighted that many children of divorced parents grow up without experiencing any male role model until young adulthood.

Family judges tend to consider economic and emotional stability as most important for the child and decide that children remain in the family accommodation with their mothers. But how can the negative consequences of father absence ever be ignored? Why do the results of thirty years of father research have so little effect on legislation and on legal practice? Why hasn't it become common practice to attribute equal rights and duties to both parents? Concerning the new legislation in family law it appears contradictory that the legislator has not subsumed the family accommodation under the category of matrimonial property regime. If we take into account that most households are privately owned, why is the house or flat not part of the joint property to be divided in the case of divorce?

The new legislation enables couples to get divorced rapidly and promotes private autonomy. At the same time the state favours a private housing market which is hardly accessible for divorced people. In other words, the legislator promotes values of personal freedom and autonomy and simultaneously impedes indirectly new forms of individual life experience. After divorce the ex-spouses remain still linked by a long-term contract as regards the family accommodation. As a consequence the economic resources of the non-resident parent are restricted to such an extent that is hardly possible to make a long-term commitment in a new relationship.

The results of the study showed that in the majority of cases custody was attributed to mothers with fathers exercising their legal authority according to a visiting plan. Only in few cases did parents opt for joint custody. Therefore the introduction of this regime in the new legislation did not produce an increase of joint custody. Custody was mostly bestowed to mothers with the fathers keeping the right of contact. The custodial parent was attributed the accommodation in the majority of cases.

Divorce seems to work for most couples as a solution to a relationship in crisis and point of no return. Most ex-spouses recover from the detrimental effects of divorce over time. It is essential that the parents – and especially the father – stay in contact with their children.

It is striking how many divorces occur in families with lower income levels in Spain. The economic consequences for single earner households are particularly precarious. It seems inappropriate that two adult parents after their divorce still remain linked by a long-term bank contract. As a consequence, the debtor spouse can neither fully separate from the other, nor can he make commitments in a new relationship because this would exceed his financial capacity. Although an important aim of divorce is to enable a new start, the debtor spouse is actually sanctioned by the legislator. The aim of the new law on family mediation is to promote consensual divorce in order to guarantee the best interests of the child. Two characteristic features may complicate family mediation in Spain, such as a tendency to implicit transfer of information and a high level of contextualization within the culture. As the family mediation was only been introduced a few years ago it remains to be seen whether it serves as an appropriate method of conflict resolution in family disputes. This task seems difficult in cultures that are highly contextualized, such as in Spain, and in which a great deal of relevant knowledge is transferred by way of implicit information.

Appendix

Divorce Sentences in Autonomous Communities (2007)

	Total	Consensual divorce	Non-consensual divorce
Total	125.721	79.945	45.776
ANDALUCÍA	21.601	12.069	9.532
Almería	1.642	943	699
Cádiz	3.286	1.813	1.473
Córdoba	1.854	963	891
Granada	2.389	1.385	1.004
Huelva	1.393	662	731

(*continued*)

	Total	Consensual divorce	Non-consensual divorce
Jaén	1.422	763	659
Málaga	4.552	2.802	1.750
Sevilla	5.063	2.738	2.325
ARAGON	2.799	1.948	851
Huesca	432	307	125
Teruel	203	114	89
Zaragoza	2.164	1.527	637
ASTURIAS (PRINCIPADO DE)	3.470	2.169	1.301
BALEARS (ILLES)	3.490	2.353	1.137
CANARIAS	7.682	4.202	3.480
Palmas (Las)	4.096	2.211	1.885
Santa Cruz de Tenerife	3.586	1.991	1.595
CANTABRIA	1.514	1.019	495
CASTILLA Y LEÓN	4.717	2.752	1.965
Ávila	195	105	90
Burgos	646	416	230
León	1.166	628	538
Palencia	265	154	111
Salamanca	607	358	249
Segovia	210	120	90
Soria	154	102	52
Valladolid	1.159	698	461
Zamora	315	171	144
CASTILLA-LA MANCHA	3.892	2.414	1.478
Albacete	874	586	288
Ciudad Real	931	500	431
Cuenca	316	181	135
Guadalajara	589	410	179
Toledo	1.182	737	445
CATALUÑA	23.833	17.058	6.775
Barcelona	18.109	12.970	5.139
Girona	2.131	1.600	531
Lleida	1.099	745	354
Tarragona	2.494	1.743	751
COMUNITAT VALENCIANA	15.511	10.595	4.916
Alicante/Alacant	5.543	3.546	1.997
Castellón/Castelló	1.601	1.116	485
Valencia/València	8.367	5.933	2.434
EXTREMADURA	1.943	1.100	843
Badajoz	1.209	716	493
Cáceres	734	384	350
GALICIA	7.236	4.007	3.229
Coruña (A)	3.044	1.754	1.290
Lugo	776	435	341
Ourense	753	423	330
Pontevedra	2.663	1.395	1.268
MADRID (COMUNIDAD DE)	17.056	11.175	5.881
MURCIA (REGION DE)	3.456	1.992	1.464
NAVARRA (COMUNIDAD FORAL DE)	1.309	947	362
PAIS VASCO	4.952	3.385	1.567

(*continued*)

	Total	Consensual divorce	Non-consensual divorce
Álava	667	444	223
Guipúzcoa	1.529	1.133	396
Vizcaya	2.756	1.808	948
RIOJA (LA)	763	520	243
CEUTA	259	136	123
MELILLA	238	104	134

Table of Divorce Sentences

Sentencia/Judgement
SAP Las Palmas 24-9-2007 (JUR\2007\353964)
SAP Santa Cruz de Tenerife 5-6-2007 (JUR\2007\337915)
SAP Las Palmas 28-5-2007 (JUR\2007\344134)
SAP Las Palmas 17-5-2007 (JUR\2007\288195
SAP Las Palmas 23-2-2007 (JUR\2007\151664)
SAP Islas Baleares 29-5-2007 (JUR\2007\321875)
SAP Islas Baleares 19-4-2007 (JUR\2007\296931)
SAP Islas Baleares 27-2-2007 (JUR\2007\254010)
SAP Islas Baleares 6-3-2007 (JUR\2007\282547)
SAP Islas Baleares 13-3-2007 (JUR\2007\273221)
SAP Barcelona 20-7-2007 (JUR\2007\284258)
SAP Barcelona 19-7-2007 (JUR\2007\316774)
SAP Barcelona 17-7-2007 (JUR\2007\284499)
SAP Barcelona 19-7-2007 (JUR\2007\284371)
SAP Barcelona 18-7-2007 (JUR\2007\284433)
SAP Barcelona 17-7-2007(JUR\2007\341881)
SAP Barcelona 25-9-2007 (JUR\2007\329627)
SAP Barcelona 12-9-2007 (JUR\2007\330479)
SAP Barcelona 20-7-2007 (JUR\2007\284277)
SAP Barcelona 20-7-2007 (JUR\2007\284309)
SAP Barcelona 25-7-2007 (JUR\2007\284101)
SAP Barcelona 25-7-2007 (JUR\2007\284103)
SAP Barcelona 14-6-2007 (JUR\2007\72181)
SAP Barcelona 20-9-2007 (JUR\2007\329851)
SAP Barcelona 13-9-2007 (JUR\2007\330384)
SAP Barcelona 15-6-2007 (JUR\2007\65225)
SAP Barcelona 28-9-2007 (JUR\2007\334918)
SAP Barcelona 25-9-2007 (JUR\2007\329641)
SAP Barcelona 28-9-2007 (JUR\2007\329460)
SAP Barcelona 15-6-2006 (JUR\2007\65213)
SAP Barcelona 14-6-2006 (JUR\2007\18852)
SAP Barcelona 12-6-2006 (JUR\2007\18969)

SAP Barcelona 9-6-2006 (JUR\2007\11058)
SAP Girona 24-5-2006 (JUR\2007\12010)
SAP Girona 26-5-2006 (JUR\2007\65509)
SAP Girona 8-6-2006 (JUR\2007\11132)
SAP Tarragona 23-5-2006 (JUR\2007\19825)
SAP Tarragona 24-5-2006 (JUR\2007\19791)
SAP Tarragona 31-5-2006 (JUR\2007\65469)
SAP Tarragona 12-7-2007 (JUR\2007\336713)
SAP Tarragona 25-7-2007 (JUR\2007\292342)
SAP Tarragona 25-7-2007 (JUR\2007\292348)
SAP Tarragona 31-7-2007 (JUR\2007\364429)
SAP Lugo 27-4-2007 (JUR\2007\252972)
SAP A Coruña 7-5-2007 (JUR\2007\279653)
SAP A Coruña 13-7-2006 (JUR\2007\134868)
SAP A Coruña 31-7-2006 (JUR\2007\297896)
SAP A Ourense 14-7-2006 (JUR\2007\40301)
SAP Pontevedra 6-3-2007 (JUR\2007\265018)
SAP Asturias 31-5-2007 (JUR\2007\302934)
SAP Asturias 20-6-2007 (JUR\2007\306985)
SAP Asturias 29-11-2006 (JUR\2007\23523)
SAP Valencia 25-7-2007 (JUR\2007\341234)
SAP Valencia 24-7-2007 (JUR\2007\316313)
SAP Valencia 12-9-2007 (JUR\2007\340148)
SAP Valencia 6-9-2007 (JUR\2007\340308)
SAP Valencia 5-9-2007 (JUR\2007\340356)
SAP Valencia 5-9-2007 (JUR\2007\340349)
SAP Valencia 16-7-2007 (JUR\2007\317375)
SAP Valencia 17-7-2007 (JUR\2007\317134)
SAP Valencia 27-3-2007 (JUR\2007\213572)
SAP Valencia 18-9-2007 (JUR\2007\340034)
SAP Valencia 20-9-2007 (JUR\2007\339999)
SAP Valencia 20-9-2007 (JUR\2007\339980)
SAP Castellón 7-9-2007 (JUR\2007\340230)
SAP Alicante 20-9-2006 (JUR\2008\140754)
SAP Alicante 20-9-2006 (JUR\2008\118681)
SAP Alicante 9-5-2007 (JUR\2007\261473)
SAP Madrid 26-7-2007 (JUR\2007\336153)
SAP Madrid 16-10-2007 (AC\2007\2324)
SAP Madrid 13-9-2007 (JUR\2007\346268)
SAP Madrid 16-7-2007 (JUR\2007\336589)
SAP Madrid 27-3-2007 (JUR\2007\313894)
SAP Madrid 21-9-2007 (JUR\2007\329739)
SAP Madrid 7-7-2007 (JUR\2007\25887)
SAP Madrid 19-7-2006 (JUR\2007\32432)
SAP Madrid 20-7-2006 (JUR\2007\32345)

SAP Madrid 19-4-2007 (JUR\2007\313629)
SAP Madrid 14-7-2006 (JUR\2007\25424)
SAP Madrid 13-7-2006 (JUR\2007\167719)
SAP Madrid 14-7-2006 (JUR\2007\25374)
SAP Madrid 13-7-2006 (JUR\2007\266461)
SAP Madrid 19-7-2006 (JUR\2007\32431)
SAP La Rioja 12-2-2003 (JUR\2003\93756
SAP La Rioja 18-2-2008 (JUR\2008\217672)
SAP Guipúzcoa 19-12-2006 (JUR\2007\102814)
SAP Guipúzcoa 21-12-2007 (JUR\2007\117075)
SAP Álava a 27-4-2007 (JUR\2007\226393)
SAP Vizcaya a 22-9-2006 (JUR\2007\100066)
SAP Vizcaya a 27-7-2006 (JUR\2007\95898)
SAP Vizcaya a 26-7-2006 (JUR\2007\95901)
SAP Murcia a 23-5-2007 (JUR\2007\344200)
SAP Murcia a 30-4-2007 (JUR\2007\313484)
SAP Murcia a 6-3-2007 (JUR\2007\265019)
SAP Murcia a 21-6-2007 (JUR\2007\320524)
SAP Zaragoza a 24-7-2007 (JUR\2007\306816)
SAP Zaragoza a 24-7-2007 (JUR\2007\336334)
SAP Zaragoza a 27-3-2007 (JUR\2007\263758)
SAP Huesca a 14-6-2007 (JUR\2007\311867)
SAP Cantabria a 16-3-2007 (JUR\2007\125849)
SAP Cantabria a 19-6-2007 (AC\2007\2242)
SAP Navarra a 8-11-2007 (JUR\2008\127839)
SAP Navarra a 27-8-2007 (JUR\2008\7079)
SAP Valladolid a 12-7-2007 (JUR\2007\307507)
SAP Valladolid a 12-7-2007 (JUR\2007\307507)
SAP Valladolid a 28-7-2007 (JUR\2007\309909)
SAP Burgos a 9-4-2007 (JUR\2007\282062)
SAP Burgos a 27-2-2007 (JUR\2007\282623)
SAP León a 26-2-2007 (JUR\2007\249673)
SAP León a 26-2-2006 (JUR\2007\60650)
SAP Salamanca a 30-11-2006 (JUR\2007\144094)
SAP Cáceres a 11-4-2007 (JUR\2007\262787)
SAP Cáceres a 5-3-2007 (JUR\2007\265115)
SAP Badajoz a 21-11-2006 (JUR\2007\14327)
SAP Toledo a 8-6-2007 (JUR\2007\301561)
SAP Toledo a 25-4-2007 (JUR\2007\262101)
SAP Ciudad Real a 12-6-2007 (JUR\2007\312105)
SAP Albacete a 8-11-2007 (JUR\2007\46117)
SAP Guadalajara a 16-10-2007 (JUR\2007\314485)
SAP Almería a 28-7-2006 (JUR\2007\47227)
SAP Córdoba a 12-6-2007 (JUR\2007\78867)
SAP Granada a 9-6-2006 (JUR\2007\48774)

SAP Granada a 29-9-2006 (JUR\2007\129153)
SAP Córdoba a 10-7-2006 (JUR\2007\185823)
SAP Jaén a 7-5-2007 (JUR\2007\359838)
SAP Jaén a 8-6-2006 (JUR\2007\41959)
SAP Cádiz a 23-5-2007 (JUR\2007\359197)
SAP Cádiz a 23-5-2007 (JUR\2007\359197)
SAP Cádiz a 23-5-2007 (JUR\2007\359197)
SAP Sevilla a 12-6-2007 (JUR\2007\78867)
SAP Sevilla a 23-11-2006 (JUR\2007\181805)
SAP Sevilla a 23-11-2006 (JUR\2007\181814)
SAP Sevilla a 8-11-2006 (JUR\2007\182538)
SAP Málaga a 24-5-2006 (JUR\2007\27758)
SAP Málaga a 30-11-2006 (JUR\2007\163774)
SAP Málaga a 3-5-2007 (JUR\2007\359929)
SAP Toledo a 2-2-2007 (JUR\2007\81018)
SAP Barcelona a 20-12-2006 (JUR\2007\143259)
SAP Vizcaya a 28-6-2007 (JUR\2007\348645)
SAP Santa Cruz de Tenerife a 8-6-2007 (JUR\2007\349436)
SAP Madrid a 18-5-2007 (JUR\2007\313112)
SAP Cádiz a 29-1-2007 (JUR\2007\156390)
SAP Vizcaya a 28-6-2007 (JUR\2007\348645)
SAP Barcelona a 29-6-2007 (JUR\2007\342682)
SAP Toledo a 3-7-2007 (JUR\2007\308821)
SAP Madrid a 19-9-2007 (JUR\2007\329883)
SAP Barcelona a 5-3-2007 (JUR\2007\120785)
SAP Madrid a 20-3-2007 (JUR\2007\313970)
SAP Barcelona a 4-7-2007 (JUR\2007\285163)
SAP Vizcaya a 27-3-2008 (JUR\2008\130045)
SAP Murcia a 27-6-2006 (JUR\2006\240424)
SAP Madrid a 31-1-2002 (JUR\2002\111924)

Table of Cases

Sahin *v*. Deutschland & Sommerfeld *v*. Deutschland, EGMR, 08.07.2003, Beschwerdenr./Aktenzahl: 30943/96 und 31871/96.

Andrzej Cernecki gg. Österreich (Zulässigkeitsentscheidung), EGMR, 11.07.2000 Beschwerdenr./Aktenzahl: 31061/96.

Elsholz gg. Deutschland (Große Kammer) EGMR, 13.07.2000. Beschwerdenr./Aktenzahl: 25735/94.

P. E. v. Österreich, EKMR, 03.12.1997, Beschwerdenr./Aktenzahl: 31179/96.

OLG Bamberg vom 28.3.1996, 7 WF 49/96.

OLG München vom 8.5.1996 – 12 WF 712/96.

OLG Karlsruhe vom 21.1.2000 – 16 WF 102/99.

OLG Frankfurt vom 4.5.2000 – 3 UF 146/99.

OLG Frankfurt am Main vom 3.9.2002 – 1 UF 103/00.

Table of Statutes

Comunidad Autónoma de las Illes Balears (Ley 18/2006), de 22 de noviembre, de Mediación Familiar.

Comunidad Autónoma del Galicia Decreto 159/2003, de 31 de enero, por el que se regula la figura del mediador familiar, el Registro de mediadores familiares de Galicia y el reconocimiento de la Mediación gratuita. (DOG n° 34, de 18 de febrero de 2003)

Recommendation n° R (98) 1 of the Committee of Ministers to Member States on Family Mediation

Recommendation No. R (99) 19 of the Committee of Ministers to member States concerning mediation in penal matters

Recommendation Rec (2001)9 of the Committee of Ministers to member states on alternatives to litigation between administrative authorities and private parties

Recommendation Rec (2002) 10 of the Committee of Ministers to member States on mediation in civil matters

Directive 2008/52/EC of the European Parliament and of the Council of 21 May 2008 on Certain Aspects of Mediation in Civil and Commercial matters

Código Civil, de 24 de Julio de 1889

Código Civil Ley 30/1981, de 7 de Julio (BOE n° 172, de 20 de Julio)

Código Civil Ley 30/1981, de 7 de Julio (BOE n° 172, de 20 de Julio) Art. 81.

Código Civil Ley 30/1981, de 7 de Julio (BOE n° 172, de 20 de Julio). Art. 82.

Código Civil Ley 30/1981, de 7 de Julio (BOE n° 172, de 20 de Julio). Art. 83.

Código Civil Ley 30/1981, de 7 de Julio (BOE n° 172, de 20 de Julio). Art. 84.

Código Civil Ley 30/1981, de 7 de Julio (BOE n° 172, de 20 de Julio). Art. 85.

Código Civil Ley 30/1981, de 7 de Julio (BOE n° 172, de 20 de Julio). Art. 86.

Código Civil Ley 30/1981, de 7 de Julio (BOE n° 172, de 20 de Julio). Art. 87.

Código Civil Ley 30/1981, de 7 de Julio (BOE n° 172, de 20 de Julio). Art. 88.

Código Civil Ley 30/1981, de 7 de Julio (BOE n° 172, de 20 de Julio). Art. 89.

Código Civil Ley 30/1981, de 7 de Julio (BOE n° 172, de 20 de Julio). Art. 90.

Código Civil Ley 30/1981, de 7 de Julio (BOE n° 172, de 20 de Julio). Art. 91.

Código Civil Ley 30/1981, de 7 de Julio (BOE n° 172, de 20 de Julio). Art. 92.

Código Civil Ley 30/1981, de 7 de Julio (BOE n° 172, de 20 de Julio). Art. 93.

Código Civil Ley 30/1981, de 7 de Julio (BOE n° 172, de 20 de Julio). Art. 94.

Código Civil Ley 30/1981, de 7 de Julio (BOE n° 172, de 20 de Julio). Art. 95.

Código Civil Ley 30/1981, de 7 de Julio (BOE n° 172, de 20 de Julio). Art. 96.

Código Civil Ley 30/1981, de 7 de Julio (BOE n° 172, de 20 de Julio). Art. 97.

Código Civil Ley 30/1981, de 7 de Julio (BOE n° 172, de 20 de Julio). Art. 98.

Código Civil Ley 30/1981, de 7 de Julio (BOE n° 172, de 20 de Julio). Art. 99.

Código Civil Ley 30/1981, de 7 de Julio (BOE n° 172, de 20 de Julio). Art. 100.

Código Civil Ley 30/1981, de 7 de Julio (BOE n° 172, de 20 de Julio). Art. 101.

Código Civil Ley 30/1981, de 7 de Julio (BOE n° 172, de 20 de Julio). Art. 102.
Código Civil Ley 30/1981, de 7 de Julio (BOE n° 172, de 20 de Julio). Art. 103.
Código Civil Ley 30/1981, de 7 de Julio (BOE n° 172, de 20 de Julio). Art. 104.
Código Civil Ley 30/1981, de 7 de Julio (BOE n° 172, de 20 de Julio). Art. 105.
Código Civil Ley 30/1981, de 7 de Julio (BOE n° 172, de 20 de Julio). Art. 106.
European Convention on the Exercise of Children's Rights
Ley 15/2005, de 8 de julio, por la que se modifican el Código Civil y la Ley de Enjuiciamiento Civil en materia de separación y divorcio (BOE, núm. 163, de 09-07-2005, pp. 24458–24461).
Ley 30/1981, de 7 de julio, por la que se modifica la regulación del matrimonio en el Código Civil y se determina el procedimiento a seguir en las causas de nulidad, separación y divorcio (BOE v. 20. Juli 1981)
Decreto 139/2002, de 14 de mayo, por el que se aprueba el Reglamento de la Ley 1/ 2001, de 15 de marzo, de Mediación Familiar de Cataluña (DOGC n.° 3641, de 23 de mayo de 2002; correcciones de errores en DOGC n.° 3867, de 17 de abril de 2003, y n.° 3898, de 4 de junio).
Decreto 159/2003, de 31 de enero, por el que se regulan la figura del mediador familiar, el Registro de Mediadores Familiares de Galicia y el reconocimiento de la mediación gratuita (DOG n.° 34, de 18 de febrero de 2003; corrección de errores en DOG n.°44, de 4 de marzo).
Decreto 93/2005, de 2 de septiembre, por el que se regulan los Puntos de Encuentro Familiar (BOPA n.° 214, de 15 de septiembre de 2005).
Decreto 41/2007, de 13 de abril, por el que se desarrolla la Ley 7/2001, de 26 de noviembre, reguladora de la Mediación Familiar en el ámbito de la Comunidad Valenciana (DOGV n.° 5.492, de 18 de abril de 2007).
Ley 15/2003, de 8 de abril, de la Mediación Familiar (BOC n.° 85, de 6 de mayo de 2003; BOE n.° 134, de 5 de junio). Decreto 144/2007, de 24 de mayo, por el que se aprueba el Reglamento de la Ley de la Mediación Familiar (BOC n.° 114, de 8 de junio de 2007).
Ley Foral 22/2002, de 2 de julio, para la adopción de medidas integrales contra la violencia sexista de Navarra (BON n.° 84, de 12 de julio de 2002; BOE n.° 199, de 20 de agosto).
Ley 18/2006, de 22 de noviembre, de Mediación Familiar (BOIB n.° 169, de 30 de noviembre de 2006; BOE n.° 303, de 20 de diciembre).
Decreto 50/2007, de 17 de mayo, por el que se aprueba el Reglamento de desarrollo de la Ley 1/2006, de 6 de abril, de Mediación Familiar (BOCL n.° 99, de 23 de mayo de 2007)
Navarra Foral Law 1/1973 of 1.3.1973, Compilación de Derecho Civil Foral de Navarra
Aragón Law 3/1985 Compilación de Derecho Civil de Aragón
Balearic Islands, decree 79/1990 of 6.9.1990, Compilación de Derecho Civil de Baleares
Law of the Basque Country 3/1992, del Derecho Civil Foral del País Vasco
Galicia Law 4/1995, de Derecho Civil de Galicia

Ley Orgánica 10/1995, de 23 de noviembre, del Código Penal, Libro III., Faltas y Sus Penas, Título I. Faltas contra las Personas, Artículo 618.2.

Criminal Law, Article 618.2, Ley Orgánica 10/1995, de 23 de noviembre, del Código Penal, Libro III., Faltas y Sus Penas, Título I. Faltas contra las Personas.

Catalan Law 9/1998 of 15.7.1998, del Codí de família

Comunidad Autónoma de Cataluña (Ley 9/1998), de 15 de julio, del Código de Familia de Cataluña.

Ley 9/1998, de 15 de julio, del Código de Familia de Cataluña (DOGC n.° 2.687, de 23 de julio de 1998; BOE n.°198, de 19 de agosto).

Ley 1/2000, de 7 de enero, de enjuiciamiento Civil (BOE n° 7, de 8 de enero de 2000; corrección de errores en BOE n° 90, de 14 de abril).

Ley 1/2000, de 7 de enero, de enjuiciamiento Civil (BOE n° 7, de 8 de enero de 2000; corrección de errores en BOE n° 90, de 14 de abril). Art. 748.

Ley 1/2000, de 7 de enero, de enjuiciamiento Civil (BOE n°7, de 8 de enero de 2000; corrección de errores en BOE n° 90, de 14 de abril). Art. 749.

Ley 1/2000, de 7 de enero, de enjuiciamiento Civil (BOE n° 7, de 8 de enero de 2000; corrección de errores en BOE n° 90, de 14 de abril). Art. 750.

Ley 1/2000, de 7 de enero, de enjuiciamiento Civil (BOE n° 7, de 8 de enero de 2000; corrección de errores en BOE n° 90, de 14 de abril). Art. 751.

Ley 1/2000, de 7 de enero, de enjuiciamiento Civil (BOE n° 7, de 8 de enero de 2000; corrección de errores en BOE n° 90, de 14 de abril). Art. 752.

Ley 1/2000, de 7 de enero, de enjuiciamiento Civil (BOE n° 7, de 8 de enero de 2000; corrección de errores en BOE n° 90, de 14 de abril). Art. 753.

Ley 1/2000, de 7 de enero, de enjuiciamiento Civil (BOE n° 7, de 8 de enero de 2000; corrección de errores en BOE n° 90, de 14 de abril). Art. 754.

Ley 1/2000, de 7 de enero, de enjuiciamiento Civil (BOE n° 7, de 8 de enero de 2000; corrección de errores en BOE n° 90, de 14 de abril). Art. 755.

Ley 1/2000, de 7 de enero, de enjuiciamiento Civil (BOE n° 7, de 8 de enero de 2000; corrección de errores en BOE n° 90, de 14 de abril). Art. 769.

Ley 1/2000, de 7 de enero, de enjuiciamiento Civil (BOE n° 7, de 8 de enero de 2000; corrección de errores en BOE n° 90, de 14 de abril). Art. 770.

Ley 1/2000, de 7 de enero, de enjuiciamiento Civil (BOE n° 7, de 8 de enero de 2000; corrección de errores en BOE n° 90, de 14 de abril). Art. 771.

Ley 1/2000, de 7 de enero, de enjuiciamiento Civil (BOE n° 7, de 8 de enero de 2000; corrección de errores en BOE n° 90, de 14 de abril). Art. 772.

Ley 1/2000, de 7 de enero, de enjuiciamiento Civil (BOE n° 7, de 8 de enero de 2000; corrección de errores en BOE n° 90, de 14 de abril). Art. 773.

Ley 1/2000, de 7 de enero, de enjuiciamiento Civil (BOE n° 7, de 8 de enero de 2000; corrección de errores en BOE n° 90, de 14 de abril). Art. 774.

Ley 1/2000, de 7 de enero, de enjuiciamiento Civil (BOE n° 7, de 8 de enero de 2000; corrección de errores en BOE n° 90, de 14 de abril). Art. 775.

Ley 1/2000, de 7 de enero, de enjuiciamiento Civil (BOE n° 7, de 8 de enero de 2000; corrección de errores en BOE n° 90, de 14 de abril). Art. 776.

Ley 1/2000, de 7 de enero, de enjuiciamiento Civil (BOE n° 7, de 8 de enero de 2000; corrección de errores en BOE n° 90, de 14 de abril). Art. 777.
Ley 1/2000, de 7 de enero, de enjuiciamiento Civil (BOE n° 7, de 8 de enero de 2000; corrección de errores en BOE n° 90, de 14 de abril). Art. 778.
Official Journal of the European Communities C 364/13, 18.12.2000
Comunidad Autónoma de Cataluña (Ley 1/2001), de 15 de marzo, de Mediación Familiar de Cataluña.
Ley 1/2001, de 15 de marzo, de Mediación Familiar (DOGC n.° 3.355, de 26 de marzo de 2001, con corrección de errores en DOGC n.° 3.548, de 8 de enero de 2002; BOE n.° 91, de 16 de abril de 2001).
Comunidad Autónoma del Galicia (Ley 4/2001), de 31 de mayo, de Mediación Familiar de Galicia.
Ley 4/2001, de 31 de mayo, reguladora de la Medición Familiar (DOG n.° 117, de 18 de junio de 2001; BOE n.° 157, de 2 de julio).
Comunidad Autónoma Valenciana (Ley 7/2001), de 26 de noviembre, reguladora de la mediación familiar, en el ámbito de la Comunidad Valenciana.
Ley 7/2001, de 26 de noviembre, reguladora de la Mediación Familiar en el ámbito de la Comunidad Valenciana (DOGV n.° 4.138, de 29 de noviembre de 2001; BOE n.° 303, de 19 de diciembre).
Comunidad Autónoma de Castilla-La Mancha (Ley 4/2005), de 24 de mayo, del Servicio Social Especializado de Mediación Familiar.
Ley 4/2005, de 24 de mayo, del Servicio Social Especializado de Mediación Familiar (DOCM n.° 111, de 3 de junio de 2005; BOE n.° 203, de 25 de agosto).
Ley 13/2005 of 1 July (published in BOE, Nr. 157, de 02-07-2005, pp. 23632–23634).
Ley 1/2006, de 6 de abril, de Mediación Familiar (BOCL n.° 75, suplemento, de 18 de abril de 2006; BOE n.° 105, de 3 de mayo, con corrección de errores en BOE n.° 135, de 7 de junio).
Comunidad de Madrid (Ley 1/2007), de 21 de febrero, de Mediación Familiar de la Comunidad de Madrid.
Ley 1/2007, de 21 de febrero, de Mediación Familiar (BOCM n.° 54, de 5 de marzo de 2007; BOE n.° 153, de 27 de junio).
Decreto 2/2007, de 26 de enero, por el que se regulan los Puntos de Encuentro Familiar (BOR n.° 14, de 30 de enero de 2007).
Comunidad Autónoma del Principado de Asturias (Ley 3/2007), de 23 de marzo, de Mediación Familiar.
Ley 3/2007, de 23 de marzo, de Mediación Familiar (BOPA n.° 81, de 9 de abril de 2007; BOE n.° 170, de 17 de julio).
Ley 4/2007, de 22 de marzo, de prevencion y protección integral de las mujeres víctimas de violencia en Aragón (BOA n. 41, de 9 abril de 2007; BOE n. 141, de 13 de junio).
Ley 1/2008, de 8 de febrero, de Mediación Familiar (BOPV n. 34, de 18 febrero de 2008.)
Comunidad Autónoma de Andalucía (Ley 1/2009), de 27 de Febrero, reguladora de la Mediación Familiar en la Comunidad Autónoma de Andalucía.

Principle 2:2, Principles of European Family Law Regarding Divorce and Maintenance between Former Spouses

Homepages

http://www.econ.upf.edu/docs/papers/downloads/986.pdf
http://mediate.com/articles/zumeta.cfm
http://conventions.coe.int/Treaty/en/Treaties/Html/160.htm
http://www.ipfe.org. Report on the Evolution of the Family in Europe 2008, Institute for Family Policies (2008: 32).
http://ec.europa.eu/employment_social/news/2006/oct/consultation_reconciliation_en.pdf
http://factfinder.census.gov
http://conventions.coe.int/Treaty/en/Summaries/Html/005.htm
http://ec.europa.eu/civiljustice/divorce/divorce_spa_de.htm
http://epp.eurostat.ec.europa.eu
http://noticias.juridicas.com/base_datos/Admin/constitucion.html
http://noticias.juridicas.com/base_datos/Privado/lo1-1996.html
http://www.europarl.europa.eu/charter/pdf/text_en.pdf
http://www.gencat.net/justicia/normes/angl/l9e.htm
http://www.ine.es
http://www.mjusticia.es/
http://www.poderjudicial.es
http://www.pon.harvard.edu
http://www.whenparentspart.org.uk
http://www2.ohchr.org/english/law/crc.htm
http://www3.uakron.edu/witt/fc/fcnote5.htm
http://ec.europa.eu/employment_social/news/2006/oct/consultation_reconciliation_en.pdf
Recommendation No. R (98) 1 of the Committee of Ministers to Member States on Family Mediation adopted by the Committee of Ministers on 21 January 1998.
http://bundesrecht.juris.de/bundesrecht/lpartg/gesamt.pdf
http://www2.law.uu.nl/priv/cefl/
http://www2.law.uu.nl/priv/cefl/Reports/pdf/SpainApp02.pdf

Abbreviations

AA VV	Autores Varios
ABGB	Bürgerliches Gesetzbuch (Austria)
ABl	Amtsblatt
ABl.EG	Amtsblatt der Europäischen Gemeinschaften

AC	Aranzadi Civil
Act. Civ.	Actualidad Civil
AcP	Archiv für civilistische Praxis
ADC	Anuario de Derecho Civil
Amtsbl.	Amtsblatt
art./arts.	artículo/artículos
Art	Artikel
ASPD	Antisocial personality disorder
BB OO	Boletines Oficiales
BCEHC	Boletín del Centro de Estudios Hipotecarios de Cataluña
BGB	Bürgerliches Gesetzbuch (Germany)
BGBl	Bundesgesetzblatt (Germany)
BIMJ	Boletín de Información del Ministerio de Justicia
BOA	Boletín Oficial de Aragón
BOCAIB	Boletín Oficial de la Comunidad Autónoma de las Islas Baleares
BOGAN	Boletín Oficial de Canarias Aranzadi
BOCM	Boletín Oficial de la Comunidad de Madrid
BOCyL	Boletín Oficial de Castilla y León
BOE	Boletín Oficial del Estado
BOJA	Boletín Oficial de la Junta de Andalucía
Bol. (UE)	Boletín (de la Unión Europea)
BON	Boletín Oficial de Navarra
BOPA	Boletín Oficial del Principado de Asturias
BOPV	Boletín Oficial del País Vasco
BOR	Boletín Oficial de La Rioja
BORM	Boletín Oficial de la Región de Murcia
cap./caps	capítulo/capítulosCC Código Civil
CC AA	Comunidades Autónomas
CCJC	Cuadernos Civitas de Jurisprudencia Civil
CE	Constitución Española
CEE	Comunidad Económica Europea
CEEP	European Centre of Enterprises with Public Participation and of Enterprises of General Economic Interest
CEDH	Convenio Europeo para la Protección de los Derechos Humanos y Libertades Fundamentales
CGPJ	Consejo General del Poder Judicial
CJ	Colección de Jurisprudencia Civil, publicada por la RGLJ
CL	Colección Legislativa
Com. CC I	Comentario del Código Civil. Ministerio de Justcia, t. I
Com. CC II	Comentario del Código Civil. Ministerio de Justcia, t. II
Comp.	Compilación
CP	Código Penal
D	Decreto/Digesto
DFCPY	Derecho Foral Civil del País Vasco

DG	Dirección General
DIPr	Derecho Internacional Privado
Diss.	Dissertation
disp. adic.	disposición adicional
disp. derog.	disposición derogatoria
disp. final	disposición final
disp. transit.	disposición transitoria
DOC	Diario Oficial de las Comunidades Europeas, serie "Comunicaciones e Informaciones"
doc./docs.	documento/documentos
DOCE	Diario Oficial de las Comunidades Europeas
DOCM	Diario Oficial de Castilla-La Mancha
DOE	Diario Oficial de Extremadura
DOG	Diario Oficial de Galicia
DOGC	Diario Oficial de la Generalitat de Cataluña
DOGV	Diario Oficial de la Generalitat Valenciana
DOL	Diario Oficial de las Comunidades Europeas, serie "Legislación"
EE AA	Estatutos de Autonomía
et al.	*et alii* (y otros)
ECtHR	European Court of Human Rights
EE 02/05	Edición Especial
EheG	Ehegesetz
etc.	Etcétera
ETUC	European Trade Union Confederation
f./ff.	following
FamRÄndG	Familienrechtsänderungsgesetz
fig./figs.	figura/figuras
hab./habs.	habitante/habitantes
ibid.	*ibidem* (allí mismo, en el mismo lugar)
id.	*idem* (el mismo, lo mismo, la misma)
INE	Instituto Nacional de Estadíatica (Spain) National Statistics Institute
Inf. Gen.	Informe General
JURA	Juristische Ausbildung
LAN	Legislación de Andalucía Aranzadi
LArb	Ley de Arbitraje
LARG	Legislación de Aragón Aranzadi
LCAT	Legislación de Cataluña Aranzadi
LCEur	Legislación de las Comunidades Europeas Aranzadi
LCLM	Legislación de Castilla-La Mancha Aranzadi
LCM	Legislación de Madrid Aranzadi
LCV	Legislación de la Comunidad Valenciana
LCyL	Legislación de Castilla y León Aranzadi
LDCF	Ley de Derecho Civil Foral
LDCG	Ley de Derecho Civil de Galicia

LDCFPV	Ley de Derecho Civil Foral del País Vasco
LECiv	Ley de Enjuiciamiento Civil
LECrim	Ley de Enjuiciamiento Criminal
LEXT	Legislación de Extremadura Aranzadi
LG	Legislación de Galicia Aranzadi
LIB	Legislación de las Islas Baleares
LLR	Legislación de La Rioja Aranzadi
LNA	Legislación de Navarra Aranzadi
LO	Ley Orgánica
loc. cit.	*loco citato* (en el lugar citado)
LOPJM	Ley Orgánica de Protección Jurídica del Menor
LORPM	Ley Orgánica Responsabilidad Penal de los Menores
LOTC	Ley Orgánica del Tribunal Constitucional
LPAS	Legislación del Principado de Asturias
LRC	Ley de Responsabilidad Civil
LRJ-PAC	Ley de Régimen Jurídico de las Administraciones Públicas y del Procedimiento Administrativo Común
LRM	Legislación de la Región de Murcia Aranzadi
N.B.	*nota bene* (nota, observa, advierte bien)
n°/n^{os}	número/números
O	Orden
OM	Orden Ministerial
ONU	Organización de las Naciones Unidas
op. cit.	*opere citato* (en la obra citada)
p./pp.	página/páginas
p. ej.	por ejemplo
RCL	Repertorio Cronológico de Legislación Aranzadi
RDLey	Real Decreto Legislativo
RDley	Real Decreto-ley
RDP	Revista de Derecho Privado
Rep. JCE	Repertorio Doctrinal y Legal de la Jurisprudencia Civil Española
Rec.	Recopilación (de la Jurisprudencia del Tribunal de Justicia)
RGD	Revista General de Derecho
RGLJ	Revista General de Legislación y Jurisprudencia
RJ	Repertorio de Jurisprudencia Aranzadi
RJC	Revista Jurídica de Cataluña
RR DD	Reales Decretos
RTC	Repertorio Aranzadi del Tribunal Constitucional
s./ss.	siguiente/siguientes
SAP	Sentencia de Audiencia Provincial
SI	Symbolic Interaction Theory
STEDH	Sentencia del Tribunal Europeo de Derechos Humanos
TC	Tribunal Constitucional

TCE	Tratado Constitutivo de la Comunidad Europea
TEDH	Tribunal Europeo de Derechos Humanos
TRRL	Texto Refundido de las disposiciones legales
TS	Tribunal Supremo
UEAPME	European Association of Craft, Small and Medium-Sized Enterprises
UNICE	Union of Industrial and Employers' Confederation
VOC	*'value-of-children'-theory*
v. gr.	*verbi gratia* (por ejemplo)
vid. vide	(véase)
vol./vols.	volumen/volúmenes

Spanish Civil Code 1889 (CC)

Ley 15/2005[1]
Book I: Persons
Title IV: Marriage

Chapter IV
Rights and Duties of Spouses

Article 66

The spouses have equal rights and duties.

Article 67

Spouses should respect and help each other and act in the interest of the family.

Article 68

The spouses are obliged to live together, be faithful and help each other. They must also share domestic responsibilities and the care and attention of ascendants and descendants and other dependents.

Chapter VII: Separation

Article 81

Separation shall be judicially decreed, regardless of the form in which the marriage was contracted:

1. At the petition of both spouses, or of one of them with the other's consent, at the expiration of 3 months after the marriage was contracted. The petition for separation must be accompanied by a proposal for a regulatory agreement to govern the separation in accordance with Article 90 of this Code.

[1]See: Ley 15/2005, de 8 de julio, por la que se modifican el Código Civil y la Ley de Enjuiciamiento Civil en materia de separación y divorcio. BOE núm. 163, Sábado 9 julio 2005: 24458–24461.

2. At the petition of one of the spouses, after 3 months of marriage. There is no requirement to wait for the expiration of 3 months after the marriage in order to file the claim if it can be proved that a spouse's life is in danger, there is a risk against the physical integrity, freedom, moral integrity or sexual indemnity of the claimant, the children of both, or any of the members of the marriage.

The petition must be accompanied by a proposal based on the measures that regulate the effects of separation.

Article 82

(This Article was repealed by Law 15/2005)

Article 83

A decree of separation suspends the spouses' life in common, and terminates the possibility of binding the assets of the other spouse in the exercise of domestic prerogative (*potestad doméstica*).

Article 84

Reconciliation puts an end to the separation proceedings and leaves what may have been decided therein without further effect. Both parties must, however, separately notify the court of the reconciliation before which the proceedings are or have been held.

The above notwithstanding, the measures taken in relation to the children shall be maintained or modified by judicial resolution whenever there exists just cause therefore.

Chapter VIII: Dissolution of Marriage

Article 85

Marriage is dissolved by the death or declaration of death of one of the spouses, and by divorce, regardless of the manner and time in which it was contracted.

Article 86

The divorce court decree, whatever form of marriage, the petition of one spouse only, both or one with the consent of the other, where the conditions and circumstances prescribed in Article 81.

Article 87

(This Article was repealed by Law 15/2005)

Article 88

The action for divorce is terminated by the death of any of the spouses and by their reconciliation. Reconciliation must be express when it takes place after the filing of the demand.

Reconciliation after divorce does not produce legal effects, although the divorced parties may contract a new marriage between each other.

Article 89

Dissolution of marriage by divorce can only take place by means of a decree of divorce so declaring and shall produce effects from the time this decree becomes final. It shall not prejudice third parties in good faith until it is recorded in the Civil Registry.

Chapter IX: Effects Common to Nullity, Separation, and Divorce

Article 90

The regulating agreement to which Articles 81 and 86 of this Code make reference must deal with, at least, the following subjects:

(a) The determination of the person in whose custody the children under parental authority of both spouses are to remain; the exercise of parental authority; and the regime of visitations, communications, and children's periods of stay with the parent who does not live with them.
(b) The use of the family dwelling and furnishings.
(c) Contributions to the expenses of marriage and support obligations, as well as the basis for updating them and guarantees, when appropriate.
(d) The liquidation of the matrimonial property regime, when appropriate.
(e) Maintenance which, pursuant to Article 97, must eventually be discharged by one of the spouses.

Matrimonial agreements, entered into for the purpose of regulating the consequences of nullity, separation, or divorce, shall be approved by the court, unless they should be detrimental to the children or seriously damaging to one of the spouses. The rejection must be made by reasoned opinion, and, in such a case, the spouses must submit a new proposal to the consideration of the court for approval, where appropriate. From the moment it receives court approval, the agreement may be enforced by compulsory executory process (*vía de apremio*).

The measures adopted by the court in the absence of agreement, as well as those agreed upon by the spouses, may be modified judicially or by a new agreement when there is a substantial change in the circumstances.

The court may establish the real or personal guarantees that the performance of the agreement may require. [....]

Article 91

If the spouses fail to present an agreement in judgments of nullity, separation or divorce, or their performance, the judge will determine the following measures to be taken according to the following articles: The relation to the children, the family accommodation, the duty to pay child support, liquidation of the matrimonial economic regime, cautionary and mutual guarantees. The judge will determine all these concepts if the parents have not decided on these concepts. These orders may be modified when circumstances have altered substantially.

Article 92

1. The separation, annulment and divorce do not discharge parents of their obligations for their children.
2. If the judge adopts any decisions on custody, child care and education of the minor children, he or she has to ensure that the right of the child to be heard is guaranteed.
3. In the judicial decision will be agreed on the withdrawal of the legal authority if during the process is revealed that there is any cause for it.
4. Parents may agree in the regulatory agreement or the judge may decide, in the best interests of the children that legal authority is fully or partially exercised by one of the spouses.

5. The joint exercise of child custody is bestowed if the parents propose it in the regulating agreement or if both reach an agreement during the process. In the agreement of joint custody and after giving reasons for his resolution his, the judge adopts the appropriate precautions for the effective accomplishment of the established custody regime, intending not to separate brothers.
6. In any case, before the establishing a custody arrangements, the judge shall obtain the report of the prosecutor, hears the children who are old enough to judge, when deemed necessary or requested by child or the team of specialists, the judge assesses the arguments of the parties expressed at the hearing and the evidence brought in and the relationship that parents have among each other and to their children to determine their suitability in the custody regime.
7. There shall be no joint custody if either parent is under criminal proceedings for crimes against life, physical integrity, freedom, moral integrity or sexual indemnity against the other spouse or the children who live with both. Neither will be joint custody if there is evidence of domestic violence.
8. Exceptionally, if paragraph five is not the case, the judge, at the request of a party and with a favourable report of the Public Prosecutor may agree to bestow joint custody on the ground that only in this way the interests of the child can be guaranteed.
9. Before the judge takes any decisions concerning the previous paragraphs may request the report of a qualified specialist about the suitability of the way in which parental authority and custody of the minor children is exercised.

Article 93

In any case, the judge will determine the contribution of each parent to cover the cost for alimentation and takes appropriate measures to ensure the effectiveness and adaptation of payment according to the economic circumstances and needs of children at all times.

If adult children live in the family home or emancipated adult children who have no income, the judge determines in the same resolution the child support according to Article 142 and subsequent Articles of this Code.

Article 94

The parent who does not have custody of minor or disabled children has the right to visit them, communicate with them and have them in company. The judge will determine the time, manner and place of exercising this right, which may be limited or suspended if there was any serious circumstance that gives evidence that there has been repeated failure to meet the duties imposed by the court decision.

The judge may also determine, after hearing the parents and grandparents, who shall consent, that the grandchildren have the right of communication and visitation of grandparents, according to Article 160 of the Code, keeping in mind the best interest of the child.

Article 95

The judicial decision produces the final decision concerning the matrimonial property, the dissolution of the matrimonial regime.

If the decree of nullity declares the bad faith of only one of the spouses, the one who has acted in good faith may choose to apply provisions in the liquidation of the matrimonial property concerning a participation in the profit of the property and the one who has acted in bad faith is not entitled to participate in the profit of the property earned by the other spouse.

Article 96

In the absence of an agreement among the parties, the judge approves that the use of the family home and the objects of ordinary use in it are attributed to the children and the spouse in whose company they are.

When some of the children remain in the company of one and the other in that of the other, the court shall decide as appropriate.

If there are no children, it can be agreed that the use of such property, for as long as prudently be set, corresponds to the spouse who does not own it, provided that the circumstances require it and the spouse is in need of protection.

For a spouse to make use of a accommodation and property of which he is not the owner requires the consent of both parties or, where appropriate, judicial authorization.

Article 97

The spouse to whom the separation or divorce produces an economic imbalance in relation to the position of the other, which involves a worsening of the situation he or she had during the marriage, has a right to maintenance which shall be fixed in the judicial decree, taking into account, among other, the following circumstances:

1. The agreements that the spouses may have reached.
2. Their age and state of health.
3. Professional qualifications and the probabilities of gaining employment.
4. Past and future dedication to the family.
5. Collaboration, by his or her own labour, with the commercial, industrial, or professional activities of the other spouse.
6. The duration of the marriage and their marital life.
7. The eventual loss of a right to a pension
8. The wealth and economic means and necessities of both spouses

The judicial decree shall establish the bases for updating the award of maintenance, and the guarantees for its effectiveness.

Article 98

The spouse in good faith whose marriage has been declared null shall have a right to an indemnification award, if there has been marital life, taking into account the circumstances provided by Article 97.

Article 99

The substitution of an annuity, the usufruct of certain property, or the delivery of capital in assets other than in money, instead of the judicially fixed award pursuant to Article 97, may be agreed upon at any time.

Article 100

After maintenance and the bases for updating it are fixed in the judgement on separation or divorce, the award may only be modified when there are substantial alterations in the economic capability of either spouse.

Article 101

The right to receive maintenance terminates on the cessation of the cause that gave raise to it, by the subsequent marriage of the spouse entitled to it or by his or her marital cohabitation with another person.

The right to receive maintenance does not end on the death of the person who is obliged to make this payment. Nevertheless, the debtor's heirs may request the reduction or suppression of the award from the court if the hereditary assets were insufficient to discharge the debt or if their right to the legitimate portion would be affected.

References

Ahrons, C. (1979). The binuclear family. *Alternative Lifestyles, 2*, 499–515.

Ahrons, C. (1981). The continuing coparental relationship between divorced spouses. *American Journal of Orthopsychiatry, 5*, 415–427.

Ahrons, C., & Tanner, J. (2003). Adult children and their fathers: relationship changes 20 years after parental divorce. *Family Relations, 52*, 340–351.

Albaladejo, M. (2008). *Curso de Derecho Civil IV. Derecho de Familia.* Madrid: Edisofer.

Allen, D. (1992). Marriage and divorce: comment. *American Economic Review, 82*, 679–685.

Alberdi, I., Matas, N. (2002). La violencia doméstica. Informe sobre los malos tratos a mujeres en España. Fundación la Caixa.

Allen, K. (1993). The dispassionate discourse of children's adjustment to divorce. *Journal of Marriage and Family, 55*(1), 46–50.

Alwin, D., Braun, M., & Scott, J. (1992). The separation of work and the family: attitudes towards women's labour-force participation in Germany, Great Britain and the United States. *European Sociological Review, 8*(1), 13–37.

Amato, P. (1993). Family structure, family process, and family ideology. *Journal of Marriage and the Family, 55*, 50–54.

Amato, P. (1994). "Life-span adjustment of children to their parents' divorce". *The Future of Children, Children and Divorce, 4*(1), 143–164.

Amato, P. (2000). The consequences of divorce for adults and children. *Journal of Marriage and the Family, 62*, 1269–1287.

Amato, P., & Booth, A. (1991). Consequences of parental divorce and marital unhappiness for adult well being. *Social Forces, 63*, 895–914.

Amato, P., & Gilbreth, J. (1999). Nonresident fathers and children's well-being: a meta-analysis. *Journal of Marriage and the Family, 61*, 557–573.

Amato, P., & Keith, B. (1991a). Parental divorce and the well-being of children: a meta-analysis. *Psychological Bulletin, 110*, 26–46.

Amato, P., & Keith, B. (1991b). Parental divorce and adult well-being: a meta-analysis. *Journal of Marriage and the Family, 53*, 43–58.

Amato, P., & Rezac, S. (1994). Contact with non-resident parents, interparental conflict, and children's behaviour. *Journal of Family Issues, 15*, 191–207.

Amato, P., Loomis, L., & Booth, A. (1995). Parental divorce, marital conflict, and offspring wellbeing in early adulthood. *Social Forces, 73*, 895–916.

Andreß, H., Borgloh, B., et al. (2006). The economic consequences of partnership dissolution – a comparative analysis of panel studies from Belgium, Germany, Great Britain, Italy, and Sweden. *European Sociological Review, 22*(5), 533–560.

Anxo, D., & Carlin, P. (2004). Intra-family time allocation to housework: French evidence. *Electronic International Journal of Time Use Research, 1*(1), 14–36.

Aquilino, W. (1994). Impact of childhood family disruption on young adults' relationships with parents. *Journal of Marriage and the Family, 56*(2), 295–314.

Aquilino, W. (2006). The noncustodial father–child relationship from adolescence into young adulthood. *Journal of Marriage and Family, 68*, 929–946.

Arch Marin, M., & Jarne Esparcia, A. (2008). Opinión y valoración de los diferentes sistemas de guarda y custodia por psicólogos forenses y juristas españoles. Un estudio piloto. *Derecho de Familia, 41*, 25–33.

Arditti, J. (1992). Factors related to custody, visitation, and child support for divorced fathers: an exploratory analysis. *Journal of Divorce and Remarriage, 17*, 23–42.

Arditti, J. (1999a). Rethinking relationships between divorced mothers and their children: capitalizing on family strengths. *Family Relations, 48*, 109–119.

Arditti, J. (1999b). Parental divorce and young adults' intimate relationships: towards a new paradigm. *Marriage and Family Review, 29*(1), 35–56.

Arditti, J., & Keith, T. (1993). Visitation frequency, child support payment, and the father–child relationship post-divorce. *Journal of Marriage and the Family, 55*, 699–712.

Argys, L., Peters, H., et al. (1998). The impact of child support on cognitive outcomes of young children. *Demography, 35*, 159–173.

Aseltine, R., & Kessler, R. (1993). Marital disruption and depression in a community sample. *Journal of Health and Social Behavior, 34*, 237–251.

Asociacion de Mujeres Juridistas THEMIS. (1999). *Respuesta penal a la violencia familiar*. Madrid: Consejo de la Mujer de la Comunidad de Madrid.

Astone, N., & McLanahan, S. (1994). Family structure, residential mobility, and school dropout: a research note. *Demography, 31*, 575–584.

Bader, M., Berger, J., et al. (1980). *Einführung in die Gesellschaftstheorie. Gesellschaft, Wirtschaft und Staat bei Marx und Weber*. Frankfurt: Campus Verlag.

Baizán, P., Michielin, F., & Billari, F. (2002). Political economy and life course patterns: the heterogeneity of occupational, family and household trajectories of young spaniards. *Demographic Research, 6*(8), 191–240.

Baker, A. (2005). The long-term effects of parental alienation on adult children: a qualitative research study. *The American Journal of Family Therapy, 33*, 289–302.

Bandura, A., & Walters, R. (1963). *Social learning and personality development*. New York: Holt, Rinehart and Winston.

Barisic, P. (2008). Philosophy and democracy. Does globalization threaten democracy? *Synthesis Philosophica, 46*(2), 297–303.

Barrett, M. (2002). How a woman can protect herself and her children in divorce. *American Journal of Family Law, 8*(14), 212–217.

Bartholomew, K. (1990). Avoidance of intimacy: an attachment perspective. *Journal of Social and Personal Relationships, 7*, 147–178.

Bastine, R. (2005). Familienmediation heute – Leistungsfähigkeit und Barrieren in der Praxis. *Zeitschrift für Konflikt-Management, 8*, 11–14.

Bastine, R., Haynes, J., Link, G., & Mecke, A. (Eds.). (2002). *Scheidung ohne Verlierer. Familienmediation in der Praxis*. München: Kösel.

Baumgärtel, F. (1994). Trennung und Scheidung – Ein Massenphänomen ohne kultiviertes Ritual – im Umbruch? *SpielRäume, 11*, 1.

Bausermann, R. (2002). Child adjustment in joint-custody versus sole-custody arrangements: a meta-analytic review. *Journal of Family Psychology, 16*, 91–102.

Beck, U. (2003). *Risikogesellschaft. Auf dem Weg in eine andere Moderne*. Frankfurt a.M: Suhrkamp.

Beck, N., & Hartmann, J. (1999). Die Wechselwirkung zwischen Erwerbstätigkeit der Ehefrau und Ehestabilität unter der Berücksichtigung des sozialen Wandels. *Kölner Zeitschrift für Soziologie und Sozialpsychologie, 51*(1999), 655–680.

Becker, G. (1973). A theory of marriage, Part I. *Journal of Political Economy, 81*(4), 813–846.
Becker, G. (1991). *A treatise on the family*. Cambridge, MA: Harvard University Press.
Becker, G., Landes, E., & Michael, R. (1977). An economic analysis of marital instability. *Journal of Political Economy, 85*(6), 1141–1187.
Beck-Gernsheim, E., & Beck, U. (1998). *Das ganz normale Chaos der Liebe*. Frankfurt: Suhrkamp.
Belsky, J., Campbell, S., Cohen, J., & Moore, G. (1996). Instability of infant–parent attachment security. *Developmental Psychology, 32*, 921–924.
Bercovitz Rodríguez-Cano, R. (2006). *Comentarios al Código Civil*. Aranzadi: Navarra.
Bidwell, L., & Vander Mey, B. (2000). *Sociology of the family: investigating family issues*. Boston: Allyn and Bacon.
Biller, H. (1974). *Paternal deprivation: family, school, sexuality, and society*. Lexington, MA: Lexington Books.
Biller, H. (1981). The father and sex-role development. In M. Lamb (Ed.), *The role of the father in child development* (pp. 319–358). Wiley: New York.
Blow, K., & Daniel, G. (2002). Frozen narratives. Post-divorce processes and contact disputes. *Journal of Family Therapy, 24*, 85–103.
Boele-Woelki, K. (2005). The principles of European family law: its aims and prospects. *Utrecht Law Review, 1*(2), 160–168.
Boele-Woelki, K., Martiny, D., Ferrand, F., et al. (2004). *Principles of European family law regarding divorce and maintenance between former spouses*. Intersentia: Antwerp.
Boele-Woelki, K., Braat, B., & Curry-Summer, I. (Eds.). (2005). *European family law in action. Vol. III: parental responsibilities*. Intersentia: Antwerp.
Boettger, U. (2004). Efficiency versus party empowerment – against a good faith-requirement in mandatory mediation. *The Review of Litigation, 23*, 1–46.
Booth, A., Johnson, D., & Edwards, J. (1983). Measuring marital instability. *Journal of Marriage and the Family, 45*, 387–393.
Bowlby, J. (1951): "Maternal care and mental health", *World Health Organization Monograph* (Serial No. 2). Geneva.
Bowlby, J. (1958). The nature of the child's tie to his mother. *International Journal of Psycho-Analysis, 39*, 350–373.
Bowlby, J. (1982). *Attachment and loss 1: attachment*. New York: Basic Books.
Braver, S., Griffin, W., & Cookston, J. (2005). Prevention programs for divorced non-resident fathers. *Family Court Review, 43*, 81–96.
Brines, J., & Joyner, K. (1999). The ties that bind: principles of cohesion in cohabitation and marriage. *American Sociological Review, 64*(3), 333–356.
Brinig, M., & Allen, D. (2000). These boots are made for walking: why most divorce filers are women. *American Law and Economics Review, 2*, 126–169.
Brinig, M., & Buckley, F. (1998). No-fault laws and at-fault people. *International Review of Law and Economics, 18*, 325–340.
Buchanan, C., Maccoby, E., & Dornbusch, S. (1991). Caught between parents: adolescents' experience in divorced homes. *Child Development, 62*(5), 1008–1029.
Buchanan, C., Maccoby, E., & Dornbusch, S. (1996). *Adolescents after divorce*. Cambridge, Mass: Harvard University Press.
Burgess, E., Locke, H., & Thomas, M. (1971). *The family: from traditional to companionship*. New York: Van Nostrand Reinhold Co.
Burkhauser, R., Duncan, G., et al. (1991). Wife or frau, women do worse: a comparison of men and women in the United States and Germany after marital dissolution. *Demography, 28*, 353–360.
Bush, K., & Peterson, G. (2007). Family influences on child development. In T. Gullotta & G. Blau (Eds.), *Handbook of childhood behavioral issues. evidence-based approaches to prevention and treatment* (pp. 43–68). New York: Routledge.

Camera, K., & Resnick, G. (1989). Styles of conflict resolution and cooperation between divorced parents: effects on child behaviour and adjustment. *American Journal of Orthopsychiatry, 59*, 560–574.

Campbell, T. (2005). Why doesn't parental alienation occur more frequently? The significance of role discrimination. *The American Journal of Family Therapy, 33*, 365–377.

Campo Izquierdo, Á. (2009). Guarda y custodia compartida. Se debe condicionar su concesión a que exista un informe favorable del Ministerio Fiscal? *Diario La Ley, 12960*, 10–12.

Carbonne, J. (1994). A feminist perspective on divorce. *The Future of Children, 4*, 183–209.

Carrasco Perera, Á. (1986). La Reforma Francesa de los Regimenes Económicos Matrimoniales. *Anuario Derecho Civil, 39*, 582–614.

Carrasco Perera, Á. (2006). *Derecho de Familia: Casos, Reglas y Paradojas*. Madrid: Editorial Dilex.

Carrasco Perera, Á. (2005a): "La custodia compartida", In *Aranzadi, Civil*, 22/2004. BIP. 2004/1797. Parte Editorial Aranzadi SA: Pamplona.

Carrasco Perera, Á. (2005b): "Sobre custodia compartida", *Actualidad Jurídica Aranzadi*, n° 648: 3.

Castillo Martínez, C. (2007). La determinación en la guarda y custodia de los menores en los supuestos de crisis matrimonial o convivencial de sus progenitores. Especial consideración de la guarda y custodia compartida tras la Ley 15/2005, de 8 julio. *Actualidad Civil, 15*, 1738–1760.

Claxton, A., & Perry-Jenkins, M. (2008). No fun anymore: leisure and marital quality across the transition to parenthood. *Journal of Marriage and Family, 70*(1), 28–43.

Coester, M. (1983). *Das Kindeswohl als Rechtsbegriff. Die richterliche Entscheidung über die elterliche Sorge beim Zerfall der Familengemeinschaft*. Frankfurt/M: Alfred Metzner Verlag.

Coester-Waltjen, D. (2002). Die internationale Zuständigkeit und Anerkennung von Sorgerechtsentscheidungen in der europäischen Union. In P. Gottwald (Ed.), *Aktuelle Entwicklungen des europäischen und internationalen Zivilverfahrensrechts* (Vol. 14, pp. 163–236). Bielefeld: Verlag Ernst und Werner Gieseking.

Coester-Waltjen, D. (2006). Voraussetzungen der Ehescheidung, *Jura*, 105–108.

Coester-Waltjen, D. (2008). *Familienrecht. Textausgabe mit ausführlichem Sachverzeichnis und einer Einführung*. München: Beck.

Cohen, O. (1999). Suitability of divorcing couples for mediation: a suggested typology. *The American Journal of Family Therapy, 27*, 329–344.

Cohen, L., & Cohen, L. (2002). Marriage: the long-term contract. In A. Dnes & R. Rowthorne (Eds.), *The law of economics of marriage and divorce* (pp. 10–34). Cambridge: CUP.

Cohen, O., & Finzi-Dottan, R. (2005). Parent–child relationships during the divorce-process: from attachment theory and intergenerational perspective. *Contemporary Family Therapy, 27*(1), 81–99.

Cohn, D., Cowan, P., et al. (1992). Mother's and father's working models of childhood attachment relationships, parenting styles, and child behavior. *Development and Psychopathology, 4*, 417–431.

Coleman, J. (1988). Social capital in the creation of human capital. *American Journal of Sociology, 94*, 95–120.

Collins, M. (1999): Unveiling the Hidden Data on Domestic Violence in the European Union. Final Report. European Centre pour la promotion d'une politique contre la violence à l'égard des femmes, Brussels.

Coysh, W., Johnston, J., et al. (1989). Parental postdivorce adjustment in joint and sole physical custody families. *Journal of Family Issues, 10*(1), 52–71.

Crane, D., Soderquist, J., & Gardner, M. (1995). Gender differences in cognitive and behavioural steps toward divorce. *The American Journal of Family Therapy, 23*(2), 99–105.

Crowell, J., & Feldman, S. (1988). Mothers' internal models of relationships and children's behavioral and developmental status: a study of mother–child interaction. *Child Development, 59*, 1273–1285.

Cummings, E., Davies, P., & Simpson, K. (1994). Marital conflict, gender, and children's appraisals and coping efficacy as mediators of child adjustment. *Journal of Family Psychology, 8*(2), 141–149.

Davies, P., & Cummings, E. (1994). Marital conflict and child adjustment: an emotional security hypothesis. *Psychological Bulletin, 116*(3), 387–411.

Davies, P., & Cummings, E. (1995). Children's emotions as organizers of their reactions to interadult anger: a functionalist perspective. *Developmental Psychology, 31*(4), 677–684.

Davies, P., & Cummings, E. (1996). Emotional security as a regulatory process in normal development and the development of psychopathology. *Development and Psychopathology, 8*, 123–139.

Davies, P., & Cummings, E. (1998). Exploring children's emotional security as mediator of the link between marital relations and child adjustment. *Child Development, 69*(1), 129–139.

Davies, P., & Windle, M. (2001). Interparental discord and adolescents adjustment trajectories: the potentiating and protective role of intrapersonal attributes. *Child Development, 72*(4), 1163–1178.

Davies, P., Myers, R., & Cummings, E. (1996). Responses of children and adolescents to marital conflict scenarios as a function of the emotionality of conflict endings. *Merrill-Palmer Quarterly, 42*(1), 1–21.

De Armas Hernández, M. (2003). La mediación en la resolución de conflictos. *Educar, 32*, 125–136.

de Graaf, P., & Kalmijn, M. (2006). Divorce motives in a period of rising divorce. Evidence from a Dutch life-history survey. *Journal of Family Issues, 27*(4), 483–505.

De Ussel, J. (2005). Qué pasa con las familia en España? *Cuadernos de pensamiento político, 7*(9), 39–60.

DeGarmo, E., Patras, J., & Eap, S. (2008). Social support for divorced fathers' parenting: testing a stress-buffering model. *Family Relations, 57*, 35–48.

Consejo General del Poder Judicial (2009): *Informe sobre víctimas mortales de la violencia de género y de la violencia doméstica en el ámbito de la pareja o ex pareja en 2009*. Madrid

Delgado Martín, J. (2008): "La patria potestad compartida en los procedimientos matrimoniales", In C. Martínez de Aguirre, *Novedades legislativas en materia matrimonial* (pp. 153–197). Madrid: Consejo General del Poder Judicial.

Dema-Moreno, S., & Díaz-Martínez, C. (2010). Gender inequalities and the role of money in Spanish dual-income couples. *European Societies, 12*(1), 65–84.

Demo, D., Acock, A. (1988). The Impact of Divorce on Children. *Journal of Marriage and the Family*, 50, 619–648.

Demo, D., & Acock, A. (1996). Family structure, family process, and adolescent well-being. *Journal of Research on Adolescence, 6*, 457–488.

Diez-Picazo, L., & Gullón, A. (2004). *Sistema de derecho Civil IV: Derecho de familia. Derecho de sucesiones*. Madrid: Tecnos.

Dillon, P., & Emery, R. (1996). Divorce mediation and resolution of child custody disputes: long-term effects. *American Journal of Orthopsychiatry, 66*, 131–140.

Dnes, A., & Rowthorn, R. (2002). *The law and economics of marriage and divorce*. Cambridge: Cambridge University Press.

Dolgin, J. (2002). The constitution as family arbiter: a moral in the mess? *Columbia Law Review, 102*, 337–407.

Domínguez-Folgueras, M., & Castro-Martín, T. (2008). Women's changing socioeconomic position and union formation in Spain and Portugal. *Demographic Research, 19*(41), 1513–1550.

Duncan, G. and Hoffman, S. (1985). "Economic Consequences of Marital Instability", In M. David, T. Smeeding (Eds.), *Horizontal Equity, Uncertainty and Well-Being* (pp. 427–470). Chicago: University of Chicago Press.

Edwards, J. (1987). Changing family structure and youthful well-being: assessing the future. *Journal of Family Issues, 8*, 355–372.

Ellman, I., & Lohr, S. (1998). Dissolving the relationship between divorce laws and divorce rates. *International Review of Law and Economics, 18*, 341–359.
Ellwood, M., & Stolberg, A. (1993). The effects of family composition, family health, parenting behavior and environmental stress on children's divorce adjustment. *Journal of Child and Family Studies, 2*(1), 23–36.
Emery, R. (1988). *Marriage, divorce, and children's adjustment*. Newbury Park: Sage Publications.
Emery, R. (1994). *Renegotiating family relationships: divorce, child custody and mediation*. New York: Guildford.
Emery, R., & Wyer, M. (1987). Child custody mediation and litigation: an experimental evaluation of the experience of parents. *Journal of Consulting and Clinical Psychology, 55*, 179–186.
Escrivá-Ivars, J. (2001). *Matrimonio y mediación familiar*. Madrid: Ediciones Rialp.
Esser, H. (2002a). Ehekrisen: Das (Re-)Framing der Ehe und der Anstieg der Scheidungsraten. *Zeitschrift für Soziologie, 31*(6), 472–496.
Esser, H. (2002b). In guten wie in schlechten Tagen? Das Framing der Ehe und das Risiko zur Scheidung. Eine Anwendung und ein Test des Frames der Frame-Selektion. *Kölner Zeitschrift für Soziologie und Sozialpsychologie, 54*, 27–63.
Esteve, A., & Cortina, C. (2006). Changes in educational assortative mating in contemporary Spain. *Demographic Research, 14*(17), 405–428.
Eurostat Yearbook (2008): Europe in figures. Luxembourg: Office for Official Publications of the European Communities. (http://epp.eurostat.ec.europa.eu/cache/ITY_OFFPUB/KS-HA-08-001/EN/KS-HA-08-001-EN.PDF)
Eurostat Yearbook (2008): Europe in figures. Luxembourg: Office for Official Publications of the European Communities. (http://epp.eurostat.ec.europa.eu/cache/ITY_OFFPUB/KS-CD-07-001/EN/KS-CD-07-001-EN.PDF)
Eurostat Yearbook (2009): Europe in figures. Luxembourg: Office for Official Publications of the European Communities. (http://epp.eurostat.ec.europa.eu/cache/ITY_OFFPUB/KS-CD-09-001/EN/KS-CD-09-001-EN.PDF)
Falco, E. (2003). Commentary: children and divorce. *The Journal of the American Academy of Psychiatry and the Law, 31*, 171–172.
Ferrer i Riba, J. (2005). "Familienrechtliche Verträge in den spanischen Rechtsordnungen", In S. Hofer, et al, *From Status to Contract ? – Die Bedutung des Vertrages im europäischen Familienrecht* (pp. 271–292). Geseking: Bielefeld.
Farmer, S., & Galaris, D. (1993). Support groups for children of divorce. *The American Journal of Family Therapy, 21*(1), 40–50.
Ferguson, N., Douglas, G., & Lowe, N. (2004). *Grandparenting in divorced families*. The Policy Press: University of Michigan.
Fernández Campos, J. (2008). Sentencia de 27 de junio de 2007: Derecho de uso sobre vivienda familiar y partición ganancial. *Cuadernos Civitas de Jurisprudencia Civil, 77*, 585–594.
Figdor, H. (1991). *Kinder aus geschiedenen Ehen: Zwischen Trauma und Hoffnung. Wie Kinder und Eltern die Trennung erleben*. Grünewald: Mainz.
Figdor, H. (1997). *Scheidungskinder – Wege der Hilfe*. Gießen: Psychosozial.
Finley, G., & Schwartz, S. (2007). Father involvement and long-term young adult outcomes: the differential contributions of divorce an gender. *Family Court Review, 45*(4), 573–587.
Fischer, T., de Graaf, P., & Kalmijn, M. (2005). Friendly and antagonistic contact between former spouses after divorce. Patterns and determinants. *Journal of Family Issues, 26*(8), 1131–1163.
Fisher, R., Ury, W., et al. (1991). *Getting to yes: negotiating agreement without giving in*. Boston: Houghton Mifflin Harcourt.
Folberg, J., Milne, A., & Salem, P. (2004). *Divorce and family mediation. Models, techniques and applications*. New York: Guilford Press.
Folger, J., & Bush, R. (1996). Transformative mediation and third-party intervention: ten hallmarks of a transformative approach to practice. *Mediation Quarterly, 13*(4), 263–278.

Folk, K., Graham, J., et al. (1992). Child support and remarriage: implications for the economic well-being of children. *Journal of Family Issues, 13*, 142–157.

Foucault, M. (1981). *Sexualität und Wahrheit. Bd. 1: Der Wille zum Wissen*. Frankfurt: Suhrkamp.

Freud, S. (1970). *Psychologische Schriften. Vol. IV, Studienausgabe*. Frankfurt a.M: Fischer Verlag.

Freud, S. (1972). *Sexualleben. Vol. V, Studienausgabe*. Frankfurt a.M: Fischer Verlag.

Freud, S. (1975). *Psychologie des Unbewußten. Vol. III, Studienausgabe*. Frankfurt a.M: Fischer Verlag.

Freud, S. (1982). *Vorlesungen zur Einführung in die Psychoanalyse Und Neue Folge. Vol. I, Studienausgabe*. Frankfurt a.M: Fischer Verlag.

Friedberg, L. (1998). Did unilateral divorce raise divorce rates? Evidence from panel data. *American Economic Review, 88*, 608–627.

Friedman, G. (1993). *A guide to divorce mediation. How to reach a fair, legal settlement at a fraction of the cost*. New York: Workman Publishing.

Friedman, D. (1995). *Towards a structure of indifference: the social origins of maternal custody*. New York: Aldine de Gruyter.

Friedman, D., Hechter, M., & Kanazawa, S. (1994). A theory of the value of children. *Demography, 31*, 375–401.

Fromm, E. (2004). *Haben oder Sein. Die seelischen Grundlagen einer neuen Gesellschaft*. München: Dtv.

Fthenakis, W. (1985a). *Väter. Zur Psychologie der Vater-Kind-Beziehung* (Vol. 1). Wien: Urban & Schwarzenberg.

Fthenakis, W. (1985b). *Väter. Zur Vater-Kind-Beziehung in verschiedenen Familienstrukturen* (Vol. 2). Wien: Urban & Schwarzenberg.

Fthenakis, W., Niesel, R., & Kunze, H. (1982). *Ehescheidung: Konsequenzen für Eltern und Kinder*. Wien: Urban & Schwarzenberg.

Fürstenberg, F., & Kiernan, K. (2001). Delayed parental divorce: how much do children benefit? *Journal of Marriage and the Family, 63*, 446–457.

Fürstenberg, F., & Nord, C. (1985). Parenting apart. *Journal of Marriage and the Family, 47*, 893–904.

Gaffal, M. (1990): Die Vater-Kind-Beziehung aus der Sicht 10 bis 15-jähriger Schülerinnen und Schüler. Unpublished Magister Thesis, Paris-Lodron-Universität, Salzburg.

Gager, C., & Sanchez, L. (2003). Two as one? Couples' perceptions of time spent together, marital quality, and the risk of divorce. *Journal of Family Issues, 24*(1), 21–50.

García García, L. (2003). *Mediación familiar. Prevención y alternativa al litigio en los conflictos familiares*. Madrid: Dykinson.

García-Longoria Serrano, M., Sánchez Urios, A. (2004): La mediación familiar como forma de respuesta a los conflictos familiares. *Portularia, 4*, 261–268.

García Rubio, M. (2006). Las uniones de hecho en España. Una visión jurídica. *Anuario de la Facultad de Derecho de la Universidad Autónoma de Madrid Derecho, sociedad y familia: cambio y continuidad, 10*, 113–138.

García Rubio, M. (2009). "Viejos y nuevos apuntes sobre la constitucionalidad del matrimonio homosexual. In: S. Alvarez González, *Estudios de derecho de familia y de sucesiones: dimensiones interna e internacional* (pp. 171–198). Malaga: Fundación Asesores Locales.

García Rubio, M., & Otero Crespo, M. (2006). Apuntes sobre la referencia expresa al ejercicio compartido de la guarda y custodia de los hijos en la Ley 15/2005. *Revista Jurídica de Castilla y León, 8*, 69–105.

García Tomé, M. (2008). La mediación familiar en los conflictos de pareja. *Documentación Social, Revista de Estudios Sociales y de Sociología Aplicada, 148*, 43–60.

García, M., & de Leonardo, T. (2008). Problemas que genera la actual regulación de la guarda y custodia compartida en el proceso contencioso. *Diario La Ley, 40228*, 4–14.

Garfinkel, I., Oellerich, D., & Robins, P. (1991). Child support guidelines: will they make a difference? *Journal of Family Issues, 12*, 404–429.

Garrity, C., & Baris, M. (1995). *Caught in the middle: protecting the children of high-conflict divorce*. New York: Lexington.

Gernhuber, J., & Coester-Waltjen, D. (2006). *Familienrecht*. München: Beck.

Glasl, F. (2004). *Konfliktmanagement. Ein Handbuch für Führungskräfte, Beraterinnen und Berater*. Bern: Paul Haupt.

Glass, S., & Wright, T. (1997). Reconstructing marriages after the trauma of infidelity. In K. Halford & H. Markham (Eds.), *Clinical handbook of marriage and couples interventions* (pp. 471–507). Chichester: John Wiley and Sons.

Glezer, H., & Wolcott, I. (1999). Work and family life: reciprocal effects. *Family Matters, 52*, 69–74.

Goldstein, J., Freud, A., & Solnit, A. (1974). *Jenseits des Kindeswohls*. Frankfurt: Suhrkamp.

Gómez Magán, P. (2008). Síndrome de Alienación Parental. *Derecho de Familia, 38*, 63–78.

González de Pozo, J. (2009). El derecho de uso de la vivienda familiar en los supuestos de guarda y custodia compartida. *Diario La Ley, 12968*, 16–19.

González, L. and Viitanen, T. (2006) "*Divorce Legislation and Marriage Rates in Europe*". Universitat Pompeu Fabra, Mimeo. http://www.econ.upf.edu/docs/papers/downloads/986.pdf.

Goode, W. (1969). The theoretical importance of love. *American Sociological Review, 24*, 38–47.

Gove, W., & Shin, H. (1989). The psychological well-being of divorced and widowed men and women. *Journal of Family Issues, 10*, 122–144.

Gray, J. (1998). Divorce-law changes, household bargaining, and married women's labor supply. *American Economic Review, 8*, 628–642.

Gray, J., & Silver, R. (1990). Opposite sides of the same coin: former spouses' divergent perspectives in coping with their divorce. *Journal of Personality and Social Psychology, 59*, 1180–1191.

Greenstein, T. (1990). Marital disruption and the employment of married women. *Journal of Marriage and the Family, 52*(3), 657–676.

Gruber, J. (2000). *Is making divorce easier bad for children?* Cambridge, MA: Mimeo, Department of Economics, MIT.

Gruber, J. (2004). Is making divorce easier bad for children? The long run implications of unilateral divorce. *Journal of Labor Economics, 22*(4), 799–833.

Grych, J., & Fincham, F. (1990). Marital conflict and children's adjustment: a cognitive-contextual framework. *Psychological Bulletin, 108*, 267–290.

Grych, J., & Fincham, F. (1992). Marital dissolution and family adjustment: an attributional analysis. In T. L. Orbuch (Ed.), *Close relationship loss: theoretical approaches* (pp. 157–173). Springer: New York.

Gschnitzer, F. (1979). *Österreichisches Familienrecht*. Wien: Springer Verlag.

Guilarte Martín-Calero, C. (2005). Comenatrios del nuevo artículo 92 del Código Civil. In V. Guilarte Gutiérrez (Ed.), *Comentarios a la reforma de la separación y el divorcio (Ley 15/2005, de 8 de julio)* (pp. 113–179). Editorial Lex Nova: Valladolid.

Habermas, J., & Luhmann, N. (1979). *Theorie der Gesellschaft oder Sozialtechnolgie*. Frankfurt: Surhrkamp.

Hanson, T. (1999). Does parental conflict explain why divorce is negatively associated with child welfare? *Social Forces, 77*, 1283–1316.

Hanson, M., & Lynch, E. (1992). Family diversity: implications for policy and practice. *Topics in Early Childhood Special Education, 12*(3), 283–306.

Hanson, T., McLanahan, S., & Thomson, E. (1996). Double jeopardy: parental conflict and stepfamily outcomes for children. *Journal of Marriage and the Family, 58*, 141–154.

Hardesty, C., Wenk, D., & Stout Morgan, C. (1995). Paternal involvement and the development of gender expectations in sons and daughters. *Youth and Society, 26*(3), 283–297.

Harold, G., & Conger, R. (1997). Marital conflict and adolescent distress: the role of adolescent awareness. *Child Development, 68*, 333–350.

Harold, G., & Shelton, K. (2008). Interparental conflict, negative parenting and children's adjustment: bridging links between parents' depression and children's psychological distress. *Journal of Family Psychology, 22*(5), 712–724.

Hawkins, D., Amato, P., & King, V. (2006). Parent–adolescent involvement: the relative influence of parent gender and residence. *Journal of Marriage and Family, 68*, 125–136.
Haynes, J. (1994). *The fundamentals of family mediation*. New York: Suny Press.
Haynes, J. (1995). *Fundamentos de la mediación familiar. Manual práctico para mediadores.* Madrid: Gaia Ediciones.
Haynes, J., & Haynes, G. (1997). *La Mediación en el Divorcio. Estrategias para negociaciones familiares exitosas basadas en casos reales.* Barcelona: Gránica S.A.
Hazan, C., & Shaver, P. (1992). Broken attachments: relationship loss from the perspective of attachment theory. In T. L. Orbuch (Ed.), *Close relationship loss: theoretical approaches* (pp. 90–110). New York: Springer.
Hedeen, T., & Salem, P. (2006). What should family-lawyers know? Results of a survey of practitioners and students. *Family Court Review, 44*(4), 601–611.
Hernando Ramos, S. (2009). El informe del Ministerio Fiscal en la guarda y custodia compartida. *Diario La Ley, 12953*, 7–9.
Hertfelder de Alcedoa, E. (2009). La familia y la vida de hoy en España. *Familia y sociedad, 6*, 1–4.
Hetherington, E., & Kelly, J. (2002). *For better or for worse: divorce reconsidered.* New York: Norton.
Hetherington, E. (2003). Intimate Pathways: Changing Patterns in Close Personal Relationships Across Time. Issue. Family Relations, *52*(4), 318–331.
Hetherington, E., & Stanley-Hagan, M. (1999). The adjustment of children and divorced parents: a risk and resilience perspective. *Journal of Child Psychology and Psychiatry, 40*(1), 129–140.
Hetherington, E., & Tryon, A. (1989). His and hers divorces. *The Family Therapy Networker, 13*(6), 58–62.
Hetherington, E., Law, T., & O'Connor, T. (1997). Divorce: challenges, changes, and new chances. In A. Skolnick & H. Skolnick (Eds.), *Family in transition* (pp. 163–172). New York: Longman.
Hill, R. (1949). *Family under stress.* New York: Harper.
Hill, S. (1992). The role of economic resources and remarriage in financial assistance for children of divorce. *Journal of Family Issues, 13*, 158–178.
Hofer, S., Schwab, D., & Henrich, D. (Eds.). (2005). *From Status to Contract? – Die Bedeutung des Vertrages im europäsichen Familienrecht.* Gieseking: Bielefeld.
Hofstede, G. (1991). *Cultures and organizations. Intercultural cooperation and its importance for survival.* London: Harper Collins Publishers.
Hughes, K. (2007). Mothering mothers: an exploration of the perspectives of adult children of divorce. *Australian Journal of Social Issues, 42*(4), 563–579.
Ivars Ruiz, J. (2008). Guarda y custodia compartida. Valencia: Editorial Tirant lo Blanch.
Irwin, H., & Benjamin, M. (1992). An evaluation of process and outcome in a private family mediation service. *Mediation Quarterly, 10*, 35–55.
Jeynes, W. (1999). Effects of remarriage following divorce on the academic achievement of children. *Journal of Youth and Adolescence, 28*(3), 385–393.
Joas, H. (1991). Mead's position in intellectual history and his early philosophical writings. In M. Aboulafia (Ed.), *Philosophy, social theory and the thought of George Herbert Mead* (pp. 57–88). New York: Suny Press.
Johnston, J. R. (1990). Role diffusion and role reversal: structural variations in divorced families and children's functioning. *Family Relations, 39*(4), 405–414.
Johnston, J., Kline, M., & Tschann, J. (1989). Ongoing post divorce conflict: effects on children of joint custody and frequent access. *American Journal of Orthopsychiatry, 59*, 576–592.
Kalmijn, M. (1998). Intermarriage and homogamy: causes, patterns, trends. *Annual Review of Sociology, 24*, 395–421.
Kalmijn, M. (2005). "The effects of divorce on men's employment and social security histories". *European Journal of Population, 21*(4), 347–366.
Karney, B., & Bradbury, T. (1995). The longitudinal course of marital quality and stability: a review of theory, method and research. *Psychological Bulletin, 118*, 3–34.

Katz, E. (2007). A family therapy perspective on mediation. *Family Process, 46*(1), 93–107.

Kelly, J. (1991). Parent interaction after divorce: comparison of mediated and adversarial divorce processes. *Behavioural Science and Law, 9*, 387–398.

Kelly, R., Redenbach, L., & Rinaman, W. (2005). Determinants of custody arrangements in a national sample. *American Journal of Family Law, 19*, 25–43.

Kiernan, K., & Hobcraft, J. (1997). Parental divorce during childhood: age at first intercourse, partnership, and parenthood. *Population Studies, 51*, 41–55.

Kindler, H., Schwabe-Höllein, M., (Eds.) (2002): "Eltern-Kind-Bindung und geäußerter Kindeswille in hochstrittigen Trennungsfamilien", *Kindschaftsrechtliche Praxis, 5*(1): 10–17.

Kitson, G. (1992). *Portrait of divorce: Adjustment to marital breakdown.* New York: Guilford Press.

Kitson, G., & Morgan, L. (1990). The multiple consequences of divorce: a decade review. *Journal of Marriage and the Family, 52*, 913–924.

Kitson, G., Babri, K., Roach, M., & Placidi, K. (1989). Adjustment to widowhood and divorce. *Journal of Family Issues, 10*, 5–32.

Klenner, W. (2002). Szenarien der Entfremdung im elterlichen Trennungsprozess. Entwurf eines Handlungskonzepts von Prävention und Intervention. *Zentralblatt für Jugendrecht, 89*(2), 48–57.

Kline, M., Tschann, J., et al. (1989). Children's adjustment in joint and sole custody families. *Developmental Psychology, 25*, 430–435.

Klosinski, G., Günter, M., & Karle, M. (Eds.). (2001). *Scheiden tut weh. Zur Situation von Kindern in auseinanderbrechenden Familien.* Tübingen: Attempto.

Koch, M., & Lowery, C. (1984). Evaluation of mediation as an alternative to divorce litigation. *Professional Psychology: Research and Practice, 15*, 109–120.

Kodjoe, U. (2002). Elternentfremdung nach Trennung und Scheidung. Ein Überblick zur aktuellen Forschungslage bei Elternentfremdung. *Das Jugendamt, 75*(9), 386–390.

Koropeckyj-Cox, T. (2002). Beyond parental status: psychological well-being in middle and old age. *Journal of Marriage and Family, 64*, 957–971.

Krause, M. (2002). PAS und seine Geschwister. Strukturell systemische Überlegungen zur Gefährdung des Kindeswohls durch sechs verschiedene Muster pathologischer Trennungsbewältigung". *Das Jugendamt, 75*(1), 2–6.

Kressel, K., et al. (1980). A typology of divorcing couples: implications for mediation and the divorce process. *Family Process, 19*, 101–116.

Kühne, A. (2006). Psychologische Aspekte der elterlichen Sorge. In T. Fabian & S. Nowara (Eds.), *Neue Wege und Konzepte in der Rechtspsychologie* (pp. 187–198). Berlin: LIT-Verlag.

Kürthy, T. (1978). *Geschlechtsspezifische Sozialisation: alte Normen und neue Vorstellungen in der Entwicklung und Erziehung von Kindern und Jugendlichen* (Vol. 1 and 2). Paderborn: Schöningh.

Lamb, E. (Ed.). (2004). *The role of the father in child development.* New York: John Wiley and Sons.

Lamb, M., Pleck, J., Charnov, E., & Levine, J. (1987). A biosocial perspective on paternal behavior and involvement. In J. Lancaster, J. Altmann, et al. (Eds.), *Parenting across the lifespan: biosocial dimensions* (pp. 111–142). Hawthorne, NY: Aldine de Gruyter.

Lathrop Gómez, F. (2008). *Custodia Compartida de los Hijos.* Madrid: Wolters Kluwer.

Lauer, R., & Lauer, J. (1986). Factors in long-term marriages. *Journal of Family Issues, 7*(4), 382–390.

Lehrer, E. L. (2006): "Age at Marriage and Marital Instability: Revisiting the Becker-Landes-Michael Hipotesis", IZA DP No. 2166, Institute for the Study of Labor: Bonn.

Leibenstein, H. (1957). *Economic backwardness and economic growth.* New York: John Wiley.

Leinfellner, W., & Köhler, E. (1998). *Game theory, experience, rationality. foundations of social sciences, economic and ethics.* Dordrecht: Kluwer.

Leite, R., & McKenry, P. (2002). Aspects of father status and postdivorce father involvement with children. *Journal of Family Issues, 23*, 601–623.

Levinger, G., & Moles, O. (Eds.). (1979). *Divorce and separation. Context, causes, and consequences.* New York: Basic Books.

Long, N., Forehand, R., Fauber, R., & Brody, G. (1987). Self-perceived and independently observed competence of young adolescents as a function of parental marital conflict and recent divorce. *Journal of Abnormal Child Psychology, 15*(1), 15–27.

Lowe, N., & Douglas, G. F. (2006). *Bromley's family law* (10th ed.). Oxford University Press: Oxford.

Lowe, N., Boele-Woelki, K., et al. (2007). *Principles of European family law regarding parental responsibilities*. Portland: Intl Specialized Book Service Inc.

Luhmann, N. (1973). *Vertrauen. Ein Mechanismus zur Reduktion sozialer Komplexität*. Stuttgart: Ferdinand Enke Verlag.

Luhmann, N. (1982). *Liebe als Passion. Zur Codierung von Intimität*. Frankfurt: Suhrkamp.

Luhmann, N. (1984). *Soziale Systeme. Grundriß einer allgemeinen Theorie*. Frankfurt: Suhrkamp.

Maccoby, E., & Mnookin, R. (1994). *Dividing the child: social and legal dilemmas of custody*. Cambridge, MA: Harvard University Press.

Maccoby, E., Buchanan, C., et al. (1993). Postdivorce roles of mothers and fathers in the lives of children. *Journal of Family Psychology, 7*, 24–38.

Main, M., & Solomon, J. (1990). Procedures for identifying infants as disorganized/disoriented during the Ainsworth Strange Situation. In M. Greenberg, D. Cicchetti, & E. Cummings (Eds.), *Attachment in the preschool years: theory, research, and intervention* (pp. 121–160). Chicago: University of Chicago Press.

Mandell, B. (1988). "Mothers post-divorce: the challenges of adjustment". *Journal of Rational-Emotive & Cognitive-Behavior Therapy, 6*(1–2), 81–101.

Marcus, M. et al. (2007). To mediate or not to mediate: financial outcomes in mediated versus adversarial divorces. *Conflict Resolution Quarterly, 17*(2), 143–152.

Marín-López, M. J. (2006). Capítulo IX. De los efectos comunes a la nulidad, separación y divorcio. Artículos 90 a 101. In R. Bercovitz Rodríguez-Cano (Ed.), *Comentarios al Código Civil* (pp. 209–233). Navarra: Aranzadi.

Marín López, J. J. (Ed.). (2008). *Legislación sobre Mediación Familiar*. Madrid: Tecnos.

Marín López, P., & Lorente Acosta, M. (2008). *La valoración del daño en las víctimas de la violencia de género*. Madrid: Consejo General del Poder Judicial.

Marks, G., & Fleming, N. (1999). Influences and consequences of well-being among Australian young people: 1980–1995. *Social Indicators Research, 46*, 301–323.

Martín-Casals, M. (1999). Grundzüge der vermögensrechtlichen Situation von Ehegatten und nichtehelichen Lebensgemeinschaften im spaischen und katalanischen Recht. In D. Henrich & D. Schwab (Eds.), *Eheliche Gemeinschaft, Partnerschaft und Vermögen im europäischen Vergleich* (pp. 283–298). Bielefeld: Gieseking.

Martín-Casals, M., & Ribot, J. (2006). Ehe und Scheidung in Spanien nach den Reformen von 2005. *Zeitschrift für das gesamte Familienrecht, 53*(18), 1331–1336.

Martin, S., Parashar, S. (2006). Women's Changing Attitudes towards Divorce, 1974–2002: Evidence for an Educational Crossover. *Journal of Marriage and the Family*, 68, 29–40.

Martínez de Aguirre, C. (2008). *Novedades legislativas en materia matrimonial*. Madrid: Consejo General del Poder Judicial.

Maslow, A. (1943). A theory of human motivation. *Psychological Review, 50*, 370–396.

Maslow, A. (1954). *Motivation and personality*. New York: Harper.

Maxwell, D. (1992). Gender differences in mediation style and their impact on mediator effectiveness. *Mediation Quarterly, 9*, 353–364.

Mazur, E., Wolchik, S., & Sandler, I. (1992). Negative cognitive errors and positive illusions for negative divorce events: predictors of children's psychological adjustment. *Journal of Abnormal Child Psychology, 20*(6), 523–542.

McCubbin, H., & McCubbin, M. (1989). Theoretical orientations to family stress and coping. In C. Figley (Ed.), *Treating stress in families* (pp. 3–43). New York: Brunner & Mazel.

McCubbin, H., & Patterson, J. (1983). Stress and the family. In F. McCubbin (Ed.), *Family stress, coping, and social support* (pp. 5–25). Thomas: Springfield.

McCubbin, H., Cauble, A., & Patterson, J. (1982). *Family stress, coping, and social support.* Springfield: Thomas.

McDonald, R. (2006). Young children's appraisals of interparental conflict: measurement and links with adjustment problems. *Journal of Family Psychology, 20*(1), 88–99.

McEwen, C., Mather, L., & Maiman, R. (1994). Lawyers, mediation, and the management of divorce practice. *Law and Society Review, 28*, 149–183.

McIntosh, J. (2003). Enduring conflict in parental separation: pathways of impact on child development. *Journal of Family Studies, 9*(1), 63–80.

McLanahan, S., Adams, J. (1987). Parenthood and Psychological Well-Being. *Annual Review of Sociology, 13*, 237–257.

McLanahan, S., & Sandefur, G. (1994). *Growing up with a single parent: what hurts, what helps.* Cambridge, MA: Harvard University Press.

McNeal, C., & Amato, P. (1998). Parents' marital violence: long-term consequences for children. *Journal of Family Issues, 19*, 123–139.

McPhail Gray, M., & Coleman, M. (1985). Separation through divorce: supportive professional practices. *Child and Youth Care Forum, 14*(4), 248–261.

McWinney, R. (1995). The winner–loser syndrome: changing fashions in the determination of child custody. *Family and Conciliation Courts Review, 33*, 298–307.

Mead, G. H. (1934). Mind, self, and society: From the standpoint of a social behaviorist. Charles W. Morris (Ed.). Chicago: University of Chicago Press.

Mechoulan, S. (2005). Economic theory's stance on no-fault divorce. *Review of Economics of the Household, 3*(3), 337–359.

Mederer, H., Hill, R. (1983). "Critical transitions over the family life span: Theory and practice", In H. McCubbin, M. Sussman, J. Patterson (Eds.), *Social stress and the family, advances and developments in family stress theory and research* (pp. 39–60). Abingdon: Haworth Press.

Menaghan, E., & Lieberman, M. (1986). Changes in depression following divorce: a panel study. *Journal of Marriage and the Family, 48*, 319–328.

Messer, A. (1989). Boys' father hunger: the missing father syndrome. *Medical Aspects of Human Sexuality, 23*, 44–47.

Meyer, D. (1993). Child support and welfare dynamics: evidence from Wisconsin. *Demography, 30*, 45–62.

Meyer, D., & Bartfeld, J. (1996). Compliance with child support orders in divorce cases. *Journal of Marriage and the Family, 58*, 201–212.

Mies, T. (1990). Familie. In J. Sandkühler (Ed.), *Europäische Enzyklopädie zu Philosophie und Wissenschaften* (pp. 15–53). Hamburg: Felix Meiner Verlag.

Mitscherlich, A., Richards, A., & Strachey, J. (Eds.). (1975). *Sigmund Freud. Band III Psychologie des Unbewussten.* Frankfurt/M: Fischer.

Montero Aroca, J. (2002). *El Convenio Regulador en la Separación y en el Divorcio. La aplicación práctica del artículo 90 del Código Civil.* Valencia: Tirant Lo Blanch.

Moore, C. (2003). *The mediation process. Practical strategies for resolving conflict.* San Francisco: Jossey-Bass.

Morgan, L., Kitson, G., & Kitson, T. (1992). "The economic fallout from divorce: issues for the 1990s". *Journal of Family and Economic Issues, 13*(4), 435–443.

Mott, F. (1990). When is a father really gone? Paternal–child contact in father-absent homes. *Demography, 30*, 719–735.

Moyer, S. (2004). *Child custody arrangements: Their characteristics and outcomes.* Canada: Background Paper. Department of Justice.

Muñoz-Eguileta, A. (2009). Personas Divorciadas: Análisis de las Características del Proceso de Ruptura. *Intervención Psicosocial, 18*(1), 65–74.

Nakonezny, P., Shull, R., & Rodgers, J. (1995). The effect of non-fault divorce law on the divorce rate of the 50 states and its relation to income, education and religiosity. *Journal of Marriage and the Family, 57*, 477–488.

Napp-Peters, A. (1988). *Scheidungsfamilien. Interaktionsmuster und kindliche Entwicklung. Aus Tagebüchern und Interviews mit Vätern und Müttern nach Scheidung*. Frankfurt: Dt. Vereins für öffentliche und private Fürsorge.

Napp-Peters, A. (1995). *Familien nach der Scheidung*. München: Verlag Antje Kunstmann.

Nauck, B. (2001). Der Wert von Kindern für ihre Eltern. "Value of Children" als spezielle Handlungstheorie des generativen Verhaltens und von Generationenbezihungen im interkulturellen Vergleich. *Kölner Zeitschrift für Soziologie und Sozialpsychologie, 53*, 407–435.

Neubauer, E. (1988). *Alleinerziehende Mütter und Väter. Eine Analyse der Gesamtsituation* (Schriftenreihe des Bundesministers für Jugend, Familie, Frauen und Gesundheit, Vol. 219). Stuttgart: Kohlhammer.

Newman, H., & Langer, E. (1981). Post-divorce adaptation and the attribution of responsibility. *Sex Roles, 7*(3), 223–232.

Nichols, W. (1989). A family systems approach. In C. Figley (Ed.), *Treating stress in families* (pp. 67–97). New York: Brunner & Mazel.

Nichols, K. (2007). Breaking impasses: strategies for working with high conflict personalities. *American Journal of Family Law, 20*, 226–233.

Nock, S. (2001). The marriages of equally dependent spouses. *Journal of Family Issues, 22*, 756–777.

Nock, S., & Brinig, M. (2002). Weak men and disorderly women: divorce and the division of labour. In A. Dnes & R. Rowthorn (Eds.), *The law and economics of marriage & divorce* (pp. 171–190). Cambridge: Cambridge University Press.

O'Connor, et al. (1999). Parental divorce and adjustment in adulthood: findings from a community sample. *Journal of Child Psychology and Psychiatry, 40*, 777–790.

Oerter, R., & Montada, L. (1982). *Entwicklungspsychologie. Ein Lehrbuch*. Wien: Urban & Schwarzenberg.

Oldham, M. (2007). *Blackstone's statutes on family law. 2006–2007*. Oxford: Oxford University Press.

Olson, D. (1972). Empirically unbinding the double bind: a review of research and conceptual formulations. *Family Process, 11*, 69–94.

Oppenheimer, V. (1988). A Theory of Marriage Timing. *American Journal of Sociology, 94*(3), 563–591.

Oppenheimer, V. (1994). Women's rising employment and the future of the family in industrial societies. *Population and Development Review, 20*, 293–342.

Orbuch, T. (1992). A symbolic interactionist approach to the study of relationship loss. In T. L. Orbuch (Ed.), *Close relationship loss: Theoretical approaches* (pp. 90–110). New York: Springer.

Ott, N. (1992). *Intrafamily bargaining and household decisions*. New York: Springer.

Padilla-Gálvez, J. (2008). Die Freiheit des Spiels oder das Spiel der Freiheit. In W. Lütterfelds (Ed.), *Das Sprachspiel der Freiheit* (pp. 55–77). Frankfurt/Main: Peter Lang.

Padilla-Gálvez, J., & Gaffal, M. (2005). *Spanienknigge. Sozioökonomische Einführung in die Interkulturalität*. München: Oldenbourg.

Papoušek, H., & Papoušek, M. (1984). Learning and cognition in the everyday life of human infants. In J. Rosenblatt et al. (Eds.), *Advances in the study of behaviour* (Vol. 14, pp. 127–163). New York: Academic.

Parkman, A. (1992). Unilateral divorce and the labour force participation rate of married women. Revisited. *American Economic Review, 82*, 871–678.

Parkman, A. (2002). Mutual consent divorce. In A. W. Dnes & R. Rowthorn (Eds.), *The law and economics of marriage & divorce* (pp. 57–69). Cambridge: Cambridge UP.

Parley, L. (2001). Commentary: a rose of a different color. *The Journal of the American Academy of Psychiatry and the Law, 29*, 29–32.

Parsons, T. (1951). *The Social System*. New York: Free Press.

Parsons, T. (1968). *Sozialstruktur und Persönlichkeit*. Frankfurt: Europäische Verlagsanstalt.

Parsons, T. (1986). *Aktor, Situation und normative Muster. Ein Essay zur theorie sozialen Handelns*. Frankfurt: Suhrkamp.
Pearson, J., & Thoennes, N. (1984). Mediating and litigating custody disputes: a longitudinal evaluation. *Family Law Quarterly, 17*, 497–524.
Pérez Galván, M. (2009). Problemas prácticos en el régimen de guarda y custodia compartida. *Diario La Ley, 12977*, 19–20.
Peters, E. (1986). Marriage and divorce: informational constraints and private contracting. *American Economic Review, 76*, 437–454.
Peters, E. (1992). Marriage and divorce: reply. *American Economic Review, 82*, 686–693.
Pfeifer, G., & Abrams, L. (1984). School-based discussion groups for children of divorce: a pilot program. *Group, 8*(4), 22–28.
Pfiffner, L., McBurnett, K., & Rathouz, P. (2001). Father absence and familial antisocial characteristics. *Journal of Abnormal Child Psychology, 29*(5), 357–367.
Piaget, J. (2003). *Das Weltbild des Kindes*. München: Dtv.
Plummer, L., & Koch-Hattem, A. (1986). Family stress and adjustment to divorce. *Family Relations, 35*, 523–529.
Price, S., & McKenry, P. (1988). *Divorce*. London: Sage.
Putnam, R. (1995). Bowling alone: America's decline of social capital. *Journal of Democracy, 6*(1), 65–78.
Quiñónez Escámez, A. (2005). *Crisis matrimoniales. Protección del menor en el marco europeo*. Buenos Aires: La Ley.
Ram, B., & Hou, F. (2003). Changes in family structure and child outcomes: roles of economic and familial resources. *Policy Studies Journal, 31*(3), 309–330.
Rasmusen, E. (2002). An economic approach to adultery law. In A. Dnes & R. Rowthorn (Eds.), *The law and economics of marriage and divorce* (pp. 70–91). Cambridge: CUP.
Rice, J. (2001). Family roles and patterns: contemporary trends. In J. Worell (Ed.), *Encyclopedia of women and gender* (Vol. I, pp. 411–424). San Diego: Academic Press.
Rieck, C. (1992). *Spieltheorie. Eine Einführung*. Eschborn: Christian Rieck Verlag.
Rivero Hernandez, F. (2007). *El Interés del Menor*. Madrid: Dykinson.
Roca i Trias, E. (1996). Las consecuencias economicas del divorcia: la pension compensatoria. In M. Cervilla Garzón (Ed.), *La situación jurídical de la mujer en los supuestos de crisis matrimonial* (pp. 145–198). Jerez de la Frontera: Publicaciones de la Universidad de Cádiz.
Rodgers, K., & Rose, H. (2002). Risk and resiliency factors among adolescents who experience marital transitions. *Journal of Marriage and Family, 64*(4), 1024–1037.
Rogers, S. (2004). Dolars, dependency and divorce: four perspectives on the role of wives' income. *Journal of Marriage and the Family, 66*, 59–74.
Rogers, S., & DeBoer, D. (1999). Changes in wives' income: effects on marital happiness, psychological well-being, and the risk of divorce. *Journal of Marriage and the Family, 63*, 458–472.
Roth, M. (2005). Future divorce law – two types of divorce. In K. Boele-Woelki, B. Braat, & Curry-Summer (Eds.), *European Family Law in Action* (Parental Responsibilities, Vol. III, pp. 41–50). Antwerp: Intersentia.
Rüedi, J. (Ed.) (2007): Alfred Adler. Menschenkenntnis (1927). Göttingen: Vandenhoeck & Ruprecht.
Ruiz Corbella, M. (2005). La familia en el contexto español y europeo. In J. Buché Peris & F. Hidalgo Mena (Eds.), *Mediación y Orientación Familiar* (pp. 41–62). Madrid: Dykinson.
Ruschena, E., Prior, M., et al. (2005). A longitudinal study of adolescent adjustment following family transitions. *Journal of child psychology and psychiatry, and allied disciplines, 46*(4), 353–363.
Rutter, M. (1987). Psychosocial resilience and protective mechanisms. *American Journal of Orthopsychiatry, 57*, 316–331.
Sabatelli, R. M., & Shehan, C. L. (1993). Exchange and resoure theories. In P. G. Boss, W. J. Doherty, R. LaRossa, W. Schumm, & S. K. Steinmetz (Eds.), *Sourcebook of family theories and methods. A contextual approach* (pp. 385–411). New York: Plenum.

Sandkühler, J. (Ed.). (1990). *Europäische Enzyklopädie zu Philosophie und Wissenschaften*. Hamburg: Felix Meiner Verlag.

Sarkadi, A., Kristiansson, R., et al. (2008). Fathers' involvement and children's developmental outcomes: a systematic review of longitudinal studies. *Acta Paediatrica, 92*(2), 153–158.

Sayer, L., & Bianchi, S. (2000). Women's economic independence and the probability of divorce. A review and reexamination. *Journal of Family Issues, 21*(7), 906–943.

Schmidbauer, W. (2007). *Mobbing in der Liebe. Wie es dazu kommt und was wir dagegen tun können*. Gütersloh: Gütersloher Verlagshaus.

Schoen, R., Astone, N., Rothert, K., Standish, N., & Kim, Y. (2002). Women's employment, marital happiness, and divorce. *Social Forces, 81*, 643–662.

Schulz von Thun, F. (1981). *Miteinander reden 1 – Störungen und Klärungen*. Reinbek: Allgemeine Psychologie der Kommunikation. Rowohlt.

Scott, M., Booth, A., et al. (2007). Postdivorce father–adolescent closeness. *Journal of Marriage and Family, 69*(5), 1194–1209.

Segal, J. (2004). Melanie Klein. London: Sage Publication.

Segura, C., Gil, M., & Sepúlveda, M. (2006). El síndrome de alienación parental: una forma de maltrato infantil. *Cuaderno Medico Forense, 12*(43/44), 117–128.

Seltzer, J., Schaeffer, N., & Charng, H. (1989). Family ties after divorce: the relationship between visiting and paying child support. *Journal of Marriage and the Family, 51*, 1013–1032.

Shapiro, A., & Lambert, J. (1999). Longitudinal effects of divorce on the quality of the father–child relationship and on fathers' psychological well-being. *Journal of Marriage and the Family, 61*(2), 397–408.

Shaver, P., & Mikulincer, M. (2002). Attachment-related psychodynamic. *Attachment and Human Development, 4*, 133–161.

Sieder, R. (1987). *Sozialgeschichte der Familie*. Frankfurt a.M: Suhrkamp.

Silverberg Koerner, S., Wallace, S., et al. (2002). Mother-to-daughter disclosure after divorce: are there costs and benefits? *Journal of Child and Family Studies, 11*(4), 469–483.

Silverstein, L., Auerbach, C. (1999). Deconstructing the essential father. *American Psychologist, 6*, 397–407.

Simons, R., Lin, K., et al. (1999). Explaining the higher incidence of adjustment problems among children of divorce compared with those in two-parent families. *Journal of Marriage and the Family, 61*, 1020–1033.

Siow, A. (2003). *The economics of marriage 30 years after Becker*. Toronto: University of Toronto. http://www.chass.utoronto.ca/cepa/Economics.pdf.

Sitorus, B. (2002). Trennung und Scheidung bei binationalen Familien. Auswirkungen der besonderen Lebenssituation auf Hilfebedarf und Unterstützungsangebote. *Das Jugendamt, 75*(9), 390–393.

Sixtl, F. (1996). *Der Mythos des Mittelwertes. Neue Methodenlehre der Statistik*. München: Oldenbourg.

Smock, P. (1994). Gender and the short-run economic consequences of marital disruption. *Social Forces, 73*(1), 243–262.

Soria, M., Villagrasa, C., & Armadans, I. (2008). *Mediación familiar. Conflicto: técnicas, métodos y recursos*. Barcelona: Bosch.

South, S., Krowder, K., & Trent, K. (1998). Children's residential mobility and neighborhood environment following parental divorce and remarriage. *Social Forces, 77*(2), 667–693.

Sprenkle, D., & Storm, C. (1983). Divorce therapy outcome research: a substantive and methodological review. *Journal of Marital and Family Therapy, 9*, 239–258.

Steward, D. (1991). Single custodial females and their families: housing and coping strategies after divorce. *International Journal of Law and the Family, 5*, 296–317.

Stewart, A., Copeland, N., et al. (1997). *Separating together: how divorce transforms families*. New York: Guilford Press.

Størksen, I., Røysamb, E., Holmen, T., & Tambs, K. (2006). Adolescent adjustment and well-being: effects of parental divorce and distress. *Scandinavian Journal of Psychology, 47*, 75–84.

Stull, D., & Kaplan, N. (1987). The positive impact of divorce mediation on children's behavior. *Mediation Quarterly, 18*, 53–59.

Sviggum, G. (2000). How children view their parents' divorce. *Family Matters, 55*, 62–67.

Sweeney, M. (2002). Remarriage and the nature of divorce: does it matter which spouse chose to leave? *Journal of Family Issues, 23*, 410–440.

Tamayo Haya, S. (2008). El interés del menor como criterio de atribución de la custodia. *Derecho de Familia, 41*, 35–79.

Teachman, J. (1991). Contributions to children by divorced fathers. *Social Problems, 38*, 358–371.

Textor, M. (1991). *Scheidungszyklus und Scheidungsberatung: Ein Handbuch.* Göttingen: Vandenhoeck & Ruprecht.

Teyber, E. (1983). Effects of the parental coalition on adolescent emancipation from the family. *Journal of Marital and Family Therapy, 9*, 305–310.

Themis (1999). Asociación de Mujeres Juristas. Respuesta penal a la violencia familiar. Madrid: Themis.

Thomas, K. (1976). *Handbook of industrial & organizational psychology. Conflict & conflict management.* Chicago: Rand McNally.

Thompson, L. (1991). Family work: women's sense of fairness. *Journal of Family Issues, 12*(2), 181–196.

Thompson, B. (1997). Couples and the work-family interface. In K. Halford & H. Markman (Eds.), *Clinical handbook of marriage and couples interventions* (pp. 273–290). Chichester: John Wiley and Sons.

Thomson, E., Hanson, T., & McLanahan, S. (1994). Family structure and child well-being: economic resources versus parental behaviours. *Social Forces, 73*, 221–242.

Thomson, E., Hanson, T., & McLanahan, S. (2003). Family structure and child well-being: economic resources vs. parental behaviour. In D. Cheal (Ed.), *Family. Critical concepts in sociology* (pp. 177–199). Oxon: Routledge.

Tiedje, L., & Darling Fisher, C. (1996). Fatherhood reconsidered: a critical view. *Research in Nursing & Health, 1996*(19), 471–484.

Trommsdorff, G. (2001). Eltern-Kind-Beziehungen aus kulturvergleichender Sicht. In S. Walper & R. Pekrun (Eds.), *Familie und Entwicklung: Aktuelle Perspektiven der Familienpsychologie* (pp. 36–62). Göttingen: Hogrefe.

Tschann, J., Johnston, J., & Wallerstein, J. (1989). Resources, stressors, and attachment as predictors of adult adjustment after divorce: a longitudinal study. *Journal of Marriage and the Family, 51*, 1033–1046.

Tschann, J., Johnston, J., Kline, M., & Wallerstein, J. (1990). Conflict, loss, parent–child relationships: predicting children's adjustment during divorce. *Journal of Divorce, 13*, 1–22.

Turkat, D. (2002). Shared parenting dysfunction. *The American Journal of Family Therapy, 30*(5), 385–393.

Uunk, W. (2004). The economic consequences of divorce for women in the European union: the impact of welfare state arrangements. *European Journal of Population, 20*(3), 251–285.

V.V.A.A. (2009). El acuerdo sobre la custodia compartida y su eficacia en los tribunales. *Derecho de Familia, 43*, 259–263.

Vassiliou, D., & Cartwright, G. (2001). The lost parents' perspective on parental alienation síndrome. *The American Journal of Family Therapy, 29*, 181–191.

Veenhoven, R. (1991). Is happiness relative? *Social Indicators Research, 24*, 1–34.

Velarde, L. (2006). *Informe Evolución de la Familia en Europa 2006.* Madrid: Institúto Politica Familia. IPF.

Wagner, M. (1997). *Scheidung in Ost- und Westdeutschland. Zum Verhältnis von Ehestabilität und Sozialstruktur seit den 30er Jahren.* Frankfurt: Campus.

Waldman Rich, B., et al. (2007). Conducting a children's divorce group: one approach. *Journal of Child and Adolescent Psychiatric Nursing, 20*(3), 163–175.

Walker, J., McCarthy, P., Timms, N. (1994). *Mediation: The making and remaking of co-operative relationships.* Centre for Family Studies: University of Newcastle Upon Tyne.

Wallerstein, J. (1986). Women after divorce: preliminary report from a ten-year follow-up. *The American Journal of Orthopsychiatry, 56*, 65–77.

Wallerstein, J., Lewis, J., & Blakeslee, S. (2000). *The unexpected legacy of divorce*. New York: Hyperion.

Wallerstein, J., Lewis, J., & Blakeslee, S. (Eds.). (2002). *Scheidungsfolgen – Die Kinder tragen die Last. Eine Langzeitstudie über 25 Jahre*. Münster: Votum.

Walters, J., Tasker, F., et al. (2001). Too busy? Fathers' attendance for family appointments. *Journal of Family Therapy, 23*, 3–20.

Wang, H., & Amato, P. (2000). Predictors of divorce adjustment: stressors, resources, and definitions. *Journal of Marriage and the Family, 62*, 655–668.

Ward, M., & Carlson, E. (1995). Associations among adult attachment representations, maternal sensitivity, and infant–mother attachment in sample of adolescent mothers. *Child Development, 66*, 69–79.

Watson, N., & Greeff, A. (2004). An analysis of schema theory and learning theory as explanations for variant in adolescent adjustment to divorce. *The American Journal of Family Therapy, 32*, 437–448.

Watzlawick, P., Weakland, J., & Fisch, J. (2009). *Lösungen – Zur Theorie und Praxis menschlichen Wandels*. Bern: Hans Huber Verlag.

Weber, M. (1976). *Wirtschaft und Gesellschaft*. Tübingen: Mohr Siebeck.

Wehler, H. (2003). *Deutsche Gesellschaftsgeschichte. Vierter Band: Vom Ersten Weltkrieg bis zur Gründung der beiden deutschen Staaten 1914–1949*. München: Beck.

Weltner, J. (1982). A structural approach to the single parent. *Family Process, 21*, 203–210.

Westberg, H., Nelson, T., & Piercy, K. (2002). Disclosure of divorce plans to children: what the children have to say. *Contemporary Family Theory, 24*(4), 525–542.

Wheaton, B. (1990). Life transitions, role histories, and mental health. *American Sociological Review, 55*, 209–223.

White, L. (1990). Determinants of divorce: a review of research in the eighties. *Journal of Marriage and the Family, 52*, 904–912.

White, S., & Mika, K. (1983). Family divorce and separation: Theory and research. In H. McCubbin, M. Sussman, & J. Patterson (Eds.), *Social stress and the family, advances and developments in family stress theory and research* (pp. 175–192). New York: Haworth Press.

Whitehead, B. (1997). *The divorce culture*. New York: Knopf.

Wilcox, W., & Nock, S. (2006). What's love got to do with it? Equality, equity, commitment and women's marital quality. *Social Forces, 84*(3), 1321–1345.

Willi, J. (1998). *Die Zweierbeziehung. Spannungsursachen, Störungsmuster, Klärungsprozesse, Lösungsmodelle*. Reinbeck: Rohwolt.

Wodak, R. (1981). Die Beziehung zwischen Mutter und Tochter: eine sozio- und psycholinguistische Studie auf der Textebene. *Folia Linguistica, XV*, 39–87.

Wodak, R. (1982). Relationships between mothers and daughters from a socio- and psycholinguistic point of view. *Sigmund Freud Bulletin, 6*(1), 11–25.

Wodak, R. (1983). Eigentlich habe ich meine Mutter sehr gerne". Sozio- und psycholinguistische Aspekte der Partikelverwendung. In H. Weydt (Ed.), *Partikeln und Interaktion* (pp. 203–221). Tübingen: Niemeyer.

Wodak, R. (1984). *Hilflose Nähe? – Mütter und Töchter erzählen*. Deutike: Wien.

Wolchik, S., Tein, J., Sandler, I., & Doyle, K. (2002). Fear of abandonment as a mediator of the relations between divorce stressors and mother–child relationship quality and children's adjustment problems. *Journal of Abnormal Child Psychology, 30*(4), 401–418.

Wood, J., Repetti, L., & Roesch, S. (2004). Divorce and children's adjustment problems at home and school: the role of depressive/withdrawn parenting. *Child Psychiatry and Human Development, 35*(2), 121–142.

Wu, Z., Schimmele, C., Wu, Z., & Schimmele, C. (2005). Repartnering after first union disruption. *Journal of Marriage and Family, 67*, 27–36.

Yahm, H. (1984). Divorce mediation: a psychoanalytic perspective. *Mediation Quarterly Issue, 6*, 59–63.

Yogman, M., Kindlon, D., & Earls, F. (1995). Father involvement and cognitive behavioral outcomes of premature infants. *Journal of the American Academy Child and Adolescent Psychology, 34*, 58–66.

Zarraluqui Sánchez-Eznarriaga, L., Abril Campoy, J., et al. (2006). *Temas de Actualidad en Derecho de Familia*. Madrid: Dykinson.

Zhang, Z., & Hayward, M. D. (2001). Childlessness and the psychological well-being of older persons. *Journal of Gerontology: Social Sciences, 56B*(S), 311–320.

Zill, N. (1986). Marital disruption parent–child relationships, and behaviour problems in children. *Journal of Marriage and the Family., 4*, 295–307.

Zumeta Z. (2000). Styles of mediation: facilitative, evaluative and transformative mediation. http://mediate.com/articles/zumeta.cfm.

Index

FSC
www.fsc.org
MIX
Papier | Fördert
gute Waldnutzung
FSC® C083411

Kolibri 360 GmbH
Ferdinand-Jühlke-Straße 7
99095 Erfurt, Deutschland
produktsicherheit@kolibri360.de